# Financial Services: Regulating Investment Business

*Second Edition*

## Simon Morris

*Partner in Cameron Markby Hewitt*

**LAW & TAX**

© S Morris 1995

ISBN 0752 000411

*Published by*
FT Law & Tax
21–27 Lamb's Conduit Street
London WC1N 3NJ

A Division of Pearson Professional Limited

*Associated offices*
Australia, Belgium, Canada, Hong Kong, India, Japan, Luxembourg,
Singapore, Spain, USA

First published 1989
Second edition 1995

Printed in Great Britain by Mackays of Chatham

# *Contents*

# *Preface*

Much water has flowed under the regulatory bridge since the first edition of this book was published in 1989. While there are still relatively few reported cases on the FSA, and we therefore lack a useful source of interpretative guidance, there has been no shortage of other developments to record.

First, the directives intended to complete the single European market in financial services are either implemented or in the course of being implemented. Second, there have been a number of alterations to the primary legislation, not least the restructuring of the rulebook regime consequent upon the Companies Act 1989, and the introduction of the Public Offers of Securities Regulations.

But the greatest single change compared to five years ago is the growing maturity of the regulatory system. The Large Report has ushered in a change in the style and pace of self-regulation. SIB's reforms of the retail investment sector are bedding down as it shifts its focus to the wholesale markets. The regulators have accumulated sufficient experience to display a surer touch and to formulate and publish clearer policies. The regulated, in turn, have a better understanding of what is expected of them.

In preparing this second edition I have sought to reflect these evolving changes. I have added chapters describing how a compliance function should operate and another summarising the regulators' powers of monitoring, enforcement and discipline. Also included are new sections looking at complaints, compensation, insider dealing and money laundering. I have tried to produce a reasonably comprehensive yet concise overview of the FSA regulatory regime.

I have once again been greatly helped by my colleagues and would like to thank Nigel Berger, Guilherme Brafman, James Carter, Jo Chattle, Andrew Crawford, Pauline Dall, Chris Ffinch, Stephen Hallam, James Lever, Catherine Lomas, Barney Hearnden, Andrea MacAuley, Julia Miller, Humphrey Morrison, Elisabeth Ruiz, Victoria Schroter, Derek Stone and Philip White who have very kindly written or revised particular sections.

I would also like to mention Sue Lyons, my secretary, who typed endless amendments and Jean Berwick and Sarah Knowles in our library who plied me with the source material.

I have endeavoured to state the law as at 21 June 1995.

Simon Morris
Cameron Markby Hewitt
Midsummer Day 1995

# Abbreviations

| | |
|---|---|
| ADR | American Depository Receipt |
| AFBD | Association of Futures Brokers and Dealers |
| CAD | Capital Adequacy Directive |
| CGT | capital gains tax |
| CIS | collective investment scheme |
| DIE | designated investment exchange |
| DTI | Department of Trade and Industry |
| EEA | European Economic Area |
| EU | European Union |
| FIMBRA | Financial Intermediaries, Managers and Brokers Regulatory Association |
| FRN | floating rate notes |
| IFA | independent financial adviser |
| IMRO | Investment Management Regulatory Organisation |
| ICS | Investors Compensation Scheme |
| ISD | Investment Services Directive |
| LAUTRO | Life Assurance and Unit Trust Regulatory Organisation |
| LIFFE | London International Financial Futures Exchange |
| LME | London Metal Exchange |
| LTOM | London Traded Options Market |
| MLRO | money laundering reporting officer |
| PIA | Personal Investment Authority |
| RCH | recognised clearing house |
| RIE | recognised investment exchange |
| RPB | recognised professional body |
| SFA | Securities and Futures Authority |
| SIB | Securities and Investments Board |
| SRO | self-regulating organisation |
| TSA | The Securities Association |
| UCITS | Undertakings for Collective Investment in Transferable Securities |

# Table of Cases

# Table of Statutes

# Table of European Provisions

# Table of Statutory Instruments

# 1 Background to the Act

The Financial Services Act 1986 (FSA) was the first comprehensive investor protection legislation in the United Kingdom for nearly 50 years. This chapter examines the background to the legislation, changes to the regime subsequent to enactment and the principal criticisms to which the FSA is subject.

What distinguishes the FSA from most other recent regulatory legislation is the breath of its scope. In consequence it affects many industrial, commercial and banking activities which would not be viewed as mainstream investment business. To take just one instance, unlike the Consumer Credit Act 1974, it is not limited to protecting private individuals.

The Act has five principal objectives. These are:

(1) It requires people who carry on investment business (as defined) to be authorised (in other words, to obtain a licence), subject only to a few exceptions.
(2) It establishes a regulatory structure of industry-based self-regulating organisations (SROs) and recognised professional bodies (RPBs) overseen by a Securities and Investments Board (SIB).
(3) It regulates the carrying on of investment business through conduct of business, financial and other rules.
(4) It restricts the marketing of investments and regulates the operating and marketing of unit trusts and other collective investment schemes.
(5) It regulates the issue of listing particulars for the admission of securities to official listing.

## 1 HOW DID WE GET HERE?

The structure of the new regulatory regime is to a large extent a response to two factors. The first is the growth in disposable wealth and expansion of retail investment business over recent years. The second is the need to ensure that the United Kingdom, and the City of London in particular, remain attractive markets for international financial business, for which well-regulated markets are essential.

A review of the reports, discussion documents and White Papers that preceded the introduction of the FSA is instructive.

In July 1981 Professor Gower was appointed by the Government to review investor protection and generally to consider new investor protection legislation. The background to his appointment was as follows:

(1)  Increasing sales of life assurance and unit trusts.
(2)  The growth of disposable wealth which was leading to increasing holding of investments by individuals, more frequently indirect (for instance in unit trusts) and in derivatives such as options.
(3)  In common with most investor protection legislation, it was preceded by some sensational scandals, such as the collapse of Signal Life in 1979.

In January 1982 Professor Gower produced a Green Paper discussion document. It said that the Prevention of Fraud (Investments) Act 1958 (PFA 1958) was complicated, obscure, and too narrow in its scope. It dated from 1939 and was intended to combat the then prevalent abuses of share pushing and selling participations of dubious worth in speculative enterprises. The key provisions restricting the distribution of circulars were 'notoriously unclear' and there was no proper regulation for unit trusts.

Professor Gower was also concerned that the licensing body under the PFA 1958, the Department of Trade and Industry (DTI), operated a fairly 'light' regime, of which Barlow Clowes may turn out to be the most notorious example. There were, moreover, too many exemptions from the requirement to be licensed. For example, no licence was needed for an intermediary acting through a Stock Exchange member.

Gower also considered that the other statutory controls in the field of investor protection were less than satisfactory. The rules contained in the Companies Acts 1948–81 (CAs 1948–81) relating to public issues of shares were confusing and inconsistent. They were only concerned with primary issues for cash and did not regulate takeovers. It was also felt that the CAs 1948–81 typified the 'reactive' school of legislative control: transgressions were punished after the event, not prevented in advance. The investment activities of companies were subject to minimal supervision, while the CAs 1948–81 relied on formulistic disclosure obligations backed up by criminal penalties.

The Banking Act 1979 (BA 1979) regulated deposit taking. Unlike the CAs 1948–81, it provided for detailed supervision (by the Bank of England) and required deposit takers to satisfy the Bank of England that they were fit and proper and financially adequate prior to commencing business. Advertisements were regulated and depositors were protected by a Depositors Protection Fund if a bank became insolvent. In some ways the BA 1979 formed a model for the FSA.

The Insurance Companies Acts 1974–81 were similar to the BA 1979 since they provided for the authorisation of insurers and continuing supervision of insurance companies' financial stability. The Policy Holders' Protection Act 1975 provided for compensation in insolvency. However, Professor Gower felt that life assurance was very easy to sell in comparison to shares, and he was concerned with the lack of control over life assurance intermediaries and advertisements.

The non-statutory regulation provided by, among others, the Stock Exchange, the Panel on Takeovers and Mergers, the Council for the Securities Industry and the 'recognised' associations of dealers was also considered to be unsatisfactory.

## 1.1 What was wrong?

Professor Gower identified five key faults in the then regulatory structure. There was, he said:

(1) No single system for regulating investment media and the securities industry, no single prosecuting authority, no clear civil remedy for compensating investors in the event of loss, and what he described as a thoroughly defective structure.

(2) No satisfactory legislation regulating the conduct of takeover bids.

(3) Insufficient regulation of the investment marketing carried on by building societies, banks, and insurance, unit trust and investment companies, even though actual operation of these companies was regulated.

(4) A growing number of largely unregulated firms which were willing to advise on and manage investments for private investors.

(5) No provision for the proliferation of investment media and the movement from direct to indirect personal investment. Options and futures were becoming more common and, with the lifting of exchange control, foreign and offshore funds were now available for retail investments. The sales of indirect investment vehicles, such as unit trusts, commodity funds, linked policies and occupational pension schemes were also increasing.

## 1.2 The recommendation

Professor Gower's most significant recommendation was that the law must regulate the investment markets and market participants to prevent loss occurring in the first place. Investors, he said, were best protected where market participants were subject to initial vetting and continuing supervision. A regulatory system based on the requirement to disclose information, such as by the registration of prospectuses and the imposition of penalties for failure to comply, was *ex post facto* control. Furthermore, disclosure of information on its own was often insufficient—investors were not always well-placed to judge the information they were given. The growth and yield of investments would often depend on the future strength of the company or the investment managers rather than on past performance and, in any case, the seller may well not be worth suing by the time a default came to light.

Gower envisaged a new Act of Parliament establishing a detailed regulatory structure, with the Government supervising industry-based self-regulators who in turn would exercise day-to-day regulation over their members.

## 1.3 The Gower Report

Professor Gower's formal report, which examined individual segments of the investment market in great detail, was presented to Parliament in January 1984. The discussion and consultation that followed the Green Paper was generally favourable to the earlier proposals, and the intended regulatory structure was further confirmed. The principal alteration was to propose that surveillance and regulation of investment businesses should be undertaken by an independent commission—eventually SIB—rather than by a department of Government.

## 1.4 The White Paper

The Government's proposal for the new legislation, entitled 'Financial Services in the United Kingdom. A New Framework for Investor Protection' was published in January 1985.

The features of the new regime were becoming clearer. The proposed Bill would include a wide definition of investments and regulate a number of activities including managing and advising. It would be an offence to carry on investment business without authorisation.

Regulation would take place within a statutory framework administered by practitioner-based organisations. The Government would delegate its authority to SIB and the practitioner-based self-regulating organisations who would together lay down conduct of business and financial rules.

Businesses would have to pass a 'fit and proper' test before being authorised, and would thereafter be subject to detailed rules governing the conduct of their business.

## 1.5 The Financial Services Bill

The Bill was published in November 1985 in substantially the same form as that envisaged in the White Paper. It underwent lengthy committee stages in both Houses of Parliament and was subject to a substantial number of amendments. The protagonists can roughly be divided into two camps.

On the one hand was what might be termed the Consumer Lobby. This comprised the DTI, representatives of the Consumers Association, the Opposition and some Conservative peers and Members of Parliament. They sought to preserve the rigours of the first draft of the Bill which was distinguished by widely drawn definitions and very limited exclusions. In particular some Conservative backbenchers were concerned that the new regime should be rigorous so that the Government could not be viewed as being 'soft' on the City.

The other camp can be viewed as the Industry Lobby, which was reasonably successful in obtaining amendments to the Bill as it passed through Parliament. The Confederation of British Industry and the Association of Corporate Treasurers succeeded in campaigning to exclude some activities of industrial and commercial companies from the Bill, such as corporate treasury and export finance work. The major banks successfully resisted the imposition of some restrictions on the marketing of life assurance and unit trusts, and the finance houses resisted the introduction of a blanket ban on stabilisation.

These amendments achieved what were, from their promoters' point of view, a number of significant alterations to the detailed drafting of the Bill. It is nonetheless fair to say that they did not affect, and were not intended to affect, the basic structure of the proposed new system, nor did they diminish the overall effect of the legislation. At that stage the full impact of the Bill had not yet been assessed, and three further series of amendments had to be made to s 75 and Sched 1 of the FSA by the DTI shortly before the principal parts came into effect.

## 1.6  The legislative timetable

The FSA received the Royal Assent in November 1986. However, in common with most other detailed legislation, the Act was brought into force in stages, with over a dozen Commencement Orders.

The principal of these was the eighth Commencement Order which brought into force the main provisions of the Act on 29 April 1988.

At the time of writing the main part of the FSA not in force is that relating to the offering of unlisted securities, Part V. As discussed in Chapter 14 it has been repealed.

From 29 April 1988 (known as 'A' date) it became an offence (subject to the FSA's exclusions) to carry on investment business without obtaining authorisation or being exempted. Because it was only possible to obtain the necessary authorisation from that date, some transitional provisions had to be devised. It was not practicable to provide that every person holding authorisation under the PFA 1958 was deemed authorised for a transitional period, since many persons needing authorisation under the new Act fell outside the PFA 1958's regulatory scope.

It was therefore decided that persons who would require authorisation under the FSA from 'A' date had to apply for authorisation by an earlier date, set at 27 February 1988 (known as 'P' date). Provided a person had properly filed an application to be authorised by 'P' date, then it was provisionally authorised from 'A' date until either its application had been accepted, or until its application for authorisation was rejected, in which case it had to cease investment business immediately, or be in breach of the FSA.

Any person who applies for authorisation after 'P' date is not provisionally authorised. That person must wait until full authorisation is obtained before carrying on investment business as regulated by the FSA.

## 2  FINANCIAL SERVICES ACT

As Andrew Large, Chairman of SIB, commented in his report on financial services regulation (May 1993: discussed below), the FSA regime has had a short but turbulent past. Over a period of eight years there have been a number of significant changes as attempts have been made to adjust or revise the ways in which investor protection is achieved, and we now examine some of the principal areas of change.

### 2.1  Amendments to the Financial Services Act

There have been three main sources of alteration since enactment in October 1986.

(1) Alterations to s 75 (definition of collective investment scheme) and Sched 1 (definition of regulated investments, investment activities and the exclusions). They have been altered by eight statutory instruments and the versions current at the time of writing are discussed in Chapters 7 to 10.

(2) Alterations introduced by the Companies Act 1989, which are discussed below.

(3) Alterations necessary to implement the Second Banking Coordination Directive, the Investment Services Directive, the Capital Adequacy Directive and the Third Life Directive. These are summarised in Chapter 2 and each is mentioned when the section or paragraph amended is referred to.

In addition responsibility for the FSA was transferred from the DTI to HM Treasury in June 1992. The intention behind this move was for a single department to have oversight over both SIB and the Bank of England, the United Kingdom's regulators of securities and banking business.

### 2.2  Restructuring the rules

The rulebooks of SIB and the SROs have undergone significant alteration over the years. The original SIB rulebook was put together in considerable haste and before the workings and consequences of the new regime and the rules themselves were fully understood. The SIB rulebook was of key importance because the rulebooks of each SRO and RPB were largely based upon it and originally were not permitted to offer less rigorous investor protection than the SIB rulebook. Much detailed criticism of the SROs' and RPBs' conduct of business rules arose from the requirement to make them equivalent to SIB's rules. Paragraphs 3(1) of Scheds 2 and 3 to the FSA, which contain requirements which have to be fulfilled before an SRO or RPB is recognised by SIB, originally provided that the rules of an SRO or RPB governing its members' conduct of investment business must give investor protection at least equivalent to SIB's rules. Equivalent does not, of course, mean identical but this requirement was interpreted by SROs (and to a lesser extent by RPBs) as requiring them to replicate the SIB's rulebook both in terms of legalistic approach and detailed provisions.

There have been several attempts to reform the SIB, SRO and RPB rulebooks. The first was when SIB produced, towards the end of 1988, in an attempt to make its rulebook less cumbersome and legalistic, a draft simplified version of its conduct of business rules which sought to clarify the wording and set the rules out in coherent order, but did not alter their substance. The draft, contained in a consultative document entitled *Conduct of Business Rules: A New Approach*, proposed reducing the conduct of business rules to 115 pages containing 93 clearly-worded principles of conduct with 'plain English' explanations. The intention was that the new-style rules would, by emphasising clear statements of principle, reduce the ability of an investment business to exploit loopholes or inconsistencies. The draft also sought to emphasise that the spirit of a rule was more important that the letter. However, the proposal was subject to criticism on the ground that the new draft rules were no more than a cosmetic compression and repackaging of the pre-existing SIB rules. SIB responded to this point by proposing entirely to restructure its conduct of business rules. A further impetus was the publication of the draft Investment Services Directive. If the United Kingdom rules were simplified they could, it was thought, form a precedent for conduct of business rules throughout the EU.

In March 1989 the DTI published a consultative document setting out possible changes to the FSA. This envisaged a major alteration to the basis of SRO rulebooks which was intended to address the criticism that the rulebooks were too legalistic. The proposal was that SRO rules were to offer protection that was *adequate* rather than *equivalent* to that in SIB's rulebook and, furthermore, the cost of compliance was to be taken into consideration in devising the rules. SIB would also be empowered to issue statements of principle which were originally intended to be enforced both by discipline and by civil action. These statements of principle were intended to be the foundation of the rulebooks, to promote clarity and provide focus, and to enable the SROs to produce detailed rules closely tailored to the relevant market sector, so producing an adequate and cost-effective regime. The test adopted by SIB in approving an SRO's rulebook would be the adequacy of investor protection provided by SIB's statements of principle in combination with that SRO's rules. The basis of this was set out in *A Wider Role for SIB's Principles of Conduct: the next stage of the new approach* issued in March 1989.

This was coupled with a proposal to restrict the right of action under s 62 FSA to private investors, so that a professional investor could not bring a civil claim against a firm for loss caused by breach of its rulebook. The existence of the s 62 remedy was perceived as a major contributor to the complexity of the rulebooks: the rules were drafted with this legal consequence in mind and were generally interpreted with the intention of minimising the possibility of civil claims. Restriction of the s 62 remedy to private investors had already been achieved to an extent by SIB and the SROs amending their rulebooks to provide that their members were deemed to have acted in accordance with their conduct of business rules in relation to non-private investors if they had taken all reasonable steps to comply with a strict or absolute rule (for example, that disclosure of remuneration must be made), and had acted in accordance with other rules. This had the effect of restricting the application of s 62 by virtue of limiting the circumstances where an investment business would be in breach of the conduct of business rules.

SIB's proposals for revising the rulebooks were further formulated in *Regulation of the Conduct of Investment Business: a proposal* in August 1989. This envisaged that greater flexibility was to be given by SIB to SROs and RPBs, while maintaining a high level of investor protection and consistent standards. This would be achieved by adopting a common core of obligations drafted in straightforward language which individual regulatory bodies might adopt. The regulators would be permitted greater scope to set detailed requirements to reflect the characteristics of the industries which they regulated and, in particular, this would enable a clear distinction to be drawn between the requirements of the rules in relation to wholesale and retail business. SIB's paper contained the first draft of the principles and core rules which are similar, but not identical, to those eventually adopted. SIB intended to take advantage of the Companies Bill, then going through Parliament, to lay down statements of principle which would apply to all authorised persons, and to designate core rules which would apply to persons regulated by SIB and the SROs.

The amendments to the FSA which were eventually introduced by the Companies Act 1989 relevant to this area are as follows:

(1) Section 47A empowers the Secretary of State to issue Statements of Principle. The Principles came into effect in April 1990 and the power to issue them has been transferred to SIB. They are discussed in Chapter 3. Section 47B, which allows Statements of Principle to be modified or waived in particular circumstances has not been brought into force.

(2) Section 62A, which restricts the civil right of action for breach of certain rules under s 62, is discussed at Chapter 11.

(3) Section 63A empowers the Secretary of State, whose functions have been transferred to SIB, to designate certain rules (the core rules) as applicable to members of SROs. These are discussed in Chapter 3. These are the conduct of business and financial resources rules, together with the client money rules and unsolicited calls regulations. IMRO published a rulebook based upon Principles, the core rules and third tier rules in August 1991 which came into force in November 1991 when SIB designated the core rules as applicable to IMRO members. SFA published its revised rulebook in December 1991 and SIB designated the core rules as applicable to SFA members in April 1992. No other regulator has adopted core rules and, as discussed in Chapter 3, they are being de-designated.

(4) Section 63B empowers an SRO to modify or waive core rules.

(5) Section 63C empowers the Secretary of State (who has transferred this power to SIB) to issue codes of practice. None has yet been issued.

(6) Schedules 2 and 3 contain the criteria for recognition of SROs and RPBs. These were amended by the Companies Act 1989 to require the SRO or RPB to have rules governing its members' investment business which, together with the Principles, afford an adequate level of investor protection. In considering this, regard must be had to the kind of investment business it regulates, its effectiveness as a regulator and the cost of compliance.

## 2.3 Reorganisation of the SROs

In the document *SIB's Approach to its Regulatory Responsibilities* (February 1987) SIB confirmed its approach of seeking to promote a system of regulation which combined the best aspects of statutory and self regulation, offering flexibility within a legal framework. SIB emphasised that the system was to be one of practitioner-based self-regulation with specialist, function-based SROs covering the whole range of investment business. Between December 1987 and April 1988 five SROs were recognised: the Securities Association (TSA), the Financial Intermediaries, Managers and Brokers Regulatory Association (FIMBRA), the Association of Futures Brokers and Dealers (AFBD), the Investment Management Regulatory Organisation (IMRO) and the Life Assurance and Unit Trust Regulatory Organisation (LAUTRO). They together received over 13,000 applications for authorisation with only 138 firms seeking direct authorisation or regulation by SIB.

In April 1991 AFBD and TSA merged to form the Securities and Futures Authority (SFA). AFBD was the smallest SRO and had considerable overlap in scope with TSA, which was further emphasised by the merger of the London markets for futures and traded options (LIFFE and LTOM).

In October 1991 SIB commenced an enquiry into the regulatory scope and boundaries of SROs with a view to considering whether the regulation of retail products was best undertaken by a new SRO with a wide financial base. This arose out of the early stages of SIB's retail review, which is discussed below. This proposal received some impetus from FIMBRA's financial difficulties: life offices were having to support FIMBRA's finances, and in 1991 LAUTRO members agreed to assume part of the responsibility for compensation costs relating to the defaults of FIMBRA members. The outcome of this enquiry was announced in March 1992 when Sir Kenneth Clucas recommended the formation of a new SRO regulating retail products. It was to be known as the Personal Investment Authority (PIA) and to be formed from the membership of LAUTRO and FIMBRA. PIA was recognised by SIB in July 1994 and, as part of the drive for higher regulatory standards, LAUTRO and FIMBRA members have not been automatically accepted for PIA membership but, rather, required to apply for membership and satisfy PIA that they fulfil its stringent requirements. It is likely that LAUTRO and FIMBRA will remain SROs until late 1995 when they will be de-recognised, and any remaining members who have not otherwise obtained authorisation will no longer be authorised persons under the FSA.

## 2.4 Marketing of retail products

Particular importance is attached to the regime under which investment products are sold to the general public. The products themselves—personal pensions, life assurance, unit trusts and PEPs—are complicated; private investors are often ill-equipped to understand what they need or whether the investment sold is what they need; suitability (or otherwise) of the product sold may not be apparent for many years; the initial value of the product may be significantly less than premiums paid; and the financial pressure upon the salesperson to make the sale can be considerable. While there have been detailed and exacting rules covering the sale of retail products since 'A' Day, there has nonetheless remained an underlying concern as to whether investor protection has been consistently achieved.

In March 1989 SIB announced that it would be undertaking a review of the ways in which retail investments are marketed with the intention of formulating a more consistent and coherent regulatory regime. Against the background of constant development of new products and intensive marketing, SIB was concerned to ensure that investors were protected by a regime that was consistent between products and did not distort competition. SIB's Review Committee published a discussion document in March 1990 which outlined a number of possible alterations to the regulation of marketing of investment products. No firm proposals were made, although the importance of disclosure of information to enable an investor to take an informed decision, and of an intelligible and straightforward marketing regime, were emphasised.

In April 1991 SIB commenced a further review of retail regulation, focusing on requirements for:

- disclosure of information about charges and expenses, commission, and status of adviser as tied or independent;
- polarisation;
- standards of advice;
- regulatory boundaries;
- funding of the compensation scheme.

Detailed discussion documents were produced covering these various aspects and in SIB Consultative Paper 60, published in March 1992, SIB set out its proposals on disclosure, polarisation and standards of advice. The issue of regulatory boundaries and funding of the Investors Compensation Scheme had been addressed by the decision to create a new SRO (as discussed above) which would be financially viable and able to meet compensation liabilities, while financing of the compensation scheme was to be separately reviewed. The principal features of the proposals were:

(1) Investors should be provided with detailed information prior to purchase of retail products, including an explanation of surrender values and the effect of costs on the value of the product.

(2) The existing polarisation regime was to remain unchanged.

(3) Rules which obliged advisers to recommend only suitable retail products should also remain unchanged, but guidance on fulfilment of this duty should be issued. A new feature would be to require the adviser to provide a written statement of why the product suited that particular customer's circumstances.

(4) The current commission disclosure requirements would remain unchanged. They oblige independent intermediaries to disclose that they are remunerated by commission, and on request to state the amount; and product providers to state the amount of commission a salesperson will receive. This proposal was, however, subsequently altered.

The current regime for marketing retail products is discussed in Chapter 17.

A further issue which has highlighted the importance of advice given to retail customers is that of pension transfers and opt-outs. Between 1989 and 1992, it is estimated that some 300,000 investors transferred £5.5 billion worth of benefits into personal pension schemes. Towards the end of 1993 SIB undertook a study on the sale of personal pension products to investors who are or were members of occupational pension schemes, and which were paid for by the transfer of a preserved benefit under that scheme. This study involved the review of a sample of 735 client files drawn from the records of product providers and independent advisers. The study revealed that roughly half of the files did not contain sufficient information to justify the recommendation, and roughly one-third of the files indicated that the sale was inappropriate. While the SIB study indicated significant concerns over the quality of advice given, it was not possible to determine whether any investor had been disadvantaged from the study of files alone. SIB has approached this issue by publishing guidance on handling future pension transfer sales, and on identifying high priority cases for investigation. In October 1994, SIB published further guidelines requiring firms to make appropriate redress to investors who had suffered loss as a result of being sold a personal pension product in breach of the conduct of business rules.

## 2.5 Review of regulation: Maxwell and the Large Report

In December 1991 details of Robert Maxwell's thefts from pension funds within his group began to emerge and a series of enquiries into various aspects of this affair were set in train.

IMRO was responsible for the regulation of the two Maxwell fund management companies. There had been serious weaknesses in its monitoring arrangements, which had been too mechanistic and uncritical, and substantial strengthening of IMRO's regulatory capability was required. SIB acknowledged that it, too, was at fault in that it had failed to detect these weaknesses at IMRO.

In July 1992 the Chancellor asked the chairman of SIB, Andrew Large, to review how SIB carried out its regulatory responsibilities in view of the problems at IMRO, and to make recommendations for improvements. The report was published in May 1993.

While acknowledging that the United Kingdom financial services industry conducted each day a huge amount of investment business properly, effectively and in the interests of investors, the Large Report recognised widespread concern that the system was not achieving its goals, and that cost-effective investor protection was not always attained. However, Mr Large was anxious not to prescribe over-regulation as a response to the Maxwell affair, and recognised that the regulator's duty was to provide a clean market for risk investment, and not to eliminate market risk altogether.

The view taken in the report was that the FSA regime could deliver investor protection, but that a change in attitude and approach was needed. In particular SIB should retreat from direct regulation and concentrate upon supervising the regulatory bodies and enforcing standards.

Having discussed a number of criticisms in the financial services regime (see below) the report stated that the new settlement (see 2.2 above) which comprised the promotion of ten Principles, 40 core rules and the 'adequacy' test had not worked as intended. While the clearly written rules were preferable to the earlier legalistic ones, SIB had retained greater involvement in the rule-making process than had been envisaged, and the SROs had not been adequately supervised by SIB. Against this background Large proposed four key changes:

(1) SIB would set standards and would establish 'goalposts' for recognised bodies so that they would be accountable for their performance, and against which the adequacy and effectiveness of their regulation could be judged.
(2) SIB would supervise the regulators systematically and fairly.
(3) SIB would exercise its powers of enforcement more frequently.
(4) SIB would withdraw from rule-making and direct regulation. Writing rules diverted SIB's attention from supervision and setting standards of investor protection. Regulation of a few directly regulated firms also conflicted with SIB's role as a supervisor of regulation.

SIB has proceeded to implement these steps as follows:

(1) SIB has endorsed the promotion of PIA as a significant step in improving standards of advice in the retail sector.
(2) Persons regulated by SIB are being encouraged to apply to SROs, principally to PIA.

(3) SIB has prepared statements of objectives for each SRO, which are in turn preparing regulatory plans setting out how they will fulfil their regulatory tasks, and to what standards.

(4) SIB has exercised powers under 59 FSA to prohibit the employment of persons for the first time.

(5) SIB has announced its intention to de-designate the core rules.

# 3  AREAS OF CRITICISM

The financial services regime has attracted an extraordinary amount of comment and criticism during its brief existence, which can perhaps be explained by its novelty, complexity and wide application. By imposing detailed rules and requirements where none was previously required it is possible to understand how, from a practitioner's point of view, it may be said to impose restraint and expense. From a consumer's point of view its failures seem to be manifest. On the criminal front the Maxwell and Levitt affairs and other frauds have been perpetrated, while widespread misselling of retail products seems to have persisted undiminished—for example the inappropriate sale of personal pensions, and the significant number of disciplinary cases based upon alleged misselling heard before the IMRO and LAUTRO disciplinary tribunals.

While there is an element of truth in each of these views neither is a wholly appropriate criticism. First, the financial services regime probably fulfils nearly all of the criteria identified by Professor Gower as being lacking prior to its introduction. The one exception to this is the continuing multiplicity of agencies responsible for the investigation and prosecution of fraud and insider dealing. Secondly, the regulators have taken significant steps to improve the standard of advice given in retail sales. Clear rules were promulgated from 'A' day, and the action taken by the regulators in response to systematic failure to ensure adequate advice—whether disciplinary action or requiring that redress be made—indicates their determination that standards should rise and investors be protected.

The Large Report identified no fewer than 14 areas of criticism and concern. These, and other expressions of dissatisfaction, can be considered under a number of themes.

## 3.1  There is over-regulation

This argument, which principally emanates from the investment industry, can be supported by reference to the complexity of the rules and the lack of distinction between the regimes for retail and wholesale business. By way of response it can be argued that:

(1) The rules are necessarily detailed because they have to sustain legal analysis, for example if a private customer brings a claim under s 62, or

an SRO takes disciplinary action for breach of a rule. Furthermore they must be drafted with sufficient precision to enable a firm to determine what is the appropriate course of action in any circumstances, and for a regulator to judge whether its requirements have been fulfilled.

(2) The wording of the rules has been considerably simplified under the new settlement, although it must be recognised that the underlying requirements of the rules have, if anything, become more rigorous.

(3) There is ample distinction between the regimes for private and non-private customers, as summarised in Chapter 3.

A further limb to this argument is that the regulators are 'moving the goalposts' and are continually increasing their requirements. This is true, but only in part. To take the example of selling retail products, the basic rules which are to know your customer, to ensure suitability of the sale and to keep records, are little changed since 'A' Day. What has certainly altered is the standard to which the regulators expect their rules to be fulfilled. The quality of advice and record-keeping for a sale of a retail product which might have been acceptable to a regulator in, for example, 1990 would not be acceptable today.

The regulators constantly seek to increase standards of compliance in the interests of investor protection, and issue guidance and consultative documents which outline their evolving requirements. Nonetheless occasions do arise when firms feel that the regulator has not made its requirements clear, or explained the increase in standards with sufficient clarity.

## 3.2 There is under-regulation

Contrary to the last argument is the claim that there is under-regulation. This can be supported by reference to pension transfers and other instances of misselling. Reference could also be made to scandals such as Barlow Clowes and BCCI, but these either happened before the FSA was introduced or are the responsibility of other regulators. As mentioned above, the Maxwell affair did demonstrate a weakness in the regulatory system which SIB has sought to address.

There is certainly some substance to this argument, although it is submitted that it does not indicate that self-regulation does not work. The FSA has established a structure for monitoring and detecting missales and market abuses cases, and for ensuring that appropriate remedial action is taken. Furthermore it is the regulators' continually increasing standards which have highlighted practices which might have been acceptable in previous years but are no longer so.

## 3.3 Regulation is not cost-effective

For the investment industry, as Large comments, costs are evident while benefits are harder to see. This is a difficult argument to rebut, although it can be stated that one of Large's aims is to ensure that regulation is as cost-effective as possible.

Some independent studies have been undertaken to assess whether the FSA regime places an undue financial burden upon firms. In March 1993 the London Business School published a report on *The Costs and Effectiveness of the United Kingdom Financial Regulatory System* which found that overall United Kingdom regulatory costs were not substantially different from those of the United States or France.

## 3.4 Self-regulation equates to self-interest

The argument goes that the SROs are trade associations which seek to protect the interests of their members rather than investors. This is not a fair point, although the arguments within PIA as to the composition of its board and whether there should be more public interest directors than industry directors do illustrate this concern. There can be little doubt that the promulgation of detailed conduct of business rules by SIB and the SROs, and their effective enforcement, operates in the public interest. Any firm which has been subjected to a SIB or SRO investigation or disciplinary action will know that there is no question of the regulator having regard to the interests of its members rather than the interests of the public.

## 3.5 Statutory regulation is needed

Some critics of the present system call for statutory regulation, arguing that a British equivalent of the US Securities and Exchange Commission is needed. Interpreted as a call for higher standards this is understandable, but taken literally it is confusing. First, the current system is one of self-regulation within a statutory framework. The powers of the SROs are based in statute and it is difficult to see what changes should be made, other than perhaps to eliminate practitioner involvement in SROs, to convert this into statutory regulation.

Secondly, SIB possesses most if not all of the powers of the US Securities and Exchange Commission, and indeed some of SIB's powers are wider than the SEC's. Although there are certainly some anomalies, such as SIB's lack of power over SRO members and its inability to fine persons it regulates, it is submitted that there is little merit to this argument.

## 3.6 Investors may lose their investment

This is true but, as stated by Large, the objective of the FSA is to provide a clean market for risk investment, and not to eliminate market risk altogether.

Rules which are intended to offer a measure of protection to a private customer include ones obliging a firm to:

–   take reasonable steps to enable a private customer to understand the risks involved in a transaction;

- take reasonable steps to ensure any transaction is suitable in light of a private customer's circumstances.

Provided these rules are fulfilled a customer who makes an unwise or speculative investment, or whose investment loses value, will have no redress. The doctrine of *caveat emptor*—let the buyer beware—continues to have a role under the FSA. The annual reports of the Investors Compensation Scheme (discussed in Chapter 2) urge investors to be vigilant for signs of dishonesty or insolvency, and set out in an annex entitled 'Advice to Investors' points which investors should consider when dealing with a firm. They recommend an investor to do the following:

- check the firm is authorised;
- understand the transaction: if you do not understand the transaction do not sign the documents;
- obtain a full written explanation of what your money is being invested in, and request regular reports on performance;
- insist on full documentation and receipts;
- only make payments to an adviser authorised to hold client money;
- keep records of payments made and received;
- understand that a guarantee is only as valuable as the person giving it has the resources and ability to meet it;
- beware of exceptionally high promised returns;
- if in doubt take advice from an independent person.

## 3.7   The system is not working

The House of Commons Treasury and Civil Service Committee endorsed this view in relation to retail financial services in its Interim Report on Retail Financial Services Regulation when it said:

> Parts of the retail sector of the financial services industry have for too long and too often been characterised by incompetence and misselling. It is disappointing that such a heavy superstructure of regulation has had only limited success in affecting what happens in the market place.
>
> (Fourth Report 23 May 1994 paragraph 65)

It went on to endorse the creation of PIA as the single regulator for the retail sector, while calling for greater public interest and consumer representation on its board, and expressing concern as to whether PIA would actually be effective.

While the House of Commons Committee was expressing a genuine concern, it is submitted that a wider view can be taken. It is possible to identify a number of achievements of the system. The Large Report includes reference to the following:

- Creating an infrastructure for the delivery of investor protection.

- Weeding out many dubious operators. FIMBRA, for example, rejected over 3,000 firms as prospective members and terminated the membership of 600 others.
- Resolving many cases of investor risk.
- Providing £36 million in compensation.
- Establishing a programme for the training and competence of salesforce.
- Raising standards of dealing with customers.

If the present system does have an Achilles' heel, it is this: there is no single body charged with investigating and prosecuting offences like insider dealing, market manipulation and financial fraud. The creation of an agency to pursue such cases, and to bring civil rather than criminal proceedings (with the lower civil standard of proof), would go some way towards addressing this issue.

It is not easy to reach a firm overall conclusion on the effectiveness of the FSA regime. It is, however, suggested that the FSA has made a significant contribution to regulating the United Kingdom investment markets and to enhancing investor protection. That said, though, it must be admitted that progress has been uneven, cumbersome and more successful in some areas than in others.

# 2 Structure of the FSA Regime

This chapter considers the overall structure of the FSA 1986 and then examines:

- the powers and functions of SIB and the SROs;
- methods of obtaining authorisation;
- the 'fit and proper' test;
- regulation of persons subject to more than one regulator;
- permitted persons;
- regulation of employees;
- exempted persons;
- operation of the Investors Compensation Scheme;
- requirements for the handling of complaints;
- implementation of EU Directives.

## 1 BASIC STRUCTURE

The new financial services regime is perhaps best considered as a structure comprising three layers of regulation.

## 1.1 The Financial Services Act

Subject to a few exclusions, the FSA prohibits the carrying on of investment business in the United Kingdom without authorisation. It sets out the few categories which are exempted from this general prohibition, and specifies the different methods of obtaining authorisation.

It also specifies a number of criminal offences and certain civil consequences for contravention. These are discussed in detail in Chapter 11, but here are the principal ones:

*(a) Criminal offences*
The Act's principal criminal offence is to carry on investment business in the United Kingdom without being authorised or exempted (s 4). Directors and

officers of, and partners in, an investment business can be personally liable for this offence if the company or partnership commits an offence on account of their own consent, connivance or neglect (s 202).

*(b) Civil remedies*
The investment contracts of an unauthorised person, or of an authorised person which are induced by an unauthorised person, can be unenforceable against the customer, who may recover compensation (s 5).

If a private investor (or certain other categories of investor) suffers loss because an authorised person breaches its conduct of business rules then the investor may claim compensation for the loss from that person (s 62).

## 1.2 The Securities and Investments Board

The FSA vested regulatory powers in the Secretary of State for Trade and Industry. The Secretary of State's functions under the FSA and certain other legislation were transferred to the Treasury on 7 June 1992 by the Transfer of Functions (Financial Services) Order (SI No 1315). The Secretary of State was empowered by s 114 to transfer to a designated agency his functions contained in ss 3–113 of the Act, together with powers in relation to permitted persons (para 23 of Sched 1), certifying publications (para 25(2)), and certain transitional provisions. These functions generally relate to recognition of other bodies capable of granting authorisation; recognition of investment exchanges and clearing houses; formulation of conduct of business and other rules; promotion of collective investment schemes; and powers of intervention and enforcement. Functions to which s 114 do not apply are stated as:

(1) certifying equivalence of investor protection in other EU States for the purpose of the 'automatic' authorisation of certain EU investment businesses (s 31(4));
(2) making or revoking recognition orders for overseas investment exchanges and clearing houses (s 40);
(3) adding to, removing and restricting the categories of exempt persons (s 46(1));
(4) amending the classes of investment which may be stabilised (s 48(8));
(5) exempting categories of advertisement from the general restriction in s 57 (s 58(3));
(6) restricting the right of action under s 62 (s 62(A));
(7) prescribing requirements for recognising collective investment schemes constituted in other EU member states (s 86(1)) and designating territories (s 87(1));
(8) operating the Financial Services Tribunal (s 96);
(9) making rules imposing duties on auditors to disclose information to the Minister (s 109(2)).

In order to determine which functions have been transferred to SIB, and on what terms, and whether any function not so transferred is exercisable by the DTI, the Treasury or jointly, it is necessary to consult the Transfer of Functions (Financial Services) Order and the delegation orders SI 1987 No 942; SI 1988 No 738; SI 1991 No 200 and No 1256.

The designated agency is the SIB. For the reasons identified by Professor Gower, it was felt that the DTI should not be the enforcing body under the FSA, while a statutory US-style Securities and Exchange Commission would be unacceptable to the investment industry as a whole. The distinction, however, is not that obvious. SIB's ability to make rules and investigate breaches, and its powers of enforcement, make it no less powerful than a statutory body.

SIB is a private body vested with rule-making functions. It is not to be regarded as acting on behalf of the Crown when performing any of the functions which have been transferred to it (Sched 9 para 1).

SIB is formally constituted as a company limited by guarantee. It is funded by fees and levies and is not in receipt of public finance. However while not subject to Government control, it is nonetheless accountable to the Treasury, Parliament and the courts. SIB must provide an annual report which is laid before parliament (s 117). The Treasury may under s 115 resume all or any transferred functions.

The Chairman of SIB and members of its Board are appointed and liable to removal by the Treasury and Governor of the Bank of England acting jointly. SIB's board must include persons with experience of investment business and others who are users of investment services, and there must be a balance between practitioners and public interest board members (Sched 7, para 2).

SIB is required to be able and willing to promote and maintain high standards of integrity and fair dealing in relation to investment business—the same duties imposed upon SROs and RPBs (Sched 7 para 5). In relation to persons whom SIB regulates (see below) SIB is required to have a satisfactory system for monitoring and enforcing compliance (Sched 7 para 3).

In order to facilitate the performance of its duties SIB and its staff are granted by s 187(3) statutory immunity from action in damages other than when acting in bad faith. This does not exclude the right to seek an injunction or a declaration of the court, nor does it preclude an application for judicial review.

'Bad faith' in this context would probably include acting unreasonably or perversely as in *Associated Provincial Picture Houses v Wednesbury Corporation* [1948] 1 KB 223 and *UKAPE v ACAS* [1981] AC 424.

SIB and certain other persons are placed under an express duty of confidence by s 179 FSA. This provides that information obtained by a person listed in s 179(3) for the purpose of, or in the discharge of his functions under, the FSA and which relates to the business or affairs of another person:

- may not be disclosed by such person (termed 'the primary recipient'); or
- any person obtaining the information directly or indirectly from the primary recipient;

without the consent of whoever supplied the information to the primary recipient and, if different, the person to whom it relates.

SIB and the other persons listed in s 179(3) are permitted to disclose information which is subject to s 179 in over two dozen situations specified in s 180(1).

The only sanction for breach of s 179 is criminal prosecution (s 179(6)) and there is no civil action (*Melton Medes v SIB* (July 1994) unreported).

Section 179 does not apply to the SROs, each of which is instead bound by a duty of confidentiality set out in its rulebook.

A myriad of powers and functions under the FSA have been transferred to SIB. The four principal ones are:

(1) To recognise the SROs and RPBs (ss 10 and 18). SIB may revoke recognition (ss 11 and 19) and may apply to the court for an order that an SRO or RPB properly performs its functions (ss 12 and 20).

(2) To authorise persons to carry on investment business under ss 25–30. In 1994 SIB was responsible for the authorisation of 75 persons. SIB is additionally responsible for the regulation of persons who are authorised under other legislation or EU Directives (see 2.1 below) and who do not join an SRO. For the reasons discussed in 2.5 below SIB is encouraging those persons whom it authorises to transfer to one of the SROs.

(3) To publish statements of principle (s 47A), conduct of business rules (s 48), financial resources rules (s 49), cancellation rules (s 51), notification regulations (s 52), indemnity rules (s 53—but not brought into force), compensation rules (s 54), client money regulations (s 55) and unsolicited call regulations (s 56). These rules and regulations are discussed in Chapter 3.

SIB's conduct of business rules regulate persons who obtain authorisation to carry on investment business directly from SIB, as well as (to a greater or lesser extent in each case):

(i) Insurance companies authorised under s 22 which do not join PIA.

(ii) Operators and trustees of EU-recognised collective investment schemes authorised under s 24.

(iii) Persons authorised in other EU states who obtain automatic authorisation under s 31. In practice, however, this section is not used on account of 'passport' rights—see (iv).

(iv) EU persons who exercise 'passport' rights under the Second Banking Coordination Directive, the Third Life Directive and (on its coming into force on 1 January 1996) the Investment Services Directive and who choose not to join an SRO.

When making such rules and regulations SIB is required to promote high standards of integrity and fair dealing in the conduct of investment business (Sched 8 para 1A). Schedule 8 also contains specific requirements for the making of the other rules and regulations.

(4) To take enforcement action against persons generally (as distinct from persons authorised by it). These powers include seeking injunctions halting unauthorised investment business and restitution orders (s 6), prohibiting

the employment of persons who are not fit and proper (s 59), and seeking injunctions and restitution orders in relation to rule breaches (s 61).

SIB's role is considerably wider than a strict review of these statutory provisions might suggest, and its annual reports set out the range of its activities. SIB's main purpose, as published in its statement of objectives, is to ensure that the other regulatory bodies deliver high standards of investor protection. As discussed in the Large Report (May 1993, see Chapter 1) SIB is concentrating on setting standards of regulation and supervising the other regulators, and is withdrawing so far as possible from directly authorising persons and making rules.

## 1.3  The self-regulating organisations

Formed on private initiative, the SROs are legal entities financed and controlled by their members, hence the description 'self-regulating'. There were originally five SROs but this has been reduced to four and is currently being reduced to three.

An SRO is defined as a body which regulates the carrying on of investment business by enforcing binding rules (s 8(1)). A member of an SRO will be subject to its rules because of the contract of membership, while the employees or appointed representatives of the member can be made subject to them by virtue of entering into a contract with the member.

An SRO is recognised by SIB if it satisfies the requirements of Sched 2 FSA (s 10) and membership of a recognised SRO (subject to three exceptions) confers authorisation upon that member to carry on investment business (s 7(1)). The exceptions are:

(1) An insurance company authorised under s 3 or 4 Insurance Companies Act (s 22) which chooses to join an SRO (now PIA) to be regulated by its rules on the marketing of retail products rather than those of SIB.

(2) A friendly society authorised under the Friendly Societies Act which chooses to join an SRO rather than to be regulated by SIB's rules on the marketing of retail products (s 23).

(3) An insurance company authorised in another member state operating in the United Kingdom on a services basis only (s 31). As mentioned, this section is not now used.

In addition a European institution properly exercising its 'passport' rights under the Second Banking Coordination Directive, Investment Services Directive or Third Life Directive will not require authorisation under the FSA when carrying on home-authorised business in the United Kingdom. It may join an SRO in order to be subject to its rather than SIB's applicable host-state rules, but membership of the SRO will not of itself confer authorisation on that firm.

The SROs and their staff are granted immunity from liability in damages in defined circumstances unless acting, or omitting to act, in bad faith (the meaning of which is discussed at 1.2 above). Decisions of an SRO are nonetheless amenable to judicial review—for example *R v AFBD ex parte Mordens* (1990) (*Financial*

*Times*, 11 July); *R v LAUTRO ex parte Ross* (1992) 2 WLR 549. However, it seems that a regulator may not be liable in negligence or breach of statutory duty to customers of a firm which it regulates (*Yuen Kun Yeu v Attorney General of Hong Kong*) [1988] 1 AC 175; *Davis v Radcliffe* [1990] 1 WLR 821).

The requirements for recognition of an SRO are set out in Sched 2 to the FSA and, in summary, require:

(1) It must have rules and practices to ensure its members are fit and proper persons (para 1).

(2) Its conduct of business rules, together with SIB's Statements of Principle and other rules, must afford an adequate level of protection for investors, having regard to the kind of investment business it regulates and the SRO's effectiveness (para 3).

(3) It must have adequate arrangements to monitor and enforce compliance (para 4).

(4) It must promote and maintain high standards of integrity and fair dealing in the carrying on of investment business (para 7).

The SROs' powers of monitoring, enforcement and discipline are discussed in Chapter 12. The rules to which SRO members are subject are discussed in Chapter 3.

## 2  OBTAINING AUTHORISATION

There are five distinct ways of becoming authorised to carry on investment business under the FSA. They are:

(1) Authorisation with other legislation.
(2) Authorisation under an EU Directive.
(3) Authorisation by SIB.
(4) Authorisation by membership of a recognised SRO.
(5) Authorisation by membership of a recognised professional body.

While some of these are suitable for persons who carry on investment business as a sole or principal activity, others are only appropriate for people who carry on investment business incidentally to some other activity.

### 2.1  Authorised under other legislation

Two persons are automatically authorised under the Act. These are:

*(a) Insurance companies*
Section 22 provides that an insurance company which is authorised in the UK to carry on insurance business under s 3 or s 4 of the Insurance Companies Act 1982 is authorised in respect of such of its insurance business which is regulated by the

FSA, and other business which it may carry on without contravening s 16 of the Insurance Companies Act 1982. This will normally be business concerned with life assurance policies, which fall within para 10 of Sched 1. Life assurance companies are granted automatic authorisation for this kind of business as they are already subject to financial and prudential control by the DTI.

### (b) Friendly societies

A friendly society is granted authorisation under s 23 FSA in relation to investment business which it carries on for or in connection with any of the activities mentioned in Sched 2 to the Friendly Societies Act 1992.

## 2.2 EU persons

Three limited classes of EU persons are granted authorisation. These are:

(1) Persons who validly exercise 'passport' rights under the Second Banking Coordination, Investment Services and Third Life Directives, discussed below. These permit an EU institution to carry on in the United Kingdom an activity falling within the scope of the Directive which it is authorised or permitted to carry on in its home member state. To this extent ss 3 and 4 of the FSA will not apply to that institution.

(2) The operator or trustee of a collective investment scheme constituted in a member state other than the United Kingdom which is recognised under s 86 (which implements the UCITS Directive). This person is authorised (by s 24) to operate the scheme, act as trustee and carry on investment business in relation to the scheme. Once recognised, the SIB conduct of business rules will apply to their United Kingdom marketing activities (s 86(7)). This is discussed further in Chapter 16.

(3) A person with its head office in a member state other than the United Kingdom, whose law recognises him as an EU national and who is authorised to carry on investment business by its law, is granted authorisation by s 31. As mentioned above, this section is not used as it is significantly less advantageous than the 'passport' regime.

## 2.3 Authorisation by SIB

This is covered by ss 25–30 of the FSA. At the time of writing there are some 75 persons authorised by SIB to carry on investment business. These may be persons which do not conveniently fall within the scope of any SRO or prefer regulation by SIB rather than by their peers in an SRO. As mentioned above, SIB is encouraging all persons whom it regulates to transfer to an SRO. Those who decline to leave cannot be compelled to go, but SIB is empowered by Sched 7 para 3 of the FSA to delegate monitoring to another person (who may be an SRO) and SIB may require that they observe the rules of that SRO.

The procedure for obtaining authorisation from SIB is to make an application in the prescribed form (s 26). SIB is empowered to grant or refuse the application, and shall grant authorisation if satisfied that the applicant is a fit and proper person (s 27). The meaning of this expression is discussed below. SIB may withdraw or suspend authorisation (s 28).

## 2.4 Authorisation from an SRO

A member of an SRO recognised by the SIB is, with the exceptions mentioned at 2.1 and 2.2 above, an authorised person.

In order to join an SRO an applicant must generally satisfy it that it is a fit and proper person and, in addition, the applicant must carry on investment business of a kind with which the SRO is concerned. The meaning of fit and proper is discussed below.

The applicant must file with the SRO details of its ownership, directors, senior employees, financial projections and a business profile indicating what kind of investment business it wishes to carry on. Once authorised, the member must only transact the categories of business set out in the statement of permitted business agreed with its regulator. If it engages in other investment business, it will be contravening its SRO's rules and exposing itself to liability under s 62 and to disciplinary action by its regulator.

The description of the kinds of business which an SRO can authorise, set out below, indicate the SRO's scope. A person authorised by an SRO may only carry on such business falling within its scope as set out in its statement of permitted business.

## 2.5 The individual SROs

The membership and scope of IMRO, SFA and PIA are considered here. The membership and scope of the earlier SROs (AFBD, TSA, LAUTRO and FIMBRA) are discussed in the first edition of this book. Each SRO has detailed scope rules which are intended to minimise overlap with other SROs, and these should be consulted in each case.

*(a) Investment Management Regulatory Organisation (IMRO)*
IMRO is principally responsible for regulation of investment managers: its statement of scope provides that it regulates those firms whose main investment business falls within the categories of:

- managing investments;
- managing assets of an occupational pension scheme (this is relevant to trustees of an occupational pension scheme who manage its assets themselves rather than engage a professional manager);
- acting as manager or trustee of an authorised unit trust scheme;
- acting as manager or operator of other collective investment schemes;
- providing investment advice to non private investors.

On 31 March 1994 IMRO had 1,142 members, of whom the largest categories include 494 fund managers, 168 authorised unit trust managers, 134 venture capital companies, 115 trustees who manage their own occupational pension schemes, 78 advisers and 50 banks.

*(b) Securities and Futures Authority (SFA)*
SFA is concerned with authorising persons who deal in and advise on all kinds of investments including:

- domestic and foreign equities;
- debt instruments;
- warrants;
- financial and commodity options;
- futures;
- certificates of deposits.

SFA will also authorise persons who engage in corporate finance activities.

On 31 March 1994 there were 1,275 member firms. The largest categories were 372 'broad scope' (ie mainly dealing) firms; 192 banks; 177 corporate finance advisers; 162 arrangers and 152 agency brokers.

*(c) Personal Investment Authority (PIA)*
PIA was recognised as an SRO in July 1994 and is at the time of writing still processing applicants. It was created to regulate investment business primarily carried on with or for a private investor. Because both SFA and IMRO have previously regulated firms which deal with or manage for private investors, PIA has had to devise elaborate scope rules in order to draw up appropriate lines of demarcation.

In summary PIA will regulate any firm whose business involves, to a substantial extent, marketing of packaged products to private customers. This is deemed to be the case automatically for life offices and friendly societies. It will also regulate the marketing activities of unit trust managers obtaining business through a direct sales force or by direct marketing. In other cases, managers of unit trusts may be able to select IMRO as their regulator. In addition PIA will regulate the activities of dealing, arranging deals in, managing and advising on a wide range of investments (shares, warrants, debt instruments and certain derivatives), primarily for private customers, but with the exception of the following:

- establishing, operating and winding up collective investment schemes;
- market making;
- provision of clearing services;
- business as a member of an exchange dealing in securities or derivatives;
- corporate finance activities;
- management of occupational pension scheme assets (except small schemes as defined);
- writing options.

PIA's likely membership will be in the order of 200 life assurance companies, 180 unit trust managers, 200 friendly societies and some 5,000 independent financial advisers.

## 2.6 Recognised Professional Bodies (RPBs)

A body which regulates the practice of a profession which does not mainly or wholly consist of investment business may apply to SIB to be a recognised professional body (RPB) (ss 16(1), 17(1)). A person who holds an investment business certificate issued by an RPB is an authorised person (s 15(1)). Merely being a member of an RPB does not on its own confer authorisation. The requirements for recognition of a professional body are set out in Sched 3 of the FSA. It was felt undesirable to require such professionals to obtain individual authorisation as the weight of numbers of solicitors and accountants would overburden the SROs.

An RPB is empowered, by s 187(6), to make it a condition of issuing a certificate that neither it nor its staff or governing body is liable in damages except in the case of bad faith.

There are nine RPBs, listed below:

(1) Law Society of England and Wales (English solicitors)
(2) Law Society of Scotland (Scottish solicitors)
(3) Law Society of Northern Ireland (Northern Ireland solicitors)
(4) Institute of Chartered Accountants in England and Wales
(5) Institute of Chartered Accountants in Scotland
(6) Institute of Chartered Accountants in Ireland
(7) Chartered Association of Certified Accountants
(8) Institute of Actuaries
(9) Insurance Brokers Registration Council

Each RPB imposes a limit on the quantity of investment business which a member may carry out pursuant to holding an investment business certificate. This is measured by reference to fee income and is intended to ensure that the member's main business is indeed practice of a profession and not investment business. This limit varies between RPBs and the different RPB rulebooks contain detailed regulations regarding how it is calculated.

This is a summary of the different kinds of investment business which holding an investment business certificate from an RPB will authorise its members to carry on.

### (a) Law Society of England and Wales

Limit on fee income from investment business: not more than 20 per cent.
  Scope of authorisation: all activities constituting investment business except:

(a) market making in investments;
(b) dealing as principal where the firm holds itself out as engaging in the business of buying such investments with a view to selling them;
(c) entering into margined transactions as agent for a client other than through a permitted third party;
(d) acting as a stabilising manager in relation to any issue of relevant securities;
(e) acting as the trustee or manager of a regulated collective investment scheme; and
(f) entering into a broker funds arrangement.


### (b) Law Society of Scotland

Limit on fee income from investment business: not more than 49.9 per cent.
  Scope of authorisation: all activities constituting investment business, except:

(a) dealing with a client;
(b) market making in investments;
(c) dealing or arranging a deal in derivatives otherwise than by way of introducing a client to an appropriately authorised person;
(d) acting as a manager or a trustee of a regulated collective investment scheme;
(e) entering into a broker funds arrangement.

### (c) Law Society of Northern Ireland

Limit on fee income from investment business: not more than 20 per cent.
  Scope of authorisation:

(a) dealing, arranging deals or advising in relation to:

   (i) any investment commonly used as security for mortgages of immovable property, for pension provision or inheritance tax planning;
   (ii) any readily realisable investment in relation to the administration or winding up of any estate or fund;
   (iii) any investment where the dealing is part of a commercial transaction between two or more participants which is for business rather than investment purposes and where the matter is dealt with by the firm in its capacity as solicitors;

(b) Dealing or arranging deals in relation to any investment of any kind, other than a derivative or margined transaction, for an execution only client.

*(d) Institute of Chartered Accountants in England and Wales*
Limit on fee income from investment business: not more than 20 per cent.
Scope of authorisation: all activities constituting investment business except:

(a) market making;
(b) dealing as principal with a client;
(c) dealing with a client in derivatives other than through an authorised third party;
(d) stabilising investments;
(e) acting as trustee or manager of an authorised unit trust or recognised collective investment scheme.

There are, however, limits on the quantity of discretionary management which a firm may carry out.

*(e) Institute of Chartered Accountants in Ireland*
The authorisation is identical to that granted by the Institute of Chartered Accountants in England and Wales.

*(f) Institute of Chartered Accountants in Scotland*
The authorisation is identical to that granted by the Institute of Chartered Accountants in England and Wales.

*(g) Chartered Association of Certified Accountants*
Limit on fee income from investment business: not more than 20 per cent.
Scope of authorisation: all activities constituting investment business except:

(a) market making in investments;
(b) dealing as principal where the firm holds itself out as engaging in the business of buying such investments with a view to selling them;
(c) entering into margined transactions as agent for a client other than through a permitted third party;
(d) acting as a stabilising manager in relation to any issue of relevant securities;
(e) acting as the trustee or manager of a regulated collective investment scheme; and
(f) acting for or on behalf of a person authorised otherwise than pursuant to an Investment Business Certificate issued by the Association or an equivalent certificate issued by another RPB accountancy body as a locum or similar.

*(h) Institute of Actuaries*
Limit on fee income from investment business: not more than 20 per cent.
  Scope of authorisation:

  (a)  advising on all investments;
  (b)  arrange deals in any investment, other than derivatives.

*(i) Insurance Brokers Registration Council*
Limit on fee income from investment business: not more than 49 per cent.
  Scope of authorisation:

  (a)  dealing as agent in life assurance policies, units in a regulated collective
       investment scheme and securities in an open ended investment company;
  (b)  making arrangements for another person to deal in such investments;
  (c)  advising on such investments.

## 2.7  Identifying an authorised person

The writing paper, business cards, publications and advertisements of an
authorised person (and its appointed representative) should normally state by
whom it is authorised in accordance with the rules of SIB or its SRO or RPB.

SIB maintains (pursuant to s 102) a central register of persons authorised to
carry on investment business, including those authorised by SIB, by SROs, by
RPBs, permitted persons and EU institutions exercising their 'passport' rights.
Also included on the register are:

  −  recognised clearing houses;
  −  recognised investment exchanges;
  −  authorised unit trusts;
  −  recognised collective investment schemes;
  −  persons disqualified under s 59.

The register can be consulted personally; by writing to SIB; on Prestel; or by
telephoning 0171–929 3652.

The registered entry will normally disclose the name, address, and telephone
number of the authorised person, together with brief details of the investment
business which it carries on. It does not, however, give the names of the investment
business's directors, managers or sales force as it is felt that such information
would get out of date too quickly.

## 3  THE FIT AND PROPER TEST

One of the principal means by which the FSA seeks to achieve investor protection
is by ensuring that only suitable persons are authorised to carry on investment
business. The second key method is the requirement that, once authorised, firms
comply with detailed conduct of business and other rules, and this is discussed in
Chapter 3.

The prerequisite for obtaining authorisation through membership of an SRO (or directly from SIB) is to demonstrate that you are a fit and proper person both on admission and thereafter. Someone who obtains authorisation other than through SRO membership, such as an authorised insurer or an EU institution exercising 'passport' rights, is not subject to this test because that person will already have satisfied its regulator (the DTI or its home-state authorities) that it is fit and proper. However such persons will be expected to satisfy the prospective SRO on other matters, for example their ability to observe SIB's Principles and the SRO's conduct of business and other rules. SFA and IMRO additionally require applicants for individual registration to demonstrate that they are fit and proper.

The term 'fit and proper' is not defined in the FSA, but was considered by the Financial Services Tribunal when it was ruling upon an unsuccessful appeal for authorisation by SIB (*Re Noble Warren Investments Limited* (1988) BJIBFL July 1989, p 334). The tribunal held that 'fit and proper' 'extends to the conduct of an applicant both in its dealings with the public and in the ordering of its internal affairs'. The tribunal stated that the test to be applied was an objective one and unrelated to 'a subjective view that an applicant may hold of his own conduct and methods, or even to an opinion that his customers hold'.

Each SRO is required to have rules and practices which secure that persons who obtain authorisation through membership are fit and proper persons to carry on investment business of the kind it regulates (Sched 2, para 1) and this is reflected in the SROs' rules. SFA, for example, requires applicants to satisfy it that they are fit and proper persons to carry on investment business of the kind and scale for which they seek authorisation (rule 2.2). In determining whether an applicant is fit and proper the SROs take a number of factors into consideration. The following list is drawn from the published statements of SFA (rulebook, Appendix 3) IMRO (rulebook, Appendix A) and PIA's rulebook (in the Statements section).

Any matter which suggests that authorisation (or personal registration) of the applicant may be detrimental to investors is relevant to determine whether they are fit and proper and accordingly, while the SROs consider fitness and properness under the following broad headings, this must be seen as indicative of the issues taken into account rather than definitive.

*(a) Financial integrity and reliability*
The applicant's solvency should not be in question. The applicant should have sufficient financial resources to meet its commitments on a continuing basis and to withstand likely financial risks.

*(b) Competence*
All applicants must demonstrate sound internal compliance arrangements. Applicants for individual registration must have suitable experience and qualifications.

### (c) Good reputation and character

Civil liabilities and criminal convictions, refusal of a licence to carry on business or being subject to an investigation or disciplinary procedures may be relevant with this heading. Contravention of the FSA, of conduct of business or of other rules, provision of false or misleading information to the regulator and failure to observe good market practice will also be taken into account.

### (d) Efficiency, honesty and fairness

The regulator must believe that the applicant will conduct its business fairly, operate efficiently and deal candidly with it.

These tests are to be considered in light of information concerning the applicant, its employees, associates and directors. The applicant, in relation to whom the tests are to be applied, may be a firm seeking authorisation or an individual seeking personal registration.


## 4 REGULATION OF A FIRM SUBJECT TO MORE THAN ONE REGULATOR

Where a firm is a member of more than one SRO, or is authorised under the FSA but also supervised under a separate regulatory regime, steps must be taken to ensure that it is effectively regulated.

### (a) Information sharing

First, regulators with an interest in the same group or firm will consult with each other and share information. Principally in relation to financial information, this will also include matters relevant to conduct of business. The intention is to ensure that regulators are fully informed about the workings of a firm or the group as a whole, which is particularly important where the regulator has oversight over only one part of the firm or group.

### (b) Lead-regulation

If more than one regulator has responsibility for monitoring the financial position of a firm or a group, that supervision may be performed by a single regulator in order to avoid any duplication or conflict between different rules or reporting requirements. Where an SRO has entered into a lead-regulator agreement with another regulator, its financial rules will be largely disapplied. An example of this is an authorised United Kingdom banking institution for whom the Bank of England is the lead financial regulator and which joins an SRO in order to be authorised to conduct investment business.

*(c) Prudential regulation*

The regulator responsible for a firm's prudential regulation has oversight of the firm's fitness and properness. Where a firm is authorised under the FSA other than by joining an SRO, such as a life assurance company, then its 'non-FSA' regulator—in this example the DTI—and not the SRO will be its prudential regulator. Where a firm subject to prudential regulation under the FSA joins two SROs then one will assume responsibility for carrying out prudential regulation. An example of this could be a unit trust manager who joins IMRO to be authorised to manage funds and joins PIA to be authorised to market them.

*(d) Conduct of business rules*

A firm which is a member of two or more SROs for different kinds of investment business will be subject to only the conduct of business rules of the SRO which regulates that particular kind of business.

*(e) EU institutions*

Where an EU firm exercises a 'passport' to establish a branch or provide services in another member state, its home state supervisor will retain responsibility for prudential supervision. The United Kingdom regulators will be responsible for other areas of regulation of it and any subsidiary which is allowed to exercise the 'passport' in terms of the directive.

By way of illustration, an EU firm which validly exercises its passport under the Second Banking Coordination Directive, and which chooses to join SFA rather than to be subject to SIB's rules, must observe the following SFA rules in relation to its passported investment business: in other words its home-state regulated business which it carries on in the United Kingdom. If it did not join SFA it would be subject to the corresponding SIB rules.

(1) It is not subject to the fit and proper test when applying for membership of SFA.
(2) Notification requirements relating to prudential regulation do not apply.
(3) The financial rules are substantially disapplied.
(4) The client money and conduct of business rules apply.
(5) The complaints, arbitration and enforcement rules substantially apply.

In addition it will be subject to:

(1) SIB's Principles, save to the extent that they cover matters subject to home-state prudential regulation (probably Principles 8 and 9).
(2) Cancellation, notification, compensation and unsolicited calls regulations in relation to its carrying on home-state regulated business in the UK.

A similar regime will apply to EU firms exercising passport rights under the Investment Services Directive and currently applies to those exercising passport rights under the Third Life Directive.

# 5 PERMITTED PERSONS

A permitted person is a person exempted from the application of para 12 of Sched 1 of the FSA and who has been granted permission by the SIB to deal in investments (as defined by para 12 of Sched 1), but not to engage in any other investment business. A permitted person may only buy, sell or subscribe for or underwrite regulated investments as principal or agent, or offer to agree to do so.

The details of this category are contained in para 23 of Sched 1 to the FSA, which is set out below.

In summary, SIB will grant permitted person status if it is satisfied that the main business of the applicant or its group is not investment business for which it requires authorisation under the FSA, but that the applicant is likely to deal in investments other than with the public in the course of carrying on its business in circumstances where it is inappropriate to require it to obtain authorisation. An example would be a trading company which deals in investments for the purpose of cash or risk management. There were 110 permitted persons in March 1994.

The permitted person exemption will be narrowed when the Investment Services Directive is implemented as the Directive does not include corresponding exemptions.

Paragraph 23 of Sched 1 to the Act states the following:

23(1) Paragraph 12 above does not apply to anything done by a person:
  (a) as principal;
  (b) if that person is a body corporate in a group, as agent for another member of the group; or
  (c) as agent for a person who is or proposes to become a participator with him in a joint enterprise and for the purposes of or in connection with that enterprise.
  if it is done in accordance with the terms and conditions of a permission granted to him by the Secretary of State under this paragraph.

  (2) Any application for permission under this paragraph shall be accompanied or supported by such information as the Secretary of State may require and shall not be regarded as duly made unless accompanied by the prescribed fee.

  (3) The Secretary of State may grant a permission under this paragraph if it appears to him:—
  (a) that the applicant's main business, or if he is a member of a group the main business of the group, does not consist of activities for which a person is required to be authorised under this Act;
  (b) that the applicant's business is likely to involve such activities which fall within paragraph 12 above; and
  (c) that, having regard to the nature of the applicant's main business and, if he is a member of a group, the main business of the group

taken as a whole, the manner in which, the persons with whom and the purposes for which the applicant proposes to engage in activities that would require him to be an authorised person and to any other relevant matters, it is inappropriate to require him to be subject to regulation as an authorised person.

(4) Any permission under this paragraph shall be granted by a notice in writing; and the Secretary of State may by a further notice in writing withdraw any such permission if for any reason it appears to him that it is not appropriate for it to continue in force.

(5) The Secretary of State may make regulations requiring persons holding permissions under this paragraph to furnish him with information for the purpose of enabling him to determine whether those permissions should continue in force; and such regulations may, in particular, require such persons:—

  (a) to give him notice forthwith of the occurrence of such events as are specified in the regulations and such information in respect of those events as is so specified;

  (b) to furnish him at such times or in respect of such periods as are specified in the regulations with such information as is so specified.

(6) Section 61 of this Act shall have effect in relation to a contravention of any condition imposed by a permission under this paragraph as it has effect in relation to any such contravention as is mentioned in subsection (1)(a) of that section.

(7) Section 104 of this Act shall apply to a person holding a permission under this paragraph as if he were authorised to carry on investment business as there mentioned; and sections 105 and 106 of this Act shall have effect as if anything done by him in accordance with such permission constituted the carrying on of investment business.

# 6  THE REGULATION OF EMPLOYEES

A director or employee of an authorised person will not be personally carrying on investment business (see Chapter 6) but is nonetheless subject to the regulatory regime.

The starting point is SIB Principle 9 which provides that a firm which employs staff must ensure they are suitable, adequately trained and properly supervised. This obligation extends to staff of a firm's appointed representative. A firm is therefore obliged to ensure that its personnel act in such a way that the firm will itself comply with the provisions of the FSA and its SRO. In addition there are a number of specific rules which directly affect directors and employees. The following instances, taken from the SFA rulebook, are by way of example and reference should be made to the rulebooks of the individual regulators to determine the rules applicable to firms regulated by other SROs.

### (a) Individual registration

Directors, managers and staff who manage investments, give advice or deal in investments must be individually registered with SFA. Such a person is subject to SIB's Principles and must undertake to commit no act or omission which would place his firm in breach of SFA's rules. He may not be employed by another firm without SFA's consent (rule 2.24).

### (b) Training and competence

Staff who manage investments, give advice or deal in investments may not become registered unless they have passed a prescribed examination or secured exemption from it on account of equivalent qualifications or experience (rule 2.37 and following).

### (c) Notification

A firm must immediately notify SFA in writing if a registered person commits a significant act of misconduct or a matter arises relevant to him being a fit and proper person (rule 2.46).

### (d) Personal account dealings

A firm must take reasonable steps to ensure its staff and directors observe restrictions on insider dealing and propriety in personal dealings. This is core rule 34, which is expanded by SFA rule 5.51 to require a firm to give every employee a personal account notice which regulates the way in which the employee may deal in securities.

### (e) Monitoring, enforcement and discipline

SFA will monitor the compliance of a registered person with the rules and may interview him (rule 7.8), investigate him (rule 7.9), issue an intervention order against him (rule 7.12), and may institute disciplinary proceedings against him (rule 7.23). These powers are discussed in Chapter 12.

## 7  WHO IS EXEMPT?

Unlike the PFA 1958 which it replaced, the clear policy of the FSA is to exempt as few categories as possible. There are, accordingly, only six classes of exempt person, each of whom falls within this category for a good reason, and in respect of which the investor is either at no risk or is felt to be otherwise adequately protected.

## 7.1 The Bank of England

The Bank of England is exempted by s 35.

## 7.2 Recognised investment exchanges and clearing houses

Recognised investment exchanges (RIEs) and recognised clearing houses are exempted persons in accordance with ss 36–41 in relation to any investment business carried on in that capacity.

Operating an investment exchange which is based in the United Kingdom, has an office or merely transacts business in this country, may well be carrying on investment business because, depending on the circumstances, it may be dealing or arranging deals in investments, which are two investment activities regulated by the FSA. If a recognised exchange were not an exempt person it might need to obtain authorisation.

Individual exchanges may apply to SIB to be recognised investment exchanges (and hence become exempted persons) and must satisfy SIB that they have rules which fulfil the requirements of s 37 and Sched 4 of the FSA. United Kingdom recognised investment exchanges include the International Stock Exchange and the International Petroleum Exchange.

A clearing house will normally operate in the futures and commodities markets, reconciling sales and purchases, organising margins and effecting settlements. A clearing house may need to be authorised for the same reasons as an investment exchange, and can apply to SIB to be an exempted person under s 39 on a similar basis. The ICCH is a recognised clearing house.

An exchange or clearing house with a head office outside the United Kingdom which wishes to carry on investment business in the United Kingdom can seek:

(1) authorisation from SIB under s 25 FSA; or
(2) recognition by the Treasury as an overseas investment exchange or an overseas clearing house under s 36–41 FSA which constitutes them exempted persons.

Recognition allows foreign investment exchanges and clearing houses to participate in the United Kingdom markets. Intervention by the UK authorities in the day-to-day affairs of overseas investment exchanges and clearing houses is reduced by relying substantially on the supervisory and regulatory arrangements in the country where the applicant's head office is situated.

Before granting recognition the Treasury needs to be satisfied on a number of points, including that the applicant is subject to supervision in its head-office country which, together with the applicant's rules and practices, is such that the investors in the United Kingdom are afforded the same protection as that provided by recognised investment exchanges and clearing houses whose head offices are situated within the United Kingdom. Recent applicants for recognition are the French Futures and Options Exchange and the New York Mercantile Exchange.

World trading in futures and options is expanding and further applications from overseas investment exchanges and clearing houses are expected.

If an overseas investment exchange or clearing house does not carry on investment business in the United Kingdom it will not need to apply for recognised status in order to obtain exemption. It may, however, wish to apply to the SIB for designated status.

Designation does not itself confer authorisation or recognition. Its main consequence is that firms which effect customer transactions on a designated exchange are no longer obliged to report transactions on that designated exchange to the SIB at the close of business each day. Transactions on designated exchanges are treated for the purpose of SIB rules as though they have been effected on a recognised investment exchange. Designated exchanges may not carry on investment business in the United Kingdom unless they are otherwise exempted under the FSA.

Designated investment exchanges include the Chicago Board of Trade and the Johannesburg Stock Exchange.

## 7.3 Lloyd's

The Society of Lloyd's and Lloyd's underwriting agents are exempted persons in relation to investment which they carry on in connection with or for the purpose of insurance business at Lloyd's (s 42). In Guidance Release 2/89 SIB takes the view that a Lloyd's name does not require authorisation under the FSA to manage assets provided by him as collateral for his liabilities as a name.

## 7.4 Listed money market institutions

A listed money market institution is an exempt person under s 43 in relation to certain investment business transactions.

Transactions between certain parties in wholesale money, bullion and foreign exchange markets are removed from the ambit of the FSA because they are supervised by the Bank of England. This is discussed in Chapter 15.

## 7.5 Appointed representatives

The largest category of exempted persons are those termed appointed representatives who are, in summary, exclusive or semi-exclusive sales agents of an authorised person.

44(1) An appointed representative is an exempted person as respects investment business carried on by him as such a representative.

The FSA provides for appointed representatives to be exempted rather than authorised since a tied agent of an authorised person can in principle be regulated by that firm, and thus the number of persons requiring authorisation can be kept within reasonable limits. An appointed representative has the following characteristics. It is:

(1) An independent contractor who can be an individual, a partnership or company.

(2) Employed under a contract for services. This is distinct from an employee who is engaged under a service contract. A person who is not carrying on investment business, such as the employee of an authorised person, will not require to be an appointed representative. Only persons otherwise carrying on investment business in their own right need to do so.

(3) Engaged by an authorised person (termed a 'principal' in the FSA) under a contract which allows it to carry on a limited range of investment business for which the authorised person accepts responsibility. The appointed representative's business is restricted to that which could be carried on by the authorised person in accordance with its statement of permitted business.

44(2) For the purposes of this Act an appointed representative is a person:

(a) who is employed by an authorised person (his 'principal') under a contract for services which:

(i) requires or permits him to carry on investment business to which this section applies; and

(ii) complies with subsections (4) and (5) below; and

(b) for whose activities in carrying on the whole or part of that investment business his principal has accepted responsibility in writing; and the investment business carried on by an appointed representative as such is the investment business for which his principal has accepted responsibility.

The only investment business which an appointed representative may carry out is:

(1) procuring persons to enter into investment agreements with his principal;

(2) advising persons about entering into investment agreements with his principal;

(3) advising on selling his principal's investments, or on exercising rights conferred by any investment;

(4) procuring persons to enter into investment agreements with any person, or advising persons about entering into investment agreements with any person, where this is not prohibited by his contract.

An 'investment agreement' is an agreement under which either party engages in an investment activity (such as dealing or managing) ignoring the exclusions in Sched 1 FSA (s 44(9), discussed in Chapter 13).

It will be noted that the appointed representative's activities are limited to:

(1) advising;

(2) 'procuring or endeavouring to procure ... persons ... to enter into investment agreements' which, it is submitted, means making, or trying to

make, them enter into such agreements. It seems that, as an agent authorised to procure persons to enter into agreements, an appointed representative may bind its principal to a contract. The investment agreement may be one under which the principal (or, if permitted, another person) deals, arranges deals, manages, advises or operates a collective investment scheme.

An appointed representative is not allowed by s 44 to engage in the investment activities of dealing, managing or operating a collective investment scheme although the appointed representative may presumably offer or agree to do any of these things on behalf of its principal. It may only do so for itself if it is able to take advantage of the FSA's other exclusions.

44(3) This section applies to investment business carried on by an appointed representative which consists of:

> (a) procuring or endeavouring to procure the persons with whom he deals to enter into investment agreements with his principal or (if not prohibited by his contract) with other persons;
>
> (b) giving advice to the persons with whom he deals about entering into investment agreements with his principal or (if not prohibited by his contract) with other persons; or
>
> (c) giving advice as to the sale of investments issued by his principal or as to the exercise of rights conferred by an investment whether or not issued as aforesaid.

The contract between the appointed representative and its principal must either:

> (1) prohibit the appointed representative from procuring or advising in relation to third party investment agreements; or
>
> (2) if it permits this, it must allow the principal to prohibit or restrict such activities with reference to categories of person or investment.

In practice an appointed representative of a life assurance company will be prohibited from selling or advising on packaged products other than those issued by its principal or its principal's group for reasons of polarisation. See Chapter 17.

> 44(4) If the contract between an appointed representative and his principal does not prohibit the representative from procuring or endeavouring to procure persons to enter into investment agreements with persons other than his principal it must make provision for enabling the principal either to impose such a prohibition or to restrict the kinds of investment to which those agreements may relate or the other persons with whom they may be entered into.
>
> (5) If the contract between an appointed representative and his principal does not prohibit the representative from giving advice about entering into investment agreements with persons other than his principal it must make provision for enabling the principal either to impose such a prohibition or to restrict the kinds of advice which the representative

may give by reference to the kinds of investment in relation to which or the persons with whom the representative may advise that investment agreements should be made.

The principal is responsible for the acts and omissions of its appointed representative when carrying on investment business for which it has accepted responsibility (s 44(6)). In determining whether the principal has complied with the provisions of the FSA and its SRO, the acts and omissions of the appointed representative for which it was accepted responsibility are to be taken into account (s 44(7)), although if it is a criminal offence the knowledge and intention of the appointed representative shall only be attributed to the principal if reasonable under all the circumstances (s 44(8)).

SIB Principle 9 requires a principal to have adequate arrangements to ensure that appointed representatives (being persons for whose investment business it is responsible) are suitable, adequately trained and properly supervised. This duty is expanded upon by core rule 13:

- The principal must be satisfied on reasonable grounds that an appointed representative is a fit and proper person on appointment and thereafter.
- The principal must have adequate resources to monitor and enforce its appointed representatives' compliance with high standards of business conduct.
- The principal must ensure that the appointed representative carries on its authorised business separate from unauthorised financial business (unless it is a bank or a building society) and does not engage in unauthorised investment business.

SFA expands on the core rule requirements and requires to be notified in advance of the activities of a prospective appointed representative, and requires that the appointed representative and its employees are individually registered with it.

It will be necessary to narrow the exemption for appointed representatives when the Investment Services Directive is implemented and this may affect an appointed representative who provides services falling within the Investment Services Directive, which do not include insurance. The Directive provides that the activities of a person who receives and transmits orders solely for the account of, and under the unconditional responsibility of, an authorised person are to be treated as the activities of that authorised person and not of the receiver and transmitter, who is to be regarded as exempt. The Treasury intends to allow a person who deals with more than one authorised person to be exempt, but otherwise to narrow the s 44 exemption.

## 7.6 Miscellaneous exemptions

These fall into three categories. First, a number of judicial and other officers are exempted persons under s 45(1). Secondly, the FSA contains some exemptions relating to insolvency practitioners. Thirdly, some additional exemptions have been made under s 46.

*(a) Exemptions in the FSA 1986*

Section 45(1) provides the following exemptions:

45(1) Each of the following persons is an exempted person to the extent specified in relation to that person—

   (*a*) the President of the Family Division of the High Court when acting in the exercise of his functions under s 9 of the Administration of Estates Act 1925;

   (*b*) the Probate Judge of the High Court of Northern Ireland when acting in the exercise of his functions under s 3 of the Administration of Estates Act (Northern Ireland) 1955;

   (*c*) the Accountant General of the Supreme Court when acting in the exercise of his functions under Part VI of the Administration of Justice Act 1982;

   (*d*) the Accountant of Court when acting in the exercise of his functions in connection with the consignation or deposit of sums of money;

   (*e*) the Public Trustee when acting in the exercise of his functions under the Public Trustee Act 1906;

   (*f*) the Master of the Court of Protection when acting in the exercise of his functions under Part VII of the Mental Health Act 1983;

   (*g*) the Official Solicitor to the Supreme Court when acting as judicial trustee under the Judicial Trustee Act 1896;

   (*h*) a registrar of a county court when managing funds paid into court;

   (*i*) a sheriff clerk when acting in the exercise of his functions in connection with the consignation or deposit of sums of money;

   (*j*) a person acting in his capacity as manager of a fund established under s 22 or 22A of the Charities Act 1960, s 24 or 25 of the Charities Act 1993, s 25 of the Charities Act (Northern Ireland) 1964, s 11 of the Trustee Investments Act 1961 or s 42 of the Administration of Justice Act 1982;

   (*k*) the Central Board of Finance of the Church of England or a Diocesan Authority within the meaning of the Church Funds Investment Measure 1958 when acting in the exercise of its functions under that Measure;

   (*l*) a person acting in his capacity as an official receiver within the meaning of s 399 of the Insolvency Act 1986 or in that capacity within the meaning of any corresponding provision in force in Northern Ireland.

*(b) Insolvency exemptions*

An insolvency practitioner, such as a receiver, administrator or liquidator will usually be a chartered accountant or solicitor. Provided he or his firm has obtained authorisation under the FSA by holding a certificate from the appropriate RPB, then he may carry on investment business which arises from his acting as an insolvency practitioner in accordance with that RPB's conduct of business rules.

Section 45(2) contains an exclusion which may be relevant to an insolvency practitioner:

> 45(2) Where a bankruptcy order is made in respect of an authorised person or of a person whose authorisation is suspended under section 28 above or who is the subject of a direction under section 33(1)(b) above or a winding-up order is made in respect of a partnership which is such a person, the trustee in bankruptcy or liquidator acting in his capacity as such is an exempted person but—
>
> > (*a*)  sections 48 to 71 below and, so far as relevant to any of those provisions, Chapter IX of this Part of this Act; and
> >
> > (*b*)  sections 104, 105 and 106 below,
>
> shall apply to him to the same extent as they applied to the bankrupt or partnership and, if the bankrupt or partnership was subject to the rules of a recognised self-regulating organisation or recognised professional body, he shall himself also be subject to those rules.

If a bankruptcy order is made against an authorised person, a person whose authorisation is suspended under s 28, or a person who is subject to a direction under s 33(1)(b); or if a winding-up order is made in respect of a partnership which is authorised, suspended under s 28 or subject to a s 33(1)(b) direction then, in any such case, the trustee in bankruptcy or liquidator is an exempt person. He will therefore not require to be authorised when he carries on investment business when acting as trustee or liquidator. However, because as an exempt person he would, in principle, not be obliged to observe any conduct of business rules, he will be bound by the following to the extent that they bound the bankrupt or partnership, and not by the rules of his own SRO or RPB. These rules are the SIB conduct of business rules and financial resources rules and other restrictions contained in ss 48–63. He will also be subject to the powers of intervention contained in ss 64–71 and to the jurisdiction of the Financial Services Tribunal. He will in addition be subject to the rules of the SRO or RPB (if any) which authorised the insolvent person or partnership.

Sections 45(3) and (4) adapt s 45(2) for Scotland and Northern Ireland.

It is considered that an administrator, administrative receiver, liquidator or supervisor of a voluntary arrangement of an authorised company will not require to be authorised or, if authorised, will not be governed by the rules of his SRO or RPB when acting as such because he will not thereby be carrying on investment business. Instead, he will be acting as agent of the company and will rely on, and be bound by, that company's authorisation. However an administrative receiver's agency will be terminated once the company to which he is appointed has gone into liquidation. After liquidation the administrative receiver will be trading as principal and should consider the requirement for authorisation. A supervisor of a voluntary arrangement must also ensure that the terms of the arrangement are such that he is the agent of the debtor and is empowered to run the debtor's business.

If an insolvent company owns investments regulated by the FSA 1986, the insolvency practitioner will be acting as agent of the company when managing the investments and will therefore not be carrying on the investment activity of managing the investments of another.

There are, however, circumstances where an insolvency practitioner may need to rely on authorisation from an SRO or RPB, for example where:

(1) he advises prospective purchasers of the company on the merits of buying its shares or the investments which it owns; or

(2) the insolvency practitioner advertises to sell shares in the company or investments which it owns; or

(3) if the insolvency practitioner is acting for an unauthorised company which requires, but did not obtain, authorisation, or is the trustee in bankruptcy or supervisor of a voluntary arrangement of an individual who required authorisation under the FSA but did not obtain it.

*(c) Miscellaneous exemptions in the SIs*

A substantial number of miscellaneous exemptions have been made by the Financial Services Act 1986 (Miscellaneous Exemptions) Orders SI 1988 No 350 and No 723, SI 1989 No 431, SI 1991 No 493 and No 1516 to which reference should be made.

# 8  INVESTORS COMPENSATION SCHEME

## 8.1  Introduction

The Investors Compensation Scheme (ICS), which is established by s 54 FSA, is the rescue fund for private clients of firms authorised under the FSA that have failed. The ICS is funded by a levy to which all authorised firms must contribute. It will pay up to £48,000 compensation to a private investor who stands to lose the money he or she has invested. An investor who loses money at the hands of an unauthorised investment business will have no claim on the ICS but may have a remedy under s 5 FSA, and SIB may take action under s 6 FSA.

The ICS is intended to provide the final safety net of the regulatory system. The requirement that only fit and proper persons be authorised to carry on investment business, and the imposition of conduct of business and financial resource rules monitored and enforced by a firm's regulator, are introduced to eliminate the likelihood of a firm failing to meet its obligations.

## 8.2 Constitution of the Investors Compensation Scheme

Section 54(1) FSA empowers the Secretary of State (whose functions were transferred to SIB in May 1987) to establish by rules a scheme for compensating investors where a currently or previously authorised person is unable, or likely to be unable, to satisfy civil claims arising out of its investment business.

The rules made under s 54(1) may establish a compensation fund, provide for its administration and for the levying of contributions from any class of authorised persons, and specify the terms on which compensation is payable (s 54(2)).

## 8.3 Making of rules under s 54

Schedule 8 FSA lays down the principles applicable to SIB when making rules and regulations. The specific obligation in relation to s 54 is that the rules made under it:

> must make the best provision that can reasonably be made for the [purpose of that section] (para 10).

The purpose of the ICS is stated in s 54(1) as being to compensate investors who have suffered loss because of claims arising from investment business carried on by currently or previously authorised persons. With this in mind SIB has constituted the ICS as a unitary scheme under which all authorised firms are liable to contribute to the levy that funds compensation notwithstanding how or when the claim arose.

The rules originally made by SIB under s 54 were the Financial Services (Compensation of Investors) Rules 1988, which were replaced by the Financial Services (Compensation of Investors) Rules 1990 from 15 July 1990 (the '1990 rules') which were themselves replaced by the Financial Services (Compensation of Investors) Rules 1994 (the '1994 rules') with effect from 15 September 1994.

## 8.4 Application to SRO members

Section 54(3) provides that a scheme established under s 54(1) will only apply to SRO members after consultation with that SRO and SIB must be satisfied that its rules make sufficient provision:

    (a)  for the administration of the scheme by a body on which the interests of those persons are adequately represented; and

    (b)  for securing the amounts which [SRO members] are liable to contribute reflect, so far as practicable, the amount of the claims made or likely to be made in respect of those persons.

In drawing up the ICS rules SIB interpreted the obligation in s 54(3)(b) as meaning that it should ensure that sufficient money is forthcoming from each SRO's members to meet investors' claims. Moreover members of one SRO can be called upon to pay for defaults of members of other SROs when costs of default among an SRO's members reach a point when it is no longer practicable to require members of that SRO to be exclusively responsible to pay for defaults of its own members. This requirement to contribute to defaults of other SROs' members (known as cross contribution) was a key feature of the 1990 rules and is retained in relation to defaults of FIMBRA and LAUTRO members in the 1994 rules.

## 8.5   Operation of the scheme

The 1994 rules govern defaults on or after 15 September 1994, and provide that Investors Compensation Scheme Limited ('the Management Company') will continue to be responsible for operating the ICS.

The ICS provides that compensation is payable in respect of any description of civil liability incurred on or after 18 December 1986 in connection with the investment business of a person who is or was an authorised person. This curious date was chosen by the court in *SIB v FIMBRA* [1991] 4 All ER 398 because it was when s 1 and Sched 1 FSA came into force, so defining the term 'investment business'. The court was giving judgment on a construction summons brought to determine whether FIMBRA members were liable to contribute to losses of investors in Dunsdale Securities who had invested before it was authorised by FIMBRA. The question of when civil liability arises for the purposes of the ICS was considered in *R v Investors Compensation Scheme ex parte Weyell* [1994] 1 All ER 601.

The conditions which need to be satisfied for payment of a claim are summarised as follows, although reference should in any case be made to the full text of the 1994 rules.

(1)   The firm must be in default, which is when it appears to the Management Company that it is unable, or unlikely to be able, to meet any civil liability incurred in connection with its investment business.

(2)   An eligible investor (in summary a private customer or a non unit-trust trustee) must apply for compensation. A claim should be made within six months of when he became aware, or ought to have become aware, that the firm was declared in default. The 1994 rules provide that time limits are directory and not mandatory.

(3)   The claim must relate to investment business in respect of which the firm was an authorised person, including that of a firm's appointed represent-ative for which it has accepted responsibility. Claims relating to regulated insurance companies are dealt with under the Policyholders Protection Act, discussed below.

(4)   The claim must be for property held or transactions uncompleted, and other claims are only admitted where meeting them is essential to providing fair compensation. The liability must be one that a court has recognised or would recognise. Failure to match a guarantee and loss arising because of the fluctuation in market value of investments are not compensatable.

However, if a claim falls within the ICS, the Management Company has no discretion to reject or limit a compensatable claim (*R v Investors Compensation Board ex parte Bowden* [1994] 3 WLR 1045, CA).

(5) The amount payable as compensation is the investor's overall net claim against the firm in default, limited to £30,000 plus 90 per cent of the balance up to £50,000, so that £48,000 is the maximum compensation sum payable. In addition the Management Company is subject to an overall limit of £100 million compensation in any one year in relation to the defaults of any one SRO.

(6) The Management Company may seek recovery in respect of any claim the investor may have had against a third party, for example against the firm's liquidator or trustee in bankruptcy. In 1993/94 the Management Company retrieved £629,000 in this way.

## 8.6   Funding the ICS

The Management Company is empowered to levy contributions, to borrow and to insure (Annex 1 to the 1994 rules). Its principal source of income is levies raised from the SROs, who are (subject to the Management Company's residual right to levy directly (Annex 2 para 14 1994 rules)) solely responsible for levying their own members.

Under the 1990 rules:

(a) The annual overall liability of the Scheme was set at £100 million (and between April 1990 to March 1992 the top £75 million was insured).

(b) There was a fixed limit on contributions from members of each SRO in any one year. For LAUTRO members the maximum contribution was £27 million, for FIMBRA members £19 million.

(c) Costs in excess of limits on claims from the members of any one SRO were borne by a levy on other SRO members who had not reached the upper limit of their own contribution (cross contribution). This was in force throughout the period of the 1990 rules but used only for the 1991/92 levy when FIMBRA members incurred £2 million liability over the £19 million cap.

In addition LAUTRO members agreed from 1990 to 1993 to provide up to £14 million towards the liability of FIMBRA members to contribute within their £19 million cap. LAUTRO members, other than friendly societies, who derived business from FIMBRA members were liable to be levied for this.

SIB recognised that cross contribution was unpopular and in Discussion Paper 10/93 indicated its intention to abolish it. SIB carried out consultation on this proposal in Consultative Paper 79 (February 1994). The ICS was to remain a unitary scheme but with separate SRO funds each capped at £100 million and without cross contribution, as it was hoped that three large SROs with well-balanced memberships would have a solid financial base.

Annex 2 of the 1994 rules deals with allocation of costs for levy purposes:

(1) Costs incurred and amounts received will be allocated to accounts maintained for different SRO member groups.

(2) Each SRO is responsible for levying contributions from its members and reference should be made to its rulebook to determine the basis on which this is carried out.

(3) PIA will administer the financing of compensation paid by the ICS for defaults after 18 July 1994 of FIMBRA and LAUTRO members not now regulated.

(4) Any firm regulated by SIB will be deemed to be a member of an appropriate SRO.

(5) Compensation costs otherwise allocable to the FIMBRA, LAUTRO or SIB contribution groups will be allocated to PIA.

(6) The maximum contribution costs allocable to IMRO, SFA or PIA for any year's compensation costs are £100 million.

## 8.7 Operation of the Scheme

Since the ICS was created in August 1988 it has paid compensation totalling £61.6 million to over 6,700 investors. In 1993/94 it paid £25.4 million in compensation payments to 2,276 investors.

Seventy-nine per cent of claims are for less than £15,000 and only 5 per cent for more than £30,000.

Of the 130 firms declared in default during the operation of the ICS, 87 per cent were regulated by FIMBRA, 10 per cent by SFA (including those formerly regulated by TSA or AFBD), 2 per cent by IMRO, 1 per cent by SIB and none by LAUTRO.

## 8.8 Draft EU Directive on Investors Compensation

The EU Commission has published a proposal for a Directive on investors compensation. The main feature of this would be to require the firm's home state to administer a compensation scheme covering the firm's activities both in the home state and when exercising its 'passport' rights in a host state. As currently drafted the proposed Directive would require:

– Compensation per investor of up to ECU 20,000. This is less than the ICS limit but there is no overall cap proposed.

– Compensation to be payable for claims relating to repayment of money or return of property. This is narrower than the ICS coverage of all civil liabilities.

These requirements are, of course, minima and a member state could exceed them. The draft Directive is silent on how funds are to be raised.

## 8.9 Policyholders Protection Act 1975 (PPA)

The PPA was introduced following the failure of Vehicle & General and Nation Life insurance companies in the early 1970s.

The PPA is administered by the Policyholders Protection Board which is empowered to raise levies on general or long term business of all United Kingdom authorised insurance companies in order to provide compensation funds. The amount of a levy may not exceed 1 per cent of leviable net premium income in any one year.

If an insurance company goes into liquidation, the Board is required to compensate United Kingdom policyholders to prescribed limits:

- general business policies: 100 per cent of claims in relation to compulsory cover; otherwise 90 per cent of claims where the policyholder is a private policyholder;
- long term policies: 90 per cent of claims crystallised prior to liquidation; if the policy has not crystallised the Board will try to secure continuity of 90 per cent of future benefits.

The Board has since inception compensated investors in five failed life assurance companies and policyholders of 13 general insurance companies. Prior to 1992 levies of £2.5 million were raised, but subsequent failure of the insurance subsidiaries of London United Investments is likely to entail very substantial levies.

# 9 COMPLAINTS

## 9.1 Introduction

In this section we discuss the role of complaints under the FSA regime, to which there are three particular aspects.

(1) A firm is required to handle complaints properly and to ensure appropriate remedial action is taken. It is considered important that investor grievances are effectively dealt with. It should, in principle, not be necessary for an investor to take legal action to obtain redress because the firm, its SRO or an independent complaints handling authority will investigate and resolve the investor's complaint without charge. The disciplinary tribunals of PIA and IMRO have power to award compensation in connection with a disciplinary action, which is separate from the complaints procedures discussed here.

(2) A firm should monitor complaints since they are viewed by regulators as an important indicator of unsatisfactory business practices, and are capable of providing an early indication of a problem with a firm or an individual within it. A sequence of complaints relating to a particular sales person may show he requires further training or is not fit and proper; a pattern of

complaints about a product may indicate that it is poorly designed or misleadingly advertised. In either case the firm's compliance officer should investigate the matter, determine if remedial action is needed, and ensure is is taken. Furthermore a regulator may take enforcement or disciplinary action where complaints reveal misconduct by a member.

(3) where a firm is unable to resolve a complaint to the customer's satisfaction it must advise him of further steps that can be taken in relation to that complaint. The complaint can then be investigated by the SRO or, if still unresolved, independently.

As noted by Lord Ackner in his report for PIA on 'A Unified Complaints Procedure' (July 1993, p 51),

> There is currently an excessive number of dispute resolution schemes in the financial sector which bewilder the investor and makes his task of obtaining a satisfactory settlement of his complaint unnecessary difficult.

His recommendation that PIA should, when recognised as an SRO, adopt a single complaints procedure has been adopted. However, the validity of this comment has not diminished and there is a separate complaints procedure, with different rules and criteria, for each regulator.

The system for consideration of complaints against firms by customers who have a grievance normally involves:

(1) The firm considering the complaint. We outline the requirements of IMRO, SFA and PIA.

(2) If the customer is still dissatisfied, the complaint is considered by the firm's SRO at no cost to the customer. This is only relevant to SFA but not to PIA or to IMRO.

(3) If the complaint is still not resolved, it is then considered independently and without cost to the customer. The ground rules of the PIA and IMRO Ombudsmen (the latter being known as the Investment Ombudsman) and also the Ombudsmen in other financial sectors are outlined below.

## 9.2 Consideration by the firm

A firm must have a written procedure for the proper handling of complaints. While details vary between IMRO, SFA and PIA, it should provide:

(1) A complaint should be handled by a responsible officer not concerned with the matter.

(2) A substantive response should be promptly sent which accepts the complaint and offers to remedy it, or otherwise rejects it.

(3) If the customer is dissatisfied he must (if not already informed of this) be told of his right to complain to the SRO and/or the relevant Ombudsman.

(4) The firm should keep records of complaints made and action taken.

## 9.3 Consideration by the SRO (SFA only)

If a complaint relating to an SFA member is referred to SFA, it will investigate and attempt to resolve the matter. If the customer is still not satisfied the complaint will be independently investigated. The procedure relevant to SFA is discussed below.

## 9.4 Independent consideration

The Investment Ombudsman (who handles complaints against IMRO members), the PIA Ombudsman, and the Insurance, Banking, Building Societies and Pensions Ombudsmen all operate under detailed rules or terms of reference which must be consulted in each case. They do, however, have the following points in common:

(1) Any customer or investor may refer complaints to them, although the Banking, Building Society and Insurance Ombudsman Schemes contain restrictions relating to certain non-private customers.

(2) The customer must first have tried to resolve the complaint with the firm itself.

(3) The customer is not charged for the ombudsman's services.

(4) The ombudsman will consider the complaint independently and impartially. He will try to conciliate the customer and the firm so that they reach a mutually agreed settlement. If unsuccessful he can adjudicate the complaint and if he finds in the customer's favour he can require the firm to pay compensation or make appropriate amends.

(5) The firm must cooperate with the ombudsman.

(6) The customer is not bound to accept the compensation and, if he rejects it, may pursue legal remedies. However the investor is bound by an adjudication of the Investment and Pensions Ombudsmen.

(7) There are time limits within which a complaint must have been referred to the ombudsman.

## 9.5 IMRO

A customer of an IMRO member whose complaint is not resolved by the firm could, until May 1995, refer it to IMRO. After that date IMRO will not itself investigate complaints because the transfer of its retail members to PIA is expected to result in significantly fewer complaints. They are, instead, referred straight to the Investment Ombudsman. For the year ending 31 March 1994, 874 complaints were referred to IMRO for resolution, and were investigated by IMRO's Complaints Unit with the aim of achieving a conciliated settlement. The largest categories of complaint related to maladministration (249), best advice or suitability (242), poor performance (69) and advertisements (44).

A customer of an IMRO member may from May 1995 refer a complaint to the Investment Ombudsman provided the firm has been given at least two months to try to achieve settlement, and (unless the firm agrees) the complaint must not normally involve a sum exceeding £100,000. The Investment Ombudsman first investigates the claim and seeks to achieve an informal conciliation in relation to the complaint, and the firm must cooperate in this. In 1993/94, 73 cases were referred to the Investment Ombudsman and he achieved an agreed settlement in all cases.

If conciliation does not succeed, the Investment Ombudsman can seek to adjudicate a complaint for which there is a legal remedy. A decision reached by adjudication binds both the firm and the customer, and appeal lies only on a point of law. The firm is bound to pay any sum awarded by the Investment Ombudsman up to £100,000.

## 9.6 SFA

SFA's Complaints Bureau will investigate a written complaint made by a customer against a firm relating to its authorised business once the firm has had a reasonable opportunity to investigate it.

In the year ended 31 March 1994 the Complaints Bureau received 393 complaints from customers relating to 111 firms. The three largest categories were 139 complaints relating to administration (often of personal equity plans), 72 relating to dealing and 59 regarding investment advice.

A customer may complain to the Complaints Commissioner about the way the Complaints Bureau has handled the complaint, and the Complaints Commissioner will investigate this.

A private customer may refer a claim against a firm to SFA's consumer arbitration scheme. The customer must pay a registration fee, currently £50, and is normally bound by the arbitrator's decision. In 1993/4 there were 20 consumer arbitrations.

SFA additionally operates a full arbitration scheme which is available for one firm to use for a dispute against another firm, and for a customer whose claim exceeds £50,000.

## 9.7 PIA

A customer of a PIA member may refer his complaint to the PIA Ombudsman if it is still outstanding after two months or the customer is dissatisfied with the firm's response.

The PIA Ombudsman will investigate most complaints about business carried on by a member of PIA or its appointed representative which is regulated by PIA. This includes business of a member or its appointed representative which was regulated by SIB or another SRO before the firm joined PIA. He can make an award of up to £50,000 binding on the PIA member.

PIA has not been in operation long enough at the time of writing to publish any statistics relating to complaints made against its members. Information can, however, be taken from LAUTRO and FIMBRA whose members will make up the bulk of PIA members. In the year ending March 1994 LAUTRO received 3,641 complaints against its members and FIMBRA received 2,697.

## 9.8   Other schemes

There are other ombudsman schemes relevant to the financial services sector. They are briefly summarised here.

*(a) Insurance Ombudsman*
The Insurance Ombudsman has jurisdiction to consider any complaint (including a dispute or claim) referred to him in connection with a policy of insurance provided it is with a firm which is a member of the Insurance Ombudsman Bureau (IOB) (of which there are 350) and is taken out by a private individual.

The complaint must relate to the marketing or administration of a policy, or a claim under a policy.

The Insurance Ombudsman will try to conciliate the dispute, failing which he will investigate and adjudicate the complaint. He may make a binding award up to £100,000.

In *R v Insurance Ombudsman Bureau ex parte Aegon Life Assurance Limited* ((1994) *The Times*, 7 January) it was held that the Bureau's decisions could not be challenged in the courts through judicial review.

The IOB completed 6,344 cases during 1993 and of these just under a quarter (1,557) related to life assurance, in particular complaints regarding administration and selling. The IOB acted as the complaints handling authority for LAUTRO members who had joined the IOB, but will not have jurisdiction in relation to PIA members, whose complaints will be dealt with by the PIA Ombudsman.

*(b) Building Societies Ombudsman*
The Building Societies Ombudsman operates under the Building Societies Ombudsman Scheme set up in accordance with the Building Societies Act 1986. He can deal with most complaints relating to a building society, and can award up to £100,000 compensation for financial loss.

*(c) Banking Ombudsman*
The Banking Ombudsman deals with complaints about all types of banking business carried on in the United Kingdom which concern a bank that is a member of the Banking Ombudsman Scheme. The complaint must be brought by an individual, a partnership or by a company with a turnover of less than £1 million a year. The claim must be for £100,000 or less and the Ombudsman can compel a bank to pay up to this sum in compensation.

*(d) Pensions Ombudsman*

The Pensions Ombudsman is appointed under the Pension Schemes Act 1993 to deal with complaints against, and disputes with, occupational and personal pension schemes, and employers on pension matters. He has, however, no jurisdiction in relation to social security benefits or matters more properly handled by an SRO or the Insurance Ombudsman.

# 10 IMPLEMENTATION OF THE SECOND BANKING COORDINATION, INVESTMENT SERVICES, CAPITAL ADEQUACY AND THIRD LIFE DIRECTIVES

## 10.1 Freedom of financial institutions within the EU

Articles 52 and 59 of the Treaty of Rome provide that a person established in a member state and exercising its right of freedom of establishment or to provide services in another member state must be able to do so under the same conditions as are imposed by that state on its own nationals. The various directives introducing the single passport regime have not created these freedoms but have made their exercise easier.

These freedoms are not absolute since member states may still apply to nationals of another member state the conditions they apply to their own nationals, such as professional rules of conduct. However, the European Court of Justice has limited the extent to which member states can apply their legislation to nationals of other member states who provide services in their territory. Although the main relevant judgments of the European Court of Justice concern co-insurance, it seems that the principles laid down by the court are of general application and may apply to other areas of business. In the so-called German co-insurance case (Case 205/84 *Commission of the European Communities v Germany* [1986] ECR 3755), the European Court of Justice held that the freedom to provide services is one of the fundamental principles of the Treaty of Rome and may only be restricted by provisions which meet the following cumulative criteria:

- those restrictions must be justified by the general good or public interest;
- they must be applied to all persons or undertakings operating within the territory of the state in which the service is provided (principle of non-discrimination);
- the public interest is not protected by the rules of the member state where the insurer is established (principle of non-duplication); and
- the same result could not be obtained by less restrictive rules (this is the principle of proportionality).

These are often called the 'general good' criteria.

## 10.2 Implementation of the Second Banking Coordination Directive

*(a) The single passport under the Second Banking Coordination Directive*
The Second Banking Coordination Directive, which came into force on 1 January 1993, introduced the concept of a single passport for credit institutions. The principles are very similar to those introduced by the Investment Services Directive, discussed below. A credit institution authorised in a European Economic Area (EEA) state is able to provide services or to open a branch in another EEA state and will remain subject to the supervision of its home-state regulator subject to certain limited exceptions. The single passport covers a wide range of activities including traditional banking activities and securities business.

*(b) Financial institutions benefiting from the single passport under the Second Banking Coordination Directive*
There was a risk of discrimination in favour of universal banks (such as German banks) as against banks (such as United Kingdom banks) which run their securities business through independent subsidiaries. Universal banks would have been able to take advantage of the single passport to carry out securities business across EEA borders whereas other banks would have the benefit of the single passport only in relation to their traditional banking business, their securities subsidiaries being excluded from the single passport facility as long as the Investment Services Directive was not in force.

In order to limit this risk as much as possible, art 18 of the Second Banking Coordination Directive allows financial subsidiaries of credit institutions to take advantage of the single passport subject to very strict conditions.

(1) The parent undertaking(s) must be authorised as credit institutions in the member state where the subsidiary is incorporated.
(2) The parent undertaking(s) must hold at least 90 per cent of the voting rights relating to the shares in the capital of the subsidiary.
(3) The parent undertaking(s) must satisfy the competent authorities as to the prudent management of the subsidiary and must have declared, with the consent of the relevant home member state competent authorities, that they jointly and severally guarantee the commitments entered into by the subsidiary.
(4) The subsidiary must be effectively included, for the activities in question, in the consolidated supervision of the parent undertaking, in particular for the calculation of the solvency ratio and for the control of large exposures.

The subsidiary can only use its passport in relation to the activities listed in the Annex to the Second Banking Coordination Directive which it actually carries on within its home member state. Financial subsidiaries are subject to most of the supervision requirements imposed upon credit institutions by the Second Banking Coordination Directive including, in particular, the minimum capital requirement.

Because of these stringent requirements, it is thought that most of the financial institutions which could potentially take advantage of art 18 of the Second Banking Coordination Directive have preferred to wait until the coming into force of the Investment Services Directive for two reasons. The Capital Adequacy Directive has introduced lower capital requirements than the Second Banking Coordination Directive and the list of activities covered by the single passport under the Investment Services Directive is better adapted to financial institutions business than the list annexed to the Second Banking Coordination Directive.

*(c) Implementation of the Second Banking Coordination Directive by SIB*
In March 1993, SIB issued the Financial Services (European Institutions) Instrument 1993 which made changes to the statements of principle, core rules and SIB rules necessary to comply with the requirements of the Second Banking Coordination Directive. The 1993 instrument came into force on 1 March 1993 and lays down the regime applicable to EEA credit or financial institutions which carry on investment business in the United Kingdom. It draws a distinction between prudential supervision (in particular, in respect of fitness and properness including financial resources, sound administration and accounting procedures and adequate internal controls) which will be solely the responsibility of the home-state supervisor who will enforce its own rules and other areas, where, subject to the general good requirements, United Kingdom host-state rules will be applicable. Those rules include, in particular, the Financial Services (Conduct of Business) Rules 1990 subject to various omissions.

## 10.3 Implementation of the Investment Services Directive and the Capital Adequacy Directive

*(a) Introduction*
This section examines the implementation of the Investment Services Directive (ISD) and the Capital Adequacy Directive (CAD) in the United Kingdom.

The ISD together with the CAD will complete the main EU measures introducing the single European passport in the financial sector. It follows implementation of the passport system for UCITS in 1989, banks on 1 January 1993 and for insurers and life companies on 1 July 1994. The banking passport under the Second Banking Coordination Directive already covers investment services activities where they are carried on by credit institutions. The ISD will give equivalent rights to investment firms.

The CAD provides harmonised capital requirements for investment firms but it also applies to banks (many of whom will also be concerned with some of the changes arising from the ISD). The CAD attempts to create a level playing-field between banks and investment firms by imposing the same requirements (some of which are taken from existing banking Directives) on both types of institutions.

Initial capital requirements, however, will remain much higher for credit institutions.

The main purpose of the ISD is to grant a passport, which means that a firm properly authorised in one EEA state (for instance under the FSA in the United Kingdom) may as of right conduct investment business in another EEA state through a branch or by the direct provision of services provided it observes the correct procedures. Once operating in that other EEA state (the host state) it will be subject to the host state's conduct of business rules although its regulator in the United Kingdom (the home state) will continue to supervise prudential requirements.

The ISD requires EEA states to make arrangements for firms which conduct investment business to be authorised and to observe minimum standards. The FSA already fulfils these rules in the United Kingdom. While the basic United Kingdom structure will require minimal alteration, implementation of the ISD and the CAD will lead to a number of changes to the present regime in the United Kingdom. These are discussed below and noted where relevant elsewhere in the text.

A separate Directive has been proposed to deal with the harmonisation of investor compensation schemes on the basis that firms will belong to the scheme in their home member state. This proposal reflects the provisions of the adopted Directive on deposit guarantee schemes.

In addition to preliminary notices, no fewer than nine consultation documents have been issued on the implementation of the ISD and the CAD and the amendments actually made to the FSA and SROs rulebooks will to an extent depend upon the outcome of the consultation exercise.

### (b) Overview of the Investment Services Directive

The ISD was adopted in May 1993 and implementing provisions must be adopted by 1 July 1995 to come into force by 31 December 1995.

The ISD has six key elements:

(1) It requires an EEA firm whose regular business is to provide certain specified investment services to obtain authorisation in order to do so from the authorities of the state in which it has both its head and registered office. This requires the introduction of an FSA-style regime in other member states.

(2) It provides a single 'passport' enabling firms authorised in one EEA state to carry on business, either through branches or directly, throughout the EEA states without the need for further local authorisation from any other EEA state.

(3) It creates the concept of a 'regulated market' which must meet prescribed minimum standards.

(4) It prescribes minimum standards for prudential supervision and conduct of business rules, and divides the supervisory responsibilities between the

authorities of a firm's 'home state' and the authorities of the firm's 'host state'.

(5) It aims to facilitate direct market access by ISD firms to regulated markets.

(6) It imposes transaction reporting requirements on ISD-authorised firms.

The ISD will be implemented in the United Kingdom by secondary legislation and it is not envisaged that any primary legislation will be required. The Directives will be implemented within the existing institutional framework and division of responsibilities established under the FSA. The changes made to the FSA will be made by regulations under the European Communities Act 1972, secondary legislation under s 2 of the FSA itself and through directions issued under s 192 of the FSA. The United Kingdom regulatory structure will be retained and SIB, the SROs and the Bank of England will act as competent authorities for the purposes of the ISD and the CAD although changes will have to be made to the rulebooks of the SIB and SROs and through Bank of England notices.

Many of these changes will affect firms even if they do not undertake any cross border business and some rulebook changes are likely to affect firms that fall outside the ISD altogether.

*(c) Scope of the Investment Services Directive*
The ISD applies to all 'investment firms'. Generally for the purposes of the ISD, an 'investment firm' is a firm which carries out a specified range of investment business provided that its regular occupation or business is the provision of those services for third parties on a professional basis. The relevant services are those listed in section A of the Annex to the Directive where the service relates to any of the financial instruments listed in section B.

Section A activities are:-

(1) reception and transmission, on behalf of investors, of orders in relation to one or more of the instruments covered by the Directive;

(2) execution of such orders other than for own account;

(3) dealing in any of the instruments covered by the Directive;

(4) discretionary portfolio management involving ISD investments;

(5) underwriting and/or placing of ISD investments.

The list of investments covered by the ISD is set out in section B of the Annex and comprises:

(1) transferable securities;

(2) units in collective investments undertakings;

(3) money-market instruments;

(4) financial futures contracts, including equivalent cash-settled instruments;

(5) forward interest-rate agreements;

(6) interest rate, currency and equity swaps;

(7) options to acquire or dispose of any ISD instruments including equivalent cash-settled instruments and, in particular, options on currency and on interest rates.

This activity/investment matrix under the ISD is different from that under the FSA. In most respects (but not all) FSA has a wider scope. For example FSA activities not covered by the ISD include:

- firms which only give advice;
- life assurance investment products (covered under the Third Life Insurance or 'Framework' Directive);
- collective investment schemes such as unit trusts (some of which are covered by the 1985 UCITS directive which has already been implemented).

Where a firm has ISD authorisation for any of the 'core' services in section A, it can seek approval from its regulator to provide a specific range of additional services ('non-core services') in other EEA states. The non-core services (for which EEA states are not obliged to impose authorisation requirements) are set out in section C of the Annex and comprise:

(1) safekeeping and administration of instruments covered by the ISD;
(2) safe custody services;
(3) granting credits or loans to an investor to allow him to carry out a transaction in an ISD instrument, where the firm granting the credit or loan is involved in a transaction;
(4) corporate finance advice and advice in services relating to mergers and acquisitions;
(5) services relating to underwriting;
(6) investment advice concerning ISD instruments;
(7) foreign exchange services where these are connected with the provision of investment services.

*Amendments to Schedule 1 FSA and the current FSA exemptions*    The Government proposes to extend the scope of Sched 1 to the FSA to include any activities which are covered by the Directive but not by the Act. These proposals are noted in the text of Chapters 7 to 10. For example the way in which transferable securities is defined in the Directive means that shares in some industrial and provident societies will need to be added to the list of FSA investments, and para 2 of Sched 1 will need to be extended to include bank bills (or bankers acceptances).

   Certain types of financial services activities are specifically excluded from the scope of the ISD, and these include life assurance, some corporate treasurers, unit trusts and other forms of collective investment undertakings, most pensions business, independent financial advisors who cannot handle clients' money or assets and investment business conducted by professionals which is incidental to the practice of their profession. These activities will continue to be regulated under the FSA to the present extent. It is not, however, proposed to implement the ISD outside the FSA regime so some of the excluded activities in Sched 1 FSA will need to be narrowed, which may result in some firms requiring authorisation under the FSA for the first time. The exclusion in the FSA for groups and joint enterprises at para 18 of Sched 1 FSA is wider than the equivalent ISD exemption which does not cover joint enterprises. The present permitted person regime under para 23 of Sched 1 also conflicts with the ISD. Some firms which currently rely upon para 18, particularly in relation to joint enterprises, and some permitted persons who deal in ISD business/instruments may therefore now need to seek authorisation under FSA.

The present exemptions in para 17 (dealing as principal) and 19 (sale of goods and supply of services) of Sched 1 FSA are also inconsistent with the ISD regime and will have to be narrowed. The present exemption in para 19 is of particular importance to unauthorised institutions involved in trade finance and these firms will need to consider carefully the amendments which are to be made.

The scope of the exemption in s 44 FSA for appointed representatives will also have to be reduced. The effect of this change will depend upon the type of business involved (whether it is ISD or non-ISD) and whether the activities are restricted to passing orders only to one ISD firm under that firm's full and unconditional responsibility.

There will also be changes in the present regime under s 43 FSA for the wholesale money-market activities of institutions on the Bank of England list as the Grey paper activities (see Chapter 15) may involve investment business under the ISD. In future listed institutions will have to be FSA authorised rather than exempted, although they will continue to enjoy exemption from many of the FSA obligations which apply to SIB/SRO authorised firms.

*(d) Authorisation requirements*
An investment firm which wishes to carry on investment business covered by the ISD must be authorised by its 'home' state. This authorisation must specify the core services the firm is authorised to provide, and can also cover any non-core services. It is intended that United Kingdom firms already authorised under the FSA on 31 December 1995 will be deemed to be authorised under the ISD regime. Firms which are brought into the scope of the FSA for the first time as a result of implementation of the ISD should be able to apply for authorisation in the second half of 1995 so that they are authorised by 31 December 1995.

A firm must notify its regulator of the non-core services (see the list from section C above) it intends to carry on. Some of these activities are not at present subject to authorisation under FSA (eg safe custody). This will remain the case, but such activities will form part of the business regulated by the ISD, and fall within the ISD passport. The United Kingdom Government proposes to make an order to extend the FSA to encompass these activities so as to enable conduct of business rules to be made for non-core activities. It is not thought that the effect of these changes to the responsibilities of SIB and the SROs will be significant as they already have the ability to have regard to the whole range of activities of a firm seeking authorisation.

The ISD sets out the following conditions which will need to be met by investment firms who seek authorisation after the ISD comes into force:

(a) *Location of head office*  A firm covered by the ISD must have its head office in the same EEA state as its registered office.

(b) *Fit and proper requirements*  The ISD does not prescribe detailed standards for fit and proper requirements at the authorisation stage, but rather lays down principles which each EEA state must reflect in its national requirements. The SIB and SROs are already empowered to take these criteria into account in the United Kingdom, and the Government sees no need to turn this power into an obligation in respect of firms seeking authorisation under the ISD regime. However, it will be necessary to introduce regulations relating to firms, whether natural or legal persons, who have only a single proprietor. The SIB and SROs will have to ensure that, before authorisation of such firms, there are appropriate arrangements in place to safeguard clients' interests in the event of the individual's death or incapacity. Natural persons, essentially sole traders and partnerships in the United Kingdom, will also have to meet additional conditions relating to solvency and segregation of client assets. Partners of authorised firms will be subject to individual solvency monitoring and may have to file annual solvency statements.

(c) *Capital requirements*  Firms will have to comply with the capital requirements laid down in the CAD. At present there is no explicit requirement in the FSA that a person must have an initial capital before authorisation is granted, so an express requirement will be imposed in the new regulations. Ongoing capital requirements under the CAD can be met in the case of firms authorised by SIB under SIB's existing powers and provisions will be made placing SROs under an obligation to make and apply the rules which give effect to the CAD.

(d) *Business plan*  The ISD requires a business plan to be submitted by each firm when applying for authorisation. Business plans are already a feature of the United Kingdom authorisation process, but on implementation of the ISD they will become a formal requirement.

*Controllers*  The ISD requires investment firms to notify their home state authority of the identities of all who hold 'qualifying holdings' in the firm. The ISD defines 'qualifying holdings' as 10 per cent of the capital or voting rights in a firm, including indirect holdings and holdings which enable the holder to exercise significant influence over the management of the firm. The present FSA regime is based on a controller definition of those holding 15 per cent or more and the ISD requires the threshold to be lowered and the controller definition to be widened. Firms will be obliged to identify controlling shareholders when seeking authorisation. A further change will be necessary in relation to ongoing supervision and anyone intending to become a 'controller' of an investment firm, and a controller intending to increase or reduce its holding in certain specified circumstances, will be obliged to pre-notify the firm's regulator and await approval. This will bring the FSA in line with the Banking Act 1987 and the Insurance Companies Act 1982 which already have pre-notification requirements. This is one of the areas where changes may apply to all FSA firms, including those outside the scope of the ISD.

Further requirements concerning the monitoring of group structure were introduced under the so-called 'post-BCCI' Directive, adopted in June 1995.

*(e) Prudential supervision by home-state authorities*
The ISD provides for a division of supervisory responsibility between prudential requirements (home-state authorities) and conduct of business rules (host-state authorities), which will be relevant to firms seeking to exercise the 'passport'.

The regulatory authorities in each EEA state will be responsible for applying prudential requirements to firms which they have authorised. The areas which the ISD requires to be covered under the prudential requirements include administrative and accounting procedures, arrangements for the holding of client money and other client assets, record keeping, structures for dealing with conflicts of interest, ongoing solvency and capital adequacy requirements and fitness and properness of a firm and its controllers. This supervisory function is already expressed as a power of the United Kingdom authorities in relation to United Kingdom firms; an obligation will be imposed on them to use these powers in conformity with the ISD.

*Client/investors money and other assets*   Under the ISD, client money/asset protection is the responsibility of home-state regulators (and not host regulators under their individual conduct of business rules). Changes to the current client money regulations will be required to bring them into line with the ISD and difficulties arise because the law in other EEA states may conflict with the United Kingdom rules.

For this reason, the proposals in relation to client money and assets are, at the date of writing, not finalised. The United Kingdom will need to take into account how other EEA states propose to implement these requirements. It is clear that the current possibility of an opt-out from segregation for non-private customers cannot be retained where the firm is a sole trader or a partnership. The United Kingdom regulators are considering whether to retain the present system with additional obligations on firms (as to accounting and top up) for client funds where the regulations do not apply, which would take account of the ISD's requirements that no investor's money can be used by the firm for its own account. The alternative is to have three different types of account—one for full client money regulations as at present, another under a less stringent regime for non-private/expert investors who opt out, and a third for the firm's own funds. The United Kingdom authorities will also need to determine the client money/asset rules to be followed by United Kingdom firms when they conduct investment business in other member states. Protection in the event of insolvency of a firm may be more difficult in other countries, and the concept of trust law on which the client money regulations are based may not be recognised. The alternative is either to require firms to abide by host rules or require all client money to be held in the United Kingdom, although it is recognised that the latter option would breach fundamental principles of EU law.

*Conduct of business rules*   The United Kingdom authorities will be responsible for applying conduct of business rules in respect of ISD business carried out in the United Kingdom (whether the business is being carried out by a United Kingdom authorised firm or by a firm authorised in another EU state). As in the case of prudential rules, obligations to exercise the powers in conformity with the ISD will be imposed. The ISD also lists a number of principles which must be reflected in each state's conduct of business rules. Provision will also be made for cooperation between competent authorities in home and host states for supervision of those firms taking advantage of the passport.

*(f) The Investment Services Directive Passport*
The 'passport' is the name given to the right of an investment firm authorised in the EU to operate through a branch or on a services basis in all EEA states without requiring further authorisation.

Articles 17 and 18 of the Directive set out the procedures through which investment firms need to go before they can take advantage of this passport. The ISD introduces notification procedures to enable United Kingdom firms to use the passport. FSA authorised firms which only conduct non-core activities under section C of the ISD may wish to extend their United Kingdom authorisation and undertake a small amount of a section A activity in order to obtain a right to the passport for the non-core activities which they would otherwise not have.

Many United Kingdom investment firms will be providing investment services in other EEA states when the ISD comes into force. The United Kingdom intends to make use of special provisions for such firms which means that the United Kingdom authorities will send the authorities of the other EEA state a 'bulk' notification of firms which have already established a branch or are providing services in that state. The Government also proposes that any investment firms which are subsidiaries of credit institutions and have passport rights under the Second Banking Coordination Directive should from 31 December 1995 obtain their passports under the ISD. However, those already operating under a Second Banking Coordination Directive passport on that date will continue under that regime.

The first stage for any 'new' United Kingdom authorised investment firm wishing to exercise its passport rights will be to notify the relevant United Kingdom authority of its intention, providing all the necessary information required. The home state has three months to review in the case of firms wishing to establish a new branch and one month to review in the case of a firm wishing to provide services, at the end of which period the home state must pass the notification details on to the prospective host state. The firm may then establish a branch in the host state after two months or, if the firm is merely providing ISD services in another state, then the firm may commence business as soon as the host state has received the notification.

The provisions for notification by a firm authorised in another EEA state who wishes a passport into the United Kingdom will mirror those established for United Kingdom firms wishing to operate in another EEA state. SIB will be established as the first point of contact for all incoming institutions. Regulations governing incoming firms will amend the FSA to allow such firms using the ISD passport to set up a branch or provide services in the United Kingdom on the basis of the authorisation of their own home-state supervisors. These EU firms will be subject to a measure of regulation in the United Kingdom in relation to their conduct of business and will be free to join an SRO if they wish to be governed by the SRO's rather than SIB's conduct of business and other rules. The existing regime for European institutions, which was introduced following implementation of the Second Banking Coordination Directive, will be extended to exempt incoming ISD firms from SRO rules which relate to matters of prudential supervision, and these will remain the responsibility of the home state authorities. An example of this regime is set out in Appendix 39 of the SFA rulebook.

## (g) Transaction reporting

The ISD requires a minimum coverage of transactions executed by any ISD firm to be reported to their home-state authorities. The implementation of the ISD will require some changes to the reporting requirements applicable to United Kingdom firms, in particular in relation to reporting off-market trades.

## (h) Regulated markets

The decision as to which markets are designated 'regulated markets' is to be left to the individual EEA states although certain requirements set out in the ISD must be met. In the United Kingdom it is proposed that the domestic equity market, the international equity market, the gilt edged and fixed interests markets, the traditional options market, LIFFE and OMLX be designated as regulated markets.

ISD firms and credit institutions have a right of access to regulated markets under the ISD (subject to some transitory provisions). These markets can place screens in other EEA states in order to facilitate the exercise of that right and in future they will be able to do so in the United Kingdom without needing to obtain recognition under s 40 FSA. The London Stock Exchange has stated that it will be using its rights to expand the reach of its markets and to increase order flows.

It is SIB's view that the ISD allows host EEA states to impose additional capital requirements in respect of matters outside the scope of the CAD. On this basis SIB intends to maintain additional capital requirements for clearing members of LIFFE and London Clearing House irrespective of whether the firm is authorised in the United Kingdom or in other EEA state.

The ISD standards for post-trade transparency are detailed although no new powers will be required. SIB is discussing the best way of fulfilling ISD's requirements with the London Stock Exchange where the directive will have a particular impact on the international equity market if it is to be a 'regulated' market under the ISD.

*(i) Implementation of the Capital Adequacy Directive—Background*
The Capital Adequacy Directive (CAD) establishes for the first time a harmonised capital adequacy regime for investment firms in the EEA. It also develops the existing regime for credit institutions under the Solvency Ratio Directive and the Own Funds Directive. The major change for banks will be the introduction of market risk requirements under the CAD, instead of the credit risk requirements under the Solvency Ratio Directive, on instruments they hold on their 'trading book'. The present capital/financial resources requirements for United Kingdom investment firms will have to change and some of the present banking regulations on credit risk and large exposures will also apply. In this way, the CAD seeks to establish a level playing-field between investment firms and credit institutions although initial/maximum capital requirements will remain much higher for banks.

*(j) Changes to the present structure of regulation*
The CAD is to be implemented at the same time as the ISD, no later than 31 December 1995. Implementation will require changes to the powers of SIB and the SROs, the Bank of England and the Building Societies Commission already having all the powers they need. The Treasury has identified the areas where action will be required. These relate to:

(1) SROs' ability to impose capital requirements. SIB already has adequate powers under s 49 FSA to lay down rules requiring firms to maintain particular levels of capital in conformity with the CAD. The SROs do not have a directly corresponding power. It is proposed that a direction will be issued under the FSA laying down an obligation guaranteeing that the SROs will exercise their powers in conformity with the CAD.

(2) Powers to enable the regulators to exercise greater powers on an ad hoc basis. The CAD includes a number of provisions which mean that supervisors need to be able to exercise their powers on an ad hoc basis. The SROs will be able to do this under their existing powers. It is proposed that a power should also be conferred on SIB to allow an investment firm (within the meaning of the CAD) to depart from rules it has made in implementation of the CAD. Conditions will also be imposed on firms in the exercise of this dispensation and a breach of these conditions will be treated as a contravention of requirements imposed under the FSA. The

CAD also sets limits on the extent to which an investment firm can be exposed to a single counterparty without incurring additional capital requirements. This is a principle which United Kingdom supervisors already have the powers to implement.

(3) Powers to gain information for the purposes of consolidated supervision. The final element of the CAD is the requirement that investment firms must be supervised on a consolidated basis. Where a group includes a bank, the Bank of England will be responsible for overseeing the consolidation. Otherwise, consolidation will normally be carried out by the regulator of the holding company where that company is itself a financial institution or carried out by the regulator of the preponderant regulated business. The Bank of England already has adequate powers to make the necessary changes to its consolidation regime. The FSA regulators' powers are inadequate in some respects and the Government therefore proposes to confer new powers on SIB similar to those in s 39(5) of the Banking Act to remedy these defects.

*(k) Changes to current SFA/IMRO financial resource requirements*
Substantial consultative documents have been published by SFA and IMRO, and some of the principal issues are as follows.

(1) Financial resources rules will continue to apply to investment firms on a solo basis but they will also be subject to capital requirements on a consolidated basis. This will be a major change for groups, particularly if the investment firm is not a subsidiary of a bank and they are not therefore at present subject to the existing regime under the Second Consolidated Supervision Directive. The right to a full regulatory accounting consolidation is reserved by SFA but it will normally follow a 'risk-based aggregation'. The scope of upward and downward consolidation under the CAD is limited but SFA will extend it to include subsidiaries and parents which are not investment firms/credit institutions/financial holding companies.

(2) The CAD introduces the concept of the trading book to distinguish between financial instruments which are traded and other assets. Market risk requirements on the trading book already apply to investment firms, whom SFA requires to mark to market daily all positions in financial instruments. There will be changes for these firms, but the main change is for banks where any trading book assets will in future be subject to the CAD rather than the Solvency Ratio Directive requirements.

(3) Under the CAD, non-trading assets for investment firms are subject to the 8 per cent capital requirement of the Solvency Ratio Directive, but SFA intends to maintain the right to apply a secondary requirement in relation to illiquid assets. This additional requirement is part of the 'super-equivalence' approach adopted by the United Kingdom SROs which will

probably mean that United Kingdom firms will have higher capital requirements than firms from other member states. The secondary requirement will not be applied where a firm can demonstrate it is well managed and that its activities and risks are appropriately diversified.

(4) Another area of 'superequivalence' is SFA's and IMRO's approach to the structure of the different requirements under the CAD. Whereas under the CAD firms are required to meet the highest of initial expenditure and risk requirements, IMRO will maintain the cumulative nature of its current requirements and SFA will apply a partially additional expenditure requirement.

(5) As well as a foreign exchange requirement, investment firms will also be subject to a large exposure requirement under the CAD. Large exposures (25 per cent) on the trading books of both banks and investment firms will be subject to additional capital requirements after ten days. Other large exposures will be subject to the absolute limits which already apply to banks. Large exposures will have to be monitored on a consolidated basis.

(6) Investment firms seeking authorisation under the ISD will need to meet the minimum/initial capital levels set out in the CAD (which range from ECU730,000 to ECU50,000). Investment firms already in existence before July 1995 can benefit from 'grandfathering' provisions. If these firms do not meet the relevant initial capital limit, their capital levels will be monitored at six monthly intervals and, once the CAD is in force, their levels of capital may not fall below the highest reference level established by this process, until they reach the level of the appropriate initial capital requirement.

(7) Finally, the CAD places greater emphasis than the present United Kingdom regime on capital in the form of equity and audited profits and reserves. This will mean that current year profits of investment firms will need to be audited before they can be included as part of the firm's resources. In addition the current gearing limits which restrict the amount of subordinated debt which firms can utilise will be substantially reduced.

## 10.4 Implementation of the Third Life Directive

The Insurance Companies (Third Insurance Directives) Regulations 1994 (SI No 1696), which came into force on 1 July 1994, make a number of amendments to the FSA (as well as to the Insurance Companies Act) in order to give effect to the Third Life and Non-Life Directives. One of the principal purposes of these directives is to introduce the principle of home state control whereby each EEA state has sole responsibility for the authorisation and supervision of business carried on throughout the EEA by undertakings having their head office in that state. It should also be borne in mind that these regulations make amendment to the Insurance Companies Act regime.

The main alterations to the FSA are, in outline, as follows, although reference should be made to the regulations in each case.

(1) An EEA insurer authorised in its home state to carry on insurance business which is investment business is authorised to carry on that business in the United Kingdom, together with other investment business which it may carry on under the law of its home state, provided it has observed the procedure in Sched 2(F), ICA (reg 57).

(2) If an EEA insurer seeks to join an SRO, it may not be refused admission, or subsequently expelled, for reasons relating to its fitness to carry on insurance business which is investment business. It may not be required to maintain financial resources for such business, nor may the SRO regulate any matter which is the preserve of its home state regulator (reg 56).

(3) SIB's Statements of Principle and conduct of business rules to which an EEA insurer is subject shall not provide for any matter which is the preserve of its home state regulator (reg 58).

(4) SIB's exercise of powers of intervention, under s 64 FSA, and to restrict business under s 65 FSA, are amended (reg 59).

# 3 Principles, Rules and Duties

This chapter sets out to consider the rules to which an authorised person is subject. The imposition of detailed rules regulating the conduct of persons authorised under the FSA is one of the two limbs of the investor protection regime. The other is the requirement, discussed in Chapter 2. that any person carrying on investment business demonstrates that they are fit and proper before obtaining authorisation. The exceptions to this requirement are also mentioned in that chapter.

Once a firm has obtained authorisation it is subject to detailed rules which to a greater or lesser extent regulate the conduct of its day to day investment business. In this chapter we examine the various rules which regulate an authorised person, and then consider the other duties which are relevant to investment business.

## 1 AN OVERVIEW

The rules drawn up under the FSA can be viewed as a series of layers:

(1)   The highest layer is SIB's ten Principles which are intended to lay down the required standards of conduct at a high level of generality. They apply to all authorised persons and their staff.

(2)   The next layer are the 40 core rules drafted by SIB dealing with conduct of business, together with the five core rules dealing with financial supervision. These were originally intended to form a common basis of rules which would apply to all SROs (but not RPBs). They have been adopted by IMRO and SFA but not by LAUTRO or FIMBRA nor by SIB itself in relation to persons directly regulated by it. SIB stated in section 6 of the Large Report ('Making the Two Tier System Work' May 1993) that it intended to withdraw from direct regulation (see Chapter 1) and as part of this exercise SIB has de-designated most of the core rules, the client money regulations, the supplementary client money regulations and the core financial rules. In practical terms this may make little difference to

the current regime for the foreseeable future as neither IMRO nor SFA is likely to make wholesale rule changes in consequence. Similarly while the new PIA conduct of business rules will not necessarily follow the core rules they are likely to have a number of features in common with them.

(3) The third layer is the third tier rules. These are drafted by each SRO which has adopted the core rules and are intended to build upon the core rules. Together with the core rules they form an integral part of the conduct of business rules of IMRO and SFA.

(4) The fourth layer is formal guidance issued by an SRO, of which examples are given below.

Taken together these four layers are intended to provide a regime with the following particular features:

–   Principles which set the 'tone' and guide a firm in its business.
–   Core rules which are intended to provide a common structure for all SRO members' conduct of business rules, augmented by each SRO's third tier rules. As mentioned above this position may change over time in consequence of the Large Report.
–   A regime which provides appropriate levels of protection. A private customer is entitled to benefit from a wider range of rules than an institutional customer (see section 6 below).

LAUTRO, FIMBRA and the RPBs have conduct of business rules which do not incorporate the core rules. They are, instead, based upon SIB's conduct of business rules, which do not themselves incorporate the core rules. They are broadly similar in effect to the core rules and third tier rules but are drafted with less clarity.

In addition to the Principles, core rules, third tier rules and guidance there are two other relevant sources of duties and obligations.

(5) Other rules made under the FSA. These are discussed below and include:

–   Membership rules which govern admission to membership.
–   Financial rules which are concerned with a firm's financial resources.
–   Client money regulations which oblige a firm to segregate client money and assets from its own assets.
–   Rules relating to monitoring, enforcement and discipline.
–   Rules governing the handling of complaints and resolution of disputes.
–   Regulations governing the promotion of unregulated collective investment schemes.
–   Common unsolicited calls regulations which regulate the circumstances in which a firm may cold call a customer.
–   Cancellation regulations relating to the sale of life assurance and regulated collective investment schemes to private investors.

(6)   Duties which arise outside the FSA which are:

- Contractual duties resulting from the contract between the firm and its customer or counterparty.
- Fiduciary duties. These are especially relevant where a firm provides advisory or discretionary services but have wide application. (See section 14 below.)

# 2   SIB'S TEN PRINCIPLES

These were issued by SIB on 15 March 1990 under s 47A FSA. As stated in the preamble to the Principles, they are intended to form a universal statement of the standards expected. They apply directly to the conduct of investment business and financial standing of all persons regulated by SIB, members of an SRO, and firms certified by an RPB. In addition, individual employees of a firm and its appointed representatives must also observe the Principles as failure to comply with a Principle is a ground for disqualification of an individual under s 59 (s 47A(4)(b)).

Section 47B, which provides for the modification or waiver of the Principles in particular cases, is unlikely to be brought into force.

The preamble to the Principles additionally states that they are not exhaustive of the standards expected. Following the rulebook does not necessarily equate to following the Principles, and *vice versa*.

The Government's purpose in empowering SIB to issue the Principles was stated by Mr Maude, the Minister responsible, during debate in Standing Committee D in May/June 1989 on the amendments to the FSA which were introduced by the Companies Act 1989:

> The SIB had indicated that at the outset it intends to use this power to issue broadly expressed statements of principle which briefly and clearly establish certain fundamental requirements which everyone must satisfy ... They are much the same as aims in management terms ... [and] are intended to provide a framework, at a high level of generality, for legally enforceable rules ... .

The origin of the Principles lies in the decision of the chairman of SIB to re-examine the SIB rulebook in late 1988. His stated purpose was:

> To see whether significant simplification could be achieved to introduce greater flexibility and cost-effectiveness without compromising client protection and whether greater emphasis could be placed on the underlying principle than its application in a detailed rule.

The Principles were intended to be:

> [T]he guiding light of firms engaged in investment business

as the Minister responsible said in the House of Lords (13 November 1989 col 1095) and as David Walker said in a conference speech in April 1989 to:

> describe standards of conduct of which a breach would cast doubt on the fitness and propriety of the individual or firm concerned to continue to undertake investment business

These two associated purposes are illustrated by the day-to-day application of the Principles. First, they are used by firms to guide them in the conduct of investment business. They enable directors or senior management to judge whether a proposed course of action is acceptable by providing a clearer statement of the required standards than can necessarily be derived from the conduct of business rules. In other words, they enable a firm to see the wood for the trees. Secondly, breach of a principle is used by SIB and the SROs as grounds to bring disciplinary action and for exercising powers of intervention. This is discussed in Chapter 12. The availability of the Principles for disciplinary action is set out in s 47A (3) and (4):

47A(1) The Secretary of State may issue statements of principle with respect to the conduct of financial standing expected of persons authorised to carry on investment business.

(2) The conduct expected may include compliance with a code or standard issued by another person, as for the time being in force, and may allow for the exercise of discretion by any person pursuant to any such code or standard.

(3) Failure to comply with a statement of principle under this section is a ground for the taking of disciplinary action or the exercise of powers of intervention, but it does not of itself give rise to any right of action by investors or other persons affected or affect the validity of any transaction.

(4) The disciplinary action which may be taken by virtue of sub-section (3) is:

(a) the withdrawal or suspension of authorisation under section 28 or the termination or suspension of authorisation under section 33;

(b) the giving of a disqualification direction under section 59;

(c) the making of a public statement under section 60; or

(d) the application by the Secretary of State for an injunction, interdict or other order under section 61(1);

and the reference in that subsection to powers of intervention is to the powers conferred by Chapter VI of this Part.

(5) Where a statement of principle relates to compliance with a code or standard issued by another person, the statement of principle may provide:

(a) that failure to comply with the code or standard shall be a ground for the taking of disciplinary action, or the exercise of powers of intervention, only in such cases and to such extent as may be specified; and

(b) that no such action shall be taken, or any such power exercised, except at the request of the person by whom the code or standard in question was issued.

(6) The Secretary of State shall exercise his powers in such manner as appears to him appropriate to secure compliance with statements of principle under this section.

The powers of discipline set out in subs (4) are those exercisable by SIB against persons whom it regulates and certain other persons. Their exercise is discussed in Chapter 12. The SROs may also use breach of the Principles as grounds for taking such action and are empowered to do so by their own rulebooks.

Use of the Principles in disciplinary action by SIB and the SROs has thrown into sharp focus uncertainty over their status. While most firms would consider that breach of a Principle is a more serious matter than breach of a rule, an alternative view (expressed by more than one SRO disciplinary tribunal) is that breach of a Principle is no more serious than a breach of a rule, and that rules and Principles are interchangeable for disciplinary purposes.

It is not easy to determine the role of the Principles. First, they are unique in a regulatory field; there is nothing that resembles them other than perhaps the Takeover Code, and no guidance can be derived from other sources. Secondly, the Principles arguably cannot be interpreted as rules because the legal consequence of liability does not result from their breach. They are not actionable by an investor in damages and failure to observe a Principle does not invalidate a transaction. Furthermore while guidance can be derived from the reports of SIB and SRO disciplinary actions, it is difficult to apply their general, non-specific wording to any particular factual situation.

## 2.1 The Principles

We now look at each Principle in turn, mentioning circumstances when they have been used in disciplinary action as this throws some light on their practical application:

(1) *Integrity*:   A firm should observe high standards of integrity and fair dealing.

Drawn from the wording of the FSA itself (Sched 8 para 1A) this requires a firm to act honestly and fairly. A firm must not act deceitfully. IMRO has disciplined a firm under this Principle for unreasonably charging private customers.

(2) *Skill, care and diligence*:   A firm should act with due skill, care and diligence.

Also derived from Sched 8 of the FSA (at para 2), this Principle obliges a firm to discharge its duties skillfully and carefully. A firm which causes its customer loss through carelessness will be in breach of this Principle. IMRO has disciplined a member for breach of Principle 2 where it failed to ensure customers had a suitably diversified investment portfolio.

(3) *Market practice*: A firm should observe high standards of market conduct. It should also, to the extent endorsed for the purpose of this Principle, comply with any code or standard as in force from time to time and as it applies to the firm either according to its terms or by rulings made under it.

In addition to the levels of honesty and competence required by Principles 1 and 2, a firm which trades on a commodities or securities market should comply with that market's best practice. In 1991 SFA fined five members for breach of this Principle when they carried out own-account dealing in a certain contract on a futures exchange with the object of seeking to create the impression that the contract was more frequently traded than was the case.

A firm must also comply with any code endorsed with this Principle. SIB endorsed the Takeover Code in February 1995. This would enable SIB or an SRO to take disciplinary or intervention action at the Takeover Panel's request for failure to observe the code.

(4) *Information about customers*: A firm should seek from customers it advises or for whom it exercises discretion any information about their circumstances and investment objectives which might reasonably be expected to be relevant in enabling it to fulfil its responsibilities to them.

The firm must 'know its customer' before providing advisory or discretionary services. IMRO has disciplined a member under this Principle for making unsuitable investment recommendations.

(5) *Information for customers*: A firm should take reasonable steps to give a customer it advises, in a comprehensive and timely way, any information needed to enable him to make a balanced and informed decision. A firm should similarly be ready to provide a customer with a full and fair account of the fulfilment of its responsibilities to him.

The firm must provide its customers with adequate information, for example on the nature of its services, its charges and the sources of its remuneration (such as commission from third parties). IMRO has disciplined a member for breach of Principle 5 where it failed to keep adequate records of its customers' circumstances and of the transactions carried out for them.

(6) *Conflicts of interest*: A firm should either avoid any conflict of interest arising or, where conflicts arise, should ensure fair treatment to all its customers by disclosure, internal rules of confidentiality, declining to act, or otherwise. A firm should not unfairly place its interests above those of its customers and, where a properly informed customer would reasonably expect that the firm would place his interests above its own, the firm should live up to that expectation.

Examples of conflicts of interest (discussed at section 14 below) are where a firm is dealing off its own book to a discretionary customer, or acting as broker to both sides in a transaction. This Principle requires a firm to either avoid such conflicts or to ensure fair treatment. The overriding obligation is that the firm must not unfairly place its own interests above its customers. SFA has taken disciplinary action under this Principle against a firm that encouraged customers to invest against their interests but so as to benefit the firm.

(7) *Customer assets*: Where a firm has control of or is otherwise responsible for assets belonging to a customer which it is required to safeguard, it should arrange proper protection for them, by way of segregation and identification of those assets or otherwise, in accordance with the responsibility it has accepted.

The firm must protect customer assets when appropriate.

(8) *Financial resources*: A firm should ensure that it maintains adequate financial resources to meet its investment business commitments and to withstand the risks to which its business is subject.

The firm must maintain adequate financial resources both to discharge its commitments and to withstand business risks. This Principle is implemented by the financial core rules. IMRO has disciplined a member under this Principle for failure to maintain adequate financial resources.

(9) *Internal organisation*: A firm should organise and control its internal affairs in a responsible manner, keeping proper records, and where the firm employs staff or is responsible for the conduct of investment business by others, should have adequate arrangements to ensure that they are suitable, adequately trained and properly supervised and that it has well-defined compliance procedures.

The firm must have an effective compliance system as discussed in Chapter 4. Principle 9 is frequently cited in SIB's and SROs' disciplinary proceedings. A firm that fails to maintain proper management controls, supervise its staff or keep proper records may breach this Principle.

(10) *Relations with regulators*: A firm should deal with its regulator in an open and cooperative manner and keep the regulator promptly informed of anything concerning the firm which might reasonably be expected to be disclosed to it.

This requires the firm to cooperate with its regulator; it must allow access on inspection visits and not conceal any matter. Its staff must be helpful towards the regulator. The firm additionally must promptly notify the regulator of relevant matters. This goes beyond the particular disclosure rules contained in a firm's rulebook and may include circumstances where, for example, the firm has detected misfeasance on the part of another firm. A stockbroker that failed to notify SFA that its financial position had changed from that set out on a return was held to have breached this Principle. SIB has also disciplined a firm which it regulates for breach of Principle 10 for failing to ensure that its staff were co-operative with SIB. IMRO has disciplined a firm under Principle 10 whose employee lied to it during a formal investigation.

The case of *Kaufmann v Credit Lyonnais* (1995) *The Times*, 1 February suggests that information provided by a firm to its regulator may be discoverable in litigation.

# 3   THE CORE RULES

The 40 core rules were drafted by SIB and approved on 28 January 1991. They were intended to apply to members of all SROs and persons directly regulated by SIB and to be brought into force in relation to members of particular SROs when their third tier rules were ready.

The core rules do not apply to RPBs, and have never been brought into force for persons directly regulated by SIB or for members of FIMBRA or LAUTRO. As stated in section 6 of the Large Report, SIB has mostly de-designated the core rules and they will not be brought into force for PIA (Financial Services (Dedesignation) Rules and Regulations 1994). The one exception is core rule 36, which gives statutory authority to Chinese Walls. This is necessary in light of the uncertainty over the effectiveness of Chinese Walls (see section 14.5 below).

De-designation is intended to give the SROs greater control over their rulebooks. SROs will be expected to consult with SIB before introducing changes in order to ensure investor protection. The core rules will not be revoked for the time being, and an SRO member will continue to observe its applicable rulebook which (in the case of IMRO and SFA) incorporates the core rules.

The core rules do not have any force on their own; they only apply to a firm when its SRO has adopted them and they are then reproduced in its rulebook and accompanied by the SRO's own third tier rules. For example rule 5–40 in SFA's conduct of business rules incorporates core rule 23 as 5–40(1), and its own third tier rules which expands upon the core rule as 5–40(2):

5–40(1)  A firm must ensure that a transaction it executes is promptly allocated.

   (2)  The allocation must be:
   (a)  to the account of the customer on whose instructions the transaction was executed;
   (b)  in respect of a discretionary transaction, to the account of the customer or customers with or for whom the firm had made and recorded, prior to the transaction, a decision in principle to execute that transaction; or
   (c)  in all other cases, to the account of the firm.

The core rules are arranged in logical order under 8 clear headings. They are summarised briefly here but reference should always be made to the conduct of business rules relevant to a firm in order to determine what rules are applicable. In particular consideration should be given to the following points:

(1) Do the conduct of business rules apply to the particular situation: is it regulated business or not?

(2) Is the firm's counterparty a customer of the firm and, if so, is it a private or non-private customer?

## 3.1  Independence

(1) *Inducements*:   A firm should not give or take any inducement which is likely significantly to conflict with duties owed to its customers.

(2) *Material interest*:   Where a firm has a material interest in a transaction or a conflict of interest, it must takes reasonable steps to ensure fair treatment for the customer.

(3) *Soft commission*:   A firm which deals for a customer on an advisory or discretionary basis may only deal through a broker pursuant to a soft commission agreement in defined circumstances. A soft commission agreement is one where a firm provides goods or services to another which deals in securities on a discretionary or advisory basis in return for an assurance that it will receive such business.

(4) *Polarisation*:   A firm which advises a private customer on packaged products (life assurance and unit trusts) must either do so as a product company (advising only on its own products) or as an independent intermediary.

## 3.2  Advertising and marketing

(5) *Issue and approval of advertisements*:   Where a firm issues or approves an investment advertisement, it must apply appropriate expertise and be able to show it is fair and not misleading.

(6) *Issue or approval of advertisements for an overseas person*:   A firm may issue or approve an investment advertisement about a specific investment for an overseas person only in specified circumstances.

(7) *Overseas business for UK private customers*:   A firm may only carry on unregulated investment business with a United Kingdom private customer if it has given a prescribed warning that FSA protections do not apply.

(8) *Business conducted from an overseas place of business with overseas customers*:   If a firm carries on unregulated business with an overseas private customer and indicates that it is an authorised person, it must state that the protections of the FSA do not apply.

(9) *Fair and clear communications*:   A firm may only make a promotional communication about investment business if it reasonably believes it is fair and not misleading.

(10) *Customer's understanding*:   A firm must not recommend a transaction to a private customer, or act as a discretionary manager for him, unless it has taken reasonable steps to enable him to understand the nature of the risks involved.

(11) *Information about the firm*:   A firm must take reasonable steps to ensure that a private customer to whom it provides investment services is given adequate information about its identity and business address, the identity and status of its staff and the identity of its regulator. If selling a packaged product to a private customer this includes details of the firm's polarisation status.

(12) *Information about packaged products*:   When recommending a private customer to buy a packaged product, a firm must give adequate information about the product.

(13) *Appointed representatives*:   A firm must satisfy itself on reasonable grounds that its appointed representatives remain fit and proper, and only carry on approved business.

## 3.3   Customer Relations

(14) *Customer agreements*:   Where a firm provides investment services to a private customer on written contractual terms, they must be adequately detailed. Where a firm provides a private customer with investment services involving contingent liability transactions or discretionary management it must do so under a customer agreement signed by both parties.

(15) *Customer's rights*:   A firm must not try to exclude or restrict any duty or liability to a customer under the FSA, or under the regulatory system. A firm may only exclude or restrict its duty of care to a private customer if reasonable to do so.

(16) *Suitability*:   A firm should ensure that any personal recommendation or discretionary transaction for a private customer is suitable for him in light of the facts disclosed by that customer or of which the firm should reasonably be aware.

(17) *Standards of advice on packaged products*:   This rule implements the doctrine of polarisation. A product company should advise a private customer to buy the packaged product from the product company which best meets the customer's needs. An independent intermediary should advise a private customer to buy the packaged product from any product company which best meets his needs.

(18) *Charges and other remuneration*:   A firm's charges to a private customer should be reasonable. Before a firm provides investment services to a private customer it must disclose its charges and any other remuneration receivable.

(19) *Confirmations and periodic information*:   A firm which deals in an investment other than a life policy must send a contract or confirmation note to its customer. An investment manager must provide periodic information to its customers.

## 3.4   Dealing for customers

(20) *Customer order priority*:   A firm should deal with customer and own account orders fairly and in due turn.

(21) *Timely execution*:   Once a firm has agreed or decided to effect a current customer order, it must execute it as soon as reasonably practicable.

(22) *Best execution*:   Where a firm deals with or for a private customer in securities or derivatives, or fulfils an order from a non-private customer, it must provide best execution (principally, obtain the best price).

(23) *Timely allocation*:   A firm must ensure that a transaction it executes is promptly allocated.

(24) *Fair allocation*:   Where a firm has aggregated orders for customer transactions it must not give unfair preference to itself or to any customer.

(25) *Dealing ahead of publications*:   Where a firm intends to publish a recommendation to customers it must not deal for itself until customers are likely to have had a reasonable opportunity to react to it.

(26) *Churning and switching*:   A firm must not recommend to a private customer to deal, or itself deal in the exercise of discretion for any customer, if it would reasonably be regarded as too frequent in the circumstances. A firm must also not recommend to a private customer to switch within a packaged product or between packaged products, or effect such a switch in the exercise of discretion for a private customer, unless it believes on reasonable grounds that the switch is justified from the customer's viewpoint.

(27) *Certain derivatives transactions to be on exchange*:   A firm must not deal or recommend a contingent liability transaction with or to a private customer unless it is made on a recognised or designated investment exchange or the transaction is to hedge against currency risk.

## 3.5   Market Integrity

(28) *Insider dealing*:   A firm must not effect an own account transactions when it, its associate, or an employee is prohibited from effecting that transaction by the statutory restriction on insider dealing. A firm must also not knowingly effect a transaction for a customer it knows is so prohibited.

(29) *Stabilisation of securities*:  A firm may only stabilise the price of securities in accordance with the statutory stabilisation rules.

(30) *Off-exchange market makers*:  Where a firm sells unquoted securities to a private customer as a market maker it must ensure that a reasonable re-purchase price is available for at least three months.

(31) *Reportable transactions*:  A firm must notify its regulator of transactions effected on a unrecognised investment exchange.

## 3.6   Administration

(32) *Safeguarding of customer investments*:  A firm which has custody of customer investments must keep safe title documents and ensure that any registerable investments are properly registered.

(33) *Scope of business*:  A firm must maintain a business profile describing the kind of investment business it carries on and may only carry on (and hold itself out as carrying on) investment business of that kind.

(34) *Compliance*:  A firm must take reasonable steps to ensure its staff and those of its appointed representatives act in conformity with their responsibilities under the regulatory system, and keep records to show this.

(35) *Complaints*:  A firm must ensure complaints are properly handled and that any appropriate remedial action on a complaint is promptly taken.

(36) *Chinese Walls*:  Where a firm has an established Chinese Wall arrangement which requires information obtained by it in the course of carrying on one part of its business to be withheld from persons with whom it deals in the course of carrying on another part of its business, then it may withhold information under those circumstances.

(37) *Cessation of business*:  Where a firm or its appointed representative stops providing any investment services to private customers, the firm must ensure that any outstanding business is properly completed or is transferred to another firm.

## 3.7   General

(38) *Reliance on others*:  A person will act in conformity with the core rules if it observes its regulator's formal guidance (ie written guidance issued to all, or a class of, SRO members).

(39) *Classes of customer*:  A firm may treat a private customer as a non-private customer if he has sufficient experience and understanding to waive the protections provided for private customers and has received and consented to a written warning.

(40) *Application of the core conduct of business rules*:  This core rule deals with the kinds of business which are subject to the core rules.

# 4   THE THIRD TIER RULES

The third tier rules are those rules adopted by IMRO and SFA to supplement the core rules. They form an integral part of the conduct of business rules and, as the example of SFA rule 5–40(2), set out in section 3 above, shows, are combined with the core rules.

# 5   GUIDANCE

Beneath the core rules and third tier rules in the hierarchy are the codes of practice and guidance issued by an SRO. SFA conduct of business rule 5–41 is an example of how guidance has been issued to supplement a rule:

5-41   A firm may aggregate an order for a customer with orders for other customers, or with own account orders, where:
   (a) it is unlikely that the aggregation will operate to the disadvantage of any of the customers whose orders have been aggregated; or
   (b) the firm has disclosed to the customer that his order may be aggregated and that the effect of the aggregation may operate on some occasions to his disadvantage.

*Guidance*: A firm should only aggregate customers' orders where it believes on reasonable grounds that this is in the overall best interests of its customers.

Other examples of guidance issued by an SRO are:

– SFA's guidance on the meaning of fit and proper contained in Appendix 3 to its rulebook, which is guidance issued under rule 2–2;
– IMRO's code on the contents of advertisements;

Guidance of this kind can be relied upon by a firm in ensuring that it has acted in conformity with the rule to which it relates where it reasonably believes it is doing so (core rule 38).

# 6   LEVELS OF PROTECTION

The regulators' conduct of business rules will provide different levels of protection for different customers, depending upon whether they are businesses or private individuals. In each instance the definitions must be checked to ascertain into what category the customer or counterparty falls. By way of illustration the SFA rulebook clearly sets out the different rules which apply to different categories of person.

*(a) Not a customer*

Where the person with whom the firm deals falls outside the definition of a customer, for example because they are a 'market counterparty' (as defined) then the conduct of business rules will not apply to the transaction, although the Principles will apply and fiduciary and contractual duties will be relevant.

*(b) All customers*

Many of the conduct of business rules apply to transactions with all customers, for example the rules concerning:

- the duty to ascertain the customer's circumstances and requirements;
- the requirement that advertisements be fair and not misleading;
- disclosure of material interests;
- suitability of recommendations for discretionary customers;
- issue of contract notes;
- orders to be given fair priority;
- timely execution/allocation of orders;
- prohibition on churning and on insider dealing.

*(c) Private customers*

In addition a smaller number of rules apply exclusively to private customers. These include:

- detailed requirements on the contents of advertisements;
- the requirement to use a written contract for certain transactions;
- polarisation for packaged products;
- an investment may only be recommended if suitable;
- a firm must take reasonable steps to ensure the customer understands any risks;
- charges must be reasonable and disclosed;
- the firm must obtain best execution.

## 7 LIABILITY FOR BREACH

The potential consequences of breaching the Principles, rules and guidance can be summarised as follows:

| *Principle or rule* | *Liability for breach* |
| --- | --- |
| Statements of Principle | Disciplinary action by regulator; no civil liability; does not invalidate transaction. |

| | |
|---|---|
| Core rule/third tier rule/conduct of business rule | Disciplinary action by regulator; civil liability (s 62FSA). |
| Guidance | May be relevant in determining if core rule breached, and also whether the firm has breached its duty of care to the client (see *Lloyd Cheyham & Co Ltd v Littlejohn & Co* (1987) BCLC 303). |

# 8 MEMBERSHIP RULES

Each SRO has rules governing membership. These will vary in detail but generally include the following features:

(1) In order to be admitted to membership the applicant must satisfy the SRO that it is fit and proper. This test does not apply to persons automatically authorised under the FSA or to persons subject to prudential regulation by another regulator. These are discussed in Chapter 2.

(2) The applicant must show that it will carry on business of a kind regulated by the SRO.

(3) The applicant will have a right of appeal if its application is rejected or made subject to conditions.

(4) Once admitted the member must only carry on business of a kind agreed with the SRO (unless, of course, it holds additional authorisation or can take advantage of any of the exemptions in the FSA).

(5) A firm may only resign on giving requisite notice and it will remain a member until the resignation is accepted, pending resolution of any enquiries, investigation or disciplinary action.

(6) Directors, managers and persons who deal with customers (whether employed by the firm or its appointed representative) must be individually registered with the SRO and satisfy any examination requirements. Personal registration enables the SRO to exercise a measure of direct control over these persons. FIMBRA, IMRO and SFA have introduced this requirement and PIA may do so for life assurance sales staff. The actual categories of person who must register, and the detailed regulations, are set out in each rulebook.

(7) Information of prescribed kinds must be notified to the SRO for example, change of controller 28 days in advance, and any event of insolvency or misconduct immediately.

# 9 FINANCIAL RULES

SIB's financial supervision rules came into force on 1 August 1990 and were de-designated in November 1994. Subject to certain exceptions they applied to persons authorised by LAUTRO, IMRO, FIMBRA, SFA and SIB. They did not apply in the case of regulated insurance companies, regulated friendly societies, building societies and certain categories such as oil market participants and occupation pension scheme managers. The rules also did not apply in their entirety to firms for whom another regulator is the lead financial regulator, such as the Bank of England for United Kingdom authorised banks, and they applied only in part to European institutions. Although de-designated, they are summarised here and are still reflected in regulators' rulebooks. They are unlikely to undergo major alteration for the time being.

(1) A firm must have available the amount and type of financial resources required by its regulator. For a lead–regulated firm these will normally be set out by its lead financial regulator. These are specified in detail in the rulebooks, to which reference should be made.

(2) A firm must maintain adequate records which accurately disclose its financial position. Their form will depend on the nature and complexity of a firm's business but are likely to include records of receipts and expenses, assets and liabilities, purchases and sales of investments, records of receipt and disposal of investments and of documents of title. In each case the nature of the transaction and identity of the parties should be clear. A firm must also regularly reconcile its own bank accounts and balances with brokers and exchanges it uses. These records should enable the firm to manage its risk exposure. It must provide regular financial statements to its regulator in accordance with the provisions of its rulebook.

(3) A firm must have adequate internal financial controls and systems. These must ensure that all transactions and commitments are properly recorded and that customer assets are protected.

(4) A firm must immediately notify its regulator when aware of a breach or impending breach of the preceding three rules.

(5) A firm must appoint an auditor as required by its regulator and provide the auditor with sufficient information to enable it to discharge its duties. SFA, for example, requires that it approves a firm's auditor and that the firm appoints the auditor under an engagement letter which contains prescribed terms, including that the auditor reports directly to SFA on a number of topics.

# 10 CLIENT ASSETS AND MONEY

Safeguarding of customer assets is governed by the rules of the various SROs, whereas SIB's client money regulations apply (subject to various exclusions) to all SRO members and persons regulated by SIB.

Principle 7 and core rule 32 lay down the basic requirements for safeguarding customer's investments and assets and are elaborated upon in the individual rulebooks. These can include requirements in relation to:

- providing the customer with a written statement of its obligations when offering safe custody facilities;
- use of external custodians;
- reconciliation of records

SIB has issued the Financial Services (Client Money) Regulations 1991 which are concerned with a firm's handling of client money generally. The Financial Services (Client Money) (Supplementary) Regulations 1991 apply to client money:

- received by a firm for the settlement of certain securities transactions;
- received by a firm in respect of derivatives transactions where the client may be liable to pay further amounts.

Both of these regulations (which came into force on 1 January 1992) are detailed, and reference must be made to the full text. The main provisions of the Financial Services (Client Money) Regulations 1991 (CMR) are briefly summarised below. SIB has de-designated parts of the CMR and all of the supplementary regulations. Again, this should not give rise to major changes for the time being.

(1)  The CMR apply to members of SROs, to persons directly regulated by SIB and to members of the Institute of Actuaries who hold investment business certificates, in all cases when carrying on regulated business. They do not apply to exempted persons, but a firm is responsible for ensuring its appointed representatives observe the CMR.

(2)  The CMR do not apply to an approved bank which is an authorised person and holds money with itself. Nor do they apply to insurers or friendly societies authorised under ss 22 or 23 FSA when they observe the arrangements of PIA or the Friendly Society Commission.

(3)  The CMR govern the handling of client money. This is money or cheques paid into an account in a firm's name (not the client's sole name) and which a firm holds in the course of carrying on investment business in respect of an investment agreement with the client.

(4)  All money received by a firm from a private customer who is not properly treated as a non private customer is potentially client money. In addition the money of non private customers is subject to the CMR if:

- an authorised customer requests it; or
- a non-authorised non-private customer objects to a notice sent by the firm stating that its money will not be subject to the CMR;

the firm can, of course, decline to hold their money in these circumstances.

(5)  Until client money is paid over to the client, to a third party on the client's instructions or properly paid to the firm, the firm must:

   - keep it separate from its own money and promptly pay it into a client account at an approved bank;
   - hold it as fiduciary for the client;
   - pay interest in accordance with the CMR save as otherwise agreed and subject to *de minimis* provisions;
   - account for it to the client;
   - follow the prescribed record keeping and auditing requirements.

(6)  If a firm which holds client money becomes insolvent, or its assets vest in a trustee under s 67(1)(b) FSA, or its regulator makes a direction in respect of all its client money, then the contents of its client accounts are amalgamated for distribution to clients in proportion to their claims over them. There are further provisions dealing with where a bank, overseas intermediate broker or overseas settlement agent defaults.

## 11  RULES RELATING TO MONITORING, ENFORCEMENT AND DISCIPLINE

Each SRO will have powers enabling it to:

(1)  monitor and investigate its members' activities;
(2)  intervene in their business to protect investors;
(3)  discipline members for breach of Principles and rules.

These are discussed in Chapter 12.

## 12  COMPLAINTS AND DISPUTE RESOLUTIONS

Each SRO has rules specifying how complaints are to be handled and establishing a framework for disputes between firms and customers to be resolved. These are discussed in Chapter 2.

## 13  ADDITIONAL RULES RELEVANT TO MARKETING AND OTHER ACTIVITIES

There are four further sets of rules:

(1)  The Financial Services (Promotion of Unregulated Schemes) Regulations 1991, which govern the promotion of unregulated collective investment schemes. They are discussed in Chapter 9.

(2)  The Common Unsolicited Calls Regulations, which regulate the making of uninvited personal and telephone calls. These are discussed in Chapter 17.

(3)  The Financial Services Cancellation Rules, which give customers a statutory right to a cooling off period for purchases of life assurance and regulated CIS products. These are discussed in Chapter 17.

(4)  The Stabilisation Rules, contained in Part 10 of the SIB rulebook. They set out the circumstances in which action may be taken to stabilise the price of certain investments.

# 14  FURTHER DUTIES

In addition to rules which govern a firm in the conduct of its investment business, there are two further sources of duties which govern its relationship with its customer and counterparties: contractual and fiduciary duties. The great majority of investment business services will be provided under a contract, and both a firm and its customer are, of course, bound by its express and implied terms and by the usual incidents of contract law. In addition the firm may be subject to a number of a fiduciary duties, which are discussed here.

## 14.1  When fiduciary duties arise

The law imposes fiduciary duties in two principal situations:

(a)  where one person, sometimes in a position of vulnerability, entrusts another with some task or property and relies on that other person to protect his interests; and/or

(b)  where one person in a relationship occupies a position of trust such as trustee, solicitor, agent, employee or director.

Parties to commercial transactions will generally not be subject to fiduciary duties, although this is not always the case with financial services where the customer under an advisory, discretionary or agency contract will generally be the firm's fiduciary. The fiduciary duties are considered below.

If a firm stands in a fiduciary position to its customer then, unless the customer has effectively waived its rights, breach of fiduciary duty may entitle the customer to avoid the transaction or make the firm account for its profit.

## 14.2  Law Commission's Consultative Paper

The Law Commission's Consultative Paper on Fiduciary Duties and Regulatory Rules (1992 No 124) has thrown this area into focus and identified two particular problems:

(a) a firm may owe conflicting fiduciary duties to different customers (such as in relation to confidentiality), or there may be a conflict between its own interests and those of its customers (such as self-dealing);

(b) the interrelationship between fiduciary duties and regulatory rules is unclear and a firm which observes the SIB or SRO rules and follows good market practice may nonetheless find it is in breach of fiduciary duties.

In particular, the range of products offered by a financial conglomerate, the composition of its customer base and the different capacities in which it acts combine to create a number of conflicts of interest and duty. For example, fiducuairy duties may require the disclosure of remuneration received from third parties; that no secret profits be made; and that a firm makes available all information relevant to a customer's affairs. Yet the SRO rules may countenance devices such as non-disclosure of the amount of commission received, Chinese Walls to withhold information and blanket consents in customer agreements.

## 14.3 The fiduciary duties and how they are breached

The four principal fiduciary duties are:

(1) No conflict (also called conflict of duty and interest). A fiduciary must not put himself in a position where there is a real possibility that his interest may conflict with his beneficiary's (the person to whom he owes the fiduciary duties, such as the customer).

(2) No profit (also called misuse of property held in fiduciary capacity). A fiduciary must not profit at his beneficiary's expense.

(3) Undivided loyalty (also called conflict of duty and duty). A fiduciary must not put himself in a position where his duty to one beneficiary conflicts with his duty to another beneficiary. Particular difficulties arise from the fiduciary's duty to make available to its beneficiary all information relevant to its affairs, and the rule of attribution of knowledge which provides that knowledge acquired in the course of business by an employee in one part of a firm is deemed to be known to all the firm.

(4) Confidentiality (also called misuse of confidential information). A fiduciary may only use or disclose a beneficiary's confidential information for that beneficiary's benefit.

There are many situations in which a financial services firm may breach these fiduciary duties. Circumstances identified by the Law Commission, and the particular fiduciary duty involved, include:

– dealing as principal with an advisory or discretionary customer (no conflict; no profit);
– matching orders and riskless principal transactions (undivided loyalty);
– dealing in property where the customer has an interest (no conflict);
– preferential treatment for some customers (undivided loyalty);

– not using all information available for a customer's benefit (undivided loyalty, but conflicts with duty of confidentiality);
– breach of confidentiality by using one customer's confidential information for the benefit of another customer or itself (confidentiality).

## 14.4 Contracting out of a conflict

The standard technique of drafting a customer agreement to limit fiduciary duties, and to obtain blanket advance consents, may not always be effective.

A common approach to dealing with conflicts is to draft a customer agreement:

– to exclude or limit liability for breach of fiduciary duties;
– to define the relationship to limit fiduciary duties;
– to give generalised advanced disclosure of material interests or of the possibility of conflicts arising.

The efficacy of this approach will depend on the circumstances of the fidiciary and the client. If the fiduciary relationship is constituted by a contract, it is suggested that a court will have regard to terms which define the parties' duties when determining if the relationship is fiduciary, and the scope of the fiduciary duties. A clear and specific clause which allows a firm to retain profits, deal off its own book, enter into conflicts or not disclose other customers' confidential information is potentially enforceable.

Any disclosure of conflict and obtaining of the customer's consent needs to be very specific. In the context of financial services the Law Commission considers that a very full disclosure of all material facts and fully informed consent is required, especially for private customers. In particular the kind of prior disclosure allowed by the rulebooks for soft commission, dual agency, self dealing or independence policy may not suffice. It also considers that the conflict of duties of confidentiality and full disclosure are not easy to resolve by disclosure and consent in a client agreement.

The Law Commission has considered the possibility that the rules of an SRO are incorporated into each contract between a firm and its customer, so that following the conduct of business rules would ensure that a firm does not breach its fiduciary duties. It is well established that trade customs can become the terms of a contract in this way, and this can be the case with the rules of the Stock Exchange. However, this possibility seems unlikely as Parliament included ss 62 and 62A FSA to give certain customers the right to sue for breaches. In any case the Law Commission considers that, even if SRO rules were incorporated, they would not override fiduciary duties without full disclosure and consent from the customer.

## 14.5   The efficacy of Chinese Walls and similar techniques

Chinese Walls are a central device for managing conflict. They are intended to restrict information flows within a firm, and therefore prevent the communication and attribution of knowledge, by use of physical separation and administrative procedures. Core rule 36 (which as mentioned above, SIB does not intend to de-designate) provides that a firm which uses an effective Chinese Wall will prevent the attribution of knowledge, and will not require customer consent for this. There is, however, substantial doubt whether a Chinese Wall can always be relied upon to protect a firm against liability for breach of duty, for example where it withholds information in breach of the duty of undivided loyalty, or where it enters into a transaction in which it has a material interest in conflict with that of its customer. In particular:

- Core rule 36 may have express statutory authority but, as discussed below, the effect of this is unclear;
- unless compliance with core rule 36 fulfils the firm's fiduciary duty, consent is needed and, where the customer has not given consent to the operation of the Chinese Wall after sufficient disclosure, the firm may be in breach;
- if an analyst is brought in across a Chinese Wall, or management overlooks the Wall, the rule on attribution of knowledge may cause problems where the firm's interest conflicts with its duty to customers, although the use of stop lists may help to prevent this;
- the courts have recently examined the use of Chinese Walls by firms of solicitors (*Re a Solicitor* (1987) 131 SJ 1063; *David Lee & Co Ltd v Coward Chance* [1991] Ch 259; *Re a Firm of Solicitors* [1992] 1 All ER 353) and have held that they do not protect against claims for breach of duty because of the risk of seepage, however thorough the arrangements may be.

Three further approaches to managing conflict include:

(1)   The enforced separation of function, where a firm only carries on non-conflicting activities in one entity, might in some cases avoid problems arising from attribution of knowledge. However the Law Commission recognises this would not be a practical solution since small uni-purpose firms may not be viable or competitive.

(2)   Declining to act may be appropriate where a conflict is identified in advance of acting, but will present difficulties if a firm stops acting halfway through a transaction.

(3)   A firm can adopt an independent policy to manage a conflict by subordinating its interests to those of its customers as provided for in core rules 1–4. It can restrict inducements, treat its customers fairly where it has a material interest, and observe the regulations on soft commission and

polarisation. However these steps do not eliminate the conflict, and do not fulfil a firm's fiduciary duties which impose a stricter standard.

## 14.6   Do SIB and SRO Rules override fiduciary duties?

Where the FSA gives express power to SIB to alter the common law or equitable rights and duties, and SIB has exercised this power, the answer will almost certainly be 'yes'. Some sections of the FSA which authorise SIB to make rules expressly state that they will alter the relationship between the firm and its customer. Section 55 (client money regulations) and s 81 (unit trusts) are examples of where this power is granted. In these cases SIB's rules should override the common law or fiduciary duties which would otherwise have applied, and compliance with the rules should preclude any such claim from the customer.

Other sections of the FSA are less clear. Section 48, for example, authorises SIB to promulgate conduct of business rules, but is inconsistent in stating how they will affect private law rights and leaves in doubt what is the position where the core rule does not correspond with a fiduciary duty. Core rules 2 and 25, for example, which permit material interests and front running in some circumstances, conflict with the rule that a fiduciary may not place itself in a position where there is a real possibility of conflict.

Some core rules are based on the wording of the FSA and these may alter common law and fiduciary duties. Examples are core rule 18(2) (disclosure of basis or amount of remuneration) which, although it conflicts with the duty of full disclosure, seems to be authorised by the words of s 48(2)(g) FSA. Core rule 36 (which authorises withholding of information by use of a Chinese Wall and provides for non–attribution of knowledge) conflicts with the undivided loyalty rule, and the rule on attribution of knowledge. It is, however, arguably authorised by s 48(2)(h) FSA which contemplates a rule enabling information to be withheld.

Where there is no, or unclear, statutory authority for a rule, the court will have the option to take it into account in ascertaining the scope of the firm's duty to its customer, or may disregard it altogether. Additionally, it is unclear whether SRO rules will override fiduciary duties as they operate contractually and the FSA does not expressly give SROs rule-making powers, although the Law Commission considers the Courts are likely to treat them on the same footing as SIB rules. For this reason the de-designation of most of the core rules may not alter this position.

## 14.7   Is legislation needed?

There does indeed seem little doubt that this area is thoroughly confused, given the uncertainty as to whether the rulebooks prevail over fiduciary duties, and whether Parliament did or did not intend SIB and SROs to be able to modify common law and fiduciary rights.

The Law Commission considers a number of possible legislative approaches including clarification of fiduciary duties, the validation of general advance consent and of Chinese Walls, and seems to favour requiring the Court to take a reasonable rule into account in determining the nature of a firm's duty to its customers. This, though, would not produce certainty and a more comprehensive solution would be for legislation to provide that a firm which observes the applicable regulatory rules will be deemed to have fulfilled its fiduciary duties. There is, however, little prospect of further legislation for the foreseeable future and uncertainty is therefore likely to remain.

# 4 The Compliance Function

'Compliance' is a word frequently encountered in the context of the FSA, but nowhere is it formally defined. It is submitted that it means the institution and enforcement of procedures which will enable a firm—whether an authorised or exempted person—to comply with its regulatory obligations.

The starting point in considering the scope and extent of a firm's compliance function is SIB's Principle 9, which is concerned with internal organisation. It states:

> A firm should organise and control its internal affairs in a responsible manner, keeping proper records, and where the firm employs staff or is responsible for the conduct of investment business by others, should have adequate arrangements to ensure that they are suitable, adequately trained and properly supervised and that it has well-defined compliance procedures.

The key obligation is for a firm to organise and control its internal affairs responsibly. By doing this, it will be able to discharge its regulatory obligations. Keeping records, ensuring staff and appointed representatives are suitable, trained and supervised and having well-defined compliance procedures are the means by which a firm can achieve this aim.

The compliance officer is the firm's official charged with ensuring it achieves compliance on a day to day basis; the compliance department, managed by the compliance officer, will carry out monitoring and enforcement functions in order to ensure that the firm is compliant, and the compliance manual will be the firm's formal statement of compliance procedures.

This chapter discusses the scope, structure and functions of compliance.

## 1 SCOPE AND RESPONSIBILITY

### 1.1 Scope of compliance

Taken narrowly, compliance can be understood to relate solely to compliance with the rulebook of the firm's SRO. This is a starting point, but the scope of a firm's compliance function is likely to be much wider and will usually include:

- fulfilment of SIB's Principles;
- observance of FSA requirements, for example in relation to marketing unregulated funds and avoiding market manipulation;
- fulfilment of associated legislative requirements, such as the laws relating to money laundering and insider dealing;
- observance of legislation relevant to the firm's business, such as unit trust regulations;
- fulfilment of the regulations of any exchanges on which the firm trades, such as LIFFE or LME;
- compliance, when relevant, with the Insurance Companies Act 1982, Friendly Societies Act 1992 and Building Societies Act 1986;
- if the firm has operations or business overseas, its compliance function may include observance of the regulatory laws and procedures of those overseas jurisdictions.

The breadth of a firm's compliance function can be extensive and, in addition, depth of knowledge is required. The compliance officer of a unit trust manager should be familiar not only with the rules of IMRO and PIA but, in addition, with the various unit trust regulations and the custom and practice of that market. The compliance officer of a stockbroker should understand not only the SFA rules but also money laundering and insider dealing legislation and the rules and practice of the Stock Exchange.

The responsibility for ensuring compliance may extend beyond the firm itself. Principle 9 requires a firm to ensure that its staff are suitable, trained and supervised. Compliance responsibility will generally include the activities of the firm's employees. Some SROs require them to be individually registered and examined, but in all cases the compliance officer is responsible for ensuring that they do not cause the firm to be in breach of its obligations.

Furthermore, Principle 9 extends to a firm's appointed representatives and their staff and so the firm is responsible for their activities. While a substantial appointed representative may have its own compliance officer and compliance department— such as a building society which is the appointed representative of a life office— it is the exclusive responsibility of the authorised firm to ensure that the appointed representative is complying with all applicable requirements.

The obligation to ensure compliance may extend to a firm's contractors. A fund manager which sub-contracts custodial services should take steps to ensure that the custodian is reliable and trustworthy both initially and on a continuing basis. It will also rely on brokers to buy or sell listed securities and should periodically take steps to ensure that the choice of broker is in its clients' best interests, and that the broker is when appropriate achieving best execution.

## 1.2 Responsibility for compliance

Compliance is the responsibility of the highest level of management: the firm's board or, if it is a partnership, the partners. In addition to this collective responsibility, it is desirable—and increasingly normal—for a board director to be the titular compliance officer or, if the compliance officer is not a director, for the board to receive reports directly from the compliance officer to ensure that the board is kept abreast of important compliance issues. A number of companies which have a board audit committee comprising non-executive directors require the compliance officer (or group compliance officer) to report to its meetings.

The responsibility of the board and senior management in relation to compliance issues is to 'set the tone' and to ensure that there is a compliance culture in the firm. In a compliant organisation, they will have broad awareness of the compliance issues which are relevant to the firm—eg money-laundering or the importance of factfinds when selling life assurance— and will support the operation of the firm's compliance function.

The board should make it clear to senior management that compliance is viewed as an ethical issue. This is particularly important in firms were management is sales oriented, since pressure to increase sales may lead to compliance concerns being ignored or overridden.

Senior management should, in turn, ensure that the firm's various divisions are operating in accordance with the requirements of the compliance department. For example, if the firm is a stockbroker, are the dealers obtaining best execution? If a life assurance company, are the company representatives giving best advice and is this being properly checked?

Management must be receptive of warnings and advice from the compliance department, and provide it with sufficient resources to perform its function. The head of the compliance department should regularly report to senior management for this purpose. He or she should have a reporting line which bypasses sales or operational management and have a right of access direct to the chief executive or the board to ensure that any concerns are properly aired and acted upon.

## 2 STRUCTURE AND STATUS OF COMPLIANCE

This will vary in nearly every detail between large and small firms and between wholesale and retail firms. It is, however, possible to suggest some key points.

## 2.1 Structure of compliance

At its simplest, a firm may have a single compliance officer, assisted by a small compliance department and rely upon a single compliance manual. This would be appropriate where the firm is a unit trust manager regulated exclusively by IMRO, or a futures dealer regulated solely by SFA.

If the firm is a member of two or more SROs—for example, a life assurance company which is a member of IMRO and PIA—then it may choose to have two compliance officers, each specialising in the business regulated by one of the SROs.In such circumstances, it will be important to ensure that the two compliance officers are fully aware of each other's activities, and it may be appropriate to have a single compliance department and for one compliance officer to report to the other.

A firm may have a number of separate divisions which carry on different kinds of investment business. A stockbroker or fund manager may have retail and wholesale divisions; a life assurance company may have separate divisions and sales forces for IFA, appointed representative and direct salesforce business. In circumstances like these it is desirable that either a single compliance officer is responsible for all the divisions or, alternatively, for the compliance officer to have deputies acting as compliance officers for the separate divisions. In either case, the objective is to ensure that one individual is aware, and in control, of the compliance functions of all the firm's divisions.

A financial services conglomerate may comprise a number of separate firms which carry on investment business. A common example is a life assurance company and a unit trust company. A large group might consist of an IFA, a life assurance company, a unit trust company, a stockbroker, a bank and one or more fund managers. Each separate company will be a member of an SRO and will require a compliance officer. In circumstances like these, it is necessary to devise a compliance structure which ensures that the compliance function is able to meet the requirements of a number of SROs, is familiar with the operation of a number of different investment businesses, and operates in an effective and co-ordinated way. As a single compliance officer is unlikely to be able to manage compliance in such diverse businesses, it may be appropriate for each firm, or group of firms, to have a compliance officer who in turn reports to a group compliance officer.

## 2.2   Staffing the compliance department

How much time a compliance officer should spend on compliance duties is a question that can only be answered in light of the circumstances. In a very small firm without a sales force, which only needs a compliance department comprising a part time compliance officer, it may be sufficient for the compliance officer to combine his or her compliance role with that of finance director or internal auditor. On the other hand, a firm with a substantial number of dealers or fund managers, or with a significant sales force, will require not only a number of people working full time in the compliance department but, in addition, a full time compliance officer to run it. Where a firm's titular compliance officer is, for example, a general manager or a director, then that person may have a title such as senior manager (compliance) or assistant general manager (compliance).

The size of the compliance department will, again, depend on the circumstances. It should in any case have sufficient resources to perform its duties efficiently, and size is not necessarily a guarantee of effectiveness. One approach is to consider whether all compliance functions (discussed in section 4 below) have been carried out effectively and on time. If not, additional resources in terms of quality or quantity are probably required.

## 2.3   Authority of the compliance officer

A compliance officer must have sufficient authority to perform his or her functions and to challenge senior staff and directors. This is particularly important as there is an understandable tendency for management to be supportive of the needs and requirements of income generating divisions. In addition the compliance officer must have full and unrestricted access to all parts of the firm's business.

A firm will need to devise a structure that gives its compliance officer the necessary authority. Features may include:

(1)   Staff predominantly performing compliance functions should report to the compliance officer.

(2)   The compliance officer should not be 'outranked' by sales or operational management in such a way that they can influence or obstruct the way that the compliance officer performs his or her duties

(3)   The compliance officer (if not a director) should have a clear reporting line to senior management. This may be the general manager, the finance director or a person of similar standing.

(4)   The compliance officer should have a right of access to the chief executive or a director (if not already one or reporting to one), and should also report regularly to the board on compliance issues.

All of these steps may be necessary to ensure that compliance concerns are brought to the attention of senior management and to the board when appropriate. There is, of course, no obligation on a firm to do what the compliance officer recommends on every occasion and commercial, legal or other considerations will no doubt need to be taken into account. A prudent firm will, nonetheless, always heed its compliance officer's advice and take his or her recommendations into account. A firm which ignores its compliance officer's advice, or overrules his or her judgment without good cause, is unlikely to achieve the required standards of compliance.

## 2.4   Performance of compliance

The compliance officer and the compliance department will monitor compliance, and perform a number of compliance-related functions, but the obligation to carry out compliance functions extends far wider. The compliance officer will not only centrally manage the firm's compliance function, but will also allocate compliance responsibilities throughout the firm, and the monitor the way in which they are fulfilled.

As mentioned, the board and senior management of a firm should be aware of compliance issues, set the compliance 'tone' and give support to the compliance department.

At an operational level, compliance requirements are likely to be indivisible from routine day-to-day operations. In a stockbroking firm, the dealers must when appropriate obtain and document best execution as part of their day-to-day work; the marketing department must observe the investment advertisement and cold calling regulations; the customer relations department must ensure that customer documentation is correctly completed; and the back office must swiftly effect allocation and settlement.

In a life office, the company representatives must always 'know their customer'; their factfinds should be checked by the branch manager or head office for best advice; the customer relations division must handle complaints properly; and personnel must recruit and train new sales staff in accordance with stringent requirements.

Each of these duties is circumscribed by the rules of SFA or PIA, and each person handling this work must be conversant with these requirements. It is the responsibility of the compliance officer to explain the rules to these staff, to relate them to the work in hand in the firm's compliance manual, and then to monitor compliance with those rules.

## 3 FUNCTIONS OF COMPLIANCE

### 3.1 Establishing the procedures

The first duty of a compliance officer is to study the FSA, the rules of the firm's SRO and other relevant legislation. He or she will then be able to draw up compliance procedures which relate the legislation and the rules to the firm's business and which are usually contained in a compliance manual. The purpose is to establish procedures and routines which, if properly followed and monitored, will enable the firm to comply with the regulatory requirements. These should be the 'well defined compliance procedures' referred to in SIB Principle 9.

It is important that compliance with the procedures is documented both for the firm's own records and to enable the compliance officer—and indeed the regulator—to ascertain that the procedures have been observed. Some of the SROs lay down particular requirements for records to be kept, but good practice extends beyond this. In a busy dealing room or life assurance company branch office, the temptation will be to perform the task, but not to record that it has been done. For example, a stockbroker's dealer may go to great pains to obtain best execution for private clients, and a life assurance company's branch manager may carefully go through each salesperson's persistency rate and instruct them on action required. However, if neither records the action taken, it will be difficult for the firm to prove at some future date that this has been done. It will be recalled that 'keeping proper records' is a requirement of SIB Principle 9.

## 3.2 Monitoring change

Having drawn up a compliance manual, the compliance officer must be alert to alterations, constantly keeping abreast of recent developments. The compliance officer should monitor amendments to the SRO rulebooks to ensure that the firm remains in compliance and, in addition, study discussion and consultation papers, and be aware of both United Kingdom and EU legislative proposals. Many compliance officers are members of industry-wide discussion groups for this purpose. Organisations such as the United Kingdom Association of Compliance Officers (tel 01428 684005), the Compliance Register (tel 01908 322450) and the Securities Houses Compliance Officers Group (tel 0171 956 4989) are taking a lead in establishing professional standards for compliance officers, and organise a number of conferences and study sessions.

## 3.3 Broadcasting the procedures

The compliance department is responsible, with the support of management, for ensuring that the firm's operating divisions—the dealers, the managers, the sales force and so on—are aware of relevant compliance procedures. The preparation of a compliance manual on its own is insufficient; the compliance officer must ensure that the compliance procedures are fully understood and are integrated into the firm's day-to-day operating procedures.

## 3.4 Monitoring compliance

Establishing technically correct compliance procedures is an important step, but only the first. Simply to produce a compliance manual is insufficient. The compliance manual must be observed and the compliance officer must check to see whether or not the procedures are being adhered to.

Procedures which should be carried out in accordance with compliance requirements must be monitored. Relevant procedures include those for the recruitment of new investment business staff; the issue of investment advertisements; handling new clients (including money laundering, client categorisation and issue of customer agreements); and quality of advice or of transactions. The compliance officer may monitor these procedures by sampling a number of recruitment or transaction files each month to ascertain if the procedure is being observed. The compliance officer may also carry out periodic inspections of head office departments, such as the dealing room, the back office or the personnel department. If the organisation has a branch network, then all branches should be periodically inspected. LAUTRO (in due course PIA) attached particular importance to branch visits.

## 3.5 Obtaining change

Having established the procedures and monitored them, the compliance officer will need to be satisfied that any non-observance is swiftly corrected. If a stockbroker's dealers are not obtaining or recording best execution, or if a branch manager of an insurance company is not monitoring for best advice or persistency, then action must be taken to change this.

It is, of course, easy for the compliance officer or the chief executive to issue an instruction requiring that action be taken, but without follow up action this may have little effect. Indeed 'management by memorandum' is an expression of disapproval used by several SRO disciplinary tribunals to describe organisations which take insufficient steps to achieve compliance.

If instructions for remedial action are issued they must be followed up. The compliance officer should reinspect the department or branch one week or one month later (or whatever is appropriate) to ensure that the correct procedure is being followed and, if it is not, ensure that further remedial action is taken. If necessary, the compliance officer's request for action should be supported by senior management in forceful terms.

In addition to securing future compliance and taking remedial action, it may be necessary to re-examine past transactions. If, for instance, the compliance officer determines that complaints have not been properly resolved, that customer agreements are defective or that business has been incorrectly handled as execution-only business, steps should be taken to review all such transactions, perhaps initially on a sample basis, to determine if customers have been disadvantaged. If they have, then remedial steps should be taken.

## 4 BUSINESS COVERED BY COMPLIANCE

This is likely to be the same as the firm's regulated business and it will be important for the firm to ensure that all aspects of its work are fully compliant. Particular activities, and the role of the compliance department in relation to them, are likely to include the following:

(1) *compliance manual*:   keeping this up to date;
(2) *performing compliance monitoring*:   reviewing information held on file; interviewing staff; reviewing compliance procedures; checking a random number of transaction files; reviewing accounting records for client money and assets;
(3) *alerting the authorities*:   notifying the SRO of all matters requiring notification in the rule book and, when appropriate, making other disclosures under SIB Principle 10;
(4) *financial*:   ensuring that the firm has appropriate financial controls, maintains the requisite resources and keeps the necessary records;

(5) *marketing*: ensuring that advertisements and marketing activities comply with the rules;

(6) *new clients*: ensuring they are correctly categorised and issued with appropriate client agreements;

(7) *recruitment*: ensuring that all recruits have satisfactory references, are properly trained and are individually registered as required;

(8) *money laundering*: ensuring the proper procedures are observed;

(9) *market integrity*: policing insider dealing and market manipulation;

(10) *customer relations*: ensuring when appropriate that best advice is given; that customers understand risks involved and that transactions are suitable for them;

(11) *handling transactions*: ensuring that best execution is achieved when applicable and deals properly allocated; churning must be avoided;

(12) *client money and assets*: ensuring they are held in accordance with the regulations;

(13) *polarisation*: ensuring that the rules for marketing packaged products are observed;

(14) *complaints*: ensuring they are properly handled and monitored;

(15) *conflicts of interest*: ensuring they are understood by customers, and that steps are taken to ensure the customer's interest is not overridden by that of the firm.

It may be useful to give an example of how compliance officers may handle a certain kind of business in order to ensure that it is compliant. The example of issuing an investment advertisement is taken as this is likely to be relevant to most investment businesses. The advertising rules are complex and difficult to apply. Furthermore, advertising is a marketing-run activity where decisions often have to be made against tight timetables.

(1) The compliance officer will be aware of the potential problems, which are that:

- the advertisement may be misleading: eg the service or product is misdescribed or the advertisement contains a misleading comparison;
- the advertisement may be issued without authority: eg by the marketing department or by an appointed representative without the compliance officer having authorised it;
- the firm may fail to keep records showing that the contents of the advertisement were verified and it was duly authorised.

(2) The compliance officer will appreciate the consequences of an investment advertisement failing to comply, which may be:

- the regulator requires the firm to re-contact investors to correct any misapprehension caused by the advertisement;

- the firm is required to buy back the investment or to compensate affected investors;
- the regulator may take disciplinary action against the firm over the advertisement.

(3)  The compliance officer will be familiar with the applicable rules:

- whether the advertisement relates to a product or service within the firm's business profile as agreed with its regulator;
- whether an advertisement is an investment advertisement or if any of the exemptions are relevant (see Chapter 13);
- if it promotes an unregulated collective investment scheme, then the Financial Services (Promotion of Unregulated Schemes) Regulations 1991 must be considered (see Chapter 17);

(4)  The compliance officer or a designated deputy will review the contents of the advertisement against the rules, checking:

- applicable contents requirements are observed;
- requisite warnings are present;
- that evidence is on file to substantiate all facts;
- whether it complies with any relevant guidance issued by the SRO, for instance on high income products;
- that it is, overall, fair and not misleading.

(5)  If the contents are in accordance with all requirements, the compliance officer will formally approve the advertisement and ensure that a copy of the proof together with the supporting evidence is kept in accordance with the SRO's rules.

# 5  WHEN COMPLIANCE BREAKS DOWN

The severe consequences of compliance breakdown serve to highlight the importance of achieving compliance: good compliance is good business sense and avoids both the commercial and regulatory consequences of compliance breaches.

## 5.1  Symptoms

These will vary in detail and extent depending upon the particular circumstances, but there may well be common themes:

(a)  *under resourced compliance*
the compliance officer or department does not have sufficient understanding of the business; compliance tasks are not properly carried out eg branches may not have been visited, or breaches noted on inspection visits may still be persisting;

*(b)* *unsupportive senior management*
senior management may not provide the compliance officer with sufficient resources or authority; the board may be unaware of the compliance difficulties facing the firm; the compliance officer may actually be overruled by line management for commercial reasons;

*(c)* *substantive rule breaches*
there is no limit to the number of examples which could be given, but some illustrations can be taken from recent SRO disciplinary action:

- life insurance company failing to ensure its sales recruits were fit and proper;
- life insurance company failing to ensure that its sales force gave best advice to its customers;
- building society failing to ensure that its staff were open and co-operative with its regulator;
- fund manager overcharging private customers and carrying on business for which it was not authorised;
- fund manager carrying out transactions to generate income for itself which were not in the customers' interests;
- stockbroker giving unsuitable advice to private clients;
- stockbroker failing to protect client assets and trading with insufficient capital.

## 5.2 The consequences

Where any rule is breached, the responsibility will usually lie with the firm to take remedial action to ensure that investors are not being prejudiced. This may involve considerable expense as customers may have to be contacted, transactions adjusted or reversed and compensation paid.

In severe or significant cases of rule breaches, the SRO may intervene in the member's business or take disciplinary action. This is discussed in detail in Chapter 12, and the consequences can include:

- a fine;
- payment of the SRO's costs of investigation, enforcement and discipline;
- a public reprimand.

# 5 *Approaching the Act*

Having introduced the structure of the new financial services regime, we must now go on to examine the individual elements in greater detail. Before doing that, however, it may be helpful to suggest a scheme of approach for use when considering whether any item of business is regulated by the FSA. We will then give some other sources of guidance and help.

## 1 A SCHEME OF APPROACH

The following scheme of approach may prove helpful when considering whether any item of business falls within the ambit of the FSA.

(1) Consider separately each element in the transaction.

(2) Do any of the elements involve investments which are regulated by the FSA? Consider in particular investments which fall within para 2 of Sched 1 (debentures), para 7 (options) and para 8 (futures) on account of their wide scope. Make sure that you are looking at an up-to-date version of Sched 1. The regulated investments are discussed in Chapter 7.

(3) If so, is the activity the business of dealing, arranging deals, managing, advising or operating a collective investment scheme in relation to a regulated investment? (See Chapter 6 for discussion of what constitutes a 'business', and Chapter 8 for discussion of the five different kinds of investment activity.)

(4) Is the activity carried on in the United Kingdom? This is discussed in Chapter 6.

(5) If so, consider the FSA's exclusions. These are shown in chart form at the beginning of Chapter 8, and are referred to in Chapters 6–10.

    (a) If a person is unauthorised, the existence of a relevant exclusion can make the difference between whether it needs to obtain authorisation under the FSA or not.

    (b) The exclusions are equally important if the person is authorised. If an authorised person undertakes business which falls within one of the

FSA's exclusions, then it is probably not subject to the conduct of business and other rules which would otherwise be applicable. You should, however, check the rulebook of the applicable SRO to see whether its rules do none the less apply to that situation. For example, note SFA's definition of 'associated business'.

(6) If the person is authorised and the transaction does fall within the FSA then ask:

(a) Does the transaction fall within the scope of the regulator from which it has obtained authorisation (or, if a European Institution, to whom it is subject)? (See Chapter 2.)

(b) Does the transaction fall within the statement of business which it has agreed with its SRO? If not it must be amended before proceeding.

(c) Is the authorised person infringing any general provision of the FSA, such as the restriction on unsolicited calls in s 56?

(d) Also, check whether sections of the FSA which seem applicable have been amended.

(7) (a) If the person is exempted (see Chapter 2), and the transaction does fall within the FSA, then is the transaction one that can be undertaken by such a person?

(b) If the person is exempted by virtue of a contract falling within s 44, does the contemplated transaction come within the ambit of that contract?

(c) If the exempted person is exempted only in respect of part of its investment business, then investment business in respect of which it is exempt is ignored in determining the applicability of the exclusions in paras 17–27 of Sched 1 to that person's non-exempt investment business (para 32 of Sched 1).

(8) If the transaction is structured so that property is pooled and managed by a third party, it may be a collective investment scheme even if the subject property is not a regulated investment. (See Chapter 9.)

(9) Visual or written material and some oral statements relating to regulated investments can constitute investment advertisements, irrespective of whether anyone is carrying on investment business. (See Chapter 13.)

(10) The Common Unsolicited Calls Regulations may be relevant if cold calling will be made.

(11) If the person is carrying on investment business or issuing an investment advertisement, consider the impact of the applicable conduct of business rules:

(a) Different rules apply in different circumstances, and a number of rules are disapplied for certain categories of business and of customer. For example, while most of the detailed conduct of business rules will apply when a firm is dealing with a private customer, a number are disapplied when engaging in corporate finance work. (The rules are outlined in Chapter 3.)

(b) Check through all the conduct of business rules before reaching a conclusion. They are not always cross-referenced and it is easy to miss applicable rules.

(c) Check that you are looking at the up-to-date rules. SIB, SROs and RPBs periodically amend and update their rulebooks.

(d) Ensure that the regulator has no transitional provisions in force which disapply some rules, or postpone the introduction of others, during a transitional period.

(e) Look at any guidance releases or rules bulletins which the regulator, or SIB, has issued. These can offer helpful commentary and assistance in interpreting and applying the rules.

(f) Consider whether SIB's Principles apply. A transaction may comply with the rulebook but breach a Principle.

(g) If dealing with a European Institution exercising its 'passport' rights, identify which home state and which host state rules are applicable to the activity.

(12) Consider whether other rules apply such as:

(a) client money regulations;
(b) financial rules;
(c) cancellation rules.

# 2   SOURCES OF INFORMATION

## 2.1   Treasury

The Treasury is the government department responsible for the FSA. While it can be asked to respond to enquiries by telephone or by letter, this can be a fairly lengthy process. The Treasury is reluctant to create precedents by giving definitive written responses to enquiries.

## 2.2   Securities and Investments Board

SIB regulates the SROs and RPBs. The appropriate officers of the SIB will normally try to answer enquiries over the telephone, or give a written response.

SIB has published a number of very helpful guidance releases and consultative papers on various aspects of the regime. The introduction to each guidance release states that they are issued to promote uniformity of practice and interpretation of the FSA and the rules made under it, but they have no special authority. A number of guidance releases are referred to in the following chapters.

## 2.3  SROs and RPBs

The individual SROs and RPBs will try to answer queries on their rulebooks. They are, however, generally unwilling to give answers on a no-name basis, and will normally want to know the name of the member to whom the enquiry relates. The enquiry may then be logged on that member's file. The SROs also emphasise, quite properly, that only a court can give definitive guidance on their rules, and that it is for the individual members to obtain their own legal advice.

## 3  THE VALUE OF GUIDANCE

Although advice and guidance is, to a greater or lesser extent, available from all these bodies, it is worth considering how valuable this actually is.

A letter from the Treasury or SIB confirming that, in their opinion, a certain activity falls outside the FSA or, alternatively, that a certain course of action complies with the FSA, is likely to be authoritative. It also means it is unlikely that (where this would be a possibility) a criminal prosecution will be brought against a person for following that advice, at least until either the Treasury or SIB announces a general change in policy or has issued a warning.

Similarly, a letter from an SRO or RPB stating that a certain course of action conforms to their rules is confirmation that the body is satisfied that the member is complying with the rules. This does not, though, for the purpose of the SFA or IMRO rules, constitute formal guidance upon which the member may rely.

However, the greater threat for failing to comply with the FSA or the conduct of business rules is that of civil rather than criminal liability. An investment business faced with a civil claim for compensation under s 62, or with a defence to an RSC Order 14 summons which claims that the contract is unenforceable for breach of s 3 of the FSA, may well find that a letter from SIB, or the Treasury or its SRO or RPB, is of little avail.

# 6 Carrying on Investment Business

The FSA's principal restriction, on which the financial services regime is based, is contained in s 3. This states that:

(3)    No person shall carry on, or purport to carry on, investment business in the United Kingdom unless he is an authorised person under Chapter III or an exempted person under Chapter IV of this part of the Act.

In order to understand this section we must examine the individual elements in turn and then consider the FSA's territorial scope.

## 1   CARRY ON

The words 'carry on' imply a repetition or series of acts, and connote an element of continuity, (Brett LJ in *Smith v Anderson* [1880] 15 ChD 247). The continuity can, however, be inferred (see below).

### 1.1   'Purport to carry on'

'Purport to carry on' means pretending to carry on investment business, or carrying on something which resembles (but is not) investment business: for example, where someone fraudulently pretends to sell securities.

## 2   BUSINESS

There are two inconsistent lines of authority on the meaning of business. A series of cases concerned with covenants between landlord and tenant state that profit is not a necessary element of a business (see *Bramwell v Lacy* 10 ChD 691; *Rolls v Miller* (1884) 25 ChD 206). This may be because where a school or a lodging house is causing a nuisance, it does not matter whether or not the undertaking is being run at a profit. On the other hand, a sequence of cases concerned with corporate and commercial matters hold that the intention of making a profit or avoiding a loss is a requisite of a business, and it is submitted that these cases are the better authority for interpreting the FSA.

For present purposes, business has adequately been defined as anything which occupies the time and attention and labour of a man for the purpose of profit (Jessel MR in *Smith v Anderson*). This, however, is a starting point and the proposition requires detailed consideration for the purposes of the FSA.

## 3  CARRY ON BUSINESS

As Lord Diplock said in *Town Investments v Department of Environment* [1978] AC 359 'the word "business" is an etymological chameleon; it suits its meaning to the context in which it is found'. Hence in construing this word the objective of the legislation should be considered.

It is likely that the courts will interpret 'business' and 'carrying on business' so as to enable them to regulate investment business, and to afford protection to investors, in a manner that seems appropriate in light of the facts before them. SIB would seem to support this view. Guidance Release 2/89 states that in considering what constitutes carrying on investment business in the United Kingdom, consideration should be given as to whether a person is a market participant and should be authorised in the interests of investor protection or market integrity; or whether instead it can properly be viewed as a customer of the market dealing for itself.

While guidance on the meaning of 'business' can be derived from cases arising under other legislation, some of which are referred to below, they should be treated with caution, although they do illustrate the approach adopted by the courts when seeking to apply the concept of 'carrying on business' to a variety of circumstances.

In the context of the FSA, to 'carry on business' most likely means to effect a series of actions with the intention of making a profit or avoiding a loss. There are two elements here.

(1) *Profit*:   the requirement to have an intention to make a profit or avoid a loss. Accordingly, giving occasional and gratuitous investment advice is unlikely to be viewed as carrying on investment business.

(2) *Continuity*:   the requirement that the business must be carried on. As well as the authority of *Smith v Anderson*, cited above, it was held in *Re a Debtor* [1936] 1 Ch 237 that while occasional speculation might not amount to carrying on business, frequent and systematic speculations probably did, which in that case took the form of buying and selling shares over a period of 18 months. Accordingly arranging a single investment deal, whether or not for a fee, should not be viewed as carrying on investment business. However, much will depend on the nature of the transaction or transactions under consideration. While it

may be arguable that a single sale of listed securities on the London Stock Exchange will not on its own amount to 'carrying on business', there may be other single commercial ventures which are otherwise.

SIB takes a slightly different view in Guidance Release 2/89 which states that the essential elements of 'carrying on a business' are a degree of continuity and a commercial context. In Guidance Release 4/94 SIB restates its view that commercial motivation is an essential element of a 'business' and suggests that an employer establishing a group personal pension scheme for its employees is not thereby carrying on a business in the absence of some pecuniary benefit to the employer. Commercial motivation may equate with an intention to make a profit, but seems to extend further.

It is, in addition, necessary to consider some particular circumstances.

(1) Effecting a transaction which is intended to be the first of a series of business transactions can on its own constitute carrying on a business (Esher MR in *Re Griffin* [1890] 60 LJQB 235).

(2) Effecting a series of unconnected and sporadic transactions may together amount to carrying on business. In *American Leaf Co v Director General* [1979] AC 676 a tobacco company which let surplus premises on a number of separate occasions was held to be thereby carrying on a business. In the context of the FSA, effecting a number of investment transactions in the course of business may together constitute carrying on investment business. For example, over a period of some months a manufacturing company may buy metal futures on the London Metal Exchange, advise its employees on personal pensions, buy shares on the London Stock Exchange with a view to selling them immediately for profit, and deal in traded options. Taken together (and for the purposes of illustration disregarding available exclusions) this could well amount to it carrying on investment business.

(3) In the case of a corporation, the activities which together constitute 'carrying on business' do not need to be part of the company's main business. In *American Leaf*, above, it was stated that 'any gainful use to which [a company] puts any of its assets *prima facie* amounts to the carrying on of a business'. An example is *Customs and Excise Commissioners v British Railways Board* [1976] 3 All ER 100 where it was held by the House of Lords that the provision of advice to the BR Board in relation to its pension funds was made for the purposes of a business carried out by the BR Board as providing pensions formed part of its functions as a railway undertaking.

This case related to the Board's liability for VAT, and for the purposes of the FSA one can argue that an activity which confers no commercial benefit should not be viewed as a business. There is merit to this approach, but it is submitted that a court is likely to give a wide definition to 'business' where this would enable it to take action against someone dishonestly infringing the FSA, or to compensate an investor who has unjustly suffered loss.

(4) A commercial company which acquires or disposes of investments or effects borrowing for a purpose ancillary to its corporate purposes is arguably not carrying on business when doing do. SIB in Guidance Release 1/88 comments that if, during a takeover, a bidder holds itself out as buying shares in a target's subsidiary with a view to selling them in a subsequent reorganisation, it is not thereby carrying on the business of holding itself out as buying those shares with a view to selling them. Similarly it is suggested that a listed company is not carrying on a business if, in connection with a vendor placing an open offer, it acts as agent of the vendor by offering the vendor's entitlement to ordinary shares in the company to existing shareholders.

## 3.1   Who is carrying on the business?

To 'carry on business' means to carry on one's own business (see *Le Tailleur v South Eastern Railway* 1877 3 CPD 18). As Fry LJ charmingly remarked in *Graham v Lewis* [1888] 22 QBD 1: 'A butler employed to look after his master's plate... may be a very busy man, but he could not be said to be carrying on business.'

If an individual carries on investment business in his own capacity, then he or she will in principle require authorisation, as will the partners in a partnership which carries on investment business.

In the case of a company which carries on investment business, it will be the company which in principle requires authorisation and not its directors or employees. This is because they will normally be acting in the course of their duties as agents of the company.

Quite often a company which carries on investment business is part of a larger group of companies. All employees are employed by a group services company which seconds staff to various operating subsidiaries. In such a case employees of the group services company seconded with a formal contract of secondment to a subsidiary company carrying on investment business will be viewed as agents of the subsidiary and it is the subsidiary and not them which will require authorisation under the FSA.

If a holding company and its subsidiaries are all carrying on investment business, then each of them may require authorisation under the FSA. Each is carrying on its own business, and the Act has no provision for group authorisation.

There are, however, some exceptions to the general rule that only people who carry on investment business are affected by the FSA. Two principal ones are:

(1) Investment advertisements are regulated by s 57, whether or not they are placed by persons who carry on investment business. (This is discussed in Chapter 13).

(2) Under s 191, a person who manages the regulated investment assets of an occupational pension scheme is deemed to be carrying on investment business even if he would not otherwise be regarded as doing so. This is discussed in Chapter 16.

## 4  CARRY ON INVESTMENT BUSINESS

'Investment business' is defined by s 1(2) as the business of engaging in an activity falling within Part II of Sched 1 which is not excluded by Part III of Sched 1.

The investment activities contained in Part II of Sched 1 are:

(1) dealing: buying or selling a regulated investment as principal or agent;
(2) arranging: arranging for a third party to deal;
(3) managing: managing the regulated investments of another;
(4) advising: giving specific advice on the merits of dealing;
(5) operating a collective investment scheme.

In addition, offering or agreeing to deal, arrange deals, manage or advise are also investment activities. Para 28(1)(c) of Sched 1 provides that 'offer' includes an invitation to treat. These provisions are intended to ensure that, for example, not only is the actual activity of dealing caught, but also the preliminary marketing and negotiations fall within the ambit of the FSA and are regulated by it.

The regulated investments are generally financial investments. As a rule, if one can see, touch or look after the investment, then it falls outside the scope of the FSA. Accordingly, tangibles such as land, art, houses and timeshares will fall outside the scope of the FSA provided they are not the subject of a futures contract, or a collective investment scheme. Other investments which are already regulated under other legislation, such as bank and building society accounts, are also excluded.

The investment activities, regulated investments, and the exclusions contained in paras 17–25B of Sched 1 (Part III) are discussed in Chapters 7–10.

## 5  THE FSA'S TERRITORIAL SCOPE

Section 1(3) defines the two ways of carrying on investment business in the United Kingdom. First, one can do it from a permanent place of business which one has established in the United Kingdom. Into this category will fall United Kingdom-based investment businesses. Secondly, one can be caught by the FSA when one carries on investment business *into* the United Kingdom from abroad, unless one can take advantage of one or more of the Act's detailed exclusions. These are contained in paras 17–27 Sched 1, and are discussed below.

> 1(3)  For the purposes of the Act a person carries on investment business in the United Kingdom if he—
>
> > (a)  carries on investment business from a permanent place of business maintained by him in the United Kingdom; or
> >
> > (b)  engages in the United Kingdom in one or more of the activities which fall within the paragraphs in Part II of that Schedule [Sched 1] and are not excluded by Part III or IV of that Schedule and his doing so constitutes the carrying on by him of a business in the United Kingdom.

## 5.1  Permanent place of business

The first way, set out in subs (*a*), is to carry on investment business from a permanent place of business which you maintain in the United Kingdom: in other words, you have a United Kingdom base.

Whether you are maintaining a permanent place of business will in each case be a question of fact, and the criteria should be similar to those used in determining whether a company has established a place of business for the purposes of Part 23 of the Companies Act 1985. Indeed, establishing a place of business is a necessary antecedent to maintaining it as a permanent place of business.

There are a number of decided cases which offer guidance on the concept of a 'place of business'. While these are more concerned with the narrow issue of whether a foreign company is amendable to English legal process, rather than whether it has a sufficiently close connection with the United Kingdom to require regulation under the FSA or registration under the Companies Act 1985, some guidance can be derived from them.

In recent cases (*South India Shipping Corporation Ltd v Import Bank of Korea* [1985] 2 All ER 219; *Re Oriel Ltd* [1985] 3 All ER 216) the Court of Appeal has adopted a test in determining whether an overseas corporation has established a place of business in the United Kingdom. This can be broken down into a number of separate elements and we now examine each criterion in turn. An overseas firm will, in principle, fall within the FSA if all four criteria are fulfilled.

*(a)  Does the firm have premises in the United Kingdom?*
This criterion is likely to be fulfilled:

> (i)  if the firm has a separate office visibly connected to it, particularly but not limited to where this presence is given publicity; or

(ii) if the firm operates from the premises of a third party.

In either of these cases the firm can be said to be 'maintaining' the premises in the sense of using them even if it does not formally make payment for them.

*(b) Are they the firm's permanent premises?*

It must be a permanent as distinct from a temporary place of business. An airport lounge, a hotel room or a short-term stand at an exhibition may on an occasion be places of business, but are unlikely to be considered sufficiently permanent to fall within s 1(3)(a). The Companies Act cases refer to 'establishing' or 'an established' place of business, and it is apparent that use of the word 'establishing' or 'established' connotes permanence. In *Re Oriel* a passage from the judgment in *Lord Advocate v Huron and Eric Loan and Savings Co* (1911) SC 612 was cited with approval, which indicated that this criterion is likely to be fulfilled by a 'more or less permanent location, not necessarily owned or even leased by the company, but at least associated with the company and from which habitually or at least with some degree of regularity business is conducted'.

*(c) Does the firm have personnel in the United Kingdom?*

This criterion is likely to be fulfilled:

(i) if the firm has employees in the United Kingdom; or
(ii) if a third party seconds staff to handle the firm's work in the United Kingdom.

*(d) Do those personnel conduct the firm's business from those premises?*

This criterion is likely to be fulfilled:

(i) where the personnel carry out any part of its business activities, such as public relations, gathering information, soliciting finance or identifying business opportunities. These may be only peripheral to its main business; or
(ii) where the personnel have authority to enter into contracts on its behalf for the acquisition or supply of goods or services.

Three further situations require comment. A person is unlikely to have established, or be maintaining, a permanent place of business in any of the following circumstances:

(1) where it carries on business in the United Kingdom solely through resident agents who do not work for it exclusively: *Lord Advocate v Huron and Eric Loan & Savings Company* (1911) SC 612.
(2) if it is a company and its subsidiary establishes a permanent place of business, unless the parent company itself carries on business from there: *Deverall v Grant Advertising Inc* [1954] 3 All ER 389;

(3) where it is a company just because its directors reside in the United Kingdom at a private residence unless they carry on business from it: *Re Oriel* [1985] 3 All ER 216.

Once a person has fulfilled these criteria it does not matter whether the permanent place of business is described as a branch, a representative office or a publicity office.

## 5.2 Services basis

The second way of carrying on investment business in the United Kingdom is to do so on a services basis: for instance by letters, telephone or visits and without maintaining a permanent place of business as described at 5.1 above.

Subsection (*b*) provides that someone who operates in this way will fall within the regulatory net of the FSA provided each of four elements is present. These are:

(1) You engage in the United Kingdom in one or more of the investment activities in relation to regulated investments (these are discussed in Chapters 7 and 8 respectively). These activities are dealing, arranging, managing or advising (or offering or agreeing to do any of these) or establishing, operating or winding up a collective investment scheme. It is unclear what 'engaging' in any of these activities actually means. However, bearing in mind the FSA's objective of protecting United Kingdom investors, it seems likely that a court would view an overseas person to be engaging in:

   (i) *dealing*: when the person who buys or sells is in the United Kingdom. It is submitted that the normal contractual tests, involving consideration of where the contract is made, are not applicable on account of the intention of the FSA. This view finds support in *SIB v Pantell SA* [1989] 3 WLR 698. It is, furthermore, in conformity with the proposition that a criminal offence is considered to be committed in the United Kingdom if any part of the results proscribed by the statute take place there: see *R v Ellis* [1899] 1 QB 230; *Secretary of State for Trade v Markus* [1975] 1 All ER 958 and *Diamond v Bank of India and Montreal* [1979] QB 333. This proposition is, of course, applicable to all investment activities under the FSA, and not just to dealing.

   (ii) *arranging*: when the person with whom the arrangements are made is in the United Kingdom;

   (iii) *managing*: when the actual activity or activities which constitute management take place in the United Kingdom;

   (iv) *advising*: when the advice is given to someone in the United Kingdom;

(v)   *collective investment schemes*:  as for managing;

(vi)  *offering or agreeing*: when the person receiving the offer, or making the agreement, is present in the United Kingdom. It was held in *SIB v Pantell SA* that sending circulars to people resident in the United Kingdom could be offering to deal, to arrange deals or to advise.

It should not make any difference whether the overseas person (or its representative) is physically present within the United Kingdom or not when 'engaging' in any of these investment activities.

(2)  Your doing so amounts to carrying on a business in the United Kingdom (as discussed above).

(3)  The FSA's general exclusions contained in Part III of Sched 1 (such as the dealing as principal exclusion) do not apply to your circumstances.

(4)  You do not fall within the special exclusions contained at paras 26 and 27 of Sched 1, which are termed the 'Overseas Person Exclusions' and are discussed below.

# 6   THE OVERSEAS PERSON EXCLUSIONS

If the overseas person is 'engaging' in the United Kingdom in the investment activity, and this amounts to him carrying on a business in the United Kingdom, and he cannot avail himself of the FSA's general exclusions (such as dealing as principal), then he should consider the applicability of one of the two overseas person exclusions.

These exclusions relate to overseas persons. An overseas person is defined by para 26(2) of Sched 1 to be a person who does not fall within s 1(3)(a): in other words, someone who does not carry on investment business (the business of engaging in an activity falling within Part II of Sched 1 and not excluded by Part III) from a permanent place of business he maintains in the United Kingdom.

## 6.1   Authorised and exempted counterparties

The first overseas person exclusion relates to certain transactions with or through authorised or exempted persons, and is set out at para 26 of Sched 1:

26(1)  Paragraph 12 above does not apply to any transaction by a person not falling within s 1(3)(a) of this Act ('an overseas person') with or through:—

   (a)  an authorised person; or

   (b)  an exempted person acting in the course of business in respect of which he is exempt.

(2)   Paragraph 13 above does not apply if:—

    (a) the arrangements are made by an overseas person with, or the offer or agreement to make them is made by him to or with, an authorised person or an exempted person and, in the case of an exempted person, the arrangements are with a view to his entering into a transaction in respect of which he is exempt; or

    (b) the transactions with a view to which the arrangements are made are, as respects transactions in the United Kingdom, confined to transactions by authorised persons and transactions by exempted persons in respect of which they are exempt.

This exclusion provides that, so long as you do not carry on investment business from a permanent place of business which you maintain in the United Kingdom, you may:

(1)   *deal:* the activity defined in para 12 of Sched 1:
*with or through:*` 'with' means you enter into the contract as principal or agent; 'through' is defined by para 29 of Sched 1 to mean that if you deal through me, I enter into the transaction as agent or I arrange for a third party to enter into the transaction as principal or agent;
*an authorised person or*
*an exempted person*;

(2)   *arrange deals*: the activity defined in para 13 of Sched 1 where:
*either* you make the arrangements (or offer to agree to) with an authorised or exempted person for them to deal with some third party (s (2)(a));
*or* you make the arrangements with a view to the intended deal in the United Kingdom being entered into by an authorised or exempted person (s (2)(b)).

In either case it should not matter whether you are physically present within the United Kingdom at the time of the transaction.

In all of these instances the exempted person must act in the course of business or in relation to a transaction in respect of which he is exempted.

A firm that falls within this first overseas person exclusion may solicit investment business by:

(1)   issuing investment advertisements. Article 11 of the Financial Services Act 1986 (Investment Advertisements) (Exemptions) Order 1995 provides that a non-authorised person who is not unlawfully carrying on investment business in the United Kingdom may issue an investment advertisement to a number of categories of person which include an authorised person, a journalist, a government, a public authority, or certain non-private investors.

(2) cold calling. Paragraph 1 of the Common Unsolicited Calls Regulations permits, in summary, an overseas person to cold call a non-private investor.

## 6.2 Transactions with anyone

The second overseas person exclusion is concerned with a wider category of parties. It permits an overseas person to carry on investment business (but not operate a collective investment scheme) with any United Kingdom person (who need not be authorised or exempted and who can, for example, be a company or a private individual) provided that in obtaining or carrying out the investment business the overseas person does not infringe the FSA's restrictions on advertising or cold calling. It is set out at para 27 of Sched 1.

27(1) Paragraph 12 above does not apply to any transaction entered into by an overseas person as principal with, or as agent for, a person in the United Kingdom, paras 13, 14 and 15 above do not apply to any offer made by an overseas person to or agreement made by him with a person in the United Kingdom and para 15 above does not apply to any advice given by an overseas person to a person in the United Kingdom if the transaction, offer, agreement or advice is the result of:—

(a) an approach made to the overseas person by or on behalf of the person in the United Kingdom which either has not been in any way solicited by the overseas person or has been solicited by him in a way which has not contravened s 56 or 57 of this Act; or

(b) an approach made by the overseas person which has not contravened either of those sections.

(2) Where the transaction is entered into by the overseas person as agent for a person in the United Kingdom, subpara (1) above applies only if:—

(a) the other party is outside the United Kingdom; or

(b) the other party is in the United Kingdom and the transaction is the result of such an approach by the other party as is mentioned in subpara (1)(a) above or of such an approach as is mentioned in subpara (1)(b) above.

The exclusion in subpara 27(1) permits an overseas person (defined above) to deal, arrange deals, manage or advise for or with any person provided the overseas person when obtaining the business (if it were solicited) has not breached either of:

(1) the FSA's advertising restrictions;

(2) the Common Unsolicited Calls Regulations.

We mention above the existence of 'permissions' contained in the investment advertisement and cold calling regimes which allow an overseas person to solicit non-private customers.

It is important to note that the activities of issuing an investment advertisement in the United Kingdom or making an unsolicited call on a person in the United Kingdom probably constitute engaging in an investment activity in the United Kingdom. This is because the issuer of the advertisement, or maker of the unsolicited call, may thereby be offering or agreeing to engage in an investment activity: see *SIB v Pantell SA* [1989] 3 WLR 698.

Paragraph 27(1) is drafted to differentiate between three situations:

(1) *dealing*: where the exclusion only relates to transactions, and not to offering or agreeing to deal;

(2) *arranging, managing and advising*: where the exclusion only relates to offering or agreeing to engage in these investment activities, so that the actual arranging or managing must be carried on outside the United Kingdom.

(3) *advising*: where the exclusion additionally permits the giving of advice.

It is difficult to understand the logic behind these distinctions However, in the light of the wording of this paragraph it is submitted that an overseas person, provided he observes ss 56 and 57, is free to:

(1) engage in dealing and giving advice in the United Kingdom;

(2) engage in offering or agreeing to arrange, to manage and to give advice in the United Kingdom. The arrangements and management must be engaged in wholly outside the United Kingdom, although the giving of advice can be engaged in within the United Kingdom.

Provided the overseas person observes these restrictions, it should not make any difference whether he is physically present within the United Kingdom when engaging in these activities.

There is a further restriction where the overseas person enters into a transaction not as principal with a person in the United Kingdom, but as that person's agent. The restriction is that either:

(1) the other party to the transaction is outside the United Kingdom. Presumably, though, the overseas person's principal must be in the United Kingdom; or

(2) if the other party is in the United Kingdom (in addition to the overseas person's principal being in the United Kingdom) the business must have been obtained in accordance with subparas 27(1)(a) and (b), discussed above.

To take an example, a US fund manager who qualifies as an overseas person can operate in the United Kingdom without obtaining authorisation under the FSA when carrying on the following business:

(1) It may issue an investment advertisement to, and cold call, authorised persons and substantial corporations.

(2) It can deal and arrange deals in investments for its clients with or through authorised persons.

(3) It can engage within the United Kingdom in dealing with United Kingdom individuals and can also engage in giving them investment advice. It can offer or agree to manage their investments but must carry on the management activity abroad.

# 7 *The Regulated Investments*

The FSA is concerned with regulating the carrying on of investment business in the United Kingdom. We have discussed the meaning of 'carrying on business'. We must now consider the scope of the 11 types of regulated investments which fall within the ambit of the FSA. A proper grasp of what each class of investment entails is fundamental to understanding the FSA.

The 11 classes of investment are contained in Sched 1 to the FSA. This Schedule is structured thus:

(1) Part I: the regulated investments (discussed in this chapter).
(2) Part II: the investment activities which involve the regulated investments in Part I (discussed in Chapter 8)
(3) Part III: excluded activities: those activities involving regulated investments which are excluded from the FSA's principal restriction. (These are discussed in context in Chapters 7–10.)
(4) Part IV: further exclusions which only apply to overseas persons. (These are discussed in Chapter 6.)
(5) Part V: this contains definitions and interpretation which apply to Parts I–VI (s 1(4)).

Part I of Sched 1 is structured so that each investment is given a definition, and the definition is followed by Notes which form part of the definition. This is unusual and has not met with universal approval. Donaldson MR in *City Index v Leslie* [1991] 3 All ER 180 described it as 'a novel form of legislation, and potentially somewhat confusing, at least to a lawyer'. It is submitted that one should not try to construe the definitions in too narrow or legalistic a fashion. The House of Lords has held that, when construing a criminal statute, the court should look at the mischief at which the Act is directed and then consider whether the facts fall within the ordinary meaning of the words used by Parliament: *Attorney General's Reference (No 1 of 1988)* [1989] 2 All ER 1. Bearing in mind that the object of the FSA is to protect the investor, it seems likely that a court acting in a civil matter or a criminal trial would give a wide rather than a narrow interpretation to these definitions. This view is reinforced by the observation of Steyn LJ in *SIB v Pantell* (No 2) [1993] 1 All ER 134:

> In the process of interpreting a statute there is one consideration which overshadows all others in importance. That is the need to consider the words of the statute, and the contending interpretations, in the light of the

contextual scene or setting. In a difficult case that setting will include the genesis of the statutory provision, countervailing considerations of policy and public interest and the common law and statutory framework in which the provision will operate. These propositions are self-evident. But they merit special emphasis in the approach to be adopted to the construction of a statute, such as the Financial Services Act 1986, which in some respects introduced radical new solutions for old problems.

Schedule 1 is liable to alteration. Section 2 of the FSA empowers the Treasury to alter Sched 1 and s 75, which contains the definition of collective investment schemes (s 75(9)), by extending or restricting the meaning of 'investment', the activities which constitute carrying on investment business, or the FSA's territorial scope. Schedule 1 and s 75 have been altered on a number of occasions, and further alterations will be made in connection with the implementation of the Investment Services Directive. These are noted in context and the directive is discussed in Chapter 2.

The breadth of the definitions contained in Sched 1 is the basis of the FSA's complexity. The draftsman's technique of using a 'catch all' definition followed by a series of tight exclusions has given rise to substantial doubt and uncertainty in many places.

We now set out the text of Part I of Sched 1, and follow each paragraph with a discussion of the definition. It should be borne in mind that the word 'investment' means any asset, right or interest falling within any of these paragraphs (s 1(1)), which states that this is to apply 'unless the context otherwise requires'. One such instance is Note (1) to para 8.

## 1 SHARES

Paragraph 1 in Part 1 of Sched 1 provides the following:

(1) Shares and stock in the share capital of a company.

Note: In this paragraph 'company' includes any body corporate and also any unincorporated body constituted under the law or a country or territory outside the United Kingdom but does not, except in relation to any shares of a class defined as deferred shares for the purposes of section 119 of the Building Societies Act 1986, include a building society incorporated under the law of, or of any part of, the United Kingdom, nor does it include an open-ended investment company or any body incorporated under the law of, or any part of, the United Kingdom relating to industrial and provident societies or credit unions.

This definition takes in the shares and stock in the share capital of:

(1) a United Kingdom or overseas company;
(2) an unincorporated body constituted overseas.

Excluded are shares and stock in:

(1) the capital of an open-ended investment company, which counts as a unit in a collective investment scheme, regulated under para 6 of Sched I;

(2) the capital of United Kingdom building societies (subject to the stated exemption), industrial and provident societies or credit unions. The FSA is likely to be amended to include shares in industrial and provident societies as part of the implementation of the Investment Services Directive.

The definition of 'company' is inclusive. Under English law a company is an association of persons which does not need to be incorporated. An English unincorporated company is unlikely to have what would be recognised as a share capital, although in at least one reported case 'share capital' has been given this meaning (*Wishart v Murray's Executrix* [1949] CLY 5282).

Shares and stock in the capital of a United Kingdom company are for most purposes synonymous. A share is a right to a specified amount of share capital in a company, while stock is an aggregation of shares. Section 744 Companies Act 1985 provides that references in that Act to 'shares' include 'stock' unless a distinction is intended.

Both 'shares' and 'stock' have wide meanings so it has been necessary to limit them to shares and stock in the share capital of a company which, under English law, would exclude both loan stock and debentures. Subject to this, ordinary, preference, deferred and any other kind of shares and stock are included. Whether any particular item is a share or stock in the share capital of an overseas corporate or unincorporated body should be considered in the light of the applicable law.

## 2  DEBENTURES

Paragraph 2 of Part 1 of Sched 1 is drafted as follows:

(2) Debentures, including debenture stock, loan stock, bonds, certificates of deposit and other instruments creating or acknowledging indebtedness, not being instruments falling within paragraph 3 below.

Note. This paragraph shall not be construed as applying:—

(a) to any instrument acknowledging or creating indebtedness for, or for money borrowed to defray, the consideration payable under a contract for the supply of goods or services;

(b) to a cheque or other bill of exchange, a banker's draft or a letter of credit; or

(c) to a banknote, a statement showing a balance in a current, deposit or savings account or (by reason of any financial obligation contained in it) to a lease or other disposition of property, a heritable security or an insurance policy.

This is an extremely wide definition which is generally accepted to extend to a wider category of instruments than what would be considered to be debentures under pre-existing law. The principal definition, before considering the exclusionary Note, refers to 'debentures, including debenture stock, loan stock, bonds, certificates of deposit *and* other instruments creating or acknowledging indebtedness . . .'. As part of the Investment Services Directive, this paragraph is likely to be extended to include bills of exchange and analogous instruments traded on money markets.

No one has yet laid down an authoritative and exhaustive definition of what a debenture can be, although a good starting point is probably that of Chitty J in *Levy v Abercorris Slate and Slab Company* [1888] 37 Ch, where he said a 'debenture means a document which either creates a debt or acknowledges it, and any document which fulfils either of these conditions is a debenture . . . it is not . . . a strictly technical term . . .'. In *Edmonds v Blaina Furnaces Company* [1887] 36 Ch the same judge added the following observations: 'The term itself imports a debt—an acknowledgement of a debt . . . the instrument imports an obligation or covenant to pay . . . accompanied by some charge or security.'

In each instance one must consider the substance, and not just the form or description, of the instrument. It is considered that not every document creating or acknowledging indebtedness is a debenture. For example, a document in which one simply agrees to pay money, such as a bill of exchange, a negotiable instrument or a deed of covenant is not usually viewed as a debenture, nor is a loan agreement which merely contains terms that will apply to future indebtedness. However, assuming that a document such as a loan agreement is not itself a debenture, a debenture almost certainly comes into existence when a lender is irrevocably obliged to provide funds under such an agreement pursuant to a borrower's demand. One should not, in any case, be too doctrinaire on this point. In *NV Slavenburg's Bank v National Resources Ltd* [1980] 1 All ER 955, Lloyd J was unwilling to decide that a document which merely related to future indebtedness could not be a debenture.

The policy of the FSA is to regulate investments which will, logically, include debt securities such as debenture stock, loan stock, bonds and certificates of deposit. These are similar to shares because title is constituted by entry in a register or by negotiable instrument, there can be a secondary market, and the instrument will often be one of a series of similar or identical instruments. These quite properly fall within the scope of para 2.

However, para 2 is drafted in such a way as to include items which are not normally considered debentures, including some commercial rather than investment instruments. The inclusion of the words 'and other instruments creating or acknowledging indebtedness' suggests that (subject to the (*a*)–(*c*) exclusions) every instrument creating or acknowledging indebtedness will be a debenture for the purposes of the FSA and accordingly caught, particularly since the three exclusions in the Note relate to instruments and documents which would not normally be considered to be debentures in the first place. The three exclusions contained in this Note are as follows:

(a) An instrument acknowledging or creating indebtedness which is either the price payable under a contract for the supply of goods or services, or is money borrowed to pay that price. This is very wide and rather difficult to interpret. However, it is probably intended to exclude from para 2 any instrument which involves paying, or borrowing, the price for goods or services. The person issuing the instrument need not be the one acquiring the goods or services or paying for them; nor need the supplier of the goods or services be the same person as the lender. At its simplest. Note (a) probably excludes from para 2 a receipt or 'IOU'. The wording would also seem to exclude a debenture (or other instrument falling within para 2) issued by or for a borrower to a lender in respect of a loan the lender has made to enable the borrower to acquire any goods or services. 'Instrument' and 'contract' are in the singular which, on a literal interpretation, suggests that to fall within this exclusion each debenture (or instrument) must relate to the consideration due under a single contract for either goods or services. However, given that this exclusion is intended to remove commercial borrowing from the ambit of the FSA 1986, it is submitted that these two words should be interpreted to include the plural or otherwise a single debenture relating to a single contract would be excluded, but not three debentures relating to that contract, nor one debenture issued in respect of a loan financing three contacts.

(b) A cheque, bill of exchange (subject to the impending Investment Services Directive amendment), banker's draft or letter of credit.

(c) A banknote or a statement of an account. Also excluded are leases (presumably of real or personal property), dispositions of property (which should include a contract for sale and a mortgage, assignment or novation of a debt), heritable security (arising under Scots law) and an insurance policy (which may fall under para 10). A lease, disposition of property, heritable security or insurance policy are expressed to be excluded 'by reason of any financial obligation contained in it', and it is submitted that this phrase is intended to be descriptive of these instruments rather than imposing a limitation or qualification since, if they did not contain a financial obligation, they are unlikely to create or acknowledge indebtedness in the first place.

The purposes of these three exclusions is not altogether clear. It is submitted that the correct interpretation is that they remove the excluded items from what would otherwise be an inclusionary definition. In other words, the intention of the FSA is to catch everything other than that which is expressly excluded and that, for example, in the absence of an express exclusion even a cheque or an insurance policy would count as a debenture for the purposes of the FSA. An alternative view is that the Note is, in the case of this paragraph, just guidance since the heading to the Note is 'This paragraph shall not be construed as applying' rather than the heading for other paragraphs in Sched 1 which is 'This paragraph does not apply', which suggests that Parliament did not intend to imply that the three classes in the Note would otherwise be caught by the paragraph. This, however, is an artificial approach and the Note is best viewed as an exclusion from an otherwise inclusionary definition.

This confusion is unsatisfactory and there can be little doubt that para 2 makes a substantial change to the law of what constitutes a debenture, and items which no one previously thought were debentures should now be treated as such for the purposes of the Act. It may be helpful to give some examples of how the Act's definition of debenture may operate in practice.

First, does the instrument create or acknowledge indebtedness? Instruments which do not create or acknowledge indebtedness should not fall within para 2. An example of an instrument creating indebtedness is a novation of a debt. An example of a document acknowledging indebtedness is a floating charge. The acknowledgment should come from the debtor. Covenants to repay or documents referring to prospective indebtedness do not create or acknowledge indebtedness and should not, subject to the caveat mentioned above, be debentures. However, a floating charge would appear to be a debenture as it acknowledges indebtedness.

The definition of 'instrument' given in para 28 to Sched 1 includes a record. It would therefore appear that a record acknowledging indebtedness, such as a record of a debt kept by a bank in its books, will constitute a debenture for the purposes of the FSA. Market-making in deposits between banks would appear to be caught, because the book entries will be constituted as debentures.

A mortgage or charge will, in principle, fall within para 2 because it will acknowledge the indebtedness. However, because a mortgage is a disposition of property, it should be excluded by Note (c), although a mortgage over a regulated investment probably falls within para 11. A charge is not, and is therefore caught as a debenture.

A company may issue a promissory note in return for a loan, or a bank may secure finance for a customer's exports by taking a promissory note. A promissory note is an unconditional written promise, signed by the maker, to pay a certain sum on demand or at a fixed or determinable future time. It will be a debenture for the purposes of the FSA, although (depending on the circumstances) the issuer and receiver of this debenture may be able to take advantage of the exclusions in paras 12 and 13.

We discuss the position of syndicated loan agreements in Chapter 15.

A number of the FSA's exclusions, which are discussed later, may be relevant to transactions involving debentures. Four which are particularly worthy of detailed consideration are (in summary):

(i)   Note (1) to para 12 of Sched 1: you are not dealing if you accept a debenture in respect of a loan you are making.

(ii)  Note (4) to para 13 of Sched 1: you are not making arrangements if they relate to a person accepting a debenture for a loan which that person has made or will make.

(iii) Para 28(3) of Sched 1: you are not dealing if you issue a debenture, or making arrangements if you arrange for a third party to deal in your debenture.

(iv) Para 17 of Sched 1: the dealing as principal exclusions.

## 3 GOVERNMENT AND PUBLIC SECURITIES

Paragraph 3 of Part 1 of Sched 1 deals with government and public securities as follows:

(3) Loan stock, bonds and other instruments creating or acknowledging indebtedness issued by or on behalf of a government, local authority or public authority.

Notes

(1) In this paragraph 'government, local authority or public authority' means:—
   (a) the government of the United Kingdom, or Northern Ireland, or of any country or territory outside the United Kingdom;
   (b) a local authority in the United Kingdom or elsewhere
   (c) any international organisation the members of which include the United Kingdom or another member State.

(2) The Note to paragraph 2 above shall, so far as applicable, apply also to this paragraph.

(3) This paragraph does not apply to any instrument creating or acknowledging indebtedness in respect of money received by the Director of Savings as deposits or otherwise in connection with the business of the National Savings Bank or in respect of money raised under the National Loans Act 1968 under the auspices of the Director of Savings or in respect of money treated as being so raised by virtue of section 11(3) of the National Debt Act 1972.

This paragraph takes in certain loan stock, bonds and other instruments creating or acknowledging indebtedness. In principle, this paragraph covers the same ground as para 2, so they are stated to be mutually exclusive. The point of difference is that para 3 only relates to such investments which are issued by or on behalf of certain bodies, which are:

(1) any national government; and

(2) a local or public authority in any part of the world; and

(3) any international organisation with the United Kingdom or another EC State as a member.

The Note to para 2 also applies to this paragraph, and so the three exclusions lettered (*a*)-(*c*) in that paragraph are relevant here. Note (3) excludes United Kingdom National Savings products.

Examples of investments which will normally fall within this paragraph include:

(1) promissory notes issued by the City of Vienna;

(2) United States treasury bills.

The investment must be issued by one of the prescribed bodies, or on its behalf which suggests that a third party is issuing it as agent for that body. If a third party issues its own investments backed by government debt, they will not fall within para 3 although they may fall within para 2.

The inclusion of the words 'or other instruments' creates the same problems as in para 2.

## 4  INSTRUMENTS ENTITLING TO SHARES OR SECURITIES

This category is set out in para 4 of Part 1 of Sched 1 as follows:

(4) Warrants or other instruments entitling the holder to subscribe for investments falling within paragraph 1, 2 or 3 above.

Notes

(1) It is immaterial whether the investments are for the time being in existence or identifiable.

(2) An investment falling within this paragraph shall not be regarded as falling within paragraph 7, 8 or 9 below.

These are instruments entitling one to subscribe for any of the investments contained in paras 1, 2 or 3 above, an example of which would be a warrant to subscribe for a certain number of shares at a fixed price per share, subject to customary adjustments for events occurring prior to the subscription. While para 28(4) Sched 1 refers to share and debenture warrants falling within para 4, it is submitted that 'share warrant' as used in the FSA has a different meaning from that in the Companies Act 1985 s 188, as under the latter Act a share warrant relates to securities already issued and fully paid.

Note (1) is included because such an instrument may give the holder a right to subscribe at some time in the future for an investment which does not yet exist, perhaps at a predetermined price.

Note (2) provides that a warrant or other instrument which comes within this paragraph will not fall within para 7, 8 or 9: in other words, it will not be categorised as an option, a future or contract for differences.

This paragraph only relates to warrants and other instruments which grant the right to subscribe for the specified investments and which would be recognised as having a 'holder'. Use of the word 'subscribe' indicates that the investment is to be acquired from the issuer at some future time. An agreement granting a right to acquire shares already issued would fall outside this paragraph, and may be an option under para 7. A share warrant would be caught and an option certificate issued to an employee under an employee share option scheme will usually fall within this paragraph rather than para 7.

# 5 CERTIFICATES REPRESENTING SECURITIES

The regulated investment constituted by certificates representing securities is set out in para 5 of Part 1 of Sched 1 as follows:

(5) Certificates or other instruments which confer: –
   (a) property rights in respect of any investment falling within paragraph 1, 2, 3 or 4 above;
   (b) any right to acquire, dispose of, underwrite or convert an investment being a right to which the holder would be entitled if he held any such investment to which the certificate or instrument relates; or
   (c) a contractual right (other than an option) to acquire any such investment otherwise than by subscription.

   Note: This paragraph does not apply to any instrument which confers rights in respect of two or more investments issued by different persons or in respect of two or more different investments falling within paragraph 3 above and issued by the same person.

This paragraph catches certificates and instruments conferring property rights in, and other rights in relation to, investments falling within para 1, 2, 3 or 4 above.
Examples of investments falling within this paragraph include:

(1) a legal or equitable mortgage (but not a charge) over the shares of one company, but not over the shares of two companies by reason of the Note;
(2) a depositary receipt used to permit an unlisted security to be traded. An example of this would be an American Depository Receipt: the shares will remain with the creator of the ADR while the ADR (and not the share) will circulate within the United States as a bearer instrument;
(3) an instrument which confers a right to one or more shares, debentures, government securities or warrants, subject to two provisos:
   (i) it is not an option (which may fall within para 7);
   (ii) it is not acquired on subscription ie from the original issuer (which may fall within para 4).

The Note excludes:

(1) a single instrument which confers rights in respect of investments issued by different persons. The object of this exclusion is to remove units in collective investment schemes from this paragraph, since they are dealt with in para 6, but it would also exclude, for example, a single mortgage over the shares of two companies;

(2) a single instrument which confers rights in respect of two or more investments falling within para 3 (government or public securities) issued by the same person.

# 6 UNITS IN COLLECTIVE INVESTMENT SCHEMES

Units in collective investment schemes come under para 6 of Part 1 of Sched 1. It states the following:

(6) Units in a collective investment scheme, including shares in or securities of an open-ended investment company.

This paragraph comprehends two rather different kinds of investment. The first is units—in other words, participants' rights—in collective investment schemes (defined in s 75 discussed in Chapter 9). The second is shares in or securities of an open-ended investment company, which is defined by s 75(8) as a collective investment scheme under which:

(*a*) the property in question belongs beneficially to, and is managed by or on behalf of, a body corporate having as its purpose the investment of its funds with the aim of spreading investment risk and giving its members the benefit of the results of the management of those funds by or on behalf of that body; and

(*b*) the rights of the participants are represented by shares in or securities of that body which—

(i) the participants are entitled to have redeemed or repurchased, or which (otherwise than under Chapter VII of Part V of the Companies Act 1985 or the corresponding Northern Ireland provision) are redeemed or repurchased from them by, or out of funds provided by, that body; or

(ii) the body ensures can be sold by the participants on an investment exchange at a price related to the value of the property to which they relate.

It seems that a company must possess the following elements to fall within this definition:

(1) Its funds should be invested with the aim of spreading risk.

(2) Its funds should be managed.

(3) Investors are entitled to have their units redeemed or repurchased by the company or out of funds provided by the company.

(4) The company ensures investors can sell their units on an exchange and at a price related to the underlying property.

# 7  OPTIONS

Options are dealt with in para 7 of Part 1 of Sched 1 which states the following:

(7) Options to acquire or dispose of:—

    (*a*) an investment falling within any other paragraph of this part of this Schedule;

    (*b*) currency of the United Kingdom or of any other country or territory;

    (*c*) gold, palladium, platinum or silver; or

    (*d*) an option to acquire or dispose of an investment falling within this paragraph by virtue of (a), (b) or (c) above.

An option will, depending whether it is a put or a call option, usually give the holder of the option the right to sell or buy the item in respect of which the option is granted for a specified period of time and at an agreed price.

An option to acquire or dispose of any investment falling within paras 1–6 and 8–11 is caught by this paragraph. However, an instrument entitling the holder to subscribe for investments falling within paras 1–3, whether or not presently in existence, is caught by para 4 and not by this paragraph.

Property which can be the subject of an option falling within para 7 includes:

– currency of any country or territory;
– gold, platinum, palladium or silver;

even though none of these items would, on its own, constitute a regulated investment.

An option is not always immediately identifiable as such, and it is worth bearing in mind that the grant of a right to buy or sell in due course any regulated investment may be caught, such as an option over existing shares.

# 8  FUTURES

Futures appear under para 8 of Part 1 of Sched 1 which states the following:

(8) Rights under a contract for the sale of a commodity or property of any other description under which delivery is to be made at a future date and at a price agreed upon when the contract is made.

There are four elements to this paragraph:

(1) There must be a contract for sale; hire, loan, bailment or other dealings will not be caught.
(2) The commodity or property must be capable of delivery, which suggests that tangible property is caught but not choses in action.
(3) A delivery date is agreed when the contract is made, and is some time later than the date when the contract is made.
(4) The price is agreed when the contract is made.

This paragraph gives rise to considerable practical difficulty.

Subject to the exclusions in the Notes to this paragraph, rights under any contract for the sale of deliverable property where the price and a delivery date in the future are agreed when the contract is made will be regulated by the FSA. This is wide: a bag of oats is not a regulated investment, but a contract for the forward purchase of oats is, in principle, caught by this definition. In fact, subject to the Notes below, a washing machine bought at John Lewis on Tuesday for delivery on Thursday amounts to a future.

The object of the Notes to this paragraph is to exclude commercial futures, so that only investment futures will be regulated. These Notes are unsatisfactory, and the DTI has taken the unusual step of admitting that this whole paragraph is unclear, but has nonetheless declined to amend it. On 19 January 1988 the Corporate Affairs Minister issued a press release intending to clarify that:

(1) forward foreign exchange and bullion would not normally be a future falling within this paragraph; and
(2) commercial commodity futures were not intended to be caught.

The Minister's statement is, of course, of no legal authority and it is by no means certain that either of these two propositions can be supported by construction of the Notes. We must now examine, in turn, each of the exclusions which derogate from this wide definition.

The meaning of 'a price agreed upon when the contract is made' is given an extended meaning by Note 7 to take into account methods of determining prices on a commodity exchange. It states as follows:

(7) A price shall be taken to have been agreed upon when a contract is made:—
   (a) notwithstanding that it is left to be determined by reference to the price at which a contract is to be entered into on a market or exchange or could be entered into at a time and place specified in the contract; or
   (b) in a case where the contract is expressed to be by reference to a standard lot and quality, notwithstanding that provision is made for a variation in the price to take account of any variation in quantity or quality on delivery.

These are the Notes to para 8:

(1) This paragraph does not apply if the contract is made for commercial and not investment purposes.

This Note is conclusive: rights under a contract made for commercial rather than investment purposes are not caught by para 8. 'Investment purposes' is not defined, but would probably be given its ordinary English meaning: where the object or intention of the contract relates to investment rather than commercial activity, even though the particular investment may not be regulated by the FSA. This is an instance where 'investment' does not bear the meaning in s 1(1). In determining for what purpose a contract is made, it is submitted that one should consider the purposes of the parties to the contract and, if there is more than one purpose, disregard any insignificant purpose.

Any expressions of intention made by the parties on or before entering into the contract will be relevant. It is probably sufficient for one party alone to have an investment intention when entering into the contract, since otherwise a person who has an investment intention and who deals with a counterparty with a commercial intention would not be protected under the FSA. A contract made for two predominant purposes, one investment and one commercial, would probably be caught. SIB makes the point in Guidance Release 3/88 that an insignificant investment purpose should not prevent the contract from being viewed as made for commercial purposes. If one is drafting a contract with a view to it falling within this exclusion then, among other considerations, it may be prudent to record in the contract that both parties have a commercial intention where this is the case.

Note (2) provides the following:

(2) A contract shall be regarded as made for investment purposes if it is made or traded on a recognised investment exchange or made otherwise than on a recognised investment exchange but expressed to be as traded on such an exchange or on the same terms as those on which an equivalent contract would be made on such an exchange.

This is another conclusive Note, and a futures contract will be caught by para 8 if it is made or traded on a recognised investment exchange: recognition is granted under s 36 of the FSA 1986. This will be the case where the contract is made on the floor of an open outcry market or between exchange members under its rules. A contract will also fall within this Note if it is not made on an RIE but is expressed to be 'as traded' on an RIE, or is made on the same terms as an equivalent contract made on an RIE would be. There is therefore the possibility that a contract made back-to-back with one traded on an RIE, or which incorporates the terms of an RIE's contracts, will fall within this Note.

Note (3) provides the following:

(3) A contract not falling within Note (2) above shall be regarded as made for commercial purposes if under the terms of the contract delivery is to be made within seven days.

This is a further conclusive Note. If a contract does not fall within Note (2), it is to be regarded as a commercial contract (and therefore falling outside para 8) if it provides for delivery within seven days: in other words, if it is a 'spot' contract. It is submitted that where a contract meets this test it will not matter whether:

(1) the contract contains a mechanism allowing for the date for delivery to be extended at one party's option; or

(2) delivery is actual or constructive (in other words by documents of title); or

(3) the contract is, in fact, made for investment rather than commercial purposes.

Note (4) makes the following provision:

(4) The following are indications that any other contract is made for a commercial purpose and the absence of any of them is an indication that it is made for investment purposes:—

   (a) either or each of the parties is a producer of the commodity or other property or uses it in his business;

   (b) the seller delivers or intends to deliver the property or the purchaser takes or intends to take delivery of it.

If the preceding Notes do not settle the matter, Note (4) provides that one should take into account certain other factors, no doubt giving due weight to the circumstances. If these factors are present then the contract is probably (but not conclusively) commercial. If these factors are absent then the contract is probably (but not conclusively) an investment contract. These factors are:

   (a) where either party produces the property or uses it in its business;

   (b) if either party actually gives or takes delivery, or intends to do so.

In (a) one should take into account the facts of the matter; and in (b), if delivery has not been tendered or accepted, any expressions of intent at the date of the contract will be relevant but are not conclusive.

Note (5) states as follows:

(5) It is an indication that a contract is made for commercial purposes that the price, the lot, the delivery date or the other terms are determined by the parties for the purposes of the particular contract and not by reference to regularly published prices, to standard lots or delivery dates or to standard terms.

This is a further pointer: the contract will probably (but not conclusively) be commercial (and therefore fall outside para 8) if the terms have been determined for that particular contract and are not on standard terms. This indication will not be present if the contract terms have been determined by reference to standard lots, delivery dates, terms or regularly published prices. It is submitted that the requirements of this Note would not be satisfied by a contract made by reference to the standard terms of a commodity exchange; but would be satisfied by a contract made on other standard terms which have been agreed between two business parties to represent the terms on which they will handle all business between them. The first contract would not be made for commercial purposes, but the second would be.

If this Note does not apply to a contract, then this is no indication that it is made for investment purposes.

Note (6) provides as follows:

> (6) The following are also indications that a contract is made for investment purposes:
> > (*a*) it is expressed to be as traded on a market or on an exchange;
> > (*b*) performance of the contract is ensured by an investment exchange or a clearing house;
> > (*c*) there are arrangements for the payment or provision of margin.

These are further pointers which tend to show that the contract is an investment, although the absence of these pointers does not suggest that the contract is commercial. They are as follows:

> (1) if the contract is expressed to be as traded on a market or exchange (not necessarily an RIE or DIE); or
> (2) if performance is guaranteed by an investment exchange or clearing house (which need not be an RIE, DIE or RCH); or
> (3) if the contract provides for a margin. A deposit by way of security against a customer failing to discharge its obligations is not a margin, and its inclusion may well strengthen the evidence that the contract is commercial since it would tend to indicate that the parties intend delivery.

If none of the three conclusive Notes, nor the three pointer Notes, settle the matter, one must construe the contract as a whole: the question being to consider whether the contract is, in substance, for commercial or for investment purposes.

By way of an example, we consider the application of this paragraph to forward foreign exchange contracts in Chapter 15.

When drafting a futures contract which is for commercial rather than investment purposes, one can try to highlight its commercial nature by, where appropriate, including the following points. (Including these would not, of course, operate to convert an investment into a commercial contract.)

> (1) Do not write the contract on, or in accordance with, exchange terms, nor incorporate exchange terms.
> (2) State that both parties have a commercial intention and that they intend to tender or take delivery.
> (3) Consider providing for a deposit but not one that might be viewed as a margin.
> (4) Do not grant a cancellation option.

(5) Consider whether the other party is entering into the contract for investment purposes, since this may be sufficient on its own to make it an investment contract. For instance, does the other party have a record of entering into such contracts for such purposes?

(6) Record if either party produces the property, or uses it in its business.

# 9 CONTRACTS FOR DIFFERENCES

Contracts for differences are dealt with in para 9 of Part 1 of Sched 1 as follows:

(9) Rights under a contract for differences or under any other contract the purpose or pretended purpose of which is to secure a profit or avoid a loss by reference to fluctuations in the value or price of property of any description or in an index or other factor designated for that purpose in the contract.

Notes

(1) This paragraph does not apply where the parties intend that the profit is to be obtained or the loss avoided by taking delivery of any property to which the contract relates.

(2) This paragraph does not apply to rights under any contract under which money is received by the Director of Savings as deposits or otherwise in connection with the business of the National Savings Bank or raised under the National Loans Act 1968 under the auspices of the Director of Savings or under which money raised is treated as having been so raised by virtue of section 11 (3) of the National Debt Act 1972.

This paragraph seeks to catch contracts for differences, and certain other contracts. A contract for differences is a contract for the sale or purchase of investments or commodities which is fulfilled by the payment of differences in price and not by delivery (see *City Index v Leslie* [1991] 3 All ER 180 at p 185). *Universal Stock Exchange v Strachan* [1896] AC 166, cited in *City Index v Leslie*, is an early case concerning contracts for differences.

In addition it catches a contract for making a profit or avoiding a loss by reference to fluctuations in the value of property or an index: in other words, speculating on a margin. Paragraph 33 of Sched 1 states that one is not to take into account the Gaming Acts (1845 and 1892) which provide that such contracts may be unenforceable.

Paragraph 9 overlaps with para 8: a swap providing for mutual payments in gross can be a future, whereas a contract for net differences probably falls within para 9.

Examples of contracts falling within para 9 are:

(1) A currency swap eg where I can borrow £s easily but need DMs whereas you can borrow DMs easily but need £s. We therefore each borrow the easier currency and then swap. Depending on how it is drafted, the rights under the agreement may be a contract for differences.

(2) An interest-rate swap eg where I need fixed interest money but am only offered floating rate funds. You need floating rate funds but are only offered fixed interest money. I therefore issue a floating rate note and you issue a fixed interest bond. We then swap our interest payment liabilities and pay each other's obligations.

These are frequently arranged for commercial companies with the intention of reducing the cost of funds or matching assets and liabilities without borrowing from banks.

The exclusion to para 9 contained in the Note is very narrow. There is no exclusion where the contract is for commercial purposes, so commercial hedging is caught. Furthermore, the only exclusion is where both parties intend to take delivery of the subject property, which is not always usual. Note (4) to para 10 removes linked life assurance contracts from para 9.

# 10 LONG-TERM INSURANCE CONTRACTS

Long-term insurance contracts come under para 10 of Part 1 Sched 1 which states as follows:

(10) Rights under a contract the effecting and carrying out of which constitutes long-term business within the meaning of the Insurance Companies Act 1982.

Notes
(1) This paragraph does not apply to rights under a contract of insurance if:
  (*a*) the benefits under the contract are payable only on death or in respect of incapacity due to injury, sickness or infirmity;
  (*b*) no benefits are payable under the contract on a death (other than a death due to accident) unless it occurs within ten years of the date on which the life of the person in question was first insured under the contract or before that person attains a specified age not exceeding seventy years;
  (*c*) the contract has no surrender value or the consideration consists of a single premium and the surrender value does not exceed that premium; and
  (*d*) the contract does not make provision for its conversion or extension in a manner that would result in its ceasing to comply with paragraphs (a), (b) and (c) above.

(2) Where the provisions of a contract of insurance are such that the effecting and carrying out of the contract:

(*a*) constitutes both long-term business within the meaning of the Insurance Companies Act 1982 and general business within the meaning of that Act; or

(*b*) by virtue of section 1(3) of that Act constitutes long-term business notwithstanding the inclusion of subsidiary general business provisions;

references in this paragraph to rights and benefits under the contract are references only to such rights and benefits as are attributable to the provisions of the contract relating to long-term business.

(3) This paragraph does not apply to rights under a reinsurance contract.

(4) Rights falling within this paragraph shall not be regarded as falling within paragraph 9 above.

This paragraph comprehends contracts of insurance which are long-term business under the Insurance Companies Act 1982 and it therefore includes most life assurance contracts with the exclusion only of:

(1) a protection contract which fulfils all the criteria in Note (1);

(2) reinsurance contracts.

## 11  RIGHTS AND INTERESTS IN INVESTMENTS

Paragraph 11 of Part I of Sched 1 deals with rights and interests in investments. It states the following:

(11) Rights to and interests in anything which is an investment falling within any other paragraph of this part of this Schedule.

Notes

(1) This paragraph does not apply to interests under the trusts of an occuptional pension scheme.

(2) This paragraph does not apply to rights or interests which are investments by virtue of any other paragraph of this part of this Schedule.

This paragraph takes in rights to and interests in investments which are not interests under the trusts of an occupational pension scheme, nor investments in their own right. An interest in a regulated investment under an ordinary trust, though, might be caught.

Para 11 is considered to extend the ambit of the FSA to investments which would not otherwise be caught, such as a mortgage over a regulated investment. In contrast, a charge over a regulated investment will usually fall within para 2.

The distinction between a mortgage and a charge, which is relevant for the purposes of the FSA, is that a mortgage entails a transfer or appropriation of property from mortgagor to mortgagee, while a charge only grants a proprietary interest in the charged property.

A mortgage of, or charge over, shares will at first sight fall within para 2. However, a mortgage of shares will be excluded by Note (c) since it involves the disposition of property, but a charge over shares will not be so excluded.

A mortgage of shares (but not a charge over them) may also fall within para 5, since it confers property rights in a regulated investment. Such a mortgage will only be excluded by the Note to para 5 if it is a mortgage over two or more companies' shares. If it is so excluded, then it is likely to fall within para 11 because it is an interest in a regulated investment not otherwise caught by Sched 1.

# 8    *Investment Activities*

Carrying on investment business means, subject to the points noted in Chapter 6, engaging in the course of business in one of five investment activities in relation to one or more of the regulated investments contained in paras 1–11 of Sched 1. In this chapter we review the five investment activities of dealing, arranging, managing, advising and operating a collective scheme.

Someone who engages in an investment activity in the United Kingdom in relation to one or more regulated investments in the course of business will not necessarily be caught by the FSA. First, his activity may not actually fall within the definition of the regulated investment or the investment activity on account of the exclusionary Notes to paras 1–16. Secondly, he may be able to take advantage of one or more of the exclusions contained in paras 17–27, which are examined in their context.

The significance of these exclusions is twofold. First, if a person only engages in activities which fall within an exclusion, then it will not require authorisation under the Act. Secondly, if one is authorised, then business which falls within an exclusion will (subject to the detailed provisions of the rulebook by which the authorised person is regulated) not be regulated by the conduct of business rules which govern that person's investment business.

There are three further points which should be mentioned here. These are in relation to gaming, the Crown and exempted persons.

In determining whether anything is a regulated investment, or amounts to carrying on investment business under Sched 1, the provisions of the Gaming Acts (which provides that gaming contracts are not legally enforceable) are to be disregarded (para 33 of Sched 1). Furthermore, a contract entered into by any party by way of business will not be void or unenforceable under the Gaming Acts where the making or performance of that contract by any of the parties to it falls within para 12 (dealing) ignoring the exclusions in paras 17–27 (s 63). This was applied in *City Index v Leslie* [1991] 3 All ER 180.

Part I of the FSA (ss 1–128) does not apply to any investment business carried on by a person as agent for, or on behalf of, the Crown (s 207(11)). A person will not require to be authorised or exempted in relation to such investment business, nor will he be bound by any conduct of business rules.

**Exclusion Chart**

| Sched 1 Para | Para 12 Dealing | Para 13 Arranging deals | Para 14 Managing | Para 15 Advice | Para 16 CIS | Relevant investment advertisement exclusion (see Chapter 13 at 5.6) |
|---|---|---|---|---|---|---|
| 17 Dealing as principal | ✓ | — | — | — | — | — |
| 18 Groups & joint enterprises | ✓ | ✓ | ✓ | ✓ | — | ✓ |
| 19 Sale of goods or services | ✓ | ✓ | ✓ | ✓ | — | ✓ |
| 20 Employee share schemes | ✓ | ✓ | — | — | — | ✓ |
| 21 Private company disposals | ✓ | ✓ | ✓ | ✓ | — | ✓ |
| 22 Trustees and personal representatives | ✓ | ✓ | — | ✓ | — | ✓ |
| 23 Permitted persons | ✓ | — | — | — | — | ✓ |
| 24 'Professional' advice and arranging | — | ✓ | — | ✓ | — | — |
| 25&25A Media | — | — | — | ✓ | — | ✓ |
| 26 Overseas persons – dealing with or through authorised persons etc | ✓ | ✓ | ✓ | — | — | ✓ |
| 27 Overseas persons – unsolicited etc | ✓ | ✓ | ✓ | ✓ | — | ✓ |
| Sched 5 Money-market institutions | ✓ | ✓ | ✓ | ✓ | ✓ | — |

✓ means there is an exclusion contained in Sched 1 or in the investment advertisement exclusion orders.

If someone is an exempted person in respect of only part of their investment business, then that part is to be disregarded when considering the availability of the exclusions in paras 17–27 in relation to his non-exempt investment business (para 32).

A table showing the exclusions contained in Sched 1 is set out on page 146.

# 1   DEALING IN INVESTMENTS

This is defined by para 12 as:

(12) Buying, selling, subscribing for or underwriting investments or offering or agreeing to do so, either as principal or as an agent.

Straightforward examples of dealing are:

(1) I buy your shares;
(2) I sell your shares acting as your agent;
(3) I subscribe for shares in BP;
(4) a merchant bank underwrites a share issue.

Offering or agreeing to engage in any of these activities also falls within para 12 with the intention of catching acts preliminary to a transaction and may amount to investment business where the person offering or agreeing is carrying on a business in relation to such activities. 'Offer' is defined by para 28(1)(c) to include an invitation to treat.

A person who engages in these activities as principal or as agent will be caught. A person who is principal will be dealing on its own account, either taking title or disposing of title. It is less easy to be certain as to who will count as an agent for the purposes of para 12. It is submitted that in this case an 'agent' is a person who enters into the transaction for a principal who may be disclosed or undisclosed. It therefore appears that if a principal engages an agent to buy shares from a vendor, then:

(1) The principal will be dealing within para 12 because he is buying shares as principal. For the purposes of illustration no account is taken of the dealing as principal exclusion, discussed below.
(2) The vendor will similarly be dealing within para 12.
(3) The agent will also be dealing within para 12 where he enters into the transaction. He may do this by signing the contract or stock transfer form on behalf of the purchaser. Note (1) to para 13 suggests that an agent who merely effects an introduction and does not enter into the contract will not be dealing.

It is submitted that a nominee will often be neither a principal nor an agent—the principal will enter into a contract to buy the shares and the nominee will merely complete the transaction. The position of nominees is discussed below in relation to para 22.

Paragraph 12 will include both legal and beneficial interests in investments. Paragraph 11 can include beneficial interests in investments.

'Buying' and 'selling' are defined by para 28(1)(d) as follows:

28(1) (d)　references to buying and selling include references to any acquisition or disposal for valuable consideration.

(2)　In sub-paragraph (1)(d) above 'disposal' includes:—

(a) in the case of an investment consisting of rights under a contract or other arrangements, assuming the corresponding liabilities under the contract or arrangements;

(b) in the case of any other investment, issuing or creating the investment or granting the rights or interests of which it consists;

(c) in the case of an investment consisting of rights under a contract, surrendering, assigning or converting those rights.

Investments described as consisting of rights under a contract are those falling within paras 8, 9, 10 and 11. Although para 28(2) only gives instances of 'disposal', there is no doubt that the counterparty's corresponding dealing in the same transaction will amount to 'acquiring' for the purposes of para 28(1)(d).

Further examples of activities falling within para 12 are:

(1) a life assurance company issues a life assurance policy;

(2) I surrender, assign or convert my life assurance policy: the assignment can presumably be legal or equitable;

(3) I grant an option over my shares;

(4) I charge or mortgage my shares;

(5) a collective investment scheme creates and issues units;

(6) I declare that I hold my shares on trust for another as I am thereby disposing of the beneficial interest in them.

A person is not dealing if it issues its own shares or share warrants, debentures or debenture warrants. This is set out in para 28 of Sched 1 as follows:

28 (3) A company shall not by reason of issuing its own shares or share warrants, and a person shall not by reason of issuing his own debentures or debenture warrants, be regarded for the purposes of this Schedule as disposing of them or, by reason of anything done for the purpose of issuing them, be regarded as making arrangements with a view to a person subscribing for or otherwise acquiring them or underwriting them.

(4) In sub-paragraph (3) above 'company' has the same meaning as in paragraph 1 above, 'shares' and 'debentures' include any investments falling within paragraph 1 or 2 above and 'share warrants' and 'debenture warrants' means any investment which

falls within paragraph 4 above and relates to shares in the company concerned or, as the case may be, to debentures issued by the person concerned.

Two exclusions to para 12 are of key importance. The first is contained in Notes (1) and (2), and the second are the 'dealing as principal' exclusions in para 17.

## 1.1 The Notes to paragraph 12

The Notes to para 12 are as follows:

Notes
(1) This paragraph does not apply to a person by reason of his accepting, or offering or agreeing to accept, whether as principal or as agent, an instrument creating or acknowledging indebtedness in respect of any loan, credit, guarantee or other similar financial accommodation or assurance which he or his principal has made, granted or provided or which he or his principal has offered or agreed to make, grant or provide.
(2) The references in (1) above to a person accepting, or offering or agreeing to accept, an instrument include references to a person becoming, or offering or agreeing to become, a party to an instrument otherwise than as a debtor or a surety.

This exclusion provides that one does not deal (within the meaning of para 12) if one accepts an instrument creating or acknowledging indebtedness in respect of a loan or financial accommodation one is providing.

This is an important exclusion because, on account of the width of the definitions in para 2, a borrower's acknowledgement of indebtedness could constitute a debenture. What this Note provides is that accepting an instrument such as a debenture in connection with making a loan does not amount to dealing, and accordingly most lending business carried out by a bank is not regulated by the FSA.

## 1.2 Dealing as principal exclusions

There are two exclusions which relate to dealing as principal. These are liable to be altered in connection with the implementation of the Investment Services Directive. The first exclusion relates principally to investments which are not options, futures or contracts for differences ('derivatives'), while the second relates principally to derivatives. The meaning of 'principal' is discussed above.

*(a) The first exclusion*

Paragraph 17(1) states that if one deals as principal:

(1) in the investments specified in para 17(3), which are the regulated investments other than derivatives, or

(2) in relation to life assurance provided the transaction is an assignment;

*then*, subject to the three qualifications set out in para 17(1)(a)-(c), one does not fall within para 12. SIB has stated in Guidance Release 1/88 that this is intended to exclude a firm which does not deal with or for customers, but which properly regards itself as a market customer rather than a market participant. Paragraph 17(3) limits the application of para 17(1) as follows:

17(3)  Sub paragraph (1) above applies only:—
   (a)  if the investment to which the transaction relates or will relate falls within any of paragraphs 1 to 6 above or, so far as relevant to any of those paragraphs, paragraph 11 above; or
   (b)  if the transaction is the assignment (or, in Scotland, the assignation) of an investment falling within paragraph 10 above or is the assignment (or, in Scotland, the assignation) of an investment falling within paragraph 11 which confers rights to or interests in an investment falling within paragraph 10 above.

The three qualifications set out in para 17(1)(a)–(c) are:

17(1)  Paragraph 12 above applies to a transaction which is or is to be entered into by a person as principal only if:—
   (a)  he holds himself out as willing to enter into transactions of that kind at prices determined by him generally and continuously rather than in respect of each particular transaction; or

This is generally understood to be a reference to the activity of market-making, and someone who is a market maker in relation to certain investments will therefore not be able to take advantage of the dealing as principal exclusion in relation to a transaction in those investments.

17(1)  (b)  he holds himself out as engaging in the business of buying investments with a view to selling them and those investments are or include investments of the kind to which the transaction relates; or

There are three elements to holding oneself out as engaging in the business of buying with a view to selling. SIB confirms this view in Guidance Release 1/88 and states that while advertising or conduct intended to make a firm's position known may amount to holding out, merely buying investments with a view to selling them, even on a large scale, will not. These elements are:

(1)  A person holds himself out when, by written or spoken words or by his conduct, he represents himself, or knowingly allows someone else to represent him, as someone or something. In other words, one must objectively seek to create a certain impression.
(2)  The impression must be that one is engaging in the business of buying the investments with the intention of selling rather than the intention of

holding. 'With a view to' is discussed in relation to para 13 below. 'Business' is discussed in Chapter 6. It is submitted that this paragraph should not be narrowly construed since most investments which are bought are ultimately resold. Here, the question is whether they have been bought to be held, subject to unforeseen circumstances, for the time being; or whether they have instead been bought with the object of reselling them.

(3) The person holds himself out in relation to the same kind of investments as those which are the subject of the transaction.

Accordingly, a person will not be able to take advantage of the dealing as principal exclusion in relation to investments in respect of which he seeks to create the impression that he buys with the intention of reselling rather than holding. A person comes under (c) if:

> 17(1)  (c) he regularly solicits members of the public for the purpose of inducing them to enter as principals or agents into transactions to which that paragraph applies and the transaction is or is to be entered into as a result of his having solicited members of the public in that manner.

'Regularly' connotes a degree of repetition. It may be synonymous with 'persistently' which has in certain circumstances been interpreted to mean as little as twice (*Dale v Smith* [1967] 2 All ER 1133), while 'solicits' means asking. By way of illustration, it is unlikely that making a takeover bid will be viewed as regular solicitation.

Members of the public is defined in sub-para (2), set out below, to be any person other than:

(1) authorised, exempted and permitted persons;

(2) members of the same group: this has a wide definition (see para 30, discussed in Chapter 10);

(3) participants in a joint enterprise, which has to be a commercial enterprise in accordance with para 31;

(4) a person solicited in connection with the sale and purchase of shares in defined circumstances, which should include making a takeover bid;

(5) certain overseas persons.

Paragraph 17 (2) provides that:

> 17(2)  In sub-paragraph (1) above 'buying' and 'selling' means buying and selling by transactions to which paragraph 12 above applies and 'members of the public', in relation to the person soliciting them ('the relevant person'), means any other person except—
>
> (a) authorised persons, exempted persons, or persons holding a permission under paragraph 23 below;
>
> (b) members of the same group as the relevant person;

(c) persons who are, or propose to become, participators with the relevant person in a joint enterprise;

(d) any person who is solicited by the relevant person with a view to—

   (i) the acquisition by the relevant person of 20 per cent or more of the voting shares in a body corporate (that is to say, shares carrying not less than that percentage of the voting rights attributable to share capital which are exercisable in all circumstances at any general meeting of the body); or

   (ii) if the relevant person (either alone or with other members of the same group as himself) holds 20 per cent or more of the voting shares in a body corporate, the acquisition by him of further shares in the body or the disposal by him of shares in that body to the person solicited or to a member of the same group as that person; or

   (iii) if the person solicited (either alone or with other members of the same group as himself) holds 20 per cent or more of the voting shares in a body corporate, the disposal by the relevant person of further shares in that body to the person solicited or to a member of the same group as that person;

(e) any person whose head office is outside the United Kingdom, who is solicited by an approach made or directed to him at a place outside the United Kingdom and whose ordinary business involves him in engaging in activities which fall within Part II of this Schedule or would do so apart from this part or Part IV.

In summary the effect of para 17(1)(c) is to provide that a person who canvasses persons falling outside the prescribed classes (listed in para 17(2)(a)–(e)) to buy or sell regulated investments cannot rely on the dealing as principal exclusion for any resulting transaction. If, for example, the persons solicited is an authorised person acting as agent for someone who falls outside these classes, such as an unauthorised person, then the person soliciting may fall outside the dealing as principal exclusion.

   A particular point to consider in relation to para 17(1)(c) is the motivation of the person doing the soliciting. It is submitted that the words 'for the purpose of' do not imply that inducing them to deal has to be the exclusive purpose of the person doing the soliciting. It has been held that 'purpose' connotes an intention by some person to achieve a result desired by him, while the words 'for the purpose of' denote a purpose 'which is other than quite incidental or casual or fortuitous ... but which is or has become either a significant one or a recognised one though certainly not necessarily an only one'. (*Sweet v Parsley* [1969] 1 All ER 355 per Lord Morris.) In *Chandler v DPP* [1962] 3 All ER 155 per Lord Devlin it was held that 'the results which a man appreciates will probably flow from his act are classifiable as purposes'. It therefore seems possible that a court would interpret this sub-paragraph to apply not only where members of the public are approached for the purpose of inducing them to deal, but additionally where they are approached for any purpose (which need not be related to investment business) in circumstances where it is highly likely that, as a result of the solicitation, they will enter into some transaction which falls within para 12.

The position of secured lending under the FSA illustrates the practical application of the first dealing as principal exclusion. We discuss this further in Chapter 15.

Lending secured by a mortgage or charge over shares (or the assignment of a life assurance policy) involves dealing in investments since the borrower is disposing of a regulated investment, and the lender is acquiring it, for the valuable consideration of a loan. Accordingly, taking the assignment of a life assurance policy or a mortgage or charge over shares will in principle be dealing in investments.

The lender may, however, be able to rely on the dealing as principal exclusion in para 17(1) unless:

(1) it is a market-maker in relation to such investments, which is unlikely (para 17(1)(a)); or

(2) it holds itself out as buying such investments with a view to disposing of them. It is most likely that if the lender holds itself out at all, it will be as being in the loan business. It will, furthermore, be acquiring investments with a view to holding them as security, not selling them (17(1)(b)); or

(3) it regularly solicits the public to enter into investment transactions. It is generally considered that if the lender does regularly solicit the public, it is with a view to acquiring loan business, rather than to acquire specific investments (17(1)(c)). However, it is likely that the solicitation will be caught by this sub-paragraph if the lender invariably requires the security of the assignment of a life policy, or requires security over other forms of specified regulated investment.

*(b) Second dealing as principal exclusion*

Paragraph 17(4) sets out a second exclusion:

17(4) Paragraph 12 above does not apply to any transaction, other than a transaction of a kind described in sub-paragraph (3)(a) or (b) above, which relates or is to relate to an investment which falls within paragraph 10 above or, so far as relevant to that paragraph, paragraph 11 above nor does it apply to a transaction which relates or is to relate to an investment which falls within any of paragraphs 7 to 9 above or, so far as relevant to any of those paragraphs, paragraph 11 above being a transaction which, in either case, is or is to be entered into by a person as principal if he is not an authorised person and the transaction is or is to be entered into by him:

(a) with or through an authorised person, an exempted person or a person holding a permission under paragraph 23 below; or

(b) through an office outside the United Kingdom, maintained by a party to the transaction, and with or through a person whose head office is situated outside the United Kingdom and whose ordinary business is such as is mentioned in sub-paragraph (2)(e) above.

This narrower exclusion applies to investments which do not fall within the wider dealing as principal exclusion in sub-para 17(1), (2) or (3). The investments subject to the narrower exclusion are:

(1) derivatives; and

(2) issuing, surrendering or converting life assurance contracts, since only assigning life assurance contracts falls within the wider exclusion; and

(3) rights and interests in the two foregoing categories.

This exclusion provides that you do not carry on the activity of dealing in relation to these particular investments provided:

(1) you deal as principal; and

(2) you are not an authorised person; and

(3) either you deal with or through an authorised, exempted or permitted person or certain overseas persons;

(4) or you deal with or through a person who is situated outside the United Kingdom *and* whose ordinary business is engaging in investment activities *and* you deal through your or the counterparty's office outside the United Kingdom.

'With or through' is defined by para 29 as follows:

(29) For the purposes of this Schedule a transaction is entered into through a person if he enters into it as agent or arranges for it to be entered into by another person as principal or agent.

Accordingly, 'with' means the specified person is the counterparty; 'through' means such person contracts with you as agent or arranges for a third party to contract with you as principal or agent.

Provided you can fulfil the requirements in sub-para 17(4) then you can take advantage of this exclusion. The restrictions in para 17(1)(a)-(c) are not relevant to the narrower dealing as principal exclusion.

SIB has stated in Guidance Releases 5/88 and 6/90 that a member of a recognised investment exchange who can only rely on para 17(4) should nonetheless obtain authorisation under the FSA where, under the exchange rules, members can trade with each other under open outcry.

## 2  ARRANGING DEALS IN INVESTMENTS

### 2.1  Arrangements for a particular investment

This investment activity is contained in para 13 which defines it as:

(13)    Making, or offering or agreeing to make:

(a) arrangements with a view to another person buying, selling, subscribing for or underwriting a particular investment; or

This kind of arranging (another kind is set out in para 13(b)) means making arrangements for a third party to deal in a specific investment. These arrangements will be made on each occasion that a referral takes place, as they must relate to a specific investment. Offering or agreeing to make arrangements is also an investment activity, so steps preliminary to the actual arrangements will be caught.

A company or other person should not be 'making arrangements' when it arranges for the acquisition, subscription or underwriting of its own shares, debentures or warrants (para 28(3), quoted above).

There are two qualifications to para 13(a), contained in the Notes:

(1)    It does not apply where the person who is arranging (or offering or agreeing to do so) will be a party as principal or agent to the resulting transaction (Note (1)). Being party as principal, or entering into a transaction as agent, will equate to 'dealing' for the purposes of para 12.

Note (1) states that:

'(1) This paragraph does not apply to a person by reason of his making, or offering or agreeing to make, arrangements with a view to a transaction to which he will himself be a party as principal or which will be entered into by him as agent for one of the parties.'

(2) The arrangements must bring about, or be objectively capable of bringing about, the third party dealing in a particular investment (Note (2)). 'Bring about' probably means cause to happen, so administrative or mechanical arrangements which cannot bring about the transaction may be excluded.

Note (2) states that:

'(2) The arrangements in (a) above are arrangements which bring about or would bring about the transaction in question.'

The term 'arrangement' is a very wide and indefinite one (see *Manning v Eastern Counties Railway* (1843) 13 LJ Ex 265). It need not necessarily mean a legally enforceable agreement and there may be an arrangement between two parties when they intentionally arouse in each other an expectation that they will act in a certain way (*Re British Basic Slag Ltd's Agreements* [1963] 2 All ER 807). Use of the word 'arrangements' in the plural suggests that a single referral or introduction may not be caught, although a pattern of referrals and introductions would be.

The expression 'with a view to' combines subjective intention with objective likelihood. It is submitted that a person takes action with a view to achieving a certain result if he intends that result and it is likely to occur. Depending on the circumstances it may be fulfilled if only the objective element is present.

Consideration of what constitutes the investment activity of making arrangements indicates that it is a flexible concept, and that the arranger's degree of involvement in bringing about the resulting transaction can vary greatly in the circumstances. For example:

(1) A salesperson employed by a building society which is the appointed representative of a life assurance company will make arrangements for a borrower to be issued with the life company's insurance policy. He or she will advise the borrower of the life company's standard terms and premiums, assist in the completion of a standard proposal form, but probably take no further part in the transaction beyond sending the papers to the life company and possibly issuing the policy documents to the borrower. This will constitute the investment activity of making arrangements for the borrower to acquire a life assurance contract within para 13(a).

(2) A broker in debt instruments will make arrangements for the holder to sell to a purchaser. He or she will market the instrument, seeking to identify a borrower, and then negotiate the price and fix the terms of the transaction. This will constitute the investment activity of making arrangements for the holder of instrument to sell to the purchaser under para 13(a).

These two examples illustrate that the investment activity of 'arranging' can be constituted by selling a standard product on standard terms, with little involvement beyond an initial interview; and also by marketing sophisticated financial instruments where the broker is closely involved in structuring and negotiating the deal.

For an activity to be 'arranging', the following three elements must be present.

(1) The arranger is not a party to the resulting dealing, nor entering into the transaction as agent for a party.
(2) The arrangements relate to a particular investment and not investments generally or a category of investments.
(3) The arrangements will make, or are objectively capable of making, a particular transaction happen.

I am therefore not making arrangments within para 13(a) if I introduce you to a stockbroker with a view to your discussing with that person the acquisition of a share portfolio. First, the arrangements between us do not relate to any particular investment but only to investments generally and, second, they will not bring about any particular transaction: it will be the stockbroker who will do this.

## 2.2 Arrangements for investments generally

Sub-paragraph 13(b) is concerned with a different kind of arrangment:

13(b)   arrangements with a view to a person who participates in the arrangements buying, selling, subscribing for or underwriting investments.

The 'arrangements' referred to in sub-para 13(b) are pre-established arrangements, and someone participates in these arrangements if he takes part in them or takes advantage of them. The arrangements are established in advance of the first referral, rather than constituted by it.

An example of arrangements falling within sub-para 13(b) is where a life office makes arrangements with a house builder that persons he refers to that life office will, if of appropriate status, be offered an endowment mortgage. The prospective investor will participate in the arrangements by being referred to the life office by the builder. It makes no difference whether the arrangements are documented, and it will be noted that the potential investor needs to do very little in order to become a participant in the arrangements; all he needs to do is in some way to take advantage of them.

On the other hand, a builder who responds to an occasional request by referring someone to a local building society is unlikely to be viewed as having made arrangements (see SIB Guidance Release 2/92).

This differs from sub-para 13(a) in three further respects.

(1) The person who is intended to deal must participate in the arrangements although, on account of Note (1), the person who makes the arrangements must not be, or intend to be, a party to the resulting dealing.

(2) The arrangements need only be with a view to someone dealing in investments generally and not a specific investment.

(3) Because Note (2) only applies to sub-para 13(a), the arrangements referred to in sub-para 13(b) need not actually bring about the transaction in question.

The wording of Note (3) to para 13 sheds some light on what kind of activity falls within 13(b). It suggests that introducing a person to a firm, or advising them to consult it, will amount to 'making arrangements' for the purposes of sub-para 13(b). A person will only be engaging in the investment activity of making arrangements under subpara 13(b) when it is done *with a view to* that other person dealing in investments. To illustrate this point we can pursue the example of the housebuilder who makes introductions to the life office.

The builder will only be engaging in the investment activity of making arrangements if, when referring a home buyer to a lender to obtain a mortgage, this is done 'with a view to' that person dealing in investments. It is suggested that this will be fulfilled where:

(i)   The builder actually intends this result; and/or

(ii)  The builder's referral is likely to bring about the issue of a life policy.

Some guidance on the concept of intention can be derived from cases such as *Sharp v Jackson* [1899] All ER 755, *R v Hailwood* [1928] All ER 529, *Re Cutts* [1956] 2 All ER 537, *Cunliffe v Goodman* [1950] 2 KB 237, *AG v Newspaper Publishing* [1992] 1 AC 191.

Whether the builder is making arrangements with a view to the house buyer acquiring an investment rather than just a mortgage will in each case be a question of fact. This may be the case where:

(1)  The builder encourages the house buyer to apply for an investment mortgage and the house buyer does so.
(2)  The lender's practice is to require the house buyer to effect life cover and the builder knows this.
(3)  The builder's receipt of commission depends on the issue of a life policy.
(4)  The builder can refer the house buyer to a number of lenders with the expectation that he will be granted a mortgage so as to enable the purchase to go ahead, but chooses to refer to a specific lender because he knows it will insist on life cover and the builder will be remunerated accordingly.

SIB considers that permitting an authorised person's investment advertisements to be displayed on your premises is unlikely to be making arrangements, whereas taking part in promotional activities (such as actively distributing these advertisements) may well be (SIB Guidance Release 2/92).

Sub-paragraph 13(b) operates to bring investment exchanges within the regulatory net, although recognised investment exchanges and clearing houses are exempted persons under ss 36–41. Sub-paragraph 13(b) will, in principle, catch introductions to independent intermediaries, which are therefore excluded by Note (6), and loans made to a management buyout team to enable them to purchase shares, which is accordingly excluded by Note (5).

It has been suggested that the operation of pre-emption rights under a company's articles of association may fall within sub-para 13(a) or (b). Depending on the circumstances this may be so, but it is unlikely that any of the parties making arrangements could be said to be doing so in the course of carrying on a business (see Chapter 6)

There are four further exclusions contained in the Notes which apply to both paras 13(a) and 13(b) or, in the case of Notes (5) and (6), para 13(b) alone. There are also exclusions relevant to para 13 in paras 24(2) and 25B. They are as follows.

## 2.3  Arranging lending on security of a life policy

Note (3) of para 13 specifies the following:

(3)  This paragraph does not apply to a person ('the relevant person') who is either a moneylending company within the meaning of section 338 of the Companies Act 1985 or a body corporate incorporated under the

law of, or of any part of, the United Kingdom relating to building societies or a person whose ordinary business includes the making of loans or the giving of guarantees in connection with loans by reason of the relevant person making, or offering or agreeing to make, arrangements with a view to a person ('the authorised person') who is either authorised under section 22 or 23 of this Act or who is authorised under section 31 of this Act and carries on insurance business which is investment business selling an investment which falls within paragraph 10 above or, so far as relevant to that paragraph, paragraph 11 above if the arrangements are either:-

(a) that the authorised person or a person on his behalf will introduce persons to whom the authorised person has sold or proposes to sell an investment of the kind described above, or will advise such persons to approach, the relevant person with a view to the relevant person lending money on the security of that investment; or

(b) that the authorised person gives an assurance to the relevant person as to the amount which will or may be received by the relevant person, should that person lend money to a person to whom the authorised person has sold or proposes to sell an investment of the kind described above, on the surrender or maturity of that investment if it is taken as security for the loan.

This Note excludes two situations from para 13. First, where the arrangements are between a specified lender and an authorised insurer and relate to circumstances where the lender will lend against the security of a life policy issued to a borrower introduced by the authorised person. Secondly, where the authorised person notifies the lender how much the lender will receive on surrender or maturity of the policy which the borrower has given as security for the loan.

For example, a building society may make arrangements with a life assurance company under which the life company or its agents will introduce present or potential policy-holders to the society with a view to the society making an advance to the policy-holder on security of the life policy. Provided such arrangements fall within Note (3), they will be excluded from para 13. The converse, though, does not apply. A lender introducing potential borrowers to a life company cannot take advantage of this exclusion.

## 2.4 Arranging to accept an instrument

Note (4) of para 13 deals with arranging to accept an instrument. It states:

(4) This paragraph does not apply to a person by reason of his making, or offering or agreeing to make, arrangements with a view to a person accepting, whether as principal or as agent, an instrument creating or acknowledging indebtedness in respect of any loan, credit, guarantee or other similar financial accommodation or assurance which he or his

principal has made, granted or provided or which he or his principal has offered or agreed to make, grant or provide.

(7) The references in (4) above to a person accepting an instrument include references to a person becoming a party to an instrument otherwise than as a debtor or a surety.

Someone is not making arrangements within para 13 if they are made in relation to a person taking a debenture in respect of a loan they have provided or will provide. This corresponds to the Note to para 12 discussed earlier.

## 2.5 Arranging finance

Note (5) of para 13 states:

(5) Arrangements do not fall within (b) above by reason of their having as their purpose the provision of finance to enable a person to buy, sell, subscribe for or underwrite investments.

A person who makes arrangements for the provision of finance to enable one or more of the participants in the arrangements to deal in investments will not thereby be engaging in the investment activity of arranging. This exclusion can be understood as indicating that raising finance for the purchase of investments is, in principle, the investment activity of arranging. It is suggested that the better view is that it is not, and that Note (5) is inserted to remove any uncertainty on the point.

## 2.6 Introducers

This exclusion is probably only relevant to activities potentially falling within para 13(b) since making an introduction is unlikely to fulfil the requirements of Note (2). Note (6) of para 13 states the following in regard to introducers.

(6) This paragraph does not apply to arrangements for the introduction of persons to another person if—
   (a) the person to whom the introduction is made is an authorised or exempted person or is a person whose ordinary business involves him in engaging in activities which fall within this part of this Schedule or would do apart from the provisions of Part III or Part IV and who is not unlawfully carrying on investment business in the United Kingdom; and
   (b) the introduction is made with a view to the provision of independent advice or the independent exercise of discretion either:-
      (i) in relation to investments generally; or
      (ii) in relation to any class of investments if the transaction or advice is or is to be with respect to an investment within that class.

This Note deals with the position of introducers. It provides that if:

(1) you make arrangements for the introduction of persons to an authorised or exempted person, or to someone whose ordinary business involves an investment activity but who, because they can take advantage of the exclusions in paras 17–27, is not in breach of the FSA (such as someone who can take advantage of the overseas person or dealing as principal exclusions)

(2) with the intention that they will give *independent* advice to, or exercise *independent* discretion in relation to, investments generally, or a class of investments

then you will not be making arrangements within para 13.

Accordingly, if you make arrangements to introduce me to an independent life assurance or unit trust broker with the intention that he will give me independent advice on acquiring a life policy, then you are not making arrangements within para 13. A product company which only sells or advises on its own investments is not independent.

This exclusion may be significant for lenders who require life assurance cover as security for loans. If a bank sends a customer to an independent broker for life cover to be arranged, there should be no question that it is thereby arranging deals. It makes no difference whether the referrer receives commission as it is not engaging in an investment activity in the first place.

There are, however, two provisos. First, a referral to a life assurance or unit trust company will not fall within this exclusion as it is not an independent person. Furthermore, if the referrer comments on the independent intermediary's advice or discretion, then it may well be giving investment advice so as to come within para 15.

## 2.7 Necessary arrangements

There is an exclusion in para 24(2) and (3) for making 'necessary' arrangements which states as follows:

(2) Paragraph 13 above does not apply to arrangements—
    (a) which are made in the course of the carrying on of any profession or of a business not otherwise constituting investment business; and
    (b) the making of which is a necessary part of other services provided in the course of carrying on that profession or business.

(3) ... the making of arrangements shall not be regarded as falling within sub-paragraph ... (2)(b) above if ... the making of the arrangements is remunerated separately from the other ... services.

As making an introduction to an independent adviser is already excluded by para 13 Note (6), it is implicit that this exclusion extends to include introductions to product companies in relation to their products. This exclusion is rather narrower than it seems because it provides that you are not making arrangements *only* if:

(1) you are carrying on a business or profession which does not otherwise constitute investment business (as defined by s 1(2)); and

(2) the advice is a necessary part of services you are already carrying on. The meaning of 'necessary' will depend on its context; it has been held to mean more than 'convenient' but less than 'absolutely compelling'. In this context it is likely to mean 'proper' or 'highly expedient' (*Re Wreck Recovery & Salvage Company* [1880] 15 Ch D 353; *Lewis v Weston-super-Mare Local Board* [1888] 40 Ch D 55). If a solicitor makes arrangements for his client to sell some shares, these arrangements will only be 'necessary' if the solicitor would not otherwise be properly performing his other duties; and

(3) you are not separately remunerated for making the arrangements. An example of separate remuneration would be where a product company pays a commission in return for the introduction. It is submitted that if you charge your client for your work on a time basis, for example, at an hourly rate, or on a fixed-fee basis, then you will probably not be separately remunerated for arrangements you make as part of your other services.

Paragraph 25B excludes from para 13 certain arranging carried out by an approved overseas international securities self-regulating organisation. The International Securities Market Association has been approved under this provision.

# 3  MANAGING INVESTMENTS

Managing investments is defined by para 14 to be:

(14) Managing, or offering or agreeing to manage, assets belonging to another person if:—

(a) those assets consist of or include investments; or

(b) the arrangements for their management are such that those assets may consist of or include investments at the discretion of the person managing or offering or agreeing to manage them and either they have at any time since the date of the coming into force of section 3 of this Act done so or the arrangements have at any time (whether before or after that date) been held out as arrangements under which they would do so.

The word 'managing' is not defined, but it is suggested that the investment activity of managing means assuming responsibility under a contract or some other instrument, such as a trust deed, to look after regulated investments. The activity of managing may be exercised with or without the discretion to take investment decisions. Paragraph 14 would appear to recognise this as sub-para 14(b), in the alternative to sub-para 14(a), is a description of discretionary management.

The two classes of management recognised by para 14 are:

(1) management of investments regulated by the FSA on their own or together with other assets; and

(2) management of assets (which may or may not fall within (1)) where:
   (i) they may be regulated investments at the manager's discretion; and
   (ii) the management arrangements have at any time been held out as such, or the assets actually have included regulated investments at any time since 'A' date.

Paragraph 14 would therefore appear to include the whole spectrum of management activities from non-discretionary management or portfolio review, where the manager has custody of investments and only acts on another's instructions, to full discretionary management (defined in sub-para 14(b)) where the manager will buy or sell at its discretion, although perhaps in accordance with predetermined criteria.

What amounts to management will depend on the circumstances. To take the example of managing a share portfolio, functions that can be viewed as 'management' will include those of buying, selling and valuing the investments; overseeing performance; acting as custodian; conducting correspondence; meeting and advising beneficial owners; exercising voting rights; and receiving and paying dividends.

A person who performs all of these functions will certainly be carrying on the investment activity of managing investments, but what of a person who only performs one or two of them? It is suggested that the sale and purchase of the managed investments is fundamental to the investment activity of managing. A person who buys and sells investments under its management is likely to be engaging in managing investments whether or not it or a third party takes the decisions. So too is a person who does not actually buy or sell the investments it manages but who passes instructions to a broker for execution. By way of contrast a person who performs only a few management functions is unlikely to be viewed as engaging in managing investments—for example someone who performs only secretarial, book keeping or accounting functions. Exercising the right to decide who will manage investments is not of itself managing investments.

Where management is delegated, the question may arise as to whether the appointor or the delegate is managing. If a person enters into a contract to manage investments, but delegates all functions to another who assumes entire responsibility for their management, the delegate and not the appointor is probably managing the investments provided the appointor is empowered to delegate all management decisions. If the appointor retains the right to oversee the investments, or to give instructions or detailed directions, it may still be managing them. However an appointor who retains the right to restrict sectors in which the delegate may invest, to receive quarterly reports or to attend annual meetings, is unlikely to be managing investments where the management functions are carried out by the delegate.

It seems that investment management may include dealing (regulated by para 12), or arranging deals (para 13) where the investments are not registered in the manager's name, and also advising (para 15). It is arguable that non-discretionary management and purely administrative acts will (if they amount to dealing) fall within para 12 and not within para 14. This view is, however, difficult to support and it is submitted that the better view is that the performance of all, or a number of, the management functions discussed above can amount to managing within para 14, whether carried out on a discretionary or a non-discretionary basis.

Paragraph 14 only relates to managing assets *belonging* to another: managing your own investments is not caught. 'Belonging' is a general word and will include circumstances where legal or beneficial ownership is vested in someone other than the manager. Where the manager has a beneficial interest in the property he will still be engaging in the investment activity of managing where he additionally manages the interests of other persons. Property which is legally vested in a trustee can be said to belong to the beneficiaries including where the manager does not hold unfettered beneficial ownership (*Heritable Reversionary Company v Millar* [1892] AC 598; *Barker v Archer Slee* [1927] AC 844).

The position of trustees is discussed in Chapter 10.

## 4  INVESTMENT ADVICE

Investment advice is defined by para 15 to be:

(15)  Giving, or offering or agreeing to give, to persons in their capacity as investors or potential investors advice on the merits of their purchasing, selling, subscribing for or underwriting an investment, or exercising any right conferred by an investment to acquire, dispose of, underwrite or convert an investment.

You only engage in the investment activity of giving investment advice if each of three elements is present. These are:

(1)  You are advising (or offering or agreeing to advise) investors or potential investors. This can, of course, be advice given orally or in writing. Giving advice to someone who is not an investor (in the sense that they hold an investment or have authority to buy or sell another's investment under some power they have been granted), or a potential investor (in the sense that, after receiving your advice, they may decide to become an investor) is not caught.

(2)  The advice you give must be on the merits of dealing, or exercising certain rights. If you simply state that you have no objection to, or no comment on, a particular course of action then you are unlikely to be advising, particularly if you go on to recommend that independent advice be taken.

(3) The advice must relate to one or more specific investments. Giving general advice on a client's taxation position, or giving generic advice (such as indicating that traded options are generally more risky than unit trusts) or advising on choice of stockbroker is not advising for the purposes of para 15. Similarly, provision of neutral advice is not investment advice. As SIB has stated in Guidance Release 4/89, reports of share or unit prices, or a description of the features of a life assurance policy, or an objective account of the performance of some share or unit trust or life fund in the light of various measures of performance, is not investment advice provided there is no endorsement or recommendation of any particular share or product. However, if while giving taxation or corporate finance advice you advise a corporate client on the merits of selling its shares in a subsidiary, or advise a personal client on the merits of his investing in particular US treasury bonds, you will probably be giving investment advice. Similarly, advice that purchase of a particular life policy is likely to produce a more satisfactory yield than investment in some unit trust or other, will be investment advice.

Situations which clearly fall within para 15 include:

(1) advice given by solicitors, accountants or brokers to acquire or dispose of particular investments;
(2) advice from a life assurance salesperson to buy a particular policy;
(3) a merchant bank advising on the restructuring of a group, or on a takeover.

There are two exclusions to para 15 which are set out below.

## 4.1   The 'necessary' advice exclusion

Paragraph 24 contains a necessary advice exclusion. It specifies the following:

(1) Paragraph 15 above does not apply to advice:—
   (a) which is given in the course of the carrying on of any profession or of a business not otherwise constituting investment business; and
   (b) the giving of which is a necessary part of other advice or services given in the course of carrying on that profession or business.
(3) Advice shall not be regarded as falling within sub-paragraph (1)(b) above ... if the giving of the advice ... is remunerated separately from the other advice ...

As with the exclusion to para 13, this is fairly narrow because the advice must be *necessary* and *not separately remunerated*. Accordingly, a solicitor giving investment advice to ensure his legal advice does not fall short of the standard of care and professionalism a client may expect may separately be giving *necessary* advice, but if he charges his client separately for the investment advice he will fall outside the exclusion. See 2.7 above.

## 4.2   The 'media' exclusion

This is contained in paras 25 and 25(A) and excludes from para 15 certain investment advice given in newspapers or broadcast.

SIB has stated in Guidance Release 4/89 that a journalist or publisher will normally only require authorisation where:

(1) Investment advice is being given. The meaning of investment advice is discussed above; or

(2) The business of giving investment advice is being carried on, for example by replying to readers' letters; or

(3) The advice is outside the exclusions in paras 25 and 25A discussed below.

SIB considers that persons likely to require authorisation will be publishers of 'tipsheets' which predominantly give investment advice, and certain freelance journalists.

*(a) Newspapers*
Paragraph 25 sets out the following:

(1) Paragraph 15 above does not apply to advice given in a newspaper, journal, magazine or other periodical publication if the principal purpose of the publication, taken as a whole and including any advertisements contained in it, is not to lead persons to invest in any particular investment.

(2) The Secretary of State may, on the application of the proprietor of any periodical publication, certify that it is of the nature described in sub-paragraph (1) above and revoke any such certificate if he considers that it is no longer justified.

(3) A certificate given under sub-paragraph (2) above and not revoked shall be conclusive evidence of the matters certified.

*(b) Advice given in television, sound and teletext services*
Paragraph 25(A) provides the following:

(1) Paragraph 15 above does not apply to any advice given in any programme included, or made for inclusion, in—

(a) any television broadcasting service or other television programme service (within the meaning of Part I of the Broadcasting Act 1990); or

(b) any sound broadcasting service or licensable sound programme service (within the meaning of Part III of that Act); or

(c) any teletext service.

(2) For the purposes of this paragraph, 'programme', in relation to a service mentioned in sub-paragraph (1) above, includes an advertisement and any other item included in the service.

The media will generally not carry on investment business because neither publishers nor journalists are in business to give investment advice. Paragraphs 25 and 25(A) deal with special situations where the media might otherwise be viewed as falling within para 15 by reason of giving investment advice. First, para 25 excludes investment advice given in a periodical if its main purpose is not to lead people to invest in any particular investment. A newspaper which passes this test (and most do) may therefore publish a feature or report on a particular investment or publish an investment advertisement without thereby falling within para 15. SIB may, on application, issue a certificate which is conclusive evidence that any investment advice is to be disregarded for this purpose. This exclusion does not, however, apply to advice given outside a publication. If, accordingly, the *Financial Times* 'Family Finance' column were to reply to readers' investment enquiries by telephone or by letter, rather than within their columns, then it could be giving investment advice.

Paragraph 25(A) excludes all advice given on certain television, sound and teletext services.

In the unlikely event that any broadcaster or journalist cannot take advantage of these exclusions, and does actually give investment advice, then he or she will require authorisation. Some SROs offer a special 'light' regime, disapplying the majority of its conduct of business rules, for media persons whom they authorise.

## 5  ESTABLISHING OR OPERATING COLLECTIVE INVESTMENT SCHEMES

Paragraph 16 defines this as:

(16) Establishing, operating or winding up a collective investment scheme, including acting as trustee of an authorised unit trust scheme.

The nature of a collective investment scheme is discussed in Chapter 9. The activity in para 16 differs from managing investments (para 14) because there is no requirement that the subject property belongs to someone other than the manager, although this will usually be the case with a CIS.

Paragraph 16 brings the following activities within the ambit of the FSA:

(1) Setting up or starting a collective investment scheme, for example by taking steps to constitute it. This is intended to catch the preliminary stages in the scheme's formation before it is marketed to the public. A solicitor or accountant who, in a professional capacity, advises another person on establishing a collective investment scheme will not himself be establishing it, although he may well be giving investment advice.

(2) Operating the collective investment scheme. The person operating the scheme will be actively engaged in running and managing the arrangements which constitute the scheme. The nature of the operating will depend on the subject property. Operating a scheme which is a racehorse syndicate will be radically different from operating a unit trust scheme. Operating a racehorse syndicate is likely to mean running the arrangements whereby members' contributions are collected, winnings distributed and the horses fed, stabled, trained and raced. Operating a unit trust scheme would include:

    (i) creating and selling the units;
    (ii) marketing the scheme;
    (iii) receiving and distributing participants' funds;
    (iv) purchasing the units;
    (v) managing the underlying investments.

(3) Winding up or dissolving a collective investment scheme.

Dealing in participants' rights and interests ('units') in a collective investment scheme will fall within para 12. Arranging deals in the units, managing the units and advising on the merits of buying or selling the units will also be investment activities.

There are no exclusions which relate to para 16.

We discuss the marketing of collective investment schemes in Chapters 9 and 17.

# 9 Collective Investment Schemes

A collective investment scheme ('CIS') is a category of regulated investment created by s 75 FSA. The definition given by this section is extremely wide, and the individual elements need to be considered in detail.

## 1 CHARACTERISTICS OF A CIS

The two principal characteristics of a CIS are:

- The pooling of investors' funds.
- The management of those funds (or the assets purchased with them) by someone other than the investors. The assets acquired by a CIS need not be regulated investments.

## 2 EXAMPLES OF A CIS

Before examining the detailed definition it will be useful to give some examples of a CIS:

(1) A unit trust scheme, which is constituted when a trustee holds property on trust for participants.

(2) A UCITS fund. An authorised unit trust scheme and or a UCITS fund may both be promoted to the general public by an authorised person (s 76 FSA). See 6 below.

(3) An open-ended investment company where the property belongs to the company and investors' rights are represented by shares in the company which are either redeemable or which are traded on an investment exchange. The value of shares fluctuates in accordance with the value of the company's assets.

(4) A limited partnership. A limited partnership constituted under the Limited Partnership Act 1907 is a common investment vehicle in venture capital.

CIS's such as these four examples will generally be created in the full knowledge that they are collective investment schemes, and may only be promoted in the United Kingdom in accordance with the requirements of s 76.

There are, in addition, many other instances of commercial arrangements which may have the characteristics of a CIS although, depending on the circumstances, it may be possible to structure them so that they do not possess the necessary characteristics (see section 4). Examples include:

(5) Precious stone schemes. This is where an investor buys a share in a pool of precious stones which are held by the scheme manager. The manager has full control over the holding, valuation and ultimate disposal of the stones, and none of the participants has an identifiable or severable share in them.

(6) Forward-funding arrangements for a property development. For example, a developer may enter into a rent-sharing lease with the freeholder, manage the property and pool income and expenses.

(7) Theatrical angels. A group of individuals contribute money to a promoter who pools their money and then invests it in a theatrical production in the hope that it will be successful and the contributors will realise profits.

(8) Racing syndicates. These can be structured as an arrangement under which individuals take a share in a racehorse which is managed by a trainer.

# 3 CONSEQUENCES OF A CIS

Where arrangements are a CIS, the main consequences are as follows:

(1) The rights or interests of participants, however they are described, are regulated investments falling within para 6 of Sched 1 FSA. They are called 'units' (s 75(8)).

(2) A person who engages in an investment activity in relation to these units (dealing, arranging, managing or advising) may be carrying on investment business subject to the FSA's various exclusions. If an unauthorised person carries on investment business then the consequences may include criminal liability and unenforceable contracts (see Chapter 11).

(3) Creating, operating or winding up a CIS is itself an investment activity (para 16 of Sched 1 FSA). None of the exclusions in para 17–27 of Sched 1 FSA, such as for dealing as principal or overseas persons, applies.

(4) There are restrictions on promoting a CIS discussed below. In addition, promotional material relating to a CIS may be an investment advertisement, and units in a CIS will be subject to the cold calling regulations.

(5) There are particular requirements for trustees and operators of authorised unit trust schemes and recognised collective investment schemes as discussed in Chapter 16.

(6) There may be undesirable taxation consequences. For example if the property is held on trust (such as jointly owned land), then there may be a double charge to capital gains tax on realised gains unless the scheme is structured as a limited partnership.

# 4 DEFINITION OF A CIS

This is contained in FSA s 75 (1)–(3). It is liable to alteration by an Order made under s 2 FSA (s 75(9)). There are five elements to the definition, of which the first two are particularly wide. This definition is satisfied, and the arrangements will be a CIS, if four out of five elements are present. The elements are outlined here and commented on in detail below. Exceptions are discussed in section 5 below.

(1) The arrangements relate to property of any kind. This property need not be an investment regulated by the FSA.

> 75(1) In this Act 'a collective investment scheme' means, subject to the provisions of this section, any arrangements with respect to property of any description, including money ...

(2) The purpose or effect of these arrangements is to enable the people who take part in them to participate in or receive profits or income from buying, holding, managing or selling the subject property. The participant need not own the property.

> 75(1) ... the purpose or effect of which is to enable persons taking part in the arrangements (whether by becoming owners of the property or any part of it or otherwise) to participate in or receive profits or income arising from the acquisition, holding, management or disposal of the property or sums paid out of such profits or income.

(3) All the participants do not have day-to-day control over management of the property. Where management is separate from ownership, participants will not be protected by having personal involvement in the day-to-day management and this is why the FSA seeks to safeguard them. They will not have the necessary degree of control if they merely have the right to be consulted or give directions. This point can be illustrated by reference to a unit trust. Here, an independent manager will manage the property on a day-to-day basis while the trustees will have oversight. However, the participants (the unit holders) will not have day-to-day control and their limited powers exercisable by voting at general meetings.

75(2) The arrangements must be such that the persons who are to participate as mentioned in sub-section (1) above (in this Act referred to as 'participants') do not have day to day control over the management of the property in question, whether or not they have the right to be consulted or to give directions; and the arrangements must also have either or both of the characteristics mentioned in sub-section (3) below.

(4) The participants' contributions and the profits or income out of which they receive payment are pooled.

75(3) Those characteristics are:

(a) that the contributions of the participants and the profits or income out of which payments are to be made to them are pooled;

(5) The property is managed as a whole by or on behalf of the scheme operator.

(b) that the property in question is managed as a whole by or on behalf of the operator of the scheme.

We must now examine each of the elements in this definition. Arrangements which are possibly not intended to be a CIS, such as examples (5)–(8) in section 2 above, will only be caught by s 75 if each part of this definition is fulfilled. It may be possible, depending on the circumstances, to structure arrangements so as to fall outside the definition.

## 4.1 Arrangements

The word 'arrangements', used in s 75(1), is a wide and indefinite term (see *Manning v Eastern Counties Railway Co* (1843) 13 LJ Ex 265). While the arrangement may take the form of one or more contracts, it may simply be an understanding or a course of conduct. An arrangement will not necessarily be legally enforceable. One example of an arrangement is where two parties intentionally arouse in each other an expectation that they will act in a certain way (*British Basic Slag Ltd's Agreements* [1963] 2 All ER 807).

## 4.2 Participants

A participant is someone who takes part in the arrangements. The word 'participants' in s 75(2) is in the plural, so if there is only one participant then the arrangements will not be a CIS.

It is not necessary for a participant to own all or any part of the subject property. Nor need there be a contract between the participants or between them and the operator. However, the essential feature of being a participant is that the intention (if not the practice) is that such persons will participate in profits or receive income arising from acquiring, holding, managing or disposing of the subject property, or money is paid out of such profits or income. The definition is disjunctive, and only one limb requires to be fulfilled. This is therefore a widely cast definition.

The arrangements must be such as to enable the participant to do this. If they merely facilitate what the participant could do on his own without the operator's assistance then it is arguable that it may not be a CIS.

'Profits or income' is probably meant to be all-encompassing, so all moneys a participant receives out of the arrangements will be one or the other. In this context 'income' probably means receipts in money or money's worth, while 'profit' is gain after outgoings are taken into account. Although 'income' is usually understood to connote more than one payment, it may be that a court would be prepared to interpret any money or money's worth received by a participant, even return of capital, as profit or income for the purpose of this section. However, receipt of a fee should fall outside this, so if the operator only receives a fee, then this should not make it a participant.

## 4.3  Control

The word 'control', which is used in s 75(2), is the nub. The FSA does not intend to protect people who manage their own affairs, and the arrangements will only be a CIS (and regulated by the FSA) if the people who take part in it do not control the arrangements themselves. The arrangements will not be a CIS if all the participants have day-to-day control over the management of the property. If only some participants have day-to-day control, then the arrangements may nonetheless be a CIS for the remaining participants.

The requirement in s 75(2) is that all the participants have day-to-day control over the management of the subject property. The elements are as follows:

(1) First, the participants rather than the operator must have day to day control. Where the participants have formal voting rights attached to their interests, then they will exercise control through these voting rights. Provided voting rights are not 'loaded' but, for example, relate to the size of individual investment, then in principle a person with ten per cent of the votes will fulfil this criterion, even though he may be outvoted.

(2) Secondly, although the requirement is to have rather than to exercise the day-to-day control, it must be capable of being exercised and not be a sham. If it is never intended to be exercised, or the arrangements are structured so as to hinder exercise, it is difficult to see how a court would accept that the participants have control. This will depend not only on the initial drafting of the scheme, but also how it is operated on a day-to-day basis.

(3) Thirdly, each of the participants must have control. Control means having the legal right and authority to say how something is to be done (*Dollfus Mieg et Compagnie SA v Bank of England* [1950] 1 Ch 333, *Mersey Docks and Harbour Board v Coggins and Griffith (Liverpool)* [1947] 1 AC 115). Someone controls something or someone else if he can give or refuse

consent to a proposed course of action (*R v Croydon Tramways Co* [1897] 18 QBD 39), or has the power and authority to decide what is to be done, how it should be done, and the time and place of performance (*Ready Mixed Concrete (South East) Limited v Ministry of Pensions and Insurance* [1968] 2 QB 497). It is apparent from the definition that having control is in addition to, and not fulfilled by, having the right to be consulted or to give directions.

(4) Fourthly, this control must be *day-to-day* control. Day-to-day control over the management means having control over the day-to-day aspects of the arrangements. This will be the ordinary business and trading activities not confined to control over policy or strategy, or the right to dismiss the operator of the CIS. The participants must have a continuous right to exercise control. For guidance on the concept of 'day-to-day' management see *Astor Chemicals v Synthetic Technology Limited* [1990] 1 BCLC 97; *Secretary of State for Employment v Chapman & Another* (1989) *The Times*, 11 July; *R v Governers of the Haberdashers' Aske's Hatcham Schools* (1989) *The Times*, 7 March; *R v Campbell* ([1984] BCLC 83).

(5) Finally, the day-to-day control must be exercised over the management of the property. It is suggested that 'managing' should be given its ordinary meaning of administering or dealing with something. What amounts to managing will depend on the nature of the subject property. For example:
–   if the property is a share portfolio, then the activities of buying and selling investments, acting as custodian, receiving and paying dividends and exercising voting rights will be management;
–   if the property is a shopping mall, then managing will include the usual property management functions of development, rent review, granting leases or licences and running the premises;
–   if the property is racehorses, managing will mean collecting subscribers' contributions, distributing winnings and stabling, training and racing the horses;
–   if the property is precious metals, managing will be buying, selling, valuing and safe keeping them;
–   if the property is money as in, for example, the pooling of funds for lending or for joint property development, managing will be turning it to account by lending it or using it to buy property for leasing.

## 4.4   Pooling

Pooling, referred to in s 75(3)(a), will be present where participants' contributions and profits or income out of which proceeds are paid are combined in a common account on receipt and before distribution. The two characteristics of pooling are generally understood to be the aggregation of property into a common fund, and the subsequent apportionment on an agreed basis of interests in that fund. The definition in s 75(3)(a) is cumulative and both participants' contributions and profits or income from which they are to be paid must be pooled. This criterion will not be fulfilled if funds are held in, and paid into, separate accounts.

## 4.5 Management as a whole

The criterion that the property is managed as a whole, contained in s 75(3)(b), is an alternative to 4.4 above, and is one of the key features of collectivity. This criterion will be fulfilled where the operator manages all participants' interests together, but not if each participant's interest is managed separately. The following overlapping factors may be relevant in determining this:

- Does the operator make common investment decisions, or separate decisions for each investor?
- Does each participant have separate contractual rights to the investment which it can realise at will, or does it merely have a right in a bulk investment?
- Does the viability or returns of the scheme, or generation of profits or income, depend on common management? This would seem to require more than the existence of economies of scale resulting from there being a number of investors.
- Does a participant's profit or loss relate to specific transactions on his account or to the overall performance of all participants' accounts?
- Is the scheme marketed as a pool or as a fund? For example, is there a low entry threshold to attract participants who could not otherwise participate in the scheme, which is therefore predicated on the basis of a minimum number of participants?

The word 'operator', which appears in s 75(3)(b), is given a limited definition by s 75(8) which provides that 'the operator', in relation to a unit trust scheme with a separate trustee, means the manager and, in relation to an open-ended investment company, means that company. In other cases the operator will probably be the person who manages the scheme. There is no requirement for the operator to be a participant, although a participant may agree to act as operator.

Whether the participants have day-to-day control over the management of the subject property is a question of fact to be determined in the particular circumstances of each case. If the participants collectively manage the property themselves, then they are likely to have this degree of control.

If they appoint one of their number, or a third party, to act as manager, then they need to retain day-to-day control over the way the manager performs the allocated management functions. If all the management functions, and the way they are to be performed, are definitively set out in a contract of engagement between the participants and the manager, and the participants exercise the necessary degree of control through the contract then the criterion may be fulfilled. However, the participants may not have day-to-day control if the manager retains discretion and the participants' only powers are collectively to terminate the contract or dismiss the manager, or individually to dispose of their interests.

If the manager is to act within delegated powers, or without recourse to the participants, then there should be a procedure to control him. This should probably be continuous active control entailing supervision of performance of the manager's functions and the power to give or refuse consent to the manager's proposals, which is substantially more than giving occasional strategic directions.

It is suggested that the level of control is that which would be required by a prudent man of business exercising day-to-day control over an independent contractor and, depending on the circumstances, the necessary features of this control would be:

- the participants give regular directions to the manager;
- the manager is obliged to comply with the participants' directions, which is an important element;
- the participants take major decisions and can influence or give directions in relation to other operational decisions;
- the participants have the right to receive regular reports on the manager's performance of the functions;
- where the participants have granted discretion to the manager, then they regularly review the manager's performance.

## 5  EXCLUSIONS

There are 20 total or partial exclusions from the definition of what constitutes a CIS which are contained in s 75(4)–(7) and in Sched 1 FSA paras 34 and 35. These will, of course, only fall to be considered where the definition in s 75(1)–(3) is fulfilled. The exclusions are not always easy to interpret, and it is necessary to analyse carefully any exclusion in relation to the transaction to which it is to be applied.

*(a)  Separate pooling*

> 75(4)  Where any arrangements provide for such pooling as is mentioned in paragraph (a) of sub-section (3) above in relation to separate parts of the property in question, the arrangements shall not be regarded as constituting a single collective investment scheme unless the participants are entitled to exchange rights in one part for rights in another.

This is intended to make it clear that an umbrella scheme will only constitute two or more CIS's if the participants can exchange units between the various sub-funds.

*(b) Personal equity plans*

75(5)   Arrangements are not a collective investment scheme if:

(a)   the property to which the arrangements relate (other than cash awaiting investment) consists of investments falling within any of paragraphs 1 to 5, 6 (so far as relating to units in authorised unit trust schemes and recognised schemes) and 10 of Schedule 1 to this Act;

(b)   each participant is the owner of a part of that property and entitled to withdraw it at any time; and

(c)   the arrangements do not have the characteristics mentioned in paragraph (a) of sub-section (3) above and have those mentioned in paragraph (b) of that sub-section only because the parts of the property belonging to different participants are not bought and sold separately except where a person becomes or ceases to be a participant.

This exclusion will apply where the property is shares, debentures, bonds, warrants, certificates, units in an authorised unit trust or recognised collective investment scheme or life assurance contracts, and:

(i)   each participant owns part of the property and may withdraw it at any time; and

(ii)   contributions and profits or income are not pooled, and the operator only manages the property to a specified extent.

This exclusion may be relevant to personal equity plans, and also where a managed client shares a common portfolio with other clients.

*(c) Not a business*

75(6)   The following are not collective investment schemes:

(a)   arrangements operated by a person otherwise than by way of business;

What amounts to 'business' is discussed in Chapter 6. An investment club of private individuals would probably be excluded; the participants' rights would not be caught by para 6 of Sched 1 FSA, and the operator would not fall within para 14 or 16 of Sched 1.

*(d) Commercial purposes*

75(6)(b)   arrangements where each of the participants carries on a business other than investment business and enters into the arrangements for commercial purposes related to that business.

'Investment business' is defined by s 1(2) as an activity falling within paras 12–16 Sched 1 but not excluded by paras 17–25B Sched 1. This exclusion takes in circumstances where every participant carries on a non-investment business and enters into the arrangements for related commercial purposes. This criterion must be fulfilled by all participants for so long as the arrangements continue. It is suggested that this can be fulfilled even if each of the participants also carries on investment business, provided each of them additionally carries on some other business to which the arrangements relate. For example, a bank which is a member of IMRO may carry on the investment business of fund management, but may fall within this exclusion if it enters into a CIS concerning its deposit-taking business, which falls outside the FSA. This subsection may exclude, for example,

    (i)   arrangements made by independent manufacturing companies who jointly purchase materials which are placed in a general pool from which periodical withdrawals are made;

    (ii)  arrangements made by banks in the course of ordinary bank lending such as syndicated lending.

*(e) Group*

    75(6)(c) arrangements where each of the participants is a body corporate in the same group as the operator;

'Group' is defined in s 207(1) as follows:

    207(1)   'Group', in relation to a body corporate, means that body corporate, any other body corporate which is its holding company or subsidiary and any other body corporate which is a subsidiary of that holding company;

This is a different definition of 'group' from that which applies to Sched 1.

*(f) Employee share schemes*

    75(6)(d) arrangements where:

        (i)   each of the participants is a bona fide employee or former employee (or the wife, husband, widow, widower, child or step-child under the age of eighteen of such an employee or former employee) of a body corporate in the same group as the operator; and

        (ii)  the property to which the arrangements relate consists of shares or debentures (as defined in paragraph 20(4) of Schedule 1 to this Act) in or of a member of that group;

This subsection excludes employee share schemes with the defined characteristics.

*(g) Franchise arrangements*

    75(6)(f) franchise arrangements, that is to say, arrangements under which a person earns profits or income by exploiting a right conferred by the arrangements to use a trade name or design or other intellectual property or the good-will attached to it,

Franchise arrangements usually relate to the right to carry on business under a trademark or to use a certain get-up. This paragraph goes somewhat further and includes the licence of any intellectual property.

### (h) Participants use of the property

75(6)(g) arrangements the predominant purpose of which is to enable persons participating in them to share in the use or enjoyment of a particular property or to make its use or enjoyment available gratuitously to other persons;

This excludes arrangements where the main purpose is for participants to use or enjoy a specific property. An example would be a timeshare of apartments. However if the predominant purpose is for non-participants to have use or enjoyment of the property, this must be done gratuitously.

### (i) Certificates representing securities

75(6)(h) arrangements under which the rights or interests of the participants are investments falling within paragraph 5 of Schedule 1 to this Act;

This excludes arrangements where participants' rights or interests are certificates representing securities under para 5 of Sched 1, such as ADRs.

### (j) Clearing services

75(6)(i) arrangements the purpose of which is the provision of clearing services and which are operated by an authorised person, a recognised clearing house or a recognised investment exchange;

This excludes arrangements which are clearing services operated by an authorised person, an RCH or an RIE (both defined terms). Other clearing services may be caught by s 75 when they possess the necessary characteristics.

### (k) Insurance

75(6)(j) contracts of insurance;

A long term insurance contract is a regulated investment under para 10 Sched 1, but this provides that no contract of insurance will of itself be a CIS.

### (l) Pensions

75(6)(k) occupational pension schemes;

An occupational pension scheme, which is defined in s 207(1), will not be a collective investment scheme. Furthermore, interests under the trusts of an occupational pension scheme are excluded from being regulated investments by Note (1) to para 11 in Sched 1. Arrangements relating to a personal pension scheme may, however, be a collective investment scheme.

## (m) Companies

> 75(7) No body incorporated under the law of, or of any part of, the United Kingdom relating to building societies or industrial and provident societies or registered under any such law relating to friendly societies, and no other body corporate other than an open-ended investment company, shall be regarded as constituting a collective investment scheme.

No United Kingdom building society, industrial and provident society or friendly society, and no body corporate (wherever incorporated) other than an open-ended investment company, will on its own constitute a collective investment scheme. Any of these bodies can, of course, still operate or participate in a collective investment scheme—the point is that the body on its own is not such a scheme. Accordingly, if two parties wish to engage in a venture that might otherwise be a collective investment scheme, one approach would be to vest the assets in a company which allots shares to the participants, whose rights are governed by the articles of association or a shareholders' agreement. On account of this exclusion such a company will not of itself be a collective investment scheme.

## (n) Business expansion schemes

> 34(1) For the purposes of this Schedule [ie Sched 1 FSA], arrangements are not a collective investment scheme if:
> (a) the property to which the arrangements relate (other than cash awaiting investment) consists of shares;
> (b) they constitute a complying fund;
> (c) each participant is the owner of a part of the property to which the arrangements relate and, to the extent that his part of that property:
>   (i) comprises relevant shares of a class which are admitted to the Official List of any member State or to dealings on a recognised investment exchange, he is entitled to withdraw it at any time after the end of the period of five years beginning with the date on which the shares in question were issued;
>   (ii) comprises relevant shares which do not fall within sub-paragraph (1)(c)(i) above, he is entitled to withdraw it at any time after the end of the period of two years beginning with the date upon which the period referred to in sub-paragraph (1)(c)(i) above expired;
>   (iii) comprises any other shares, he is entitled to withdraw it at any time after the end of the period of six months beginning with

the date upon which the shares in question ceased to be relevant shares; and

(iv) comprises cash which the operator has not agreed (conditionally or unconditionally) to apply in subscribing for shares, he is entitled to withdraw it at any time; and

(d) the arrangements would meet the conditions described in section 75(5)(c) of this Act were it not for the fact that the operator is entitled to exercise all or any of the rights conferred by shares included in the property to which the arrangements relate.

34(2) For the purposes of this paragraph:

(a) 'shares' means investments falling within paragraph 1 of this Schedule;

(b) shares shall be regarded as being relevant shares if and so long as they are shares in respect of which neither:

(i) a claim for relief, made in accordance with section 306 of the Income and Corporation Taxes Act 1988 has been disallowed; nor

(ii) an assessment has been made pursuant to section 307 of that Act withdrawing or refusing relief by reason of the body corporate in which the shares are held having ceased to be a body corporate which is a qualifying company for the purposes of section 293 of that Act; and

(c) arrangements shall be regarded as constituting a complying fund if they provide that:

(i) the operator will, so far as practicable, make investments each of which, subject to each participant's individual circumstances, qualify for relief by virtue of Chapter III of Part VII of the Income and Corporation Taxes Act 1988; and

(ii) the minimum subscription to the arrangements made by each participant must be not less than £2,000.

This excludes business expansion schemes which possess the defined characteristics.

*(o) Deposits*

35(a) arrangements where the entire contribution of each participant is a deposit within the meaning of section 5 of the Banking Act 1987 or a sum of a kind described in sub-section (3) of that section;

This should exclude the situation where a number of persons pool funds to get a higher interest rate when placed on deposit. It may also exclude circumstances, such as syndicated lending, where depositors or money lenders pay contributions to a central source which pools the funds, makes a profit on lending the funds out and pays interest to the depositors.

### (p) Public and other securities

35(b) arrangements under which the rights or interests of the participants are represented by the following:

(i) investments falling within paragraph 2 of this Schedule which are issued by a single body corporate which is not an open ended investment company or which are issued by a single issuer which is not a body corporate and are guaranteed by the government of the United Kingdom, of Northern Ireland, or of any country or territory outside the United Kingdom; or

(ii) investments falling within sub-paragraph (i) above which are convertible into or exchangeable for investments falling within paragraph 1 of this Schedule provided that those latter investments are issued by the same person as issued the investments falling within sub-paragraph (i) above or are issued by a single other issuer; or

(iii) investments falling within paragraph 3 of this Schedule issued by the same government, local authority or public authority; or

(iv) investments falling within paragraph 4 of this Schedule which are issued otherwise than by an open ended investment company and which confer rights in respect of investments, issued by the same issuer, falling within paragraph 1 of this Schedule or within sub-paragraph (i), (ii) or (iii) above;

This excludes arrangements where participants' rights are debentures issued by certain issuers and which are guaranteed by a government; certain convertible debentures; public securities issued by the same government or authority; and associated warrants.

An example of arrangements which may fall within this exclusion is where a special purposes vehicle issues securities backed by its assets which comprise third party securities.

### (q) Currency and interest swaps

35(c) arrangements which would fall within paragraph (b) above were it not for the fact that the rights or interests of a participant ('the counterparty') whose ordinary business involves him in engaging in activities which fall within Part II of this Schedule or would do so apart from Part III or IV are or include rights or interests under a swap arrangement, that is to say, an arrangement the purpose of which is to facilitate the making of payments to participants whether in a particular amount or currency or at a particular time or rate of interest or all or any combination of those things, being an arrangement under which:

   (i)   the counterparty is entitled to receive amounts (whether representing principal or interest) payable in respect of any property subject to the scheme or sums determined by reference to such amounts; and

   (ii)  the counterparty makes payments (whether or not of the same amount and whether or not in the same currency as those referred to in sub-paragraph (b)(i) above) which are calculated in accordance with an agreed formula by reference to the amounts or sums referred to in sub-paragraph (b)(i) above;

This exclusion is linked to the exclusion in para 35(b) above. If the special purpose vehicle enters into a currency or interest rate swap, then the counterparty may be able to take advantage of this exclusion, and hence the arrangements as a whole will not constitute a CIS.

*(r) Common account*

35(d) arrangements under which the rights or interests of participants are rights to or interests in money held in a common account in circumstances in which the money so held is held on the understanding that an amount representing the contribution of each participant is to be applied either in making payments to him or in satisfaction of sums owed by him or in the acquisition of property or the provision of services for him;

This excludes circumstances where participants' interests is money held in a common account; for example, an authorised person holding client money or the agent acting under a syndicated loan agreement.

*(s) Property trust funds*

35(e) arrangements under which the rights and interests of participants are rights and interests in a fund which is a trust fund within the meaning of section 42(1) of the Landlord and Tenant Act 1987;

*(t) Electricity privatisation*

35(f) arrangements where:

   (i)   each of the participants is a bona fide employee or former employee (or the wife, husband, widow, widower or child (including, in Northern Ireland, adopted child) or step-child under the age of eighteen of such an employee or former employee) of any of the following bodies corporate, that is to say, The National Grid Company plc, Electricity Association Services Limited or any other body corporate in the same group as either of them and which is operated by any of those bodies corporate; and

   (ii)  the property to which the arrangements relate consists of shares or debentures (as defined in paragraph 20(4) above) in or of a body corporate which is an electricity successor company for the purposes of Part II of the Electricity Act 1989(c) or a body corporate which would be regarded as connected with such an electricity successor company for the purposes of paragraph 20 above;

and for the purposes of this paragraph references to former employees shall have the same meaning as in the Financial Services Act 1986 (Electricity Industry Exemptions) Order 1990.

This is intended to exclude certain bonus schemes created as part of the electricity privatisation.

# 6   MARKETING COLLECTIVE INVESTMENT SCHEMES

There are restrictions, contained in s 76, on the promotion of collective investment schemes to the public, which are similar to those contained in s 130(1) restricting the promotion of insurance contracts.

Subject to the exclusions mentioned below, an authorised person may not issue an advertisement relating to a CIS, or advise or procure a United Kingdom person to become a participant in a CIS, unless it is:

(1) a United Kingdom unit trust scheme authorised under s 77 (discussed in Chapter 16); or

(2) a CIS constituted in another EEA member state and recognised under s 86; constituted in a designated country or territory and recognised under s 87; or recognised on an individual basis under s 88. It is irrelevant whether it is listed on the London Stock Exchange.

Section 76(1) stipulates that:

76(1) Subject to sub-sections (2), (3) and (4) below, an authorised person shall not:

(a) issue or cause to be issued in the United Kingdom any advertisement inviting persons to become or offer to become participants in a collective investment scheme or containing information calculated to lead directly or indirectly to persons becoming or offering to become participants in such a scheme; or

(b) advise or procure any person in the United Kingdom to become or offer to become a participant in such a scheme,

unless the scheme is an authorised unit trust scheme or a recognised scheme under the following provisions of this Chapter [ie Chapter VIII FSA].

The restrictions are:

(1) Against advertising (s 76(1)(a)). This is substantially similar to that contained in s 57, discussed in Chapter 13. This prohibits issuing an

advertisement or causing one to be issued. By an oversight it does not prohibit an authorised person from approving the advertisement of an unauthorised person for an unrecognised CIS. For this reason the SIB and SRO rule books generally prohibit this.

(2) Against advising anyone to become a participant.

(3) Against procuring anyone to become a participant. 'Procuring' in this context means trying to cause something to happen. (See *A-G's Reference (No 1 of 1975)* [1975] 2 All ER 684).

No criminal penalty or civil consequences are specified for breach of s 76, but s 95(1) provides that any person who contravenes any of ss 75–95 will be deemed to have contravened the SIB conduct of business rules or, if it is a member of an SRO or RPB, the rules of that body. The SIB is accordingly empowered to seek an injunction or restitution order under s 61, and an investor who suffers loss is enabled to bring an action under s 62. In this case the s 62 remedy is not restricted to private investors (the Financial Services Act 1986 (Restriction of Right of Action) Regulations 1991 (SI No 439 art 3(a)).

The restriction in s 76(1) only applies to authorised persons. Unauthorised persons who promote any CIS are liable to infringe s 3 (carrying on investment business) and s 57 (advertisements), unless they are able to rely upon any of the FSA's exclusions in the particular circumstances.

## 6.1 Exclusions

A CIS which is not an authorised unit trust scheme or recognised collective investment scheme may be promoted to certain limited classes of persons set out in sub-s 72(2)–(4) or in statutory instruments made under this section. These classes are as follows:

(1) An authorised person may promote a CIS which falls outside s 76(1) to another authorised person (such as an intermediary who is authorised by membership of PIA or an RPB) who may then promote the scheme to its own clients provided it observes the applicable conduct of business rules, and that the client falls within a category mentioned below (s 76(2)(a)). This does not permit the first authorised person to promote to anyone other than the second authorised person. It may not, for example, assist the second authorised person to promote to its clients.

76(2) Subsection (1) above shall not apply if the advertisement is issued to or the person mentioned in paragraph (b) of that sub-section is:

(a) an authorised person; or

(2) An authorised person may promote a CIS which falls outside s 76(1) to a person whose ordinary business is buying *and* selling property of the same kind as the subject property of the scheme or a substantial part of it

(s 76(2)(b)). Examples of such persons would be a diamond dealer, horse dealer, property developer or stockbroker if the subject properties of the scheme were respectively diamonds, horses, freehold or leasehold property or shares.

76(2)(b)   a person whose ordinary business involves the acquisition and disposal of property of the same kind as the property, or a substantial part of the property, to which the scheme relates.

(3) An authorised person may promote a CIS which falls outside s 76(1) to persons falling within regulations made under s 76(3).

76(3)   Sub-section (1) above shall not apply to anything done in accordance with regulations made by the Secretary of State for the purpose of exempting from that sub-section the promotion otherwise than to the general public of schemes of such descriptions as are specified in the regulations.

These regulations are the Financial Services (Promotion of Unregulated Schemes) Regulations 1991, which have considerably liberalised the promotion of unregulated CISs. An authorised person may promote an unregulated CIS to the following classes of person.

(i)   Current or previous investors: An authorised person may promote an unregulated CIS of the following kinds to someone who is or was in the past 30 months a participant in any unregulated CIS. The schemes which can be promoted to such a person are:
–   the scheme in which the person has already invested;
–   a successor scheme to such a scheme;
–   any other scheme with substantially similar underlying property (eg both schemes are based on the property market, in particular collectables or on-exchange derivatives) provided the risk profile is substantially similar both in relation to liquidity and volatility.

(ii)   Potential investors who express interest: An authorised person may promote an unregulated CIS to someone who has asked an unauthorised person (who is not an associate of the authorised person) to list him as interested in receiving details from authorised persons of schemes with particular underlying property. The authorised person must be satisfied that the investor's name did not get on this list as a result of breach of the FSA's requirements or applicable conduct of business rules. An example would be a private investor who notifies a theatre manager that he is interested in investing in theatrical productions.

(iii)   Established or newly acquired customers: An authorised person may promote an unregulated CIS to its (or its group's) established or newly acquired investment business customer, from whom (if newly acquired) it has properly obtained a written customer agreement without contravening s 76 and (in either case) for whom it has taken reasonable steps to ensure that the investment is suitable.

(iv) Permitted, exempted and non-private customers: An authorised person may promote an unregulated CIS to:
- a person holding permission under para 23, Sched 1;
- an exempted person (but not an appointed representative);
- someone who is not a private customer. This can be an individual carrying on investment business, an ordinary business investor, or a person whom an authorised person may treat as a non-private customer under the terms of its applicable conduct of business rules.

(v) Promotion of particular schemes: An authorised person may promote particular kinds of unregulated CISs to:
- CGT exempt persons;
- eligible participants under charities legislation;
- participants in employee benefit schemes.

(vi) Excluded activities: An authorised person may promote an unregulated CIS where it can take advantage of the group, sale of goods, disposal of private company, trustee, professional advising or media exclusions in Sched 1.

(4) An authorised person may promote to the public a single property scheme which conforms to the Financial Services Act 1986 (Single Property Schemes) (Exemptions) Regulations 1989 SI No 28 (s 76(4)). A single property CIS is a scheme of which the assets are solely freehold or leasehold interests in a single building or adjacent buildings, together with ancillary land and fixtures and fittings. The income of the scheme is the rental income from letting space in the building to occupation tenants.

# 10   *Exclusions*

We have already considered a number of exclusions in their context in Chapter 8. These are:

(1) dealing as principal (para 17);
(2) the necessary advice exclusion (para 24);
(3) the necessary arranging exclusion (para 24);
(4) the media exclusions (paras 25 and 25A).

We have also considered the exclusions (or, more accurately, the omissions) which arise because various items fall outside the definitions of investments and investment activities, and the exclusions contained in the Notes to paras 1–11 of Sched 1. We have discussed the overseas person exclusions, in paras 26 and 27, in Chapter 6.

We now consider the three remaining categories of exclusions which we have marshalled into corporate exclusions, commercial exclusions and those which relate principally to trustees.

The object of all these exclusions is to remove certain marginal cases from the scope of the FSA, rather than to permit any favoured category to carry on investment business outside the Act. A number of these exclusions have been in from the first draft of the Bill, while others have been included as the result of lobbying immediately before 'A' Date.

## 1   CORPORATE EXCLUSIONS

### 1.1   Groups and joint enterprises

The exclusions relating to investment activities carried on by or within groups and joint enterprises are contained in para 18. This is liable to alteration upon implementation of the Investment Services Directive as the Directive only grants an exclusion for companies who provide services exclusively to other group companies. Paragraph 18 as presently drafted states the following:

> 18(1) Paragraph 12 above does not apply to any transaction which is or is to be entered into by a person as principal with another person if:—

    (a) they are bodies corporate in the same group; or

    (b) they are, or propose to become, participators in a joint enterprise and the transaction is or is to be entered into for the purposes of, or in connection with, that enterprise.

(2) Paragraph 12 above does not apply to any transaction which is or is to be entered into by any person as agent for another person in the circumstances mentioned in sub-paragraph (1)(a) or (b) above if:—

    (a) where the investment falls within any of paragraphs 1 to 6 above or, so far as relevant to any of those paragraphs, paragraph 11 above, the agent does not:—

        (i) hold himself out (otherwise than to other bodies corporate in the same group or persons who are or propose to become participators with him in a joint enterprise) as engaging in the business of buying investments with a view to selling them and those investments are or include investments of the kind to which the transaction relates; or

        (ii) regularly solicit members of the public for the purpose of inducing them to enter as principals or agents into transactions to which paragraph 12 above applies; and the transaction is not or is not to be entered into as a result of his having solicited members of the public in that manner;

    (b) where the investment is not as mentioned in paragraph (a) above:—

        (i) the agent enters into the transaction with or through an authorised person, an exempted person or a person holding a permission under paragraph 23 below; or

        (ii) the transaction is effected through an office outside the United Kingdom, maintained by a party to the transaction, and with or through a person whose head office is situated outside the United Kingdom and whose ordinary business involves him in engaging in activities which fall within Part II of this Schedule or would do so apart from this Part or Part IV.

(3) Paragraph 13 above does not apply to arrangements which a person makes or offers or agrees to make if:—

    (a) that person is a body corporate and the arrangements are with a view to another body corporate in the same group entering into a transaction of the kind mentioned in that paragraph; or

    (b) that person is or proposes to become a participator in a joint enterprise and the arrangements are with a view to another person who is or proposes to become a participator in the enterprise entering into such a transaction for the purposes of or in connection with that enterprise.

(4) Paragraph 14 above does not apply to a person by reason of his managing or offering or agreeing to manage the investments of another person if:—

    (a) they are bodies corporate in the same group; or

(b) they are, or propose to become, participators in a joint enterprise and the investments are or are to be managed for the purposes of, or in connection with, that enterprise.

(5) Paragraph 15 above does not apply to advice given by a person to another person if:—

(a) they are bodies corporate in the same group; or

(b) they are, or propose to become, participators in a joint enterprise and the advice is given for the purposes of, or in connection with, that enterprise.

(6) The definitions in paragraph 17(2) above shall apply also for the purposes of sub-paragraph (2)(a) above except that the relevant person referred to in paragraph 17(2)(d) shall be the person for whom the agent is acting.

This exclusion removes the following from the scope of the FSA:

(1) Dealing as principal in investments with another group company (which need not be incorporated in the United Kingdom) or with another actual or intending participant in a joint enterprise where the transaction relates to the enterprise (18(1)). While 'group' is widely defined by para 30, 'joint enterprise' is given a narrow definition by para 31 of Sched 1 as follows:

> (31) In this Schedule 'a joint enterprise' means an enterprise into which two or more persons ('the participators') enter for commercial reasons related to a business or businesses (other than investment business) carried on by them; and where a participator is a body corporate and a member of a group, each other member of the group shall also be regarded as a participator in the enterprise.

A joint enterprise is a joint undertaking entered into for commercial reasons related to one or more non-investment businesses which the participants carry on. Not all joint ventures will qualify. If one participant is a member of a group then all group members are regarded as participators.

(2) Dealing as an agent in investments for a group company or participant (actual or potential) in a joint enterprise in circumstances similar to where a person can take advantage of the dealing as principal exclusion, discussed in relation to para 17. Accordingly, if the first group company enters into a transaction to deal in investments with a third party as agent for the second group company then (subject to para 18(2)(a) and (b)) neither group company will be engaging in the investment activity of dealing as para 12 is stated not to apply to the transaction.

(3) Making arrangements for another group company to deal, or another actual or intending participant in a joint enterprise to enter into a transaction which relates to the enterprise (18(3)). In consequence the first group company is not making arrangements for the second group company to deal with a third party, but the second group company will in principle be engaging in an investment activity with the third party.

(4) Managing the investments of another group company or another actual or intending participant in a joint enterprise where the managing relates to the enterprise (18(4)).

(5) Advising another group company on investments or another actual or intending participant in a joint enterprise where the advice relates to the enterprise (18(5)).

The definition of 'group' is given in para 30:

30  (1) For the purposes of this Schedule a group shall be treated as including any body corporate in which a member of the group holds a qualifying capital interest.

(2) A qualifying capital interest means an interest in relevant shares of the body corporate which the member holds on a long-term basis for the purpose of securing a contribution to its own activities by the exercise of control or influence arising from that interest.

(3) Relevant shares means shares comprised in the equity share capital of the body corporate of a class carrying rights to vote in all circumstances at general meetings of the body.

(4) A holding of 20 per cent or more of the nominal value of the relevant shares of a body corporate shall be presumed to be a qualifying capital interest unless the contrary is shown.

(5) In this paragraph 'equity share capital' has the same meaning as in the Companies Act 1985 and the Companies (Northern Ireland) Order 1986.

A group includes any body corporate in which a member of that group holds a qualifying capital interest, which entails:

(a) holding shares in any class of the equity share capital of a company;

(b) which shares carry rights to vote in all circumstances at general meetings of that company;

(c) which are held 'on a long-term basis for the purpose of securing a contribution to its own activities by the exercise of control or influence arising from that interest'. This is understood to mean that the parent benefits or intends to benefit from the subsidiary's activities through the exercise of control over a long period of time, rather than by short term speculation in those securities. A holding of 20 per cent or more of nominal value of such shares is deemed to be a qualifying capital interest unless the contrary is shown.

## 1.2  Company sales and purchases

In the White Paper which preceded the Bill, the Government undertook that the sale of businesses, or the assets of a business offered for sale as a single entity, would be excluded from the ambit of the FSA.

The exclusion in para 21 removes from the ambit of the FSA the investment activities of dealing, arranging and advising in relation to the sale or purchase of shares in any United Kingdom or overseas company (other than an open-ended investment company) in certain circumstances. 'Shares' presumably has the meaning given to it in para 1. The circumstances are:

(1) the shares must represent 75 per cent or more of the voting rights in that company (taking into account any the buyer already holds); and

(2) the parties to the transaction must be companies, partnerships, individuals or a group of connected individuals.

The exclusion is set out in para 21 as follows:

(21)(1) Paragraphs 12 and 13 above do not apply to the acquisition or disposal of, or to anything done for the purposes of the acquisition or disposal of, shares in a body corporate other than an open-ended investment company, and paragraph 15 above does not apply to advice given in connection with the acquisition or disposal of such shares if:—

    (a) the shares consist of or include shares carrying 75 per cent or more of the voting rights attributable to share capital which are exercisable in all circumstances at any general meeting of the body corporate; or

    (b) the shares, together with any already held by a person acquiring them, carry not less than that percentage of those voting rights; and

    (c) in either case, the acquisition and disposal is, or is to be, between parties each of whom is a body corporate, a partnership, a single individual or a group of connected individuals.

(2) For the purposes of subsection (1)(c) above 'a group of connected individuals', in relation to the party disposing of the shares, means persons each of whom is, or is a close relative of, a director or manager of the body corporate and, in relation to the party acquiring the shares, means persons each of whom is, or is a close relative of, a person who is to be a director or manager of the body corporate.

(3) In this paragraph 'close relative' means a person's spouse, his children and step-children, his parents and step-parents, his brothers and sisters and his step-brothers and step-sisters.

This exclusion is of significant assistance in relation to arranging and advising in company sales; if one is buying or selling the shares as principal then one may additionally be able to rely on the dealing as principal exclusion in para 17.

The shares sold must represent 75 per cent or more of voting rights exercisable in all circumstances at a general meeting.

It is difficult to understand sub-para 21(1)(c), but it is suggested that a transaction will fall within (c) where a company sells to a company or to a partnership; a company sells to a single individual; or a company and a group of connected individuals sell to a company and so on. But a transaction will not qualify if a group of unconnected individuals is a party.

# 2   COMMERCIAL EXCLUSIONS

## 2.1   Sale of goods and supply of services

Paragraph 19 excludes from the FSA people who carry on certain limited investment activities which are ancillary to the supply of non-investment goods or services. This paragraph may be altered as a result of implementation of the Investment Services Directive.

This exclusion was subject to a major amendment just before 'A' Date. Sub-paragraph (9) was added then to provide that this paragraph will not apply where the customer is an individual or where the investment activity relates to life assurance or units in a collective investment scheme.

The main business of the person seeking to rely on the exclusion ('the supplier') must be the supply of goods or services and not the business of engaging in the investment activities of dealing, arranging, managing or advising in relation to investments, or operating a collective investment scheme.

In summary, this exclusion relates to situations where the supplier engages in investment activities in defined circumstances in connection with the sale or supply of goods or services or a related third party's sale or supply of goods or services. The circumstances are:

(1)  dealing in investments as principal with a customer in connection with the sale or supply of goods or services to that customer (para 19(2));

(2)  dealing in investments as agent for a customer in connection with the sale or supply of goods or services to that customer where:

    (i)  if the investment is an option, future, contract for differences, collective investment scheme or life assurance, the supplier is dealing with or through an authorised, exempted or permitted person or certain overseas persons (para 19(3)(b)); and

    (ii) in other cases, the supplier generally does not hold itself out as buying investments of this kind with a view to selling them, or regularly solicit the public para 19(3)(a)). (The definitions of para 17(2) apply here by virtue of para 19(8));

(3)  arranging deals in investments for the customer which are connected with the sale or supply of goods or services (para 19(4));

(4) managing the customer's investments in connection with the sale or supply of goods or services (para 19(5));

(5) advising the customer (or the customer's customer) on investments in connection with the sale or supply of goods or services (para 19(6)).

If the supplier or its customer is a member of a group (as defined in para 30), then these exclusions also apply to other members of their respective groups (para 19(7)).

For example, a manufacturing company may contract to supply equipment. Its subsidiary may arrange finance and give advice on the issue of debentures to obtain funds, while the buyer's subsidiary may raise the finance. To the extent that any of them is thereby carrying on investment activities, they may be able to take advantage of this exclusion.

Paragraph 19 of Sched 1 makes the following provisions:

(19)(1) Subject to sub-paragraph (9) below this paragraph has effect where a person ('the supplier') sells or offers or agrees to sell goods to another person ('the customer') or supplies or offers or agrees to supply him with services and the supplier's main business is to supply goods or services and not to engage in activities falling within Part II of this Schedule.

(2) Paragraph 12 above does not apply to any transaction which is or is to be entered into by the supplier as principal if it is or is to be entered into by him with the customer for the purposes of or in connection with the sale or supply or a related sale or supply (that is to say, a sale or supply to the customer otherwise than by the supplier but for or in connection with the same purpose as the first-mentioned sale or supply).

(3) Paragraph 12 above does not apply to any transaction which is or is to be entered into by the supplier as agent for the customer if it is or is to be entered into for the purposes of or in connection with the sale or supply or a related sale or supply and:—

(a) where the investment falls within any of paragraphs 1 to 5 above or, so far as relevant to any of those paragraphs, paragraph 11 above, the supplier does not:—

(i) hold himself out (otherwise than to the customer) as engaging in the business of buying investments with a view to selling them and those investments are or include investments of the kind to which the transaction relates; or

(ii) regularly solicit members of the public for the purpose of inducing them to enter as principals or agents into transactions to which paragraph 12 above applies;

and the transaction is not or is not to be entered into as a result of his having solicited members of the public in that manner;

(b) where the investment is not as mentioned in paragraph (a) above, the supplier enters into the transaction:—

   (i) with or through an authorised person, an exempted person or a person holding a permission under paragraph 23 below; or

   (ii) through an office outside the United Kingdom, maintained by a party to the transaction, and with or through a person whose head office is situated outside the United Kingdom and whose ordinary business involves him in engaging in activities which fall within Part II of this Schedule or would do so apart from this Part or Part IV.

(4) Paragraph 13 above does not apply to arrangements which the supplier makes or offers or agrees to make with a view to the customer entering into a transaction for the purposes of or in connection with the sale or supply or a related sale or supply.

(5) Paragraph 14 above does not apply to the supplier by reason of his managing or offering or agreeing to manage the investments of the customer if they are or are to be managed for the purposes of or in connection with the sale or supply or a related sale or supply.

(6) Paragraph 15 above does not apply to advice given by the supplier to the customer for the purposes of or in connection with the sale or supply or a related sale or supply or to a person with whom the customer proposes to enter into a transaction for the purposes of or in connection with the sale or supply or a related sale or supply.

(7) Where the supplier is a body corporate and a member of a group sub-paragraphs (2) to (6) above shall apply to any other member of the group as they apply to the supplier; and where the customer is a body corporate and a member of a group references in those sub-paragraphs to the customer include references to any other member of the group.

(8) The definitions in paragraph 17(2) above shall apply also for the purposes of sub-paragraph (3)(a) above.

(9) This paragraph does not have effect where either:—

   (a) the customer is an individual; or

   (b) the transaction in question is the purchase or sale of an investment which falls within paragraph 6 or 10 above or, so far as relevant to either of those paragraphs, paragraph 11 above; or

   (c) the investments which the supplier manages or offers or agrees to manage consist of investments falling within paragraph 6 or 10 above or, so far as relevant to either of those paragraphs, paragraph 11 above; or

   (d) the advice which the supplier gives is advice on an investment falling within paragraph 6 or 10 above or, so far as relevant to either of those paragraphs, paragraph 11 above.

## 2.2 Employee share schemes

The impact of the FSA on such schemes, and the application of the exclusion in para 20, are discussed in Chapter 16.

## 3 TRUSTEES, PERSONAL REPRESENTATIVES, NOMINEES AND ATTORNEYS

A trustee or personal representative is likely to engage in investment activities for a number of reasons, for example:

(1) he will deal in investments because they are registered in his or her name;
(2) he will manage the investments which form part of an estate of which he is a trustee or a personal representative, unless management functions are carried out by another person;
(3) he may give investment advice to co-trustees or beneficiaries.

Whether he is additionally carrying on investment business will depend on whether he is engaging in the investment activity in the course of business.

Paragraph 22 of Sched 1 contains a number of exclusions which are, broadly speaking, intended to remove certain 'professional' trustees and personal representatives from the ambit of the FSA. Paragraph 22 does not relate to persons acting under a power of attorney, but this section is a convenient place to discuss their position.

'Holding out' and 'additional remuneration' are common elements in some of these exclusions. They are discussed in Chapter 8.

## 3.1 Dealing

Paragraph 22 sets out the following:

(22)(1) Paragraph 12 above does not apply to a person by reason of his buying, selling or subscribing for an investment or offering or agreeing to do so if:—
(a) the investment is or, as the case may be, is to be held by him as bare trustee or, in Scotland, as nominee for another person;
(b) he is acting on that person's instructions; and
(c) he does not hold himself out as providing a service of buying and selling investments.

Paragraph 22(1) is included as a bare trustee can be viewed as an agent rather than a principal (and it cannot therefore rely on the dealing as principal exclusion in para 17). A bare trustee is a person who holds property for another in circumstances where that other can call for delivery of the trust property. As discussed above in relation to para 12, a nominee will often be neither a principal nor an agent, but will complete a transaction entered into by a principal. It will in these circumstances fall outside para 12 altogether.

A personal representative, and a trustee whose powers derive from settlement or statute, will deal as principal and may, where appropriate, rely on the dealing as principal exclusion in para 17. A personal representative or trustee who is not a bare trustee cannot rely on para 22 as he will not hold an investment as bare trustee.

This sub-paragraph provides, in summary, that such person does not deal when he buys, sells or subscribes for an investment if:

(1) he holds as bare trustee for another (or, in Scotland, as nominee); and
(2) he acts on that other person's instructions. These instructions could be directly or indirectly received, but a person who acts on a third party's instructions, or who exercises his own discretion, cannot rely on this exclusion; and
(3) he does not hold himself out as providing a dealing service. If such a person is a trust company and holds itself out as providing a dealing service, it may not rely on this exclusion.

A bare trustee or Scottish nominee who falls within para 22(1)(a) and (b) may not rely on para 17. Paragraph 22(5) states the following:

22(5)  Sub-paragraph (1) above has effect to the exclusion of paragraph 17 above as respects any transaction in respect of which the conditions in sub-paragraph (1)(a) and (b) are satisfied.

## 3.2  Arranging deals

This is excluded by para 22(2) which specifies that:

22(2)  Paragraph 13 above does not apply to anything done by a person as trustee or personal representative with a view to:—
(a) a fellow trustee or personal representative and himself engaging in their capacity as such in an activity falling within paragraph 12 above; or
(b) a beneficiary under the trust, will or intestacy engaging in any such activity,
unless that person is remunerated for what he does in addition to any remuneration he receives for discharging his duties as trustee or personal representative.

A bare or other trustee or a personal representative is not making arrangements where the arrangements are for themselves or the beneficiary to deal *provided* they are not additionally remunerated. It is suggested that a trustee is not additionally remunerated for making arrangements if he charges either a flat fee or on a time basis provided making these arrangements are part of his discharging his duties as trustee, and his activities do not differ in scope from those of the other trustees.

## 3.3 Managing investments

This is excluded by para 22(3) as follows:

> 22(3) Paragraph 14 above does not apply to anything done by a person as trustee or personal representative unless he holds himself out as offering investment management services or is remunerated for providing such services in addition to any remuneration he receives for discharging his duties as trustee or personal representative.

A trustee or personal representative will normally be viewed as managing all the investments in his charge unless the management is delegated to a third party and he is empowered to make such delegation and, furthermore, he does not retain such continuing involvement with the investments that he is still managing them. As discussed in Chapter 8, investments managed by a trustee or personal representative will 'belong' to another person (a necessary element under para 14) even though legal title is registered in the trustee's or personal representative's name.

This exclusion provides that a bare or other trustee or a personal representative would not be managing investments in his charge unless he holds himself out as offering investment services, or is additionally remunerated.

As a trustee's duty is to manage investments falling within the trust it is arguable that a trustee who, along with his fellow trustees, manages investments as part of his day-to-day functions in return for his regular remuneration (be it fixed fee or on a time basis) will not be remunerated for that work in addition to remuneration he receives for his other work as a trustee. However if a particular trustee provides additional services in relation to managing investments (eg the other trustees delegate management of the trust's investments to him) and he receives additional remuneration for that additional work, then he would probably fall outside this exclusion.

## 3.4 Advising on investments

This is excluded by para 22(4);

> 22(4) Paragraph 15 above does not apply to advice given by a person as trustee or personal representative to:—
> (a) a fellow trustee or personal representative for the purposes of the trust or estate; or
> (b) a beneficiary under the trust, will or intestacy concerning his interest in the trust fund or estate,
> unless that person is remunerated for doing so in addition to any remuneration he receives for discharging his duties as trustee or personal representative.

A bare or other trustee or a personal representative will not fall within para 15 when advising fellow trustees or personal representatives for their own purposes, or when advising beneficiaries on their rights under the trust or estate unless (in either case) he is additionally remunerated (which is discussed above).

## 3.5　What is the value of para 22?

A private individual who acts as a trustee or personal representative is unlikely to be carrying on investment business, so these exclusions will normally only assist trustees or personal representatives acting professionally and who, but for these exclusions, would carry on investment business in relation to these activities.

A professional trustee or a personal representative (but not a bare trustee) may be able to rely on the dealing as principal exclusion in para 17, and a bare trustee can rely on para 22(1). However, if they are additionally remunerated, they will not be able to rely on the other exclusions in para 22.

## 3.6　Attorneys

The FSA makes no special provision for donees of a power of attorney, but their position is probably as follows. A power of attorney is a written document which constitutes the granting of agency powers. It is considered by SIB in Guidance Release 1/92.

A private individual who acts as an attorney most likely falls outside the FSA as he is not carrying on a business. Someone who acts as an attorney on a professional basis in the United Kingdom, such as a solicitor or an accountant, will most likely be carrying on a business in relation to such activities and will require authorisation if the assets over which he has authority do or may include regulated investments, and he engages in an investment activity in relation to them.

*(a) Dealing*
A donee under a power of attorney acts as agent for the principal. The exclusion in para 17 will not be available to the attorney, but may be available to the donor.

*(b) Arranging*
An attorney cannot arrange deals since it will enter into them as agent, and the donor will be a party as principal.

*(c) Managing*
If the basis of the attorney's appointment is that he will look after the donor's investments, then he may well be managing those investments.

*(d) Advising*
The attorney may, depending on the circumstances, give the donor advice as an actual or potential investor, although this is not a necessary attribute of acting as an attorney.

# 11 *Getting Caught*

Unlike earlier legislation (discussed in Chapter 1), the FSA seeks to protect investors by preventing unfit persons from commencing business in the first place, and by imposing a regulatory structure on those who pass through the initial hurdles and succeed in becoming authorised.

This chapter examines those of the FSA's provisions which are principally retrospective: those which apply once its provisions have been breached or after an investor has suffered loss.

These provisions fall into three categories. First, the FSA creates a number of criminal offences. Secondly, the FSA contains two important civil remedies, one affecting the enforceability of agreements, and the other relating to compensation. Finally, the FSA confers a number of investigative and procedural powers on the Treasury and on SIB. Some of these are, subject to the detailed points noted, exercisable against all, or all authorised, persons. Others are particular to persons whom SIB has authorised to carry on investment business, or who are otherwise subject to its rulebook and, although contained in the FSA, these powers are broadly similar to those which an SRO or RPB may exercise against its own members.

## 1 HOW CAN ONE BE FOUND OUT?

As with any legislation which contains civil remedies or criminal penalties, there will be an unlimited number of ways in which information relating to some breach or misdemeanour may become known. In particular:

(1) an investor may complain to SIB or to the relevant SRO or RPB about a person's conduct. A number of investigations and disciplinary actions have been commenced by regulators in consequence of investor complaints; see Chapter 2.

(2) the firm's compliance officer may notify the regulators either in accordance with Principle 10 or in accordance with particular notification requirements in the applicable rulebook. For an occasion when the court would not grant an injunction preventing a former employee from disclosing information to an SRO, see *In Re a Company's Application* (*Times Law Reports* 8 February 1989);

(3) a firm may be subject to enquiry on its insolvency;

(4) a firm's regulator will carry out regular and *ad hoc* monitoring visits (see Chapter 12);

(5) one regulatory body may pass information about a firm to another;

(6) a firm's breach of the FSA or of the applicable conduct of business or other rules may be made an issue in court proceedings. For example, it may be claimed that an agreement is unenforceable because the firm was not authorised, or compensation may be sought under s 62 for breach of the conduct of business rules;

(7) a firm's auditors may notify SIB or its SRO of a breach of the FSA or misconduct of which it becomes aware. The FSA contains special provisions relating to this, which are discussed below.

## 2 CRIMINAL OFFENCES

We must begin with two key points: who can commence proceedings, and who is liable? The answers are to be found in ss 201 and 202, discussed below. Jurisdiction and procedure in respect of offences is contained in s 203, and provisions relating to the service of notices (for all purposes of the FSA and not just offences) in s 204.

### 2.1 Institution of proceedings

Section 201 provides that proceedings in respect of any of the FSA's offences other than under s 133 (misleading statements made when marketing non-investment insurance contracts) or s 185 (reciprocity notices relating to banking business—see below) can only be instituted in England and Wales by or with the consent of the Treasury or the Director of Public Prosecutions. The functions of the Treasury under s 201(1) are transferred to SIB in relation to offences in Sched 3 to the Financial Services Act (Delegation) Order 1987 (SI No 942), but are exercisable concurrently with the Treasury and subject to its conditions and restrictions. Section 201 states the following:

201(1) Proceedings in respect of an offence under any provision of this Act other than section 133 or 185 shall not be instituted—

(a) in England and Wales except by or with the consent of the Secretary of State or the Director of Public Prosecutions; or

(b) in Northern Ireland, except by or with the consent of the Secretary of State or the Director of Public Prosecutions for Northern Ireland.

(2) and (3): these sub-sections relate to sections 133 and 185.

(4) The functions to which section 114 above applies shall include the function of the Secretary of State under subsection (1) above to institute proceedings but any transfer of that function shall be

subject to a reservation that it is to be exercisable by him concurrently with the designated agency and so as to be exercisable by the agency subject to such conditions or restrictions as the Treasury may from time to time impose.

This section emphasises two important points. First, the reservation of prosecutions to three specified persons or, with their consent, to third parties is intended to result in a uniform enforcement policy. Secondly, it highlights the value of obtaining written guidance from SIB or the Treasury, although they are reluctant to do this on account of the risk of creating precedents. If either body has produced a written opinion stating that in their view a particular course of action does not contravene a provision of the FSA, then it is most unlikely that they will institute proceedings under that provision without at least giving some warning.

## 2.2  Extended liability

Section 202 provides that an officer or controller of a body corporate (which may be incorporated outside the United Kingdom: s 207(1)) which commits an offence on account of his consent, connivance or neglect is also guilty of the offence. 'Consent' is normally understood to entail actual or presumed knowledge; 'connivance' connotes knowledge or suspicion of the offence coupled with acquiescence; 'neglect' means failure to perform a duty of which you knew or ought to have known. A similar section contained in the Trade Descriptions Act 1968 is analysed in *Tesco v Nattrass* HL [1972] AC 153. Section 202 provides the following:

> 202(1)  Where an offence under this Act committed by a body corporate is proved to have been committed with the consent or connivance of, or to be attributable to any neglect on the part of—
>
> (a)  any director, manager, secretary or other similar officer of the body corporate, or any person who was purporting to act in any such capacity; or
>
> (b)  a controller of the body corporate,
>
> he, as well as the body corporate, shall be guilty of that offence and liable to be proceeded against and punished accordingly.
>
> (2)  Where the affairs of a body corporate are managed by the members subsection (1) above shall apply in relation to the acts and defaults of a member in connection with his functions of management as if he were a director of the body corporate.

Where a partnership is guilty of an offence then all partners other than one who can prove he is ignorant of, or attempted to prevent, the offence are also guilty. Section 202(3) states as follows:

> 202(3)  Where a partnership is guilty of an offence under this Act every partner, other than a partner who is proved to have been ignorant

of or to have attempted to prevent the commission of the offence, shall also be guilty of that offence and be liable to be proceeded against and punished accordingly.

If an unincorporated association other than a partnership is guilty of an offence, then every officer whose breach of duty constituted the offence or, if there is no such officer, then all members of the governing body other than one who can prove he is ignorant of, or attempted to prevent, the offence, are also guilty. This is set out in s 202(4) as follows:

> 202(4) Where an unincorporated association (other than a partnership) is guilty of an offence under this Act—
> (a) every officer of the association who is bound to fulfil any duty of which the breach is the offence; or
> (b) if there is no such officer, every member of the governing body other than a member who is proved to have been ignorant of or to have attempted to prevent the commission of the offence,
> shall also be guilty of the offence and be liable to be proceeded against and punished accordingly.

'Controller' and 'Manager' are defined in s 207(5) and (6) as follows:

> (5) In this Act 'controller' means—
> (a) in relation to a body corporate, a person who, either alone or with any associate or associates, is entitled to exercise, or control the exercise of, 15 per cent or more of the voting power at any general meeting of the body corporate or another body corporate of which it is a subsidiary; and
> (b) in relation to an unincorporated association—
> (i) any person in accordance with whose directions or instructions, either alone or with those of any associate or associates, the officers or members of the governing body of the association are accustomed to act (but disregarding advice given in a professional capacity); and
> (ii) any person who, either alone or with any associate or associates, is entitled to exercise, or control the exercise of, 15 per cent or more of the voting power at any general meeting of the association;
> and for the purposes of this subsection 'associate', in relation to any person, means that person's wife, husband or minor child or step-child, any body corporate of which that person who is a director, any person who is an employee or partner of that person and, if that person is a body corporate, any subsidiary of that body corporate and any employee of any such subsidiary.

(6) In this Act, except in relation to a unit trust scheme or a registered friendly society, 'manager' means an employee who—

    (a) under the immediate authority of his employer is responsible, either alone or jointly with one or more other persons, for the conduct of his employer's business; or

    (b) under the immediate authority of his employer or of a person who is a manager by virtue of paragraph (a) above exercises managerial functions or is responsible for maintaining accounts or other records of his employer;

and, where the employer is not an individual, references in this subsection to the authority of the employer are references to the authority, in the case of a body corporate, of the directors, in the case of a partnership, of the partners and, in the case of an unincorporated association, of its officers or the members of its governing body.

## 2.3 Unauthorised business

Section 4 contains the penalty for contravening the FSA's principal restriction, contained in s 3, which is discussed in Chapter 6. Section 4(1) makes it a criminal offence to carry on (or purport to carry on) investment business in the United Kingdom without being either authorised or exempted. In 1993/94 SIB received over 300 enquiries relating to potential unauthorised investment business, which it detected in 14 per cent of these referrals. It also brought its first prosecution for breach of s 4. Section 4(1) provides the following:

4(1) Any person who carries on, or purports to carry on, investment business in contravention of section 3 above shall be guilty of an offence and liable—

    (a) on conviction on indictment, to imprisonment for a term not exceeding two years or to a fine or to both;

    (b) on summary conviction, to imprisonment for a term not exceeding six months or to a fine not exceeding the statutory maximum or to both.

It is, however, a defence to prove that you took all reasonable precautions and exercised all due diligence to avoid committing the offence. This was the defence successfully relied upon in *Tesco v Nattrass*, which the House of Lords considered was established where the company in question had:

(1) created an efficient system designed to avoid the commission of offences;

(2) allocated supervisory duties to trained employees;

(3) established an effective system of supervision to ensure that the overall system was observed.

This is stated in s 4(2):

> 4(2) In proceedings brought against any person for an offence under this section it shall be a defence for him to prove that he took all reasonable precautions and exercised all due diligence to avoid the commission of the offence.

## 2.4 Misleading statements and market manipulation

Section 47 creates two criminal offences: making misleading statements, and market manipulation. Sub-ss 47(4) and (5) deal with the territorial scope of this section. According to s 47(1) it is an offence:

(1) to make a statement which you know is misleading, false or deceptive;
(2) to dishonestly conceal material facts; or
(3) to make a statement in respect of which you are reckless as to whether it is misleading, false or deceptive

if (in any such case) you do so to induce, or are reckless as to whether you do induce, someone else to enter into (or not to enter into) an investment agreement or exercise rights (or not exercise them) in an investment. This is stated in s 47(1):

> 47(1) Any person who:
> (a) makes a statement, promise or forecast which he knows to be misleading, false or deceptive or dishonestly conceals any material facts; or
> (b) recklessly makes (dishonestly or otherwise) a statement, promise or forecast which is misleading, false or deceptive,
> is guilty of an offence if he makes the statement, promise or forecast or conceals the facts for the purpose of inducing, or is reckless as to whether it may induce, another person (whether or not the person to whom the statement, promise or forecast is made or from whom the facts are concealed) to enter or offer to enter into, or to refrain from entering or offering to enter into, an investment agreement or to exercise, or refrain from exercising, any rights conferred by an investment.

The meaning of 'investment agreement' is discussed in Chapter 13. 'Reckless' here probably means making a statement or promise regardless of whether there are any real facts on which to base it: *R v Grunwald* [1963] 1 QB 935.

It does not matter whether the person to whom the statement is made is the same person as the one who is intended to be induced as a result of the statement.

This subsection is similar to s 13 of the Prevention of Fraud (Investments) Act 1958, although it is wider in that inducements to refrain, as well as inducements to act, are covered.

An example of an activity which would probably be caught would be where someone deliberately makes an exaggeratedly optimistic statement in an offer document in a takeover bid.

There is a special provision for Chinese Walls: nothing done in conformity with rules for the withholding of information made under s 48(2)(h) is a contravention of s 47 (s 48(6)).

Section 133 contains corresponding provisions in relation to marketing insurance contracts which are not investment agreements.

A new criminal offence of market manipulation is created by s 47(2).

> 47(2)   Any person who does any act or engages in any course of conduct which creates a false or misleading impression as to the market in or the price or value of any investments is guilty of an offence if he does so for the purpose of creating that impression and of thereby inducing another person to acquire, dispose of, subscribe for or underwrite those investments or to refrain from doing so or to exercise, or refrain from exercising, any rights conferred by those investments.

There are three elements. You are committing an offence under this sub-s if you:

(1) do an act or engage in a course of conduct which creates a false or misleading impression as to market, price or value of investments. There is no need for any dishonesty or recklessness;
(2) do so to create such an impression; and
(3) have the intention of inducing another person to deal, or not to deal, or exercise rights in (or not exercise rights in) such an investment.

It is a defence to prove that you reasonably believed that your conduct would not create a false or misleading impression (s 47(3)). This is an objective test: what is relevant is what a reasonable person would have believed in those circumstances.

Chinese Walls are saved by s 48(6), and also some stabilising activities by s 48(7) (as amended by the Financial Services Act 1986 (Stabilisation) Order 1988).

This subsection is of considerable concern to practitioners. Examples of conduct which may fall within it include:

(1) a company supports its shares on its own account;
(2) an offeree arranges for a third party to buy shares in it to raise the market price beyond the bidder's resources;
(3) one bidder undersells shares of a rival bidder to depress the latter's market price;
(4) dealing to create an impression of market interest;
(5) buying shares at an inflated price to create the impression of a rising market;

(6) purchasing an offeror's shares to maintain their price;

(7) a bidder makes an announcement of his intention which is not fully candid about his long term intentions;

(8) an offeror says he does not intend to increase his bid when he is aware of circumstances when he may do so;

(9) an offeree announces a bid is inadequate unless it has been properly advised that the bid actually is financially inadequate.

## 2.5 Advertisements

Section 57 restricts the issue and approval of investment advertisements to authorised persons. It makes the following provision:

> 57(1)   Subject to s 58 below, no person other than an authorised person shall issue or cause to be issued an investment advertisement in the United Kingdom unless its contents have been approved by an authorised person.

This is discussed in detail in Chapter 13.

## 2.6 Offerings of securities

Relevant offences are discussed in Chapter 14.

## 2.7 False statements

Section 200 makes it an offence knowingly or recklessly to make a materially false or misleading statement in connection with an application under the FSA, or in purported compliance with any of the FSA's requirements. This includes making false statements to obtain authorisation from an SRO or making false returns to an SRO. Section 200 is as follows:

> 200(1)   A person commits an offence if—
>
> (a)  for the purposes of or in connection with any application under this Act; or
>
> (b)  in purported compliance with any requirement imposed on him by or under this Act,
>
> he furnishes information which he knows to be false or misleading in a material particular or recklessly furnishes information which is false or misleading in a material particular.
>
> (5)   A person guilty of an offence under subsection (1) above shall be liable—
>
> (a)  on conviction on indictment, to imprisonment for a term not exceeding two years or to a fine or to both;

(b) on summary conviction, to imprisonment for a term not exceeding six months or to a fine not exceeding the statutory maximum or to both.

It is also an offence falsely to describe or hold oneself out as being an authorised or exempted person (sub-s (2)) or as having the status of a recognised SRO, RPB, RIE or RCH (sub-s (3)). The notion of 'holding out' is discussed in Chapter 8. An offence could be committed if an individual or business were falsely to describe itself as:

(1) a member of an SRO;
(2) an appointed representative of an authorised person;

or if a body were falsely to describe itself as:

(1) a recognised professional body;
(2) a recognised clearing house.

An unauthorised person might falsely hold itself out as being authorised if, for example, it put the PIA logo on its stationery. Section 200 continues:

200(2) A person commits an offence if, not being an authorised person or exempted person, he—
   (a) describes himself as such a person; or
   (b) so holds himself out as to indicate or be reasonably understood to indicate that he is such a person.

(3) A person commits an offence if, not having a status to which this subsection applies, he—
   (a) describes himself as having that status, or
   (b) so holds himself out as to indicate or be reasonably understood to indicate that he has that status.

(4) Subsection (3) above applies to the status of a recognised self-regulating organisation, recognised professional body, recognised investment exchange or recognised clearing house.

(6) A person guilty of an offence under subsection (2) or (3) above shall be liable on summary conviction to imprisonment for a term not exceeding six months or to a fine not exceeding the fifth level on the standard scale or to both.

An offender is liable to a higher penalty where the offence under subsection (2) or (3) involves public display of an offending description, for example, use of the PIA logo on a shop fascia. This is set out in s 200(7) as follows:

200(7) Where a contravention of subsection (2) or (3) above involves a public display of the offending description or other matter the maximum fine that may be imposed under subsection (6) above shall be an amount equal to the fifth level on the standard scale multiplied by the number of days for which the display has continued.

There is a defence to proceedings brought for contravention of sub-s (2) or (3) of taking all reasonable precautions and exercising all due diligence to avoid committing the offence. It is, however, difficult to envisage circumstances where this defence would be applicable. Section 200(8) provides the following:

> 200(8)  In proceedings brought against any person for an offence under subsection (2) or (3) above it shall be a defence for him to prove that he took all reasonable precautions and exercised all due diligence to avoid the commission of the offence.

A further criminal offence may also be relevant in these circumstances. Section 19 of the Theft Act 1968 makes it an offence for officers of a company or unincorporated association to publish false or misleading statements with the intention of deceiving members or creditors.

# 3  UNENFORCEABLE AGREEMENTS

In addition to the risk of criminal prosecution, a major incentive to complying with the provisions of the FSA is the threat of civil unenforceability of agreements. A firm seeking to enforce its agreements, or collect its debts, may well find that the validity of its agreements is being disputed early in the civil process, and in particular as a defence to an application for summary judgment under RSC Ord 14.

The principal provision dealing with unenforceability is s 5 which is as follows:

> 5(1)  Subject to subsection (3) below, any agreement to which this subsection applies—
>
> (a)  which is entered into by a person in the course of carrying on investment business in contravention of section 3 above; or
>
> (b)  which is entered into—
>
> (i)  by a person who is an authorised person or an exempted person in respect of the investment business in the course of which he enters into the agreement; but
>
> (ii)  in consequence of anything said or done by a person in the course of carrying on investment business in contravention of that section,
>
> shall be unenforceable against the other party; and that party shall be entitled to recover any money or other property paid or transferred by him under the agreement, together with compensation for any loss sustained by him as a result of having parted with it.

This section provides that:

(1) if you enter into an agreement falling within sub-s (7) when you are not authorised or exempted and you should have been; or

(2) if an authorised or exempted person enters into an agreement falling within sub-s (7) in consequence of anything said or done by someone acting in breach of s 3 FSA:

then a number of consequences follow, as discussed below.

Section 5 is only concerned with agreements with, or induced by, persons who are not authorised or exempted. It has no application to agreements entered into or induced by authorised or exempted persons, even if acting outside the scope of their authorisation or exemption.

An agreement to which sub-s (1) applies is defined by sub-s (7) to be one where the person (usually the investment business) which entered into it was by making it, or would be by performing it, carrying on one of the five investment activities (dealing, arranging, managing, advising in relation to regulated investments or operating a collective investment scheme) in circumstances where it cannot rely on the exclusions in Parts III or IV of Sched 1, such as the dealing as principal or overseas person exclusions. Subsection (7) provides:

> (7) Subsection (1) above applies to any agreement the making or performance of which by the person seeking to enforce it or from whom money or other property is recoverable under this section constitutes an activity which falls within any paragraph of Part II of Schedule 1 to this Act and is not excluded by Part III or IV of that Schedule.

It should normally be straightforward to determine the application of s 5 where the person who has entered into the agreement in contravention of s 3 is neither authorised nor exempted. The position will not, however, be so clear where the contracting party is authorised or exempted, but the agreement is entered into *in consequence of* anything said or done by a third party. The FSA offers no guidance, but it is submitted that 'in consequence of' is a reference to the proximate cause of the customer entering into the agreement, and not to any remote or indirect cause (see, for instance, *Hall Brothers S S Co Ltd v Young* [1939] 1 KB 748 CA).

Accordingly, the third party's statement or action must be the principal or primary inducement. An unauthorised insurance broker who arranges for an authorised life assurance company to issue a policy to its client probably does fall within s 5(1)(b); in contrast, a person who subscribes for a share issue on the recommendation of his FSA authorised broker, but who is first alerted to the issue by an unauthorised broker, probably will not.

## 3.1 Unenforceability

The first consequence of falling within s 5 is that the agreement is, subject to the defence in sub-s (3), unenforceable against the other party ('the customer') who is relieved of his obligation to perform. The agreement is not, however, otherwise illegal or invalid as stated in sub-s (6):

(6)   A contravention of s 3 above shall not make an agreement illegal or invalid to any greater extent than is provided in this section.

This is a significant provision because, generally speaking, the courts are not prepared to enforce a contract prohibited by statute at the behest of either party, even though this may operate to prejudice the innocent party. It is relatively easy to apply s 5 to the situation where a single unauthorised or unexempted person deals with a customer, or induces him to deal with an authorised person. However s 5, subject to its defences, extends further. Presumably

(1)   a contract between two authorised persons induced by an unauthorised person will be unenforceable at the suit of either party;

(2)   if both parties to a contract are carrying on investment business in breach of s 5, then that contract is unenforceable at the suit of either party;

(3)   if a number of parties enter into a contract but only one of them infringes s 5, then the infringing party may not enforce its rights, but the arrangements between the others will not otherwise be affected by s 5 by virtue of sub-s (6).

## 3.2   Restitution

The second consequence is that the customer may recover any money or property paid or transferred to the investment business under the agreement. In cases falling within 5(1)(a) this will be from the unauthorised person; in cases falling within 5(1)(b) recovery will usually be from the authorised party rather than the unauthorised inducer.

Subsection (1) enables the customer to receive restitution under the prohibited contract, which is something that courts may be reluctant to allow. It is possible that if third party rights are involved, or the contract has been completed, the customer is more likely to receive compensation pursuant to sub-s (2) rather than restitution. Subsection (5) makes provision for circumstances where property has been transferred to a third party. Subsection (5) is as follows:

(5)   Where any property transferred under an agreement to which this section applies has passed to a third party the references to that property in subsections (1), (3) and (4) above shall be construed as references to its value at the time of its transfer under the agreement.

## 3.3   Compensation

The customer may recover compensation from the investment business for any loss he has sustained on account of parting with his money or property under the agreement. The compensation will be as agreed between the parties or as the court directs on application by either party. This is stated in sub-s (2) as follows:

(2) The compensation recoverable under subsection (1) above shall be such as the parties may agree or as the court may, on the application of either party, determine.

It is submitted that the intention of this subsection is, as a minimum, to restore the position of the customer to that before the contract was entered into, and to prevent the investment business' unjust enrichment. There are as yet no guidelines establishing what compensation may be awarded by the court for loss. However as the payment of compensation is in addition to money paid over, it seems that the compensation to which a customer may be entitled could in principle extend to loss of interest on money paid over and possibly loss of bargain and legal fees.

As the customer is entitled to compensation for 'any loss', and as the object of this section is to protect the customer, it may be that the customer will not have to establish that his loss was reasonably foreseeable.

Compensation should be determined by reference to the period from the date of the transfer to the date of judgment.

## 3.4 Repayment

If the customer chooses not to perform the agreement, or recovers money or property from the investment business, he must repay to the investment business any money or property he has received under the agreement. This is set out in sub-s (4) as follows:

(4) Where a person elects not to perform an agreement which by virtue of this section is unenforceable against him or by virtue of this section recovers money paid or other property transferred by him under an agreement he shall repay any money and return any other property received by him under the agreement.

## 3.5 Defence

The circumstances where the court may allow the agreement to be enforced, or money or other property to be retained, are set out in sub-s (3) as follows:

(3) A court may allow an agreement to which subsection (1) above applies to be enforced or money and property paid or transferred under it to be retained if it is satisfied—

(a) in a case within paragraph (a) of that subsection, that the person mentioned in that paragraph reasonably believed that his entering into the agreement did not constitute a contravention of section 3 above;

(b) in a case within paragraph (b) of that subsection, that the person mentioned in sub-paragraph (i) of that paragraph did not know that the agreement was entered into as mentioned in sub-paragraph (ii) of that paragraph; and

(c) in either case, that it is just and equitable for the agreement to be enforced or, as the case may be, for the money or property paid or transferred under it to be retained.

The first case is where the agreement is made by an unauthorised or unexempted person, and the defence will apply if he reasonably believes that his entering into the investment agreement did not contravene s 3. For the belief to be reasonable he may need to show he took, and observed, legal advice.

The second case is where the agreement is made by an authorised or exempted person but induced by an unauthorised or unexempted person. Here the defence will apply where the authorised or exempted person did not know that the agreement was induced by the unauthorised or unexempted third party. It may be difficult to establish this where the inducer has received any reward or recognition.

In addition, in either case, it must be just and equitable to enforce the agreement or to allow money or property to be retained. This may be the case where the customer was aware that he was dealing with an unauthorised business, or where the business acted in accordance with best market practice even though it was not authorised.

Section 5 does not preclude the customer taking other action where he suffers loss. This could include common law actions for misrepresentation, fraud, breach of contract or negligence, although in these cases the customer may be confronted with the problem of proving that the damage he suffered was not too remote. He may also seek the remedy of restitution.

## 4 CIVIL COMPENSATION

In principle, a person who suffers loss on account of another's breach of an Act of Parliament may have an action in tort in relation to that wrongdoing, but only where the courts consider that Parliament intended a private individual to enjoy this remedy.

In order to avoid this uncertainty, s 62 provides that if someone (here called 'the claimant') suffers loss because an investment business has contravened certain rules, then the claimant may bring an action in tort against the business for compensation for the loss which it has suffered as if it were a claim for breach of statutory duty. Section 62 also overcomes the problem of conduct of business and other rules being unenforceable by third party customers because there is no privity of contract between the claimant and the SRO or RPB.

Since breach of s 62 is expressly provided to be actionable, it is submitted that it is unnecessary to consider the usual prerequisites to an action for breach of statutory duty: the questions of whether the breach is actionable in a civil court, and whether the injury falls within the ambit of the statute. The 'defences and other incidents' applying to actions for breach of statutory duty are, however, expressly applicable and are considered below.

The majority of reported cases on breach of statutory duty relate to industrial injury and, although clear principles are apparent, it is not easy to apply them to cases involving financial loss arising under s 62.

Few claims have been brought in court for breach of s 62 and there are no reported cases on it. This is because the majority of investors with a grievance against a firm will use its complaints procedure to seek recompense. As discussed in Chapter 2, this entails the firm examining the complaint in accordance with rules laid down by its regulator, with the investor having the right to request that the regulator or an independent ombudsman seeks to conciliate or adjudicate the complaint. There is usually no charge for such services.

Section 62 nonetheless remains a cornerstone of the FSA. By establishing civil liability to private investors for rule breaches it provides a major incentive for firms to comply with the rules. Furthermore s 62 is taken as laying down the criterion by which SIB and the SROs will require a firm to pay compensation to an investor who has been disadvantaged by rule breaches. An order to this effect may be the outcome of disciplinary action (see Chapter 12) or of other action initiated by the regulator, such as SIB's Pension Transfer Review in 1994/95.

## 4.1 Breach of which rules?

Section 62 specifies the following:

(1) Without prejudice to section 61 above, a contravention of—
    (a) any rules or regulations made under this Chapter;
    (b) any conditions imposed under section 50 above;
    (c) any requirements imposed by an order under section 58(3) above;
    (d) the duty imposed by section 59(6) above,
    shall be actionable at the suit of a person who suffers loss as a result of the contravention subject to the defences and other incidents applying to actions for breach of statutory duty.

A claimant can only bring a claim under s 62 in respect of the breach of certain rules. They are:

(1) SIB's conduct of business rules (s 48);
(2) cancellation rules (s 51);
(3) notification rules (s 52);
(4) compensation rules (s 54);
(5) client money rules (s 55);
(6) cold calling rules (s 56);
(7) breach of requirements imposed by statutory instruments relating to advertising exemptions made under s 58(3): (62(1)(c));
(8) the duty to take reasonable care not to employ someone disqualified under s 59(6): (62(1)(d)).

Subsection (2) adds the following rules:

(2) Subsection (1) applies also to a contravention by a member of a recognised self-regulating organisation or a person certified by a recognised professional body of any rules of the organisation or body relating to a matter in respect of which rules or regulations have been or could be made under this chapter in relation to an authorised person who is not such a member or so certified.

(9) The corresponding rules of an RPB or an SRO which the SIB could have made, including (on account of s 8(3) and 16(3)) rules on admission, expulsion and constitution.

(10) Rules which an SRO or RPB has given itself the power to enforce even though they have not been made by the SRO or RPB (s 8(3) and 16(3)). To take an example, PIA requires that its members observe the British Code of Advertising Practice so breach of this code is actionable under s 62.

Also actionable under s 62 are:

(11) Contravention of a prohibition or requirement imposed under Chapter VI (discussed below) on directly authorised and certain other persons (s 71(1)).

(12) Contravention of a prohibition or requirement imposed by an SRO or RPB corresponding to those in ss 64–71 (s 71(2)).

(13) Contravention of ss 75–95 (relating to collective investment schemes) and regulations made under them (s 95(1)) and also s 91(4).

(14) Contravention of s 104(1) (power to call for information).

(15) Contravention of s 111(4) (member of SRO or RPB appointing a disqualified auditor).

(16) Contravention of s 154(1) restricting advertisements issued in connection with listing applications (s 154(2)).

(17) Contravention of the sections relating to offers of unlisted securities referred to in s 171(1) (which have never been in force and are now repealed).

(18) Contravention of an order not to deal with an unauthorised person who has refused to cooperate in an insider dealing investigation (s178(5)).

(19) Contravention of a restriction notice issued under reciprocity provisions (s 184(8)).

The financial resource rules are excluded. Subsection 3 stipulates that:

(3) Subsection (1) above does not apply—

(a) to a contravention of rules made under section 49 or conditions imposed under section 50 in connection with an alteration of the requirements of those rules; or

(b) by virtue of subsection (2) above to a contravention of rules relating to a matter in respect of which rules have been or could be made under section 49.

Breach of any of these rules is not a criminal offence, and does not invalidate the transaction. Subsection 4 states that:

> (4) A person shall not be guilty of an offence by reason of any contravention to which subsection (1) above applies or of a contravention of rules made under section 49 above or such conditions as are mentioned in subsection (3)(a) above and no such contravention shall invalidate any transaction.

## 4.2 Against whom can a s 62 claim be brought?

In the main it is only authorised persons against whom a claim under s 62 can be brought. However, any person can be liable under s 62 for contravention of unsolicited calls regulations (s 56) and requirements imposed by exempted advertisement regulations made under s 58(3).

## 4.3 Who can be a s 62 claimant?

Any person who suffers loss and falls within s 62A can be a claimant.

*(a)   Suffers loss*
The clearest example will be the customer of a firm who suffers loss because of its breach of conduct of business or client money rules. However there is no requirement that the claimant was the firm's customer or counterparty. It can also be a third party provided the loss is not so remote from the rule breach that it is no longer 'as a result of' the contravention.

*(b)   The s 62A restriction*
The Financial Services Act 1986 (Restriction of Right of Action) Regulations 1991 (SI No 489) limits the classes of persons who may commence a s 62 action.

The first permitted class is a private investor, who is defined in para (2) to be an investor whose cause of action arises as a result of anything he has done or suffered:

> (1) if an individual, otherwise than in the course of carrying on investment business: in other words, an individual who is not engaging in an investment activity in relation to a regulated investment in the course of carrying on a business. Investment business includes the activities of persons holding permission under para 23 Sched 1, and management activities falling within s 191 FSA (1(2));
>
> (2) if not an individual, otherwise than in the course of carrying on business of any kind. This category would include a partnership or corporation which does not carry on business, such as a charitable corporation. However, a government, local authority or public authority falling within para 3 Note (1) Sched 1 can never be a private investor (2(2)).

There are four further circumstances set out in para (3) in which action may be brought under s 62 at the suit of a person other than a private investor:

(1)  where the contravention is of a kind not mentioned in s 62(1) or (2) of the Act. This would seem to be those circumstances set out at (15) to (18) above as they are neither mentioned in s 62 nor refer to it;

(2)  where a rule or regulation prohibiting a person from seeking to make provision excluding or restricting any duty or liability has been contravened; for example by including a term in a customer agreement purporting to exclude liability under the FSA in contravention of core rule 15 or equivalent;

(3)  where a rule or regulation directed at ensuring that transactions in an investment are not effected with the benefit of unpublished price-sensitive information has been contravened;

(4)  where the action is brought at the suit of a person in a fiduciary or representative capacity, and the beneficiary was at the time of the contravention a private investor who will exclusively benefit from any recovery, and who cannot otherwise bring a s 62 action. An example could be the trustee of a unit trust bringing a s 62 action on behalf of unit holders against the scheme manager.

## 4.4   What must the claimant prove?

It is submitted that the claimant must prove two matters in order to succeed with a claim brought under s 62: first, that a provision falling within s 62 has been breached and, secondly, that he has suffered loss in consequence.

*(a)   Breach of section 62*

Taking what is likely to be the most common example, breach of the applicable conduct of business rules, we consider the following points would be relevant.

The claimant must prove on the balance of probabilities that there has been a breach of one or more of the rules within its own terms and in the context of the applicable rulebook. The claimant does not have to prove that the breach was intentional or negligent. Furthermore, as the claim is treated as one of breach of statutory duty, the defendant probably cannot argue that the breach arose on account of the negligence of agents or subcontractors (*Lockgelly Iron & Coal Co Ltd v McMullan* [1934] AC 1). In particular an authorised person is liable for the acts and omissions of its appointed representatives under s 44(6).

Each rule must be interpreted in the context of the applicable rulebook, and should not be read in isolation. For example, the SRO rulebooks contain a general *force majeure* clause excusing non-performance caused by certain supervening occurrences. If a defendant can rely on such a provision in its own rulebook, then it will not be in breach of these rules.

The rulebooks extend liability under the rules to provide that a firm is liable for its employees, agents and subcontractors acting within the scope of their engagement. An authorised person may therefore be in breach of its rules where it delegates its obligations to a third party manager who then breaches them.

Each rule is drafted differently and must be considered on its facts. For example:

(1) a rule that you *must* give a risk warning is broken if that risk warning is not given;

(2) a rule that one must *take reasonable steps* to know your customer is broken if one fails to take what amounts to objectively reasonable steps;

(3) a rule that one must *use best endeavours* to ensure that one's employees are not interested in a deal will be broken if what a court considers to be best endeavours have not been taken.

*(b)    What loss is recoverable?*

The second matter which the claimant must prove on the balance of probabilities is that it has suffered loss which was caused by the breach.

As in an action for breach of statutory duty, the defendant will only be liable for foreseeable damage arising from the breach (*Galashiels Gas Co Ltd v Millar* [1949] AC 275). The measure of damages will be as in an action in tort, which is to restore the claimant to the position he or she was in before the wrongful act took place.

*(c)    What is the necessary degree of causation?*

It is insufficient merely to show that the breach may have caused the loss. What the claimant must establish is that either:

(1) the breach caused the loss. Proving causation will require the plaintiff to show that, but for the breach in question, the loss would not have occurred. A court will need to consider what would have happened had the defendant observed the regulation falling within s 62; or

(2) the breach materially contributed to the loss. In *Bonnington Castings Ltd v Wardlaw* [1956] AC 613 it was held that the breach of statutory duty need not be the sole or main cause, and that anything too large to come within the 'de-minimis' principle was material. It has been held that this test is fulfilled where the defendant's breach materially increased the risk of the loss occurring (*McGhee v NCB* [1973] 1 WLR 1). However, in the case of a claim under s 62, the material contribution must be of such magnitude that the claimant can establish that he suffered loss as a result of the contravention.

# 4.5    What defences are available?

Liability under s 62 is strict. There is no requirement that the defendant's breach is intentional or negligent, merely that the rule or other provision falling within s 62 is broken on its terms. Furthermore, the cases on breach of statutory duty indicate that the claimant cannot consent to dispensing with the duty to observe the rules, or agree to waive claims for breach of the rules. Any attempt to exclude liability, whether in a client agreement or otherwise, is most unlikely to succeed (*ICI v Shatwell* [1965] AC 656; *Wheeler v New Merton Board Mills Ltd* [1933] 2 KB 669).

The defence of contributory negligence will, however, be available to a defendant in circumstances where it can show that the claimant's own want of care was a cause operating to produce the loss (*Caswell v Powell Duffryn* [1940] AC 152 (obiter)). Where this is the case, the claimant's contributory negligence will operate to reduce his damages to the extent he was contributorily negligent in accordance with the Law Reform (Contributory Negligence) Act 1945.

The defence of limitation will also be applicable. A claim under s 62 must normally be brought within six years after the cause of action accrued (which is usually when the damage is suffered). Where the alleged breach is negligent advice, the cause of action probably accrues when the investor acts on the advice even if loss is suffered only later (see *Forster v Outred & Co* [1982] 1 WLR 86). The Latent Damage Act 1986 may operate to extend the time from which the limitation period runs if the claimant only had the knowledge required to bring the action after the date on which the cause of action accrued.

It is conceivable that there is an additional defence: that the claimant does not come within the category of persons intended to be protected by the FSA. This is the second element that a claimant normally has to prove in order to bring a claim for breach of statutory duty but which is not needed here on account of the express wording of s 62. It is submitted that it is unlikely that this is a defence: as the remedy under s 62 is restricted to designated classes of investors, it is difficult to imagine any such claimant who was not intended by Parliament to have the benefit of this remedy.

## 4.6   Other remedies

Section 62 is not the sole remedy which an investor who suffers loss can bring against an investment business. A customer who suffers loss may also be able to bring a claim for the following:

(1)   For breach of contract, which will most likely be for breach of the implied term that the investment business will use reasonable care and skill. The courts may treat breach of the applicable conduct of business rules as breach of the contractual duty of care, or as evidence of negligence. The court viewed the Institute of Chartered Accountants' Statements of Standard Accounting Practice in this way in *Lloyd Cheyham & Co Ltd v Littlejohn & Co* [1987] BCLC 303 (QBD). Here the court held that the Statements were very strong evidence as to what is a proper standard and that, unless there is some justification, departure from the Statements will be regarded as constituting a breach of the contractual duty of care.

(2) For negligence. However, where the customer only suffers financial loss he may have to show that the loss was reasonably foreseeable and that there is a close and direct relationship between the parties (*Yuen Kun Yeu v Attorney General of Hong Kong* [1987] CLY 2580).
(3) For breach of fiduciary duty, for instance where the business fails to disclose and obtain consent to a conflict of interest.
(4) For misrepresentation.

## 4.7 Limiting liability

There are two restrictions that may be relevant to firms seeking to limit or exclude liability for breach of the FSA, for contract or for negligence:

(1) Core rule 15(1), which has been adopted by SFA and IMRO, prohibits the exclusion or restriction of any duty of liability owed to a customer under the regulatory system. A firm may also not unreasonably rely on an exclusion clause (15(3)). These rules apply to all customers, while core rule 15(2), which applies to private customers, prohibits a firm from unreasonably excluding or restricting its duty to act with care and skill. Breach of core rule 15 is actionable by any investor (Financial Services Act 1986 (Restriction of Right of Action) Regulations 1991 (SI No 489) para 3(b)).
(2) The Unfair Contract Terms Act 1977 either prohibits or subjects to a reasonableness test clauses in standard form contracts and in contracts with consumers. Schedule 1 to the Act provides that it has no application to contracts of insurance nor a contract so far as it relates to the creation or transfer of securities or any right or interest in securities. The Law Commission (Consultation Paper 124 — Fiduciary Duties and Regulatory Rules) considers that this does not prevent the Act applying to contracts for the giving of investment advice or for fund management (para 3.3.25) and cites *Micklefield v SAC Technology* [1991] 1 All ER 275 in support. It is therefore possible that the Act is relevant to a number of contracts for the provisions of activities regulated by the FSA.

## 5  SIB's POWERS OF INTERVENTION

SIB is empowered by the FSA to exercise certain powers against all persons, or all authorised persons. Reference should be made to Delegation and Transfer of Function Orders to determine whether these powers are exercisable by SIB concurrently with the Treasury or the DTI. In the Large Report (1993) the Chairman of SIB stated that it would exercise its statutory powers more frequently and it is clear that SIB is now doing so.

## 5.1 Injunction to halt an unauthorised investment business

The court may grant an injunction if it is satisfied, on application by SIB, that there is a reasonable likelihood that someone will contravene s 3, or has contravened that section and it is reasonably likely that contravention will continue or be repeated (s 6(1)). In 1993/94 SIB brought proceedings for seven injunctions to halt unauthorised investment business, and an individual was jailed for contempt of court for breaching an injunction to restrain unauthorised investment business.

> 6(1) If, on the application of the Secretary of State, the court is satisfied—
> (a) that there is a reasonable likelihood that a person will contravene section 3 above; or
> (b) that any person has contravened that section and that there is a reasonable likelihood that the contravention will continue or be repeated,
> the court may grant an injunction restraining the contravention or, in Scotland, an interdict prohibiting the contravention.

SIB's first application for an injunction under s 6 was *SIB v Pantell SA and another* [1989] 3 WLR 698. A Mareva injunction was granted, freezing the United Kingdom assets of a Swiss company, Pantell, and its English associate, on the grounds that they were carrying on investment business in the United Kingdom without being authorised or exempted.

## 5.2 Injunction to halt rule breaches

The court may, under s 61, grant an injunction if it is satisfied, on application by SIB or any other person (s 61(9)), that:

(1) there is reasonable likelihood someone will contravene the following provisions; or
(2) someone has contravened, and there is a reasonable likelihood that contravention will continue or be repeated in relation to, any of the following provisions; or
(3) someone has contravened and there are steps that could be taken to remedy the contravention of any of the following provisions.

The provisions are as follows:

(1) SIB rules and regulations made under Chapter V;
(2) section 47 (misleading statements and practices);
(3) section 56 (cold calling);
(4) section 57 (advertisements);
(5) section 59 (employment of prohibited persons);
(6) section 58(3) (requirements of the advertisement exemption orders);
(7) rules of an SRO, RPB, RIE or RCH in respect of a person whose investment business the body regulates where the body is itself unable or unwilling to take steps (s 61(2));

(8)  other sections under the FSA 1986 which refer to s 61.

As well as issuing an injunction, a court may order a person in contravention and anyone knowingly concerned in contravention to take steps to remedy it (s 61(1)).

61(1)   If on the application of the Secretary of State the court is satisfied—

(a)  that there is a reasonable likelihood that any person will contravene any provision of—

(i)   rules or regulations made under this Chapter;

(ii)  sections 47, 56, 57, or 59 above;

(iii) any requirements imposed by an order under section 58(3) above;

or

(iv) the rules of a recognised self-regulating organisation, recognised professional body, recognised investment exchange or recognised clearing house to which that person is subject and which regulate the carrying on by him of investment business,

or any condition imposed under section 50 above;

(b)  that any person has contravened any such provision or condition and that there is a reasonable likelihood that the contravention will continue or be repeated; or

(c)  that any person has contravened any such provision or condition and that there are steps that could be taken for remedying the contravention,

the court may grant an injunction restraining the contravention or, in Scotland, an interdict prohibiting the contravention or, as the case may be, make an order requiring that person and any other person who appears to the court to have been knowingly concerned in the contravention to take such steps as the court may direct to remedy it.

This power was exercised in *SIB v Vandersteen Associates* [1991] BCLC 206. SIB may not be required to give cross-undertaking in damages (see *SIB v Lloyd Wright* [1993] 4 All ER 210).

## 5.3   Restitution orders

There are two separate restitution powers: under s 6, where restitution can be ordered against someone carrying on investment business in the United Kingdom without being authorised or exempted; and under s 61, where restitution can be ordered against someone who has breached conduct of business and certain other rules.

Section 6(2) provides that if a court is satisfied on application of SIB that s 3 has been contravened, it may order a person who has entered into a transaction in contravention, and anyone else knowingly concerned in the contravention, to take steps to restore the parties to the position they were in before the transaction.

6(2)   If, on the application of the Secretary of State, the court is satisfied that a person has entered into any transaction in contravention of section 3 above the court may order that person and any other person who appears to the court to have been knowingly concerned in the contravention to take such steps as the court may direct for restoring the parties to the position in which they were before the transaction was entered into.

The scope of ss 6(2) and 61(1), and circumstances where a person could be said to be knowingly concerned in the contravention, were reviewed in *SIB v Pantell* (No 2) [1992] 3 WLR 896, CA.

The court may also order someone who has carried on business in England and Wales in breach of s 3, where *either* the person has obtained profits as a result of carrying on that business *or* investors have suffered loss or been adversely affected by contravention of s 47 (misleading statements), s 56 (cold calling) or failure to act substantially in accordance with the rules made by SIB under Chapter V, to pay over the resulting profits to the court or court appointed receiver, or compensation for the resulting loss, as the case may be (s 6(3)).

6(3)   The court may, on the application of the Secretary of State, make an order under subsection (4) below or, in relation to Scotland, under subsection (5) below if satisfied that a person has been carrying on investment business in contravention of section 3 above and—
    (a)   that profits have accrued to that person as a result of carrying on that business; or
    (b)   that one or more investors have suffered loss or been otherwise adversely affected as a result of his contravention of section 47 or 56 below or failure to act substantially in accordance with any of the rules or regulations made under Chapter V of this Part of this Act.

The procedure for enforcing s 6(3) is contained in s 6(4) for England and Wales and s 6(5) for Scotland.

6(4)   The court may under this subsection order the person concerned to pay into court, or appoint a receiver to recover from him, such sum as appears to the court to be just having regard—
    (a)   in a case within paragraph (a) of subsection (3) above, to the profits appearing to the court to have accrued;
    (b)   in a case within paragraph (b) of that subsection, to the extent of the loss or other adverse effect; or
    (c)   in a case within both paragraphs (a) and (b) of that subsection, to the profits and to the extent of the loss or other adverse effect.
  (5)   The court may under this subsection order the person concerned to pay to the applicant such sum as appears to the court to be just having regard to the considerations mentioned in paragraphs (a) to (c) of subsection (4) above.

A court may call for accounts and information (s 6(7)).

> 6(7) On an application under subsection (3) above the court may require the person concerned to furnish it with such accounts or other information as it may require for establishing whether any and, if so, what profits have accrued to him as mentioned in paragraph (a) of that subsection and for determining how any amounts are to be paid or distributed under subsection (6) above; and the court may require any such accounts or other information to be verified in such manner as it may direct.

Money recovered under s 6(4) or (5) from the person who contravened s 3 shall be paid as the court directs to persons who have entered into the transactions which led to the profit or caused the loss or other adverse effect.

Similar provisions are contained in s 61 to provide for restitution where profits are made, or an investor suffers loss, because the rules referred to in that section (as enumerated above) have been breached.

## 5.4 Prohibiting employment

SIB is empowered by s 59(1) to direct that an individual may not be employed, which is intended to include being engaged as an independent contractor (s 59(8)).

> 59(1) If it appears to the Secretary of State that any individual is not a fit and proper person to be employed in connection with investment business or investment business of a particular kind he may direct that he shall not, without the written consent of the Secretary of State, be employed in connection with investment business or, as the case may be, investment business of that kind—
>
> (a) by authorised persons or exempted persons; or
>
> (b) by any specified person or persons, or by persons of any specified description, falling within paragraph (a) above.
>
> (2) A direction under this section ('a disqualification direction') shall specify the date on which it is to take effect and a copy of it shall be served on the person to whom it relates.

SIB may make such disqualification direction where it appears that such person is not fit and proper to be employed in connection with investment business generally, or investment business of a particular kind, and either by certain authorised or exempted persons, or by authorised or exempted persons generally. This power was first exercised in 1993/94 and SIB has now used it on some ten occasions. SIB's stated purpose is to disqualify persons where there are serious fitness issues which are not already being appropriately addressed.

If someone is subject to a disqualification direction then he or she may not take part in the disqualified work without SIB's written consent.

It is a criminal offence for a disqualified individual to accept or continue in the prohibited employment or self-employment (s 59(5)). Authorised persons and appointed representatives are obliged to take reasonable care to observe any disqualification direction (s 59(6)).

The individual threatened with a disqualification direction or who is refused consent to take employment, or an application for variation of the direction under it, may refer the case to the Financial Services Tribunal (s 59(4)).

## 5.5 Power of entry

A Justice of the Peace may grant a warrant under s 199, which confers the powers mentioned below, if satisfied there are reasonable grounds to believe that an offence has been committed under certain sections of the FSA 1986, or other legislation, and relevant documents are on the premises.

The offences are under:

(1) section 4 (carrying on investment business without authorisation or exemption);
(2) section 47 (misleading statements or practices);
(3) section 57 (advertisements);
(4) section 130 (promotion of insurance contracts);
(5) section 133 (misleading statements in relation to non-investment business insurance contracts);
(6) sections 1, 2, 4 and 5 of the Company Securities (Insider Dealing) Act.

A warrant can also be granted under specified conditions in connection with investigations under s 94 (investigation of manager, trustee or operator of a collective investment scheme), s106 (general investigations), or s177 (investigations into insider dealing).

A warrant issued under s 199 empowers a police officer and other named persons to enter and search specified premises with necessary force, to remove and copy documents (including information recorded in any form) and to require persons named in the warrant to assist in explaining or finding the documents.

## 5.6 Powers of investigation

SIB may exercise wide-ranging powers of investigation granted under s 105, in relation to any person (except some exempted persons and members of an SRO or RPB other than at that body's request or unless it appears unable or unwilling satisfactorily to investigate its member: s 105(2)) who is, or was, or appears to have been, carrying on investment business, and where there is good reason for investigation. SIB has exercised s 105 powers on some 20 occasions each year.

105(1) The powers of the Secretary of State under this section shall be exercisable in any case in which it appears to him that there is good reason to do so for the purpose of investigating the affairs, or any aspect of the affairs, of any person so far as relevant to any investment business which he is or was carrying on or appears to the Secretary of State to be or to have been carrying on.

(2) Those powers shall not be exercisable for the purpose of investigating the affairs of any exempted person unless he is an appointed representative or the investigation is in respect of investment business in respect of which he is not an exempted person and shall not be exercisable for the purpose of investigating the affairs of a member of a recognised self-regulating organisation or a person certified by a recognised professional body in respect of investment business in the carrying on of which he is subject to its rules unless—

    (a) that organisation or body has requested the Secretary of State to investigate those affairs; or

    (b) it appears to him that the organisation or body is unable or unwilling to investigate them in a satisfactory manner.

It was held in *R v Secretary of State for Trade and Industry, ex parte Ritblat* (*The Independent*, 29 November 1988) that s 105 did not empower the DTI to demand the disclosure of documents relating to transactions which took place before 18 December 1986, the date the section came into force.

The person under investigation can be required to answer questions and provide information (s 105(3)). This also applies to the 'connected persons' of the person under investigation, who are defined by s 105(9) to include that person's partners, employees, bankers, auditors and solicitors; and where the person under investigation is a company, its officers and controllers, and those of related companies (again, as defined).

The person under investigation and any other person can be required to produce documents, which include records in any form (s 105(4)).

The powers of entry granted under s 199 of the FSA are exercisable in conjunction with these investigations.

It is a criminal offence to fail to comply with any requirement imposed by this section without reasonable excuse (s 105(10)).

There is an exception to these requirements which is that a person is not required to disclose information or produce a document where he could refuse on grounds of legal professional privilege, save that a lawyer can be obliged to provide a client's name and address (s 105(6)).

## 5.7 Auditors

The FSA attaches particular importance to the role of authorised persons' auditors.

### (a) Appointed auditors

SIB is empowered to make rules requiring persons authorised by it under s 25 or under s 31 (certain European persons), as well as members of SROs, to appoint an auditor with prescribed qualifications if not already required to do so (s 107(1)).

SIB has implemented the section, in relation to those firms for whose prudential regulation it is responsible, by the Financial Supervision Rules 1990. These rules do not apply to members of an SRO save as expressly designated (s 107A(1) and (4)).

Each SRO has financial rules which are principally applicable to persons for whose prudential regulation it is responsible. They will normally require a firm to appoint an auditor with prescribed qualifications and which is acceptable to the regulator. The auditor will be required to enter into an engagement letter in set form, and is placed under a duty to report directly to the regulator. The financial resources rules are discussed in greater detail in Chapter 3.

*(b)   Requiring a second audit*
SIB may require a person authorised under s 25 or 31 to submit to a second audit in relation to its accounts or information provided under s 52 (notification) or s 104 (provision of information) which has been reported or verified by the firm's auditor (s 108).

*(c)   Notifying the regulator: the auditor's right*
In principle an auditor owes its client a duty of confidentiality which would be breached by unauthorised disclosure of confidential information to any third party. This is subject to two exceptions:

(1)  *where there is a duty to the public to disclose.* For example where there is some danger to the state, or where the information subject to the duty of confidentiality relates to wrongdoing. A bank's auditors was able to rely on this exception when disclosing information about its client to an official enquiry into banking supervision (*Price Waterhouse v BCCI* [1992] BCLC 583).

(2)  *where disclosure is made under compulsion of law.* In *Parry-Jones v Law Society* [1968] 2 WLR 397 the court held that a solicitor was obliged to provide client files to the Law Society acting under its statutory powers of investigation pursuant to the Solicitors Act.

Nevertheless it was thought necessary for the FSA to empower auditors to make disclosure when appropriate to the regulators. Section 109 therefore provides that an auditor does not breach its duty to an authorised person if:

(1)  it communicates in good faith;
(2)  in response to a request or on its own initiative;
(3)  any information or opinion of a matter of which it became aware as that person's auditor;
(4)  to that person's regulator, and which is relevant to its functions as regulator.

109(1)   No duty to which an auditor of an authorised person may be subject shall be regarded as contravened by reason of his communicating in good faith to the Secretary of State, whether or not in response to a request from him, any information or opinion on a matter of which the auditor has become aware in his capacity as auditor of that person and which is relevant to any functions of the Secretary of State under this Act.

109(5)   This section applies to:

(a) the communication by an auditor to a recognised self-regulating organisation or recognised professional body of matters relevant to its function of determining whether a person is a fit and proper person to carry on investment business; and

(b) the communication to such an organisation or body or any other authority or person of matters relevant to its or his function of determining whether a person is complying with the rules applicable to his conduct of investment business,

as it applies to the communication to the Secretary of State of matters relevant to his functions under this Act.

The auditing bodies have issued guidance to assist their members to identify circumstances where disclosure under section 109 is appropriate, and reference should be made to Statement of Auditing Standards 620 and Practice Note 5 which explain the circumstances when auditors have a right to disclose to the regulator, and also when they are under a duty to do so, as discussed in (d) below.

*(d)   Notifying the regulator: the auditor's duty*

While s 109(1) gives auditors the right to make notification to the regulators, it does not require them to do so. This is a function of s 109(2) which enables the Treasury (the power is not transferred to SIB) to make rules requiring an auditor to communicate to the regulators. This power is exercisable where it appears to the Treasury that an auditor, or class of auditors, is not subject to satisfactory professional rules in relation to such disclosure.

Regulations under this section were brought into force on 1 May 1994. Auditors of banks, building societies and friendly societies have also been placed under corresponding obligations. Guidance on discharge of this duty is contained in Statement of Auditing Standards 620 and Practice Note 5.

The Auditors (Financial Services Act 1986) Rules 1994 (SI No 526) provide that an auditor must communicate a matter to which s 109 applies to a person's regulator where it believes the matter is likely to be materially significant in relation to determining whether:

(1) the person is fit and proper to carry on investment business (the issues which are relevant to this are discussed in Chapter 2); or

(2) in order to protect investors from significant risk of loss, disciplinary action should be taken or powers of intervention exercised (powers of intervention, discussed in Chapter 12 include prohibiting or restricting a

firm from carrying on investment business and can clearly be exercised to protect investors. Powers of discipline, however, are usually not exercised to protect investors but, rather, to punish transgressors and it is not easy to understand what is intended by inclusion of the reference to discipline).

*(e)   Criminal offence*
It is a criminal offence for an authorised person or any of its officers, controllers or managers knowingly or recklessly to give materially false or misleading information to an auditor appointed under s 107 or 108 and which it requires or is entitled to require (s 111(1)).

## 5.8   Reciprocity

The Treasury, and in certain cases the Secretary of State for Trade and Industry, can take action where the law or practices of any overseas country, or action or practices of any overseas body, prevent persons connected with the United Kingdom (as defined) from carrying on investment, insurance or banking business in that country on terms as favourable as persons connected with that country can carry on such business in the United Kingdom.

In appropriate cases, cessation or restriction of such business in the United Kingdom can be ordered. The detailed provisions are contained in ss 183–186.

This is a reserve power and is not related to the concept of reciprocity contained in the Investment Services Directive.

## 5.9   Insolvency proceedings

The DTI or SIB may petition the court under s 72 to wind up any authorised person or appointed representative on the grounds that it cannot pay its debts, or that it is just and equitable to do so. This power relates to specified companies and partnerships which are authorised persons or appointed representatives, but the DTI or SIB may only present a petition to wind up someone authorised by an SRO or RPB with that body's consent. Section 73 concerns proceedings relevant to Northern Ireland. In 1993/94 SIB commenced proceedings for two compulsory winding-up petitions.

In the case of *In re Walter L Jacob and Co Ltd (Times Law Report* 29 December 1988) it was held to be just and equitable to wind up a company formerly dealing in securities where it would have been just and equitable if it were still dealing.

A petition for an administration order under s 9 of the Insolvency Act 1986 may be presented in relation to a company which is an authorised person or appointed representative by the SRO or RPB which confers authorisation or, as appropriate, by SIB (s 74).

# 6 POWERS GENERALLY RELATING TO ONLY PERSONS REGULATED OR AUTHORISED BY SIB

The following powers are, except where noted, exercisable only in relation to persons directly authorised or regulated by SIB.

These powers correspond to the powers exercisable by the individual SROs and set out in their rulebooks.

## 6.1 Withdrawal and suspension of authorisation

SIB may suspend or withdraw any authorisation which it has granted if it appears that:

(1) the authorised person is not a fit and proper person in respect of the investment business which it is carrying on or is proposing to carry on; or

(2) it has contravened the FSA or any rules of SIB, an SRO or RPB as applicable, or has given SIB any false or misleading information (s 28).

SIB must first give notice under s 29, and the authorised person can require the case to be referred to the Financial Services Tribunal.

## 6.2 Powers of intervention

*(a) Exercisable against whom?*
The powers of intervention contained in ss 64–71 can be exercised by SIB against certain authorised persons and (excepting the power to restrict business contained in s 65) their appointed representatives. The powers cannot, however, be exercised against persons authorised by an SRO or RPB or their appointed representatives. The SROs or RPBs may request SIB to exercise the vesting power referred to in s 67(1) in respect of such persons (s 64(4)).

*(b) Circumstances of exercise*
SIB may exercise these powers where it appears that either:

(1) it is desirable for the protection of investors; or

(2) the authorised person is not fit; or

(3) the authorised person has contravened the FSA, any rule, regulation, prohibition or requirement made under it, or has furnished SIB with false, inaccurate or misleading information (s 64(1)).

*(c) Restriction of business*
An authorised person subject to these sections can be prohibited from entering into certain transactions, from soliciting business or from carrying on business in a certain way. This does not apply to its appointed representatives (s 65).

*(d)   Restriction on dealing with own assets*

An authorised person subject to these sections, and its appointed representatives, can be prohibited from disposing or dealing with its assets in or outside the United Kingdom other than as permitted.

This restriction only relates to the authorised person's assets, and does not cover investors' funds (s 66).

*(e)   Vesting own and client assets in a trustee*

Where an authorised person or its appointed representative is subject to these sections, SIB may order its assets or those of investors which it holds (or are held to its order), to be transferred to a specified trustee (s 67). This may include assets outside the United Kingdom and this provision can be applied to members of an SRO or RPB at that body's request. Equitable remedies may be available in relation to assets which are subject to a trust imposed under this section (s 71(3)).

*(f)   Maintenance of assets in the United Kingdom*

An authorised person or its appointed representative subject to these sections may be required to maintain specified assets in the United Kingdom to enable it to meet its liabilities (s 69).

SIB may rescind or vary any of these prohibitions or requirements (s 69).

A person who is the subject of an order made under these sections may refer the case to the Financial Services Tribunal (s 97).

If a person contravenes a prohibition or requirement imposed under ss 65–70, then action can be taken against that person pursuant to s 71 under s 60 (public statement), s 61 (injunction and restitution) and they are liable to claims under s 62 (civil action for damages). Section 62 will also apply when someone authorised by an SRO or RPB contravenes any prohibition or requirement which that body has made and which corresponds to the prohibitions or requirements contained in ss 65–70 (s 71(2)).

## 6.3   Calling for information

SIB is empowered by s 104 to do the following:

(1)   call on someone authorised under s 22 (authorised insurers), s 24 (operators and trustees of EU-recognised collective investment schemes), s 25 (authorised by SIB) or s 31 (authorised in another member state); and

(2)   call on an SRO, RPB, RIE or RCH;

to provide information which it reasonably requires to perform its functions.

The provisions of ss 60, 61 and 62 apply for contraventions relating to the first category of persons.

## 6.4 Public statement

SIB may make a public statement pursuant to s 60 where it appears that any person who is or was authorised under s 22, 24 25 or 31 has contravened any rules made under Chapter V (or any condition imposed under s 50), the cold calling regulations (s 56) or has employed a prohibited person (s 59), or has contravened other sections of the FSA which refer to s 60. SIB made a s 60 statement for the first time in 1994 in relation to a building society that it regulated.

The person about whom a statement is made must be notified in advance and may refer the case to the Financial Services Tribunal.

## 6.5 Financial Services Tribunal

The Tribunal is constituted by s 96 and comprises suitably qualified persons nominated by the Treasury, and legally qualified persons nominated by the Lord Chancellor.

The procedure which governs the Tribunal is contained in the Financial Services Tribunal (Conduct of Investigations) Rules 1988 (SI No 351). The Tribunal comprises, in any case, three members of whom the Chairman has legal qualifications, and it has the power to require any person to attend before it, give evidence and produce documents (Sched 6 para 5).

Unlike SRO disciplinary tribunals, before which the SRO will normally commence proceedings, the Tribunal is a reactive body: it only has jurisdiction after a person requests that a matter be referred to it. A further point of distinction is that, unlike SRO tribunals, it does not decide a case solely on the basis of the regulator's evidence and the member's response. Instead it will generally investigate a case 'by carrying out such enquiries as it thinks appropriate' (rule 6 of the Conduct of Investigation Rules). It then reports to the Treasury on what would in its opinion be the appropriate decision in the matter, and it is then the Treasury's duty to decide the matter forthwith in accordance with the Tribunal's report (s 98).

Those persons who can request that a matter be referred to the Tribunal are (in summary) those who have been served a notice under:

(1) Section 29: SIB proposing to refuse, withdraw or suspend authorisation in relation to persons whom it authorises.
(2) Section 34: SIB proposing to suspend or terminate a Europerson authorised under s 31.
(3) Section 59(4): SIB intending to disqualify a person from employment.
(4) Section 60(2): SIB intending to make a public statement about misconduct of a person it has authorised or whom it regulates.
(5) Section 70: SIB's exercise of powers of intervention.

These are notices that will take effect if not so referred to the Tribunal; after referral SIB can withdraw a notice but, if it does not, the Tribunal will proceed to hear the case.

The detailed procedure for making references to the Tribunal is set out in ss 97–100.

The Tribunal has met very infrequently on account of its narrow jurisdiction and the small (and diminishing) number of persons subject to SIB's direct regulation or authorisation. However its workload may increase in consequence of SIB's intention to make more s 59 disqualifications.

# 12 Monitoring, Enforcement and Discipline

In this chapter we discuss the methods by which SIB and the SROs seek to ensure that persons whom they regulate are observing the applicable rules, and what action can be taken against them if they are not.

In summary SIB and the SROs:

(1) Monitor persons they regulate by carrying out regular inspection visits, and examining periodic returns made by the firms.
(2) Carry out an *ad hoc* investigation of a firm if there appears to be misconduct.
(3) Intervene in a firm's business if this is considered necessary to protect investors.
(4) Take disciplinary action against a firm in appropriate circumstances.

These powers are exercisable:

- by SIB, in relation to firms it regulates;
- by an SRO in relation to its members;
- by an SRO in relation not only to firms, but also to persons individually registered with it in accordance with the terms of that registration.

The enforcement and disciplinary powers of the SROs are set out in their respective rulebooks and SIB's powers are different from those of the SROs. The disciplinary action SIB can take against a person whom it authorises under s 25 FSA (and against some other persons) is set out in s 60, and is to make a public statement as to that person's misconduct. SIB's powers of intervention are contained in ss 64–71 and these, together with SIB's other powers, are discussed in Chapter 11. The criminal offences created by the FSA and the civil remedies available to investors under the FSA are also discussed in Chapter 11.

In this chapter we concentrate upon the monitoring, enforcement and disciplinary powers of SFA, IMRO and PIA. LAUTRO and FIMBRA are unlikely to carry out significant further monitoring, enforcement or disciplinary action as their membership is being transferred to PIA. SIB is likewise seeking to transfer those persons whom it regulates to an SRO.

## 1  MONITORING

Monitoring is akin to auditing, and is the name given to the process by which a regulator seeks to ensure that the firms which it regulates, and any persons individually registered with it, are observing the applicable rules. The SROs perform monitoring functions not only to determine whether member firms are complying with the rules, but also to keep abreast of wider investor protection issues, whether these are products in the market or practices which could put investors at risk.

## 1.1 Standards of compliance

When carrying out monitoring the regulator will be checking standards of compliance, and the areas of business examined will depend upon the type of firm and its business.

(1) Where the regulator is responsible for the prudential regulation of a firm it will seek to monitor that firm's continuing fulfilment of the criteria relevant to it being a 'fit and proper' person. This will include examining the firm's financial resources and reviewing whether the firm's controller, directors and senior managers remain fit and proper persons.

An SRO (or SIB) is responsible for a firm's prudential regulation unless (in outline) it is a bank, building society, friendly society or insurance company, is a European institution or it is lead-regulated by an overseas regulator.

(2) In all cases a regulator will wish to examine the firm's adherence to the conduct of business rules. In the case of a fund manager this may include looking at:

- customer documentation;
- suitability of advice given;
- issue of periodic statements;
- quality of investment management.

With a stockbroker it may include examination of:

- segregation of client funds;
- aggregation of orders;
- suitability of advice for discretionary customers;
- achieving best execution.

With a seller of packaged products (whether a product company or an independent financial adviser) it may include looking at:

- recruitment of salesforce;
- observation of polarisation;
- handling complaints;
- quality of advice.

(3) In addition the regulator will examine the firm's compliance function, including consideration of whether:

- the compliance officer has sufficient status and authority and possesses sufficient expertise;
- the compliance officer performs routine monitoring satisfactorily and compliance reports are effectively followed up;
- head office departments, branches and appointed representatives are regularly inspected, reported upon and the reports followed up;
- proper records are kept demonstrating the performance of compliance tasks;
- the firm is generally observing the Principles, especially Principle 9 ie the obligation to have an effective compliance function.

## 1.2 Methods of monitoring

There are a number of means by which a regulator will monitor a firm.

(1) By monitoring information received from a firm. Firms are required in their rulebooks to notify certain transactions in investments and certain events to their regulator, such as changes in senior personnel and designated material events. In addition, they must review their business each year and report certain findings to the regulator. Furthermore SIB Principle 10, applicable to all firms, requires a firm to keep its regulator promptly informed of all matters which it could reasonably be expected to disclose. The regulator will study all this information and, if it indicates material compliance problems, may decide to undertake further enquiries, or even a formal investigation. In other cases the regulator may note that certain matters should be examined on the next formal inspection visit.

(2) By monitoring information received from investors and from other sources. A number of complaints are made directly to a firm's regulator by its customers or competitors. For instance an investor may complain about the conduct of a firm's salesperson or the quality of its service; a competitor may complain about the contents of a firm's advertisements. Information may also be passed to a regulator by an exchange on which a firm deals, or by another agency such as the Serious Fraud Office or the Department of Trade and Industry. As with information received from the firm, the regulator reviews this information and will decide what action is appropriate.

(3) By carrying out periodical inspection visits. These are routine visits which are intended to be in depth audits of the firm's compliance standards and observance of the regulatory regime. Inspections are carried out by employees of the regulator together with externally seconded staff, often accountants.

(a) *Method*: The depth and duration of an inspection will depend on the circumstances of the firm being inspected. An inspection of a large life assurance company may entail a team of eight inspectors carrying out a detailed examination of sales and recruitment records at head office and a number of branches over four or more weeks. An inspection of a futures broker may involve a team of two inspectors reviewing dealing procedures and interviewing dealers for two days.

(b) *Right of inspection*: The powers of inspection are contained in the SRO rulebooks and generally provide that a firm must allow an inspector to enter its and its appointed representative's premises with or without notice; to inspect records and other materials; and to interview staff. A firm must fully co-operate with the inspectors, and its officers and staff must fully and promptly answer all questions.

(c) *Frequency of visits*: The frequency and extent of inspection visits will depend on the regulator's assessment of the firm's potential risk. The approach of PIA, IMRO and SFA is summarised below. FIMBRA and LAUTRO are unlikely to carry out many more inspection visits as their membership is being transferred to PIA, and SIB is likewise seeking to encourage persons it regulates to join an SRO.

    (i) PIA has stated ('Approach to Regulation' March 1994) that its members will be categorised in accordance with PIA's assessment of their business risk (which includes the nature of their products, size of their network and whether they handle client money) and their operating risk (which includes complexity of operation, adequacy of controls and quality of management). Using these criteria firms will be categorised as high risk (not more than 12 months between routine inspection visits); medium risk (not more than 24 months between visits) and low risk (not more than 30 months between visits). Members will generally receive four weeks notice of visits although PIA intends that 5 per cent of members each year will receive unannounced visits to ensure they remain alert.

    (ii) IMRO has announced its intention to move away from the previous policy of conducting an extensive visit every two years (IMRO Regulatory Plan 1994/5). Instead it intends to target monitoring visits in accordance with its assessment of risk to investors. It will make greater use of shorter targeted visits and unannounced visits.

    (iii) SFA also intends to carry out a more focussed programme of monitoring (SFA Report for 1993/4 and Regulatory Plan for 1994/5). SFA will identify and target firms where it perceives the greatest regulatory risk arises, while the depth and frequency of inspection visits will depend upon a firm's risk profile.

## 1.3 Result of inspection visit

In most cases the report of the inspection visit is likely to state that a number of rule breaches have been observed. It is inevitable that a firm will not be in full compliance with all of the rules all of the time, and few compliance systems are incapable of being improved. The inspection report is likely to call upon the firm to take appropriate remedial action within a specified time. The regulator may then carry out a further inspection visit perhaps one to three months later in order to confirm that remedial action has been taken.

Where the inspection report discloses serious shortcomings and more remedial action is required than merely to bring an adequate compliance system fully up to standard, the regulator may do one or more of the following:

(a)  make a formal request for the member to take remedial action;
(b)  commence an investigation;
(c)  take intervention action;
(d)  commence disciplinary action.

## 1.4  Requesting remedial action

A regulator may request that a firm takes remedial action, perhaps after an inspection (or an investigation — see section 2 below) has revealed significant deficiencies. Examples of requests which have recently been made include:

(1)  No recruitment of salesforce until references of existing salespersons have been checked, and effective reference checking procedures introduced.
(2)  No issuing of advertisements until effective advertising vetting procedures are in place.
(3)  To check substantial quantity of sales records to see if best advice was given, and to contact any investor adversely affected.
(4)  To re-reference appointed representative network.
(5)  To contact clients to clarify nature of investments sold or services provided.
(6)  To suspend business until capital restructured to ensure financial resource requirements are met.
(7)  To cease trading in certain categories of investment until adequate back office facilities are in place.
(8)  No further sales to be made until salesforce retrained.

A firm which declines to observe a request may be liable to exercise of a power of intervention, or to disciplinary action.

## 2  INVESTIGATIONS

The regulators possess the power to carry out *ad hoc* investigations of one or more particular aspects of a member's or its appointed representative's investment business. A registered individual may also be investigated. These powers are contained in the SRO rulebooks, to which reference should be made.

A regulator may decide to carry out an investigation as a result of information which has come to light during a periodic inspection visit, or because of information received, such as investor complaints or information provided by a member itself or its auditor under s 109 FSA (see Chapter 11).

Examples of investigations recently carried out include those to determine:

(i) whether a firm has exercised sufficient control over business carried out by its appointed representative;

(ii) whether a firm adequately trains its company representatives;

(iii) whether a firm has sufficient management controls to be allowed to continue trading;

(iv) whether a firm has exercised discretionary powers in the interests of its customers;

(v) whether a firm has carried out investment business of a kind for which it was not authorised;

(vi) whether a firm has maintained sufficient financial resources.

In addition to checking records the regulator may wish to interview its staff, customers and senior management as part of its enquiries. The regulator's powers when carrying out an investigation are similar to those it has when carrying out monitoring.

Once the regulator has completed its investigation it will generally provide a report to the firm and give it the opportunity to comment upon it before deciding what action may be appropriate. This may include making a request that the firm takes remedial action (see section 1.4 above), or the exercise of formal powers of intervention and discipline, discussed below.

In 1992/3 the LAUTRO Monitoring Committee considered 31 investigation reports, and referred 14 of these cases for disciplinary action. In 1993/4 IMRO authorised 17 investigations, and SFA authorised 59 investigations, into member firms or registered individuals.

## 3   POWERS OF INTERVENTION

A regulator may exercise powers of intervention in appropriate circumstances. These powers are intended to enable the regulator to halt or remedy serious compliance failures. The circumstances where they may be exercised are set out in the SRO rulebooks including where:

(i) the firm may not be fit and proper;

(ii) a registered individual may not be fit and proper;

(iii) the firm or a registered individual has committed or may commit a breach of the FSA or the SRO's rules;

(iv) it is desirable to exercise the powers in the interests of investors.

Use of intervention powers is not a routine event and a regulator will normally resort to them if there is uncertainty as to whether the firm is willing or able to comply with the SRO's rules, or requests made by the SRO, or where the regulator feels unable to rely on the firm's voluntary undertakings.

The powers of intervention available to an SRO include:

(i) prohibiting or restricting a firm or its appointed representative from carrying on investment business;

(ii) imposing a restriction on the way a firm carries on business, eg prohibiting it from dealing with private customers, or seeking business of a particular kind;

(iii) requiring a firm to transfer assets to a trustee or to maintain assets in the United Kingdom.

An intervention order may also be made against a registered individual, requiring that specified action be taken or that they cease acting as a regulated individual. Circumstances where powers of intervention have recently been exercised include:

(i) suspending the marketing activities of a life assurance company which was engaging in sales abuses;

(ii) suspending an IFA whose directors were not fit and proper persons;

(iii) prohibiting a stockbroker which had insufficient financial resources from continuing to manage client funds.

Powers of intervention are instigated by the regulator and are effective on notification to the firm. The firm is obliged to comply and to ensure that its appointed representatives and registered individuals do likewise.

An application to rescind or vary exercise of a power of intervention may be made to the regulator's disciplinary and appeal tribunals.

In 1993/4 IMRO exercised powers of intervention on six occasions.

## 4 POWERS OF DISCIPLINE

### 4.1 Purpose of disciplinary proceedings

Some SROs have occasionally issued policy statements setting out the reasons why disciplinary action is taken. They include LAUTRO Enforcement Bulletin 14 (February 1992) and IMRO's Statement of Disciplinary Policy (May 1994). The following is drawn from IMRO's Statement but may be taken as reasonably indicative of other SROs' approaches as well. IMRO sees the fundamental principles of its disciplinary policy as being:

(1) Compensation of investors who suffer losses from rule breaches.

(2) Effective punishment. This is intended to convey the seriousness of the breach and ensure that the firm is not in a better position than firms that have not breached the rules.

(3) Deterrence, by timely and robust fines, of firms tempted by the perceived benefits of non-compliance, and thereby achieve investor protection.

(4) To be fair and timely.

(5) Publicity of its disciplinary decisions. This is considered an essential part of deterrence and will, in addition, create public awareness of the regulator's powers.

The overriding aim of disciplinary action should be, as IMRO's Annual Report for 1993 comments, to protect investors and ensure compliance, and not to exhibit severed heads on Temple Bar. Disciplinary proceedings are, however, by their nature contentious and adversarial and some firms which have undergone disciplinary action at the hands of their regulator feel that they have been unfairly picked upon, or made an example of.

## 4.2 When disciplinary proceedings are brought

Most firms will from time to time be in breach of several conduct of business or other rules, but not every rule breach gives rise to disciplinary action. A pattern is emerging of the circumstances where disciplinary action is brought:

(1) Where the rule breach is deliberate or has continued un-remedied to the knowledge of management.

(2) Where the rule breach is serious or the rule breaches are widespread. In such a case the firm may be in breach of SIB's Principles or no longer a fit and proper person.

(3) Where the firm has previously been requested to take corrective action and has not done so to an adequate standard.

(4) Where the firm is obstructive, unco-operative or untruthful in its dealings with the regulator.

(5) Where the firm does not have a compliance culture and it is considered necessary to change its attitude.

## 4.3 The charge

This will usually be for breach of the FSA, or of one or more specific rules: conduct of business, membership, financial or client money depending on the circumstances. In addition there may be a charge alleging breach of one or more of SIB's Principles. The charge served upon the member should identify the rule or Principle which the firm is alleged to have breached and set out a summary of the facts on which the regulator relies.

## 4.4 The disciplinary process

This differs between SROs and is summarised here with reference to disciplinary action taken against a member firm. Disciplinary action taken against a registered individual may follow a different course.

## (a) PIA

The disciplinary committee commences proceedings by issuing the member with a provisional order setting out the charge and penalty sought. The member may make written or oral representations in response with a view to persuading the disciplinary committee to modify or drop the charge. The disciplinary committee may withdraw or vary its order if so persuaded or, alternatively, confirm it. If the firm still contests the provisional order then the matter will be heard before PIA's disciplinary tribunal. If, however, the disciplinary committee considers that the matter is very serious or likely to be contested, it may institute proceedings before the disciplinary tribunal.

## (b) IMRO

The enforcement committee commences proceedings by sending a statement of case to the member. The member must then either:

- agree to try to settle the proceedings by 'without prejudice' negotiations and plead guilty to the charge; or
- request that the case is heard by the disciplinary tribunal, indicating whether its plea is guilty or not guilty.

A member who does neither is deemed to accept the charge and the enforcement committee may impose a penalty, subject to the member's right of appeal. If a member who seeks to settle the proceedings reaches agreement with IMRO, the settlement must then be approved by the enforcement committee. A case is heard by the disciplinary tribunal where the member requests a hearing, or fails to agree a settlement.

## (c) SFA

The enforcement committee commences proceedings by serving notice on the firm. The firm may then formally deny the charge in which case the matter is referred to the disciplinary tribunal; or may seek to negotiate a settlement. If he does neither, the notice will take effect.

The rulebooks of SFA, IMRO and PIA contain provisions for the SRO and its members to reach settlement of disciplinary proceedings. This will usually be appropriate where the member admits all or part of the charge which it may, of course, try to amend during the course of negotiations. The advantage of seeking to negotiate a settlement in these circumstances is that the member who pleads guilty is able to negotiate a penalty with the prosecutor, subject to any necessary formal approval from the tribunal, while the SRO can dispose of the case without the burden of preparing for and conducting a formal hearing.

## 4.5  The disciplinary hearing

The constitution of an SRO's disciplinary tribunal is specified in its rulebook. It will generally comprise a legally qualified chairman and two or more other members who are usually disinterested practitioners with relevant experience. It is common for a disciplinary tribunal to convene one or more preliminary hearings to give direction on procedural matters in advance of a full hearing.

The proceedings before an SRO's disciplinary tribunal vary between the SROs and depend to a large extent upon whether:

(1) The firm contests the charges and pleads not guilty. In this case the SRO will seek to prove each item in the charges and there will be a full hearing of the matter.

(2) The firm does not contest the charges and wishes to make a plea in mitigation before the tribunal. In this case there will be a full hearing of the matter but confined to the firm addressing the tribunal in mitigation and the parties addressing it on the appropriate penalty.

(3) The firm has negotiated a settlement with the prosecution. In this case (where the SRO's rules so require) the settlement is laid before the tribunal for approval. There is no formal hearing but the parties may need to justify the settlement to the tribunal.

A hearing before a disciplinary tribunal is intended to be informal. Members will represent themselves speaking through a director, company secretary or their lawyer, and the hearing is in private. The rules of evidence do not apply. The tribunal determines its own procedure although the principles of natural justice should be observed. Depending on the circumstances a hearing may last from half a day to a number of weeks. After it is completed the tribunal may take some time to reach its decision.

The case will be normally opened by the representative of the SRO. Where the firm is not contesting the charges it will then present an oral plea in mitigation. Where the charges are contested the SRO will call its witnesses who will be cross-examined by the firm and the firm will present its case in reply and call its own witnesses. If the firm is found guilty or has pleaded guilty, it should have an opportunity to address the tribunal on the penalty to be imposed.

## 4.6 The outcome

As hearings are invariably held in private, information about acquittal is not easy to determine, and the regulators do not generally publish this information. However LAUTRO's Annual Report for 1992/3 stated that during that year 11 disciplinary cases were completed, and in all cases the firm was found guilty. Ten received a fine and public reprimand, and one received a private reprimand. It seems to be the regulators' policy only to take disciplinary proceedings in cases where they consider that the evidence is sufficiently strong to obtain either a guilty plea or a conviction.

## 4.7 The penalties

The penalties available to the tribunal are set out in the SRO rulebooks and generally include:

(1) A private reprimand. This will normally only be the sole penalty where the case is not serious or the rule breach is trivial.

(2) A public reprimand. This is the usual outcome of a conviction as justice and fairness are considered to require that the outcome of disciplinary action be published. The public reprimand will take the form of a document made available to the public and to the press. A member may be able to negotiate its contents.

(3) A fine. The size of fines imposed by the regulators has been increasing as they seek to ensure that sufficient attention is paid to them. Examples of fines recently imposed are:

(i) IMRO: £750,000 for a firm with material and widespread compliance breaches.

(ii) LAUTRO: £300,000 for an insurance company which had material compliance breaches persisting for over a year.

(iii) FIMBRA: £160,000 for a firm which breached financial reporting and capital adequacy rules and had deficient internal organisation.

(iv) SFA: £100,000 for a firm which had numerous rule breaches; £200,000 for a registered individual for serious breaches of duty.

The criteria used in deciding the amount of the fine will include issues such as:

- the number and gravity of the rule breaches;
- the circumstances of the rule breaches;
- the size of the firm;
- creating a strong aversion in that firm to repetition;
- being significant in the eyes of the public.

(4) An order that remedial action be taken, eg to pay compensation.

(5) To suspend or expel a member or a registered individual. This would be appropriate in a very serious matter.

(6) To impose conditions on membership, or to restrict membership.

(7) To pay the regulator's costs of investigation and discipline, which can be substantial.

## 4.8 An appeal

A member can appeal against a finding of guilty when it has contested the charge, or against the imposition of a penalty when, having delivered a plea in mitigation or otherwise, the tribunal imposes a penalty. In some cases the SRO may also appeal. Grounds of appeal may include:

(1) The tribunal misdirected itself.
(2) Its decision was unreasonable, unsupported by the evidence or based on an error of law or a misinterpretation of the SRO's rules.
(3) The penalty was excessive.
(4) New evidence has become available.

Each SRO has an appeal tribunal whose function is to determine appeals. In order to appeal a member will be required to file a notice of appeal within the time and in the form set out in the SRO's rulebook. The appeal will be held in private and the procedure will be determined by the appeal tribunal.

## 4.9   Judicial review

The acts and decisions of an SRO are subject to judicial review (*Bank of Scotland v IMRO* 1989 SLT 432; *R v FIMBRA ex p Cochrane* (1989) *The Times,* 23 June; *R v Lautro ex p Ross* [1992] 3 WLR 549; *R v Lautro ex p Tee*(1994) *The Times*, 30 May). This remedy is available both to an SRO's members and to others in limited circumstances, such as a firm's appointed representative (*R v Lautro ex p Ross*).

The grounds for seeking judicial review can include where the SRO's tribunal:

(i)   has acted outside its statutory powers, made an error or erred in law;
(ii)  has failed to observe appropriate procedures;
(iii) has acted unreasonably in breach of the *Wednesbury* principle (see *Associated Provincial Picture Houses Ltd v Wednesbury Corp* [1947] 1 KB 223), unfairly or in bad faith.

The remedy of judicial review is available in a number of circumstances. The most relevant here is in relation to the exercise of disciplinary proceedings, although it should be noted that judicial review generally cannot be sought before appeals prescribed by the SRO's rules have been exhausted. In addition:

(i)   exercise of formal powers of investigation and enforcement; and
(ii)  refusal of admission or imposition of conditions upon membership;

are in principle subject to judicial review.

# 13   *Investment Advertisements*

A principal objective of the FSA is to restrict and regulate the marketing of investments. One of its keystones in this respect is s 57 which regulates the issue of investment advertisements. The drafting is deceptively straightforward and a number of words and phrases throw up difficult legal questions which need to be considered carefully. This chapter considers in turn:

(1) The statutory restriction on investment advertisements.
(2) Issuing and approving an advertisement.
(3) What is an investment advertisement?
(4) Consequences of breach of the restriction.
(5) The exclusions.
(6) Conduct of business rules relating to investment advertisements.

## 1   THE STATUTORY RESTRICTION

Section 57(1) of the FSA contains the restriction on investment advertisements. It states as follows:

> 57(1) Subject to section 58 below, no person other than an authorised person shall issue or cause to be issued an investment advertisement in the United Kingdom unless its contents have been approved by an authorised person.

Section 57 controls the issue of investment advertisements by providing that, subject to s 58 (which contains a number of exceptions), persons who are not authorised under the FSA are prohibited from issuing investment advertisements. An authorised person may only issue an investment advertisement or approve an unauthorised person's investment advertisement, on the terms contained in the conduct of business rules which apply to that authorised person.

## 1.1   The definition

Section 57(2) defines an investment advertisement as follows:

> 57(2) In this Act 'an investment advertisement' means any advertisement inviting persons to enter or offer to enter into an investment agree-ment or to exercise any rights conferred by an investment to acquire, dispose of, underwrite or convert an investment or containing information calculated to lead directly or indirectly to persons doing so.

## 1.2   What is an advertisement?

An advertisement is not exhaustively defined by the FSA, but probably means any kind of public announcement or activity which is intended to draw attention to an opportunity. Section 207(2) of the FSA gives a non-exhaustive list of examples. It could be:

(1)  a newspaper advertisement;
(2)  a brochure;
(3)  a broadcast announcement;
(4)  a promotional seminar;
(5)  any other act or statement which is intended to draw attention to an opportunity.

It appears that an advertisement is not restricted to material in permanent form. This view is supported by SIB's Guidance Release 3/91 on telephone-selling by telephone-marketing agencies.

There is no reason why an oral statement such as a speech, lecture or interview should not be an advertisement. An oral statement based on a prepared script almost certainly is, and is capable of prior approval in accordance with conduct of business rules. On the other hand, oral responses to genuine questions are probably not advertisements. So an interview on television consisting of replies to unprompted questions, or an unscripted discussion which was not solicited by the interviewee, should not amount to an advertisement. The position would be reversed if the interviewee has initiated the interview.

SIB's Guidance Release 3/91 on telephone-selling distinguishes between pre-recorded messages (likely to be advertisements) and scripted, guided and free form messages (unlikely to be advertisements). It is submitted that these distinctions are somewhat illogical and cannot be sustained. The better view is that they are all advertisements.

A document can be converted into an advertisement by the use to which it is put. A business plan prepared by a company's management for internal use is not, of itself, an advertisement, but it would become one if sent out to potential investors with a view to encouraging them to invest in the company.

## 2   ISSUING AND APPROVING AN ADVERTISEMENT

An advertisement is issued when it is published. Where the document is not in the nature of an advertisement, such as a draft of a share purchase agreement and a covering letter sent by one adviser to another, or to a prospective party, the activity should not amount to issuing. *Nash* v *Lynde* [1929] AC 158 offers some guidance in this respect.

## 2.1   What is approving an advertisement?

The function of approving is entirely separate from that of issuing an advertisement under the FSA:

(1) A person authorised under the FSA may issue an investment advertisement in accordance with the terms of its conduct of business rules. The advertisement does not need to be approved.

(2) Subject to the exceptions in s 58, discussed in section 5 below, an unauthorised person may only issue an investment advertisement after it has been approved by a person authorised under the FSA. This entails the unauthorised person seeking the authorised person's approval of the investment advertisement. In order to do this the authorised person must, in accordance with its own conduct of business rules, examine the investment advertisement for accuracy and accept responsibility for its contents.

## 2.2   Who issues an advertisement?

Where an advertisement is issued by a succession of persons, for example an authorised life assurance company's advertisement promoting a particular life assurance policy, the position is as follows:

(1) The life assurance company publishes the advertisement as a mailshot to the public. It is issuing it, and may do so as an authorised person in accordance with its business rules.

(2) The life assurance company also issues the brochure to a broker (who is also an authorised person) and who distributes it to its clients. The company has caused the advertisement to be issued by the broker. The broker is issuing it itself, because it is distributing it onwards to people who would not otherwise have received it. It must observe the applicable conduct of business rules (discussed in section 6 below).

(3) If the life assurance company does not publish the brochure itself, but sends it in bulk to authorised intermediaries for distribution, then they will issue it and the company is probably causing them to issue it.

(4) If the broker adds its own material to the advertisement, for example additional information, then it may be viewed as his own advertisement.

## 2.3   Who causes an advertisement to be issued?

Section 57 also restricts the act of causing an advertisement to be issued. The meaning of 'causing' was considered in *O'Sullivan* v *Truth & Sportsman Limited* [1957] 96 CLR 220 as approved in *Attorney General of Hong Kong* v *Tse Hung Lit* [1986] 3 All ER 1973 as follows.

One person ('the advertiser') will cause another person ('the publisher') to issue an advertisement where the publisher issues the advertisement *either*:

(1)  on the actual authority, express or implied, of the advertiser; *or*

(2)  in consequence of the advertiser exercising some capacity it possesses in fact or in law to control or influence the acts of the publisher;

*and* (in both cases) the advertiser contemplates or desires the publisher will issue the advertisement.

It is difficult to apply the meaning of 'causing' given in these cases to the context of s 57 without straining the natural meaning of words. For example, if a life assurance company hands leaflets to a broker, it is presumably causing them to be issued because it is implicity authorising the broker to distribute them.

It is submitted that it is unlikely that Parliament intended the word 'cause' to be interpreted as in these cases. Instances where one person passes material to another for publication without either authorising it (because no authorisation is needed) or controlling the distributor will probably be held to fall within this section.

## 3   WHAT IS AN INVESTMENT ADVERTISEMENT?

An investment advertisement is defined by s 57(2) (set out above) as an advertisement which:

(a)  invites people to enter into an investment agreement (this term is discussed in section 3.1 below); or

(b)  invites people to offer to enter into an investment agreement; or

(c)  invites people to exercise rights conferred by an investment to buy or sell, underwrite or convert an investment (but not to exercise voting rights— thus proxy solicitation is not caught—nor to hold an investment); or

(d)  containing information calculated to lead directly or indirectly to people doing the above.

It is usually easy enough to recognise advertisements falling within categories (a)–(c). It is category (d) which causes the greatest problems of interpretation.

### 3.1   What is an investment agreement?

The advertisement is only an investment advertisement if it invites people, or is calculated to lead people, to enter into an investment agreement or otherwise to exercise certain rights. The term 'investment agreement' is defined by s 44(9):

> 44(9)  In this Act 'investment agreement' means any agreement the making or performance of which by either party constitutes an activity which falls within any paragraph of Part II of Schedule 1 to this Act or would do so apart from Parts III and IV of that Schedule.

An investment agreement is an agreement where either party is, by making or performing it, dealing, arranging, managing or advising in relation to regulated investments or operating a collective scheme, ignoring:

(1) whether or not either party is carrying on a business;

(2) the exclusions contained in Parts III and IV of Sched 1 such as the exclusions for dealing as principal or overseas persons.

This is extremely wide. For example:

(1) the advertiser need not be carrying on a business;

(2) an investment advertisement can fall within s 57 even where the resulting investment activity is carried on by persons other than the advertiser;

(3) the resulting investment activity need not be carried on in the United Kingdom;

(4) an investment which contains a mixture of material, some calculated to lead directly or indirectly to people engaging in investment activities, and some not so calculated, can still be an investment advertisement.

## 3.2 Calculated to lead

'Calculated to lead' means reasonably likely to lead. This is an objective and not a subjective test. (See *R v Dawson* [1972] 2 All ER 1121, where it was held that 'calculated to deceive' means likely to deceive; and *Erven Warnick BV v John Townend & Sons (Hull) Limited* [1979] AC 371, where 'calculated' was held to mean a reasonably foreseeable consequence.)

## 3.3 Directly or indirectly

The phrase 'directly or indirectly' is problematic and difficult to interpret. Although it appears to encompass all possible outcomes, it probably bears a more restricted meaning. It is tentatively submitted that it means that the chain of causation between the advertisement and the investor entering into (or offering to enter into) the investment agreement, or exercising the rights, may be interrupted by one or more extraneous events; in other words, 'a more remote link in the chain of causation is contemplated than the proximate and immediate cause' (Scrutton J in *Coxe v Employer's Liability Assurance Corporation Limited* [1916] 2 KB 629, which considered the meaning of these words in a different context).

A line must, however, be drawn somewhere. In *Spinney's (1948) Limited v Royal Insurance Company Limited* [1980] 1 Lloyd's Reports 406 Mustill J said:

There must be some limit on the application of this clause [which excluded direct or indirect consequences] for the chain of causation recedes indefinitely into the past. The draftsman [of the insurance policy] must have intended to stop somewhere and that place must be the point at which an event ceases to be a cause of the loss and becomes merely an item of history.

Cases such as these do provide some indication of how a court might seek to approach the interpretation of s 57, although it must be emphasised that cases decided in relation to other legislation must be treated with caution.

## 3.4 An interpretation of 'calculated to lead directly or indirectly'

Where the chain of causation stops, and an advertisement would not be viewed as calculated to lead, is to be determined in accordance not only with the factual context, but also in accordance with the intention of the FSA. Here we are considering advertisements which fall into category (d) above, ie those which do not actually invite people to do anything, but just contain information. This question is particularly important for unauthorised persons. While it is also relevant to authorised persons, they may decide as a matter of policy or caution to treat advertisements as investment advertisements. A guide is offered here but until a court reviews this part of s 57 any interpretation must be conjectural:

(1) *General advertisements* Some advertisements which refer to, or discuss, investment opportunities are probably too remote from the investor's decision to count as investment advertisements. This would include examples such as a brochure outlining the economy of Mexico or describing the structure of offshore discretionary trusts. Any advertisement merely describing in general terms the services which a person has to offer is also unlikely to be an investment advertisement for this reason. An advertisement which does not have any specific investment in contemplation is unlikely to be viewed as an investment advertisement.

(2) *Advertisements for independent advice* An advertisement advising investors to seek independent advice is unlikely to be an investment advertisement where there is no specific investment in contemplation, and the advertisement is likely to make the recipient seek out more information and make a decision on the basis of that information.

(3) *Advertisements for specific investments likely to be bought* If an advertisement refers to a specific investment or category of investments and an investor is likely to make a purchase (or disposal) on the strength of the advertisement, then it is likely to be an investment advertisement. An advertisement for a unit trust capable of immediate acceptance is one such example, as the decision to invest can be made on reading the advertisement. An insurance company's advertisement for a particular kind of policy is also likely to be an investment advertisement because private investors are reasonably likely to be influenced by it and to acquire the product, which is likely to be available from the advertiser and other sources. While the test is objective, the advertiser's intention may be a useful indicator. If the advertiser's primary motivation is to get the recipient of the advertisement to enter into an investment agreement, then it is probably 'calculated to lead' to this result and is an investment advertisement.

(4) *Advertisements which refer to further material* If an advertisement contains general material relating to an investment (such as a business plan

for a new company) and indicates how further information may be obtained, it is likely to be an investment advertisement. This is because the business plan, when used in this way, is an advertisement and it is likely to lead indirectly to an investor who obtains the further material entering into an investment agreement. It is submitted that it would make no difference whether the business plan or the additional material is issued by an independent adviser or by the promoters. It is also irrelevant that the investor may have to negotiate the terms of his investment.

(5) *Advertisements of listed companies*

(a) A sales advertisement marketing the goods or services of a listed company would be unlikely in normal circumstances to lead anyone to buy shares in that company, even though by increasing public awareness of the company one of the side effects of such advertising may be to stimulate interest in its shares. The same advertisement may, however, be an investment advertisement if the company's purpose in issuing it is, at least in part, to raise its profile in connection with a planned public offering of its shares in the near future, eg the advertising campaigns in connection with the marketing of the shares in certain privatisations.

(b) There has been concern in the past as to whether listed companies' corporate image and routine financial advertising, such as year-end results advertising, would be caught by s 57 as being 'indirectly calculated to lead' the public to invest in their shares. However, the Financial Services Act 1986 (Investment Advertisements) (Exemptions) Orders 1995 include fairly wide-ranging exclusions for advertisements issued by companies whose securities are already listed on the London Stock Exchange or on most of the other major stock markets provided, of course, that they do not include an express invitation to purchase securities (see section 5.4 and section 5.6 below).

(c) Categories of advertisements relating to a listed company which remain likely to be investment advertisements are ones that give an address for obtaining further information about the company or its shares; and ones that go further than just reproducing the published results and include 'puffs' from the chairman emphasising the company's strengths and why he feels the shares are undervalued. The distinction between these examples and those in the preceding paragraphs is that here the advertisement is giving additional publicity, or publicising information, that is not otherwise available. They are therefore more likely to result in people buying the shares on the strength of the advertisement.

(6) *Summary*

    (a) If an advertisement directs the recipient to take steps to acquire or dispose of an investment (for example by including a coupon) it is more likely to be an investment advertisement than if it does not.

    (b) If the investment featured in the advertisement can be purchased direct from the advertiser, such as life assurance and unit trusts, then an advertisement for such products is probably an investment advertisement.

    (c) If there is an acid test, it is this: is any one likely to enter into an investment agreement as a result of this advertisement, or will they do so as a result of other causes? Only in the former case will it be an investment advertisement.

## 3.5   Issue in the United Kingdom

Issue in the United Kingdom means:

(1) publishing the advertisement in the United Kingdom; or

(2) publishing the advertisement outside the United Kingdom if it is directed to people in the United Kingdom. For example, a French insurance broker who posts investment advertisements to individuals in the United Kingdom is issuing them in the United Kingdom. If the advertisements are made available to people in the United Kingdom, for example by being included in magazines, newspapers or satellite television broadcasts, then they will be issued in the United Kingdom, unless the advertiser can take advantage of the exclusion in s 207(3). This is as follows:

207(3) For the purposes of this Act an advertisement or other information issued outside the United Kingdom shall be treated as issued in the United Kingdom if it is directed to persons in the United Kingdom or is made available to them otherwise than in a newspaper, journal, magazine or other periodical publication published and circulating principally outside the United Kingdom or in a sound or television broadcast transmitted principally for reception outside the United Kingdom.

Examples falling within this exclusion would include advertisements in *Paris Soir* or broadcasts on Belgian television.

## 3.6   Examples of investment advertisements

Applying these principles the following are, in principle and ignoring any available exclusions (see section 5 below), investment advertisements:

(1) a private individual advertises to sell his BP shares by putting a card in a newsagent's window;

(2) a United Kingdom listed company advertises its year's results. But rather than just offering figures, the chairman adds laudatory copy;

(3) a listed company puts an advertisement in the *Financial Times* inviting applications for its shares in connection with a new issue;

(4) a firm of Danish stockbrokers issues a brochure to United Kingdom nationals promoting certain securities listed on the Copenhagen Stock Exchange;

(5) a unit trust company inserts an off-the-page advertisement in a magazine;

(6) an accountant issues to potential investors a client's business plan with a view to attracting subscriptions for shares in that company;

(7) a newspaper gives favourable editorial coverage to a particular unit trust. The copy will not on its own be an investment advertisement. However, if the unit trust company reproduces it and hands it to its representatives for distribution to potential investors, then it will become an investment advertisement.

# 4 CIVIL AND CRIMINAL CONSEQUENCES OF BREACH OF THE RESTRICTION

These consequences relate exclusively to unauthorised persons who contravene s 57 of the FSA. An authorised person issuing an investment advertisement in contravention of the relevant conduct of business rules is liable to action by its regulator and by private investors but does not breach s 57.

It is a criminal offence under s 57 for an unauthorised person to issue (or cause to be issued) an investment advertisement which has not been approved by an authorised person:

57(3) Subject to subsection (4) below, any person who contravenes this section shall be guilty of an offence and liable:

(a) on conviction on indictment, to imprisonment for a term not exceeding two years or to a fine or to both;

(b) on summary conviction, to imprisonment for a term not exceeding six months or to a fine not exceeding the statutory maximum or to both.

Section 57(4) is an express exclusion relevant to newspapers:

57(4) A person who in the ordinary course of a business other than investment business issues an advertisement to the order of another person shall not be guilty of an offence under this section if he proves that he believed on reasonable grounds that the person to whose order the advertisement was issued was an authorised person, that the contents of the advertisement were approved by an authorised person or that the advertisement was permitted by or under section 58 below.

There is also a civil remedy contained in s 57(5) and (6). This provides that an investment agreement entered into, or an obligation to which a person becomes subject in consequence of exercising rights, after the issue of an investment advertisement which contravenes s 57 (and to which the investment agreement or exercise of rights relates) shall not be enforceable by the person who has issued or caused the advertisement to be issued. This civil remedy is only available against the person who issues or causes the advertisement to be issued. An investor who is induced to deal with a third party in consequence of an investment advertisement cannot avail himself of this remedy.

57(5) If in contravention of this section a person issues or causes to be issued an advertisement inviting persons to enter or offer to enter into an investment agreement or containing information calculated to lead directly or indirectly to persons doing so, then, subject to subsection (8) below:

(a) he shall not be entitled to enforce any agreement to which the advertisement related and which was entered into after the issue of the advertisement; and

(b) the other party shall be entitled to recover any money or other property paid or transferred by him under the agreement, together with compensation for any loss sustained by him as a result of having parted with it.

57(6) If in contravention of this section a person issues or causes to be issued an advertisement inviting persons to exercise any rights conferred by an investment or containing information calculated to lead directly or indirectly to persons doing so, then, subject to subsection (8) below:

(a) he shall not be entitled to enforce any obligation to which a person is subject as a result of any exercise by him after the issue of the advertisement of any rights to which the advertisement related; and

(b) that person shall be entitled to recover any money or other property paid or transferred by him under any such obligation, together with compensation for any loss sustained by him as a result of having parted with it.

An investor who can avail himself of this remedy may be entitled to recover his money and property handed over together with compensation for loss. The principles to be applied to recovery, restitution and third party rights should be the same as those arising under s 5 (see Chapter 11). Section 57 contains detailed provisions concerning this aspect:

57(7)  The compensation recoverable under subsection (5) or (6) above shall be such as the parties may agree or as a court may, on the application of either party, determine.

57(9)  Where a person elects to perform an agreement or an obligation which by virtue of subsection (5) or (6) above is unenforceable against him or by virtue of either of those subsections recovers money paid or other property transferred by him under an agreement or obligation he shall repay any money and return any other property received by him under the agreement or, as the case may be, as a result of exercising the rights in question.

A court may, however, allow the agreement or obligation to be enforced if either of the following situations arises (s 57(8)). First, if the customer was not influenced, or materially influenced, by the advertisement. This could be where the customer was not prejudiced by the advertisement because it merely introduced the customer to the advertiser, and the customer was induced to enter into the investment agreement at a later meeting and not by the advertisement. Secondly, if the advertisement was not misleading and fairly stated any risks, ie where the advertisement is quite fair.

57(8)  A court may allow any such agreement or obligation as is mentioned in subsection (5) or (6) above to be enforced or money or property paid or transferred under it to be retained if it is satisfied:

(a)  that the person against whom enforcement is sought or who is seeking to recover the money or property was not influenced, or not influenced to any material extent, by the advertisement in making his decision to enter into the agreement or as to the exercise of the rights in question; or

(b)  that the advertisement was not misleading as to the nature of the investment, the terms of the agreement or, as the case may be, the consequences of exercising the rights in question and fairly stated any risks involved in those matters.

# 5  EXCLUSIONS

Section 58 and the statutory instruments made under it provide exclusions from the restriction contained in s 57. An advertisement falling within any of these exclusions will not be an investment advertisement even if it possesses all the characteristics of one.

It is important to note that the general exclusions contained in paras 17–27 of Sched 1, such as the dealing as principal exclusion and the exclusion for overseas persons, have no bearing as to whether or not the advertisement is caught by s 57. There is, furthermore, no general exclusion for distributing investment advertisements to professional, business or experienced customers.

The exclusions are contained in s 58 and the two statutory instruments made under it.

Section 58 excludes advertisements issued, or caused to be issued by any of the following.

## 5.1 Government and other official bodies

Subsection 58(1)(a) excludes advertisements of governments, local authorities, central banks and international organisations of which the United Kingdom or other EU states are members relating exclusively to investments they issue such as, for example, advertisements relating to government securities or a County Council yearling bond.

58(1)(a) any advertisement issued or caused to be issued by, and relating only to investments issued by:
  (i) the government of the United Kingdom, of Northern Ireland or of any country or territory outside the United Kingdom;
  (ii) a local authority in the United Kingdom or elsewhere;
  (iii) the Bank of England or the central bank of any country or territory outside the United Kingdom; or
  (iv) any international organisation the members of which include the United Kingdom or another member State;

## 5.2 Exempted persons

Subsection 58(1)(b) excludes advertisements issued or caused to be issued by exempted persons under the FSA relating to business in respect of which they are exempted. This would exclude, for example:

(1) the advertisement of a life assurance company's appointed representative;
(2) the advertisement of a recognised investment exchange.

58(1)(b) any advertisement issued or caused to be issued by a person who is exempt under section 36, 38, 42, 43, 44 or 45 above, or by virtue of an order under section 46 above, if the advertisement relates to a matter in respect of which he is exempt;

## 5.3 EU nationals

Subsection 58(1)(c) excludes the advertisements of nationals of other EU states who are carrying on investment business lawfully in that state provided the advertisement conforms to SIB rules.

58(1)(c) any advertisement which is issued or caused to be issued by a national of a member State other than the United Kingdom in the course of investment business lawfully carried on by him in such a State and which conforms with any rules made under section 48(2)(e) above;

## 5.4 Listed securities

Certain advertisements relating to listed securities are excluded by subs 58(1)(d). These fall into two categories.

The first is an advertisement subject to s 154, which is one submitted to the London Stock Exchange and which it has approved or authorised in connection with the listing of securities.

58(1)(d) any advertisement which:
   (i) is subject to section 154 below; or
   (ii) consists of or any part of listing particulars, supplementary listing particulars, a prospectus approved in accordance with listing rules made under s 144(2) or 156A(1) below, a supplementary prospectus approved in accordance with listing rules made for the purposes of s 147(1) below as applied by s 154A or 156A(3) below or any other document required or permitted to be published by listing rules under Part IV of this Act.

The second exclusion is contained in s 58(1)(d)(ii) and is of considerable width and importance. It applies to any advertisement which consists of, or is any part of, listing particulars, supplementary listing particulars, prospectus or supplementary prospectus, or any other document required or permitted to be published by the London Stock Exchange Listing Rules. Article 11 of the Financial Services Act 1986 (Investment Advertisements) (Exemptions) (No 2) Order 1995 (SI No 1536) contains a similar exception for the advertisements of corporations whose securities are 'permitted to be traded or dealt in' on another EU or other specified foreign stock exchange, although this will not include documents such as offering circulars which are issued before a company's securities are listed. The whole or any part of the annual report, interim report, chairman's statement or other corporate announcements of a listed company should therefore be able to take advantage of this exclusion.

The exemption does not extend to an investment advertisement which contains additional material over and above the contents of, or extracts from, a document which is required or permitted to be published by listing rules. Nor does it include an advertisement which presents information taken from such documents in different wording or in a graphical or diagrammatic form which does not appear in the original document.

## 5.5 Exclusions under section 58(3)

Section 57 does not apply to an advertisement issued in the circumstances specified in any orders made by the Secretary of State (s 58(3)). This subsection states that such advertisements will, generally speaking, have defined characteristics, which is that they:

(1) are of a private character; or
(2) only deal incidentally with investments; or
(3) are issued to expert investors.

The two statutory instruments made under s 58(3) are the Financial Services Act 1986 (Investment Advertisements) (Exemptions) and (Exemptions) (No 2) Orders 1995 (SI Nos 1266 and 1536). They consolidate, with some alterations, the four 1988 and 1992 investment advertisement exemption orders which they replace. These exclusions, summarised below, are similar to some previously contained in the Prevention of Fraud (Investments) Act 1958 and exemption orders made under it, while others correspond to exclusions contained in paras 17–27 of Sched 1. It is necessary to study the full text in detail before seeking to apply an exclusion to any particular situation. They are as follows:

(1) Advertisements issued by a company to persons reasonably believed to be its existing members or creditors, or those of a group company, which relate to certain investments issued by it or its group. For instance, a company can send its shareholders a third party's takeover offer, provided the shares are to be bought for cash (SI 1995 No 1266, art 3).

(2) Corporate image and financial advertisements by companies (other than open-ended investment companies) provided they do not constitute an invitation or offer, give advice in relation to investments or any investment activity or contain information likely to result in the purchasing of, or other dealings in, any investment other than the corporate group's own securities (art 4). This exception applies to any company with securities listed on any specified EU or other foreign stock exchange and to unlisted companies provided they file accounts in the United Kingdom or other EU state and the advertisement consists of or is accompanied by part or all of such a company's annual accounts or its director's report.

(3) Communications to holders of bearer securities issued by a company in relation to its own securities or those of any other company within its corporate group, which are restricted to information about such securities. Advertisements issued in similar circumstances and containing information required by a relevant securities market are also exempt (art 5).

(4) Advertisements concerning an employees' share scheme (art 6).

(5) Advertisements issued by one group company to another (art 7). 'Group' is given the para 30 Sched 1 FSA definition.

(6) Certain advertisements issued by participants (or potential participants) in non-investment business joint ventures to similar persons (art 8).

(7) Some advertisements issued in connection with the supply of goods and services (art 9). The main business of the advertiser must not be investment business, the customer must not be an individual and the advertisement must not relate to units in a collective investment scheme or to life assurance.

(8) Advertisements issued by an overseas person to existing clients whom it recently obtained overseas (art 10).

(9) Some advertisements issued by an unauthorised person (who is not unlawfully carrying on investment business in the United Kingdom) to someone reasonably believed to be an authorised or exempted person, a government, a permitted person or a journalist, a substantial corporation or trust (corresponding to the definition in the SIB rules of a 'professional' or 'business' investor). This list does not include rich individuals and this exclusion does not apply to authorised persons' advertisements (art 11).

(10) Certain advertisements relating to shares or debentures in a private company sent to identified people with an existing common interest and which contain specified information (art 12).

(11) Some advertisements by trustees and personal representatives to other trustees, personal representatives or beneficiaries (art 13).

(12) Certain advertisements issued to existing participants by operators of a collective investment scheme recognised under s 87 or s 88 of the FSA (art 14).

(13) Advertisements relating to a programme or publication which contains information or advice (art 15).

(14) Advertisements issued by an approved market listed in the Order concerning its facilities (art 16).

(15) Advertisements for the shares of a residential property management company when acquired in conjunction with an interest in that property (art 17).

(16) Advertisements issued for the purpose of remedying injustice which the Parliamentary Commission for Administration says has happened (art 18).

(17) Advertisements issued to promote industrial or commercial activity where the advertiser has no financial interest in the business (SI 1995 No 1536, art 3).

(18) Advertisements issued in connection with the takeover of private companies and which fulfil detailed conditions (art 4).

(19) Certain advertisements to buy or sell controlling interests in private companies (art 5).

(20) Advertisements issued by a permitted person (art 6).

(21) Advertisements contained in publications sent to advertisers, and advertisements issued to people concerned with advertising (such as advertising agents) (art 7).

(22) An advertisement intended to inform or influence only a government, local or public authority; or people who deal in investments for businesses; or people whose business is to advise on dealing in investments or acting as broker in investments; provided the circulation of the advertisement is restricted to such persons. The Order sets out a number of indications which should be taken into account (art 8).

(23) An advertisement relating to shares, debt instruments, warrants or certificates traded on an exchange or market listed in the Order where the advertisement is required or permitted by its rules or by a market regulator (art 11).

(24) Advertisements relating to derivatives issued by an exchange or market listed in the Order (art 12).

(25) Certain advertisements issued by industrial and provident societies advertising their debentures (art 13).

(26) Advertisements which are prospectuses issued in accordance with the Public Offers of Securities Regulations, publications publicising such prospectuses, or documents required for admission to trading (art 14).

(27) Advertisements required or authorised under other legislation (art 15).

## 6 CONDUCT OF BUSINESS AND OTHER RULES RELATING TO ADVERTISEMENTS

### 6.1 Rules to which all advertisements are subject

When issuing an advertisement (whether or not an investment advertisement) an authorised person is subject to the following:

(1) *The Control of Misleading Advertisements Regulations 1988 (SI No 915)*: the Regulations give powers to the Director General of Fair Trading to take action against misleading advertisements if he considers that it is in the public interest to do so. He may apply for an injunction to require the publisher of an advertisement to substantiate the accuracy of any factual claims made in that advertisement. The Regulations cover most advertisements except (broadly) those which are regulated by the Independent, Television Commission, the Radio Authority, S4C and by the FSA.

(2) *The British Code of Advertising Practice*: the British Code of Advertising Practice is relevant in its entirety but section C VII of the Code, Advertising of Financial Services and Products, is particularly relevant to investment advertisements. In outline its requirements are as follows:

(a) Members of the public (which is intended to include firms and corporations) must be able fully to grasp the nature of any commitment they may enter into by responding to the advertisement.

(b) Off-the-page advertisements must be thoroughly comprehensible.

(c) An investment advertisement which may lead to consumers (which means investors and not just private individuals) making an investment should comply with the following requirements:

 (i) If an advertisement specifies an investment, or invites immediate commitment, full details on eligibility, type of contract, charges, expenses and any terms of withdrawal should be included.

 (ii) The basis of any forecasts or projections should be made clear.

 (iii) It should be stated whether the value of the investment may fluctuate or is fixed.

 (iv) References to past performance should be fair and representative and a warning given that past performance is not necessarily a guide to the future.

 (v) If the investor's request for repayment of investment moneys may be deferred, details should be stated.

 (vi) If the investment provides for withdrawal from capital as income equivalent, a clear explanation should be given.

 (vii) Claims to skill based on past performance or past advice must be capable of substantiation.

 (viii) There are restrictions on the use of the expressions 'tax free' and 'tax paid'.

 (ix) Any assumptions as to tax rates must be stated.

(3) *The Trade Descriptions Act 1968*: there is a question as to whether this covers the activity of professional persons but the general view is that it does. This Act makes it a criminal offence (s 14) for a person to make a statement in the course of carrying on a trade or business which he knows to be false or recklessly makes (in the sense of regardless as to whether it is true or false) as to:

– the provision of any services;
– the nature of any services;
– how the services will be provided;
– who will provide them (or their qualifications);
– any approval or evaluation of those services.

(4) *The ITC Code of Advertising Standards and Practice*: this will be relevant to television advertisements (broadcast, cable or non-domestic satellite).

(5) *The Radio Authority Code of Advertising Standards and Practice and Programme Sponsorship*: this will be relevant in radio advertisements.

(6) *Unregulated collective investment schemes*: an unregulated collective investment scheme may only be promoted in accordance with s 76 FSA—see Chapter 9.

## 6.2 Conduct of business rules for investment advertisements

The conduct of business rules which govern the issue or approval of an investment advertisement by an authorised person are contained in the relevant rulebook. The detailed rules vary between regulators and this section is an overview rather than a complete listing. Reference must be made to the relevant conduct of business rules. In particular, rules equivalent to the core rules on investment advertisements apply to SFA and IMRO members, but not to PIA members or to those subject to SIB rules.

(1) Two of SIB's Principles are especially relevant to advertisements and provide guidance on the application of the individual advertising rules:

- Principle 1: integrity and fair dealing. This requires a firm's advertisements to be honest.
- Principle 2: the duty to act with due skill, care and diligence. This requires a firm to take care when preparing and issuing advertisements.

(2) A key duty is that a firm must apply appropriate expertise when issuing or approving an advertisement. This is contained in a core rule, but is relevant to all firms. It requires a firm to:

- understand the subject matter of the advertisement;
- appraise the advertisement critically;
- take particular care if approving an unauthorised person's advertisement. A unit trust manager, for example, should be wary of approving the advertisement of an unauthorised futures dealer, as it may lack sufficient understanding of the services offered.

(3) The firm must be able to show that it has reasonable grounds to believe the advertisement is fair and not misleading. This, again, is contained in a core rule, but the principle here is relevant to all advertisements. The core rule is implemented in the IMRO rulebook by the IMRO Advertising Code, and by rule 5.9 of the SFA rules. In outline it requires:

- the advertisement to be factually accurate. Statements must be true and opinions reasonably held;
- the advertisement must be fair as a whole.

The advertiser must keep a proof on the file to demonstrate that the advertisement complies with this rule.

(4) A specific investment advertisement is one promoting a particular investment. Such an advertisement must identify the firm and its regulator. This is a core rule. For example, the following words should appear:

This advertisement is issued/approved by A Limited, regulated by SFA.

(5) A direct offer advertisement (one which contains an offer and specifies how to respond) to a private investor must be fair and contain adequate information. This is a further core rule.

(6) The requirement that an investment advertisement should be fair and not misleading applies to nearly all advertisements, although the extent to which information and warnings are required will depend upon the kind of investment and whom the advertisement is aimed at. The following are the main elements:

(a) *Clarity* It should clearly be an advertisement and not, for example, disguised as an editorial. The nature and type of the investment or service must be clear.

(b) *Honesty* There should be no false or misleading indication about the issuer, the services or the investment. The size of the funds under management, for example, and past performance must be true.

(c) *Visibility* Any statement required by the applicable rulebook must not be obscured or disguised.

(7) In addition, the firm's conduct of business rules may set out specific content requirements, generally for advertisements aimed at private customers. Common requirements include:

(a) A guarantee may be referred to only if a legally enforceable agreement with a third party who will meet any claim in full.

(b) Commendations must be genuine and relevant.

(c) Comparisons must be based on verifiable facts, must be fair and full, and must not be misleading.

(d) Material interests must be stated.

(e) Any reference to past performance must be relevant, fair, not selective, genuine and the source given.

(f) Tax status or relief should be stated to be variable and personal; 'tax free' must not be used if income or fund are liable to tax.

(8) Risk warnings may also be prescribed, particularly for advertisements aimed at private customers. Examples of where risk warnings may be needed are:

(a) where the investment fluctuates in value;

(b) where income yield is variable;

(c) where the investment is denominated in a foreign currency;

(d) where the investment is not readily realisable;

(e) if there may be a contingent liability.

## 6.3 Liability for approving an unauthorised person's advertisement

An authorised person should appreciate that, by approving an unauthorised person's investment advertisement, it is accepting responsibility for its contents.

If the investment advertisement for some reason does not comply with the authorised person's conduct of business rules then the authorised person may be liable to compensate investors under s 62. It may also be liable to investors in negligence if it fulfils the criteria in *Caparo Industries v Dickman* [1990] 1 All ER 568 and *Hedley Byrne & Co Ltd v Heller & Partners Ltd* [1963] 2 All ER 575.

# 14 Prospectuses, Listing Particulars and Insider Dealing

In this chapter we consider those provisions of the FSA which relate specifically to listed securities contained in Part IV of the Act. We also look briefly at the regime applicable to unlisted securities which is now contained in the Public Offers of Securities Regulations 1995 ('POS Regulations'), and examine the legislation which makes insider dealing illegal.

The distinction between a listed and an unlisted company continues to be relevant under the FSA. Part IV is only concerned with securities listed in the Official List of The International Stock Exchange of the United Kingdom and the Republic of Ireland (here referred to as the Stock Exchange). Those listed on the Unlisted Securities Market (USM) or the Third Market, traded over the counter, or for which there is no trading facility, were originally to fall under Part V FSA. However, Part V has never been brought into force and has now been repealed by the POS Regulations.

## 1 PUBLIC OFFERS OF SECURITIES

First, it may be helpful to give a brief summary of the statutory regime applying to public offers as from 19 June 1995, indicating in each case the regulations to which they are subject.

(1) *Public offers of unlisted securities*:
   (a) the POS Regulations;
   (b) s 57 FSA if not governed by the POS Regulations.
(2) *Public offers of securities to be admitted to the Official List*:
   (a) Part IV FSA, which is amended by the POS Regulations to make special provision for applications for admission associated with a public offer. The document required to be produced will be called a 'prospectus' rather than listing particulars;
   (b) the Listing Rules of the Stock Exchange;
   (c) s 57 FSA if exempt from the requirement to produce a prospectus under the new Sched 11A FSA.

(3) *Public offers of existing listed securities*:
  (a) the Listing Rules of the Stock Exchange (to the extent relevant);
  (b) s 57 FSA.
(4) *Admission to listing without a public offer or through an exempt public offer*:
  (a) Part IV FSA;
  (b) the Listing Rules of the Stock Exchange;
  (c) s 57 FSA.

## 2   THE OLD LAW ON LISTING

Prior to the FSA coming into force, the law governing the admission of securities to the Official List was contained principally in Part III of the Companies Act 1985, the Stock Exchange (Listing) Regulations 1984 (SELR 1984) and the Prevention of Fraud (Investments) Act 1958. In addition, the Listing Rules of the London Stock Exchange (referred to as the Yellow Book) had to be observed. All of the old statutory provisions regarding listed securities were replaced by Part IV FSA, supplemented by the Yellow Book.

The Companies Act laid down the basic requirement that a prospectus must accompany an offer of shares to the public: a prospectus is essentially a document issued on the occasion of making a public offer. Part IV FSA avoided the term prospectus altogether and instead referred to listing particulars. However, where securities are being offered to the public in the United Kingdom for the first time in conjunction with an application for admission to official listing, the POS Regulations have amended Part IV so that the document required to be produced is now to be referred to as a prospectus, rather than listing particulars.

Traditionally, listing of securities on the Stock Exchange was effected by means of a contract, known as the listing agreement, entered into between the prospective issuer and the Stock Exchange. The obligations arising under EC legislation referred to below were first implemented by the SELR 1984 and now by the FSA and the POS Regulations, which replace what was essentially a contract based regime with a statute based regime.

The FSA designates the Stock Exchange as the competent authority for the purposes of the EC Directives, and invests it with powers to make listing rules for the purposes of Part IV. While most of the rules that are now part of the Yellow Book are not new,their character has undergone a change in that they are now the product of the exercise of power delegated by the Minister.

## 3   EC DIRECTIVES

The FSA, the POS Regulations and the Yellow Book give effect to four EC Directives. These were made part of English law by the SELR 1984, which has been repealed. The requirements of the EC Directives are now either contained in the FSA, the POS Regulations or set out in the Yellow Book. The Directives are:

(1)  The Admissions Directive (Council Directive No 79/279/EEC of 5 March 1979) which co-ordinates the conditions for admission of securities to official exchange listing;

(2)  The Listing Particulars Directive (Council Directive No 80/390/EEC of 17 March 1980) which co-ordinates the requirements for the drawing-up, scrutiny and distribution of the listing particulars to be published for the admission of securities to official exchange listing;

(3)  The Interim Reports Directive (Council Directive No 82/121/EEC of 15 February 1985) which governs continuing disclosure obligations by companies whose securities have been admitted to official exchange listing; and

(4)  The Prospectus Directive (Council Directive No 89/298/EEC of 17 April 1989) which applies to 'transferable securities' offered to the public for the first time in a member state which are not already listed.

The Minister is empowered to require the Stock Exchange to observe EC obligations (s 192(1)).

# 4  ADMISSION OF SECURITIES TO LISTING

Applications for listing on the Stock Exchange are required to be made in accordance with the provisions of Part IV: s 142(1) states that:

142(1)  No investment to which this section applies shall be admitted to the Official List . . . except in accordance with the provisions of this Part of this Act.

The Stock Exchange is empowered to make it a pre-condition of listing that the relevant document relating to the securities is submitted to and approved by it and published.

As a result of amendments to Part IV introduced by the POS Regulations, there are now different document content requirements depending on the circumstances surrounding the application for listing. Where securities are to be offered to the public in the United Kingdom for the first time in conjunction with an application for listing on the Official List, a prospectus complying with Part IV and the content requirements in the Yellow Book is required:

144(2)  Listing rules shall require as a condition of the admission to the Official List of any securities for which application for admission has been made and which are to be offered to the public in the United Kingdom for the first time before admission—

(a)  the submission to, and approval by, the authority of a prospectus in such form and containing such information as may be specified in the rules; and

(b)  the publication of that prospectus.

Following the implementation of the POS Regulations, the only circumstances in which listing particulars are required to be submitted to and approved by the Stock Exchange and published is where there is an application for listing otherwise than in connection with a public offer, for example, on an introduction of securities to the Official List:

144(2A)   Listing Rules may require as a condition of the admission to the Official List of any other securities:

(a)   the submission to, and approval by, the authority of a document (in this Act referred to as 'listing particulars') in such form and containing such information as may be specified in the rules; and

(b)   the publication of that document;

or in such cases as may be specified by the rules, the publication of a document other than listing particulars or a prospectus.

144(2B)   Subsections (2) and (2A) have effect without prejudice to the generality of the power of the competent authority to make listing rules for the purposes of this section.

The starting point under the FSA is that, subject to the exceptions discussed below, whether securities are equity, preference, convertible or debt securities, and whether offered by way of rights, as consideration in a take over offer, in an offer for sale or in a placing, a prospectus or listing particulars (as the case may be) are required to be published containing specified information if the securities are to be admitted to the Official List.

The Stock Exchange may admit securities to the Official List if an application has been made in accordance with the Yellow Book (s 143(1)), by or with the consent of the issuer (s 143(2)), and provided both the Yellow Book and its other requirements have been complied with (s144(1)). Copies of the prospectus or listing particulars must be delivered to the Registrar of Companies (as defined in s 149(2)(a)) but only where publication is required by the Yellow Book. Failure to deliver before publication is a criminal offence for which both the issuer and any person 'knowingly a party to the publication' may be liable to prosecution. Publishers, advisers and persons responsible for the prospectus or listing particulars may be liable under this section.

Once securities have been admitted, such admission may not be challenged on the ground that any requirement or condition for their admission was not complied with (s 144(6)).

Notwithstanding the new requirement that an issuer applying for the listing of securities to be offered to the public in the United Kingdom for the first time must publish a prospectus rather than listing particulars, the provisions of Part IV (as amended by the POS Regulations) will apply in the same way to that prospectus as they do to listing particulars. The POS Regulations have introduced a new s 154A FSA which provides that the general requirements as to disclosure in listing particulars, the requirement for supplementary listing particulars, the provisions relating to compensation for false or misleading particulars and the rules of advertisements in connection with listing particulars apply in relation to prospectuses as they do to listing particulars.

154A    Sections 146 to 152 and 154 above shall apply in relation to a prospectus required by listing rules in accordance with section 144(2) above as they apply in relation to listing particulars, but as if—

(a)    any reference to listing particulars were a reference to a prospectus and any reference to supplementary listing particulars were a reference to a supplementary prospectus; and

(b)    notwithstanding section 142(7) above, any reference in section 152 above (other than in sub-section (1)(b) of that section) to the issuer of securities included a reference to the person offering or proposing to offer them.

Accordingly it should be noted that references throughout the remainder of this chapter to listing particulars and supplementary listing particulars should be read as including a reference to a prospectus or supplementary prospectus required by the Yellow Book and Part IV as amended by the POS Regulations.

## 4.1   Investments to which Part IV applies

The word 'investment' has a special meaning for the purposes of Part IV. Investments subject to Part IV are:

(1)    shares in the share capital of a company(as in para 1 of Sched 1), but here including a building society, an industrial or provident society or a credit union (s 142(3)(a)). This relates to paras 1, 4 and 5 for the purposes of Part IV;

(2)    debentures falling within para 2 of Sched 1 but including instruments falling within para 3 which are government or public securities—provided they have not been issued by an EC government or local authority (s 142(3)(b));

(3)    instruments falling within paras 4 and 5 of Sched 1 which entitle the holder to subscribe for, or which confer rights over, investments falling within para 1 of Sched 1 (s 142(3)(c)).

Some regulated investments are not covered at all by Part IV, including options, warrants to subscribe for debentures and shares in open-ended investment companies. Similarly, debentures issued by the United Kingdom government are outside its scope. Issuers of units in collective investment schemes are also not covered by the Part IV regime, but the FSA empowers the Minister to extend the application of Part IV to such investments, and units falling within the Financial Services Act 1986 (Single Property Schemes) (Exemptions) Regulations 1989 (SI No 28) are included (s 142(4)).

Part IV of the FSA only applies to these specified regulated investments, here termed 'securities'. The Stock Exchange may continue to admit investments which fall outside Part IV to the Official List and this need not be in accordance with Part IV (s 142(9)).

It may be helpful to define some terms which occur in Part IV. These are as follows:

(1) The competent authority is the Stock Exchange (s 142(6)), although this may be altered in certain circumstances under s 157.

(2) Listing Rules may be made by the Stock Exchange for the purposes of Part IV pursuant to s 156, and are contained in the Yellow Book. These listing rules implement the EC Directives mentioned above.

(3) The Official List is published daily by authority of the Stock Exchange containing details of securities fully listed on the Exchange.

(4) The issuer is the person who has issued or will issue the securities, although the issuer of an investment falling within para 5 of Sched 1 means the issuer of the underlying security, not of the certificate or instrument which relates to it, and the offeror is the person making the offer as principal, not as agent (s 142(7)).

(5) The question of whether an offer of securities to the public in the United Kingdom is being made, is to be determined in accordance with Sched 11A FSA as introduced by the POS Regulations. An offer to the public will include an offer to any section of the public, for example the shareholders or a class of shareholders of a company, but there is a multitude of exceptions specified, and reference should be made to these.

## 4.2 Advertisements

The issue of advertisements in connection with listing applications is restricted by s 154 which lays down the following:

154(1) Where listing particulars are or are to be published in connection with an application for the listing of any securities no advertisement or other information of a kind specified by listing rules shall be issued in the United Kingdom unless the contents of the advertisement or other information have been submitted to the competent authority and that authority has either:

(a) approved those contents; or

(b) authorised the issue of the advertisement or information without such approval.

An authorised person who contravenes this sub-section may be liable under s 62 (s 154(2)), while an unauthorised person is liable to prosecution (s 154(3)). There is a defence corresponding to that in s 57(4) for a publisher of such an advertisement who believes on reasonable grounds that it has been approved or authorised by the Stock Exchange (s 154(4)).

Once information has been approved or authorised, neither the person who issues it, nor any person responsible for all or part of the listing particulars, shall be civilly liable for any statements in or omission from the information, provided that when taken together the information and listing particulars are not misleading (s 154(5)). It is unclear why this sub-section only refers to 'information' and not 'advertisement or other information'. Presumably the distinction is intended and information which amounts to an advertisement is excluded. However it is difficult to identify what then remains given the wide definition of advertisement, for which see Chapter 13.

> 154(5)  Where information has been approved, or its issue has been author-
>         ised, under this section neither the person issuing it nor any person
>         responsible for, or for any part of, the listing particulars shall incur
>         any civil liability by reason of any statement in or omission from
>         the information if that information and the listing particulars, taken
>         together, would not be likely to mislead persons of the kind likely
>         to consider the acquisition of the securities in question. The refer-
>         ence above to a person incurring civil liability includes a reference
>         to any other person being entitled as against that person to be
>         granted any civil remedy or to rescind or repudiate any agreement.

Section 154 prohibits the publication of advertisements and certain other information in circumstances where listing particulars are to be published unless either it has been approved by the Stock Exchange or the Stock Exchange has indicated that it may be published without such approval. Guidance may need to be sought from the Stock Exchange on the issue of each advertisement.

The relationship between s 57 and s 154 is a problem area. Section 154 is wider than s 57 since it regulates the issue of advertisements and other information specified in the Yellow Book, while s 57 only regulates investment advertise-ments, defined by s 57(2).

Section 57, which restricts the issue of investment advertisements, does not apply to advertisements which are subject to s 154 (s 58(1)(d)(i)), and so s 57 may apply to investment advertisements where s 154 does not. Section 57 is also disapplied in relation to advertisements which consist of listing particulars or other documents required or permitted by the Yellow Book (s 58(1)(d)(ii)). This is discussed in Chapter 13).

Material which is likely, depending upon the circumstances, to fall within s 154 may include a mini prospectus, a press release giving details of a forthcoming offer for sale or placing, or a share application form.

## 4.3  When listing particulars are not required

The listing rules contained in the Yellow Book relax in some specific circumstances the general requirement that listing particulars are required. Depending upon the circumstances these may include:

(1) where listing particulars have been published within the preceding 12 months;

(2) where convertible securities are being converted, or warrants exercised and an issue is being made of shares of a class already listed;

(3) where shares of a listed class are being issued to employees;

(4) where there is a small issue of listed shares (less than 10 per cent of the then issued number);

(5) where securities are listed in another member state of the EU for not less than three years;

(6) where the issuer's shares have been traded on the USM for at least the two preceding years.

Where, there is an exemption from the obligation to publish listing particulars, then certain specified information, according to the circumstances, has to be published in printed form. This may be in an exempt listing document instead of listing particulars. The exempt listing document then has to be published as if it comprised listing particulars.

If an issuer applies for admission to listing of securities which are to be offered to the public in the United Kingdom for the first time and the issuer has published in the United Kingdom a full prospectus in respect of different securities within the preceding 12 months, then the Yellow Book (as amended following the POS Regulations) permits the prospectus relating to the securities in respect of which the application for listing is made, subject to the provisions of s 146, to contain only those differences which have arisen since the date of publication of the full prospectus and which are likely to influence the value of the securities.

## 4.4 Conditions for admission

The principal conditions for admission of securities to listing contained in the Yellow Book are:

*(a) Conditions relating to applicants*

(1) An applicant must be duly incorporated or otherwise validly established according to the relevant laws of its place of incorporation or establishment, and be operating in conformity with its memorandum and articles of association or equivalent constitutional documents.

(2) The latest financial results, subject to certain exceptions, must cover at least three years and the latest accounts must be in respect of a period ended not more than six months (12 months in the case of a USM company seeking a listing) before the date of the listing particulars.

(3) The company must be carrying on as its main activity, either by itself or through one or more of its subsidiary undertakings, an independent business which is revenue earning and must have done so for at least the period covered by the accounts. There are special rules for investment companies.

(4) A new applicant which is a company must have had continuity of management throughout the period covered by the accounts.

(5) The directors of an applicant which is a company must have, collectively, appropriate expertise and experience for the management of its business.

(6) Each of the directors must be free of conflicts between his duties to the company and private interests and other duties.

(7) The applicant must be capable at all times of operating and making decisions independently of any controlling shareholder and all transactions and relationships in the future between the applicant and any controlling shareholder must be at arm's length and on a normal commercial basis.

*(b) Conditions relating to securities*

(1) The securities to be listed must conform with the law of the applicant's place of incorporation and be issued in accordance with the applicant's constitution.

(2) The securities must be freely transferable.

(3) Except where securities of the same class are already listed, the expected aggregate market value of all securities to be listed must be at least:
   (a) £700,000 for shares
   (b) £200,000 for debt securities.

(4) Where an application for listing has been made for shares at least 25 per cent must be in the hands of the public (although this is currently subject to review).

In addition, a prospective sponsor may well have requirements for the company's minimum turnover and profits before it will sponsor the applicant.

Different conditions apply to particular issues such as mineral or property companies, scientific research based companies and investment entities.

## 4.5   Contents of listing particulars

An application for admission is subject to vetting and approval by the Stock Exchange. Listing particulars must comply with:

(1) the general duty of disclosure contained in s 146 of the FSA;
(2) the specific rules embodied in the Yellow Book; and
(3) any additional conditions imposed by the Council.

Rather than rigidly insisting on the same degree of disclosure in all cases, the FSA and Yellow Book adopt a flexible approach and permit disclosure to be tailored by reference to such factors as the nature of securities, the nature of the issuer, and the nature of persons likely to consider their acquisition. For instance, an issue targeted to professional investors, or a rights issue, will not require the same degree of disclosure as an issue which invites ordinary investors to acquire the securities.

## 4.6 General duty to disclose

Section 146(1) sets out the basic rule for the matters to be disclosed by an issuer in an application for listing. It provides as follows:

> 146(1) In addition to the information specified by listing rules or required by the competent authority as a condition of the admission of any securities to the Official List any listing particulars submitted to the competent authority under s 144 above shall contain all such information as investors and their professional advisers would reasonably require, and reasonably expect to find there, for the purpose of making an informed assessment of:
> (a) the assets and liabilities, financial position, profits and losses, and prospects of the issuer of the securities; and
> (b) the rights attaching to those securities.

Section 146(1) gives effect to the principle contained in art 4(1) of the Listing Particulars Directive, and sets out the test by reference to which the adequacy of disclosure is to be measured.

> 146(2) The information to be included by virtue of this section shall be such information as is mentioned in subsection (1) above which is within the knowledge of any person responsible for the listing particulars or which it would be reasonable for him to obtain by making enquiries.

The information that must be disclosed under this section is in addition to the information required to be disclosed by the Stock Exchange and the Yellow Book. Having fulfilled these requirements you must still consider whether you have fulfilled the 'informed assessment' test in s 146(1).

Although compliance with the Yellow Book will usually satisfy the obligation to disclose in s 146, it does not exhaustively set out the disclosure obligation. The Yellow Book recognises this by reminding issuers that, in addition to its rules, they must have regard to s 146.

The Yellow Book requires the disclosure of the following:

(1) information relating to the issuer, such as its place of incorporation, and details of the persons responsible for the listing particulars;
(2) general information about the issuer and its capital including, for instance, the amount of any convertible debt securities;
(3) a description of its principal activities;
(4) financial information concerning the issuer or its group including information with respect to profits and losses, assets and liabilities, financial record and position in the form of an accountants' report for three years up to the end of the latest audited financial period;
(5) information pertaining to the issuer's management;

(6) recent developments and prospects of the issuer or its group;

(7) additional information relating to debt securities.

There are special requirements for listing particulars issued by particular categories of issuer as referred to at 4.4 above.

There are three particular features to the test in sub-ss 146(1) and (2):

(1) It is objective—the information is such that investors and their advisers would reasonably require and expect. It is recognised that most investors only deal after consulting their advisers.

(2) It is subject to a limitation—only information known to (or reasonably obtainable by) any person responsible for the listing particulars (for whom see below) is to be included. However, this apparent limitation is deceptive. First, information within the knowledge of any person responsible must be included. Secondly, information which such a person ought to have known about is also caught: persons responsible are put under a duty of enquiry. Third, all such information reasonably needed for informed assessment is to be included: this suggests that any information which might affect the judgment of a reasonably prudent or cautious investor or adviser should be disclosed.

(3) It is flexible—in determining what information should be included in listing particulars, the nature of the securities, the issuer, potential investors and the general availability of information should be taken into account.

146(3) In determining what information is required to be included in listing particulars by virtue of this section regard shall be had—

(a) to the nature of the securities and of the issuer of the securities;

(b) to the nature of the persons likely to consider their acquisition;

(c) to the fact that certain matters may reasonably be expected to be within the knowledge of professional advisers of any kind which those persons may reasonably be expected to consult; and

(d) to any information available to investors or their professional advisers by virtue of requirements imposed under s 153 below or by or under any other enactment or by virtue of requirements imposed by a recognised investment exchange for the purpose of complying with para 2(2)(*b*) of Sched 4 to the Act.

## 4.7 Exemptions from disclosure

The Stock Exchange acting under s 148 may authorise the omission of information from listing particulars or supplementary listing particulars required by s 146 (but not if the information is required by any of the EC Directives mentioned above):

148(1)(a) on the ground that its disclosure would be contrary to the public interest.

The concept of public interest is vague. Since, in the first place, disclosure is justified on the ground that it is in the public interest for it to be made, the ground on which it could be dispensed with must be strong. It would probably permit a company having a contract with the government for the supply of defensive weapons to omit disclosing sensitive information about that contract.

> (b) subject to sub-s (2) below, on the ground that its disclosure would be seriously detrimental to the issuer of the securities.

No exemption shall be granted if non-disclosure would be likely to mislead a potential investor as to facts he needs to know to make an informed decision (s 148(2)). It is doubtful whether this sub-section is of much assistance. On the premise that the exclusion of significant information is more likely than not to mislead, it may be difficult to exempt such information on the basis of this provision.

> (c) in the case of securities which fall within para 2 of Sched 1 to this Act as modified by s 142(3)(b) above and are of any class specified by listing rules, on the ground that its disclosure is unnecessary for persons of the kind who may be expected normally to buy or deal in the securities.

This provision is intended to benefit selective marketing of Eurocurrency securities, especially Eurobonds.

## 4.8 Supplementary listing particulars

Supplementary listing particulars must be published when there has been any 'significant change' affecting a matter contained in earlier particulars, or any 'significant new matter' which should be disclosed by particulars (s 147). This covers any new factors arising between publication of the listing particulars and the commencement of dealings in the securities. Supplementary listing particulars may also be required if there is a significant change in matters previously disclosed which would affect the 'informed assessment' test in s 146(1).

> 147(1) If at any time after the preparation of listing particulars for submission to the competent authority under s 144 above before the commencement of dealings in the securities following their admission to the Official List—
> (a) there is a significant change affecting any matter contained in those particulars whose inclusion was required by s 146 above or by listing rules or by the competent authority; or
> (b) a significant new matter arises the inclusion of information in respect of which would have been so required if it had arisen when the particulars were prepared,

278

> the issuer of the securities shall, in accordance with listing rules made for the purposes of this section, submit to the competent authority for its approval and, if approved, publish supplementary listing particulars of the change or new matter.

The change or new matter must be significant in relation to investors and their advisers making an informed assessment. Section 147(2) defines the word significant as follows:

> 147(2) In subs (1) above 'significant' means significant for the purpose of making an informed assessment of the matters mentioned in s 146(1) above.

The question whether any given change is significant is one of fact: neither the FSA 1986 nor the Yellow Book offers any guidance. It will probably include any adverse court decision imposing a heavy financial burden on the issuer, such as an order to pay tax, or the loss of an important contract.

Supplementary listing particulars cannot be issued to correct an omission, or an untrue or misleading statement, in the earlier particulars unless this amounts to a change or new matter. However, it is a defence to liability for such mistakes to draw a correction to the attention of likely investors (s 151(3)) and this correction may take a form similar to that of supplementary listing particulars.

The issuer need not issue supplementary listing particulars if he is ignorant of the change or new matter, but must do so if he is notified of it by a person responsible for the particulars, who is placed under a duty to give such notification (s 147(3)). This subsection is difficult to understand: if someone other than a person responsible (such as the company's auditors or solicitors) notifies the issuer of the event then presumably the issuer's duty under s 147(1) will arise even though they are not persons responsible. It may be unwise to rely on the strict wording of this section in the light of its purpose of ensuring the availability of full information.

Supplementary listing particulars must be submitted to and approved by the Stock Exchange and then published in the same manner as listing particulars, and filed with the Registrar of Companies.

## 4.9 Refusing an application for listing, discontinuance and suspension

The Stock Exchange may refuse an application for listing for either of the following reasons:

> 144(3)(*a*) if it considers that by reason of any matter relating to the issuer the admission of securities would be detrimental to the interests of investors; or

The words 'any matter relating to the issuer' are sufficiently wide to permit the consideration of matters relating to its directors. For example, it might be proper for the Stock Exchange to take into account the fact that some or all of its directors have been convicted for fraud while being directors of another company.

> (*b*) in the case of securities already officially listed in another member state, if the issuer has failed to comply with any obligation to which he is subject by virtue of that listing.

The Stock Exchange must notify the applicant of its decision within six months from the date of the application. If the applicant was required to furnish further particulars, then the period of six months is calculated from the date on which that information is furnished (s 144(4)). The Stock Exchange shall be deemed to have refused the application where it fails to notify the applicant within this period (s 144(5)).

The Council of the Stock Exchange may discontinue the listing of securities in accordance with the Yellow Book if special circumstances preclude normal regular dealings in them, and may also suspend any listing in accordance with the Yellow Book (s 145).

## 5 UNLISTED SECURITIES

### 5.1 The POS Regulations

The POS Regulations came into force on 19 June 1995 and implement the EC Prospectus Directive which applies to 'transferable securities offered to the public for the first time in a member state provided that these securities are not already listed on the stock exchange situated or operated in a member state'. Prior to that date, implementation of the EC Prospectus Directive in the United Kingdom relied on Part IV FSA and on the Yellow Book, in the case of securities for which official listing was sought. For all other offers of securities, implementation relied on Part III of the Companies Act 1985 and on the Companies Act 1985 (Mutual Recognition of Prospectuses) Regulations 1991. The new statutory framework laid down by the POS Regulations involves the repeal (for most purposes) of both Part III of the Companies Act 1985 and also Part V of the FSA (which has never been brought into force). The main impact of the POS Regulations is on offers of unlisted securities. The POS Regulations will apply whenever unlisted securities are offered to the public in the United Kingdom for the first time and they will require anyone who makes a public offer to prepare and file a prospectus. The investment advertisement regime under the FSA continues so that where the POS Regulations do not apply because an exemption under the POS Regulations is available, the relevant document may require to be issued or approved as an investment advertisement by an authorised person under the investment advertisement regime.

## 5.2   Investments affected

Regulation 3 provides that the POS Regulations apply to any investment (including an investment which is to be admitted to dealings on an approved stock exchange—this includes the Alternative Investment Market) which is not listed nor the subject of an application for listing and which falls into any of the following paragraphs of Sched 1 FSA:

1.   Shares.
2.   Debentures.
4.   Warrants to subscribe for or purchase shares or debentures.
5.   Certificates representing securities—depository receipts.

Debt securities with a maturity of less than one year from the date of issue are expressly excluded (reg 3(2)(a)).

## 5.3   Offers of securities

The POS Regulations apply to any offer of securities to the public in the United Kingdom in any form, so that oral offers and offers made in unwritten form (for example, electronically) will be subject to the POS Regulations. Regulation 5 makes it clear that an offer of securities includes not just an offer capable of acceptance but also an invitation to treat and reg 6, like Part IV FSA, states that an 'offer to the public' includes an offer to any section of the public. However, the impact of this wide definition is lessened by the various exemptions which are referred to below.

An offer is caught if it is made to the public in the United Kingdom. An offer is treated as made to the public in the United Kingdom if any of its recipients are in the United Kingdom (reg 6). However, only those recipients need to be taken into account for the purpose of applying the exemptions referred to below. As a result if, for example, the offer is made to fewer than 50 people in the United Kingdom, no prospectus is required irrespective of the number of recipients outside the United Kingdom.

The effect of the POS Regulations is that, unless one of the exemptions applies, an offer to the public in the United Kingdom will be prohibited unless the offeror has first prepared and filed a prospectus with the Registrar of Companies.

## 5.4   Exemptions

Regulation 7 contains a long list of exemptions defining the circumstances in which an offer will not be treated as made to the public. In such cases, as mentioned above, no POS prospectus will be required and the document conveying the offer or invitation will fall into the investment advertisement regime unless there is also an exemption from that regime. The exemptions in reg 7 include the following:

(a) an offer to persons in the context of their trades, professions or occupations—investment and unit trusts, pension funds, investment managers, etc;

(b) an offer made to no more than 50 people;

(c) an offer made to a 'restricted circle of persons' reasonably believed to be sufficiently knowledgeable to understand the risks involved;

(d) an offer made in connection with a bona fide invitation to enter into an underwriting arrangement;

(e) a range of exemptions applying where the securities offered are issued by a private company;

(f) an offer where the minimum consideration per investor exceeds 40,000 ECU;

(g) an offer where the total value of the offer cannot exceed 40,000 ECU;

(h) an offer where each security has a minimum value/price under the offer of 40,000 ECU;

(i) where the offer is made to persons whose 'ordinary activities' involve them in acquiring, holding, managing or disposing of investments for the purposes of their business, or whom it is reasonable to suppose will acquire, hold, manage or dispose of them for those purposes;

(j) offers in connection with a takeover or merger;

(k) bonus issues of shares to existing shareholders;

(l) a restricted offer to employees, former employees and their families;

(m) non-transferable shares eg some partly paid;

(n) Eurobond exemption—if no retail characteristics.

Most of the exemptions may be relied on in combination, with the effect that an offer which is partly in one exemption and partly in another can be treated as exempt. For example, a limited offer to 50 private individuals can be combined with an extensive 'professionals only' marketing. As a result of the application of the two separate exemptions, the prospectus requirements will be disapplied. However, in order to prevent abuse, the POS Regulations do not allow either the 40,000 ECU total value of the offer exemption, or the '50 or fewer persons' exemption to be used more than once in any 12 month period.

In applying the exclusions in reg 7, only what is done in the United Kingdom need by taken into account so that, for example, if an offer is made only to professionals in the United Kingdom and this is combined with an offer to the public outside the United Kingdom, a United Kingdom prospectus will not be required.

## 5.5   The general duty of disclosure

For unlisted offers, where no application for mutual recognition is to be made, the POS Regulations impose a general duty of disclosure similar to that contained in s 146 which applies to listing particulars and a prospectus prepared in connection with an application for listing. This requires the POS prospectus to contain all such information as investors would reasonably require and reasonably expect to find there for the purpose of making an informed assessment of the issuer's assets and liabilities, financial position, profit/loss and prospects and the rights attaching to the securities. The general duty of disclosure does not stop at the point of issue of the prospectus. As with the listing particulars regime, a supplementary document must be produced where, following publication of the principal document, there is a significant change or new matter, or a significant inaccuracy is discovered in the prospectus, which investors need to know about.

## 5.6 Detailed requirements

In addition to the general disclosure provision, Sched 1 to the POS Regulations lays down a series of detailed requirements as to the form and contents of the prospectus. These are very similar to the requirements for prospectuses and listing particulars contained in the Yellow Book. The requirements include, in the case of a United Kingdom company, a requirement to include either the issuer's annual accounts for the preceding three financial years, together with express statements of responsibility by the issuer's directors and auditors or an accountant's report covering the preceding three financial years with, in this case, a responsibility statement by the person preparing the report. Special provisions apply to issuers with a financial record of less than three years. Interim accounts (or a separate accountant's report covering the relevant period) must be produced where more than nine months have elapsed since the end of the last financial year for which accounts were produced. There is no requirement for a table of indebtedness, nor for a summary of material contracts, nor for documents to go on display, nor for a summary of the articles of association, nor for a history of the share capital. However, there is a general duty of disclosure similar to s 146.

There are limited exemptions from the full disclosure requirements conferred by regs 8 and 11. Regulation 8(5) allows 'approved exchanges' (which includes the Alternative Investment Market) to authorise the making of an offer without a prospectus if there is a small issue, so that a company whose securities are traded on an approved exchange can issues securities having a market or nominal value of less than 10 per cent of the class traded without any requirement to prepare a prospectus. Regulation 8(6) allows an approved exchange to cut back the content requirements of a prospectus if the issuer has within the preceding 12 months published a full prospectus containing the information referred to in Sched 1 of the POS Regulations, and reg 8(4) allows information to be omitted from a prospectus in the case of pre-emptive offers if equivalent up-to-date information is available. Regulation 11 permits the grant of specific derogations by the Treasury (or the Secretary of State) or a body designated by it, namely the Stock Exchange.

## 5.7 Liability under the POS Regulations

As in the case of listing particulars or a prospectus produced under Part IV FSA, liability in the case of a false or misleading prospectus attaches to 'the persons responsible' for this prospectus. Regulation 13 states that these are:

(a) the issuer;
(b) where the issuer is a company, its directors and anyone who has agreed to be named in the prospectus as a director or as someone who has agreed to become a director;
(c) anyone who accepts, and is stated in the prospectus as accepting, responsibility for all or part of the prospectus;
(d) the offeror and, where separate from the issuer, its directors;
(e) anyone else who has authorised the contents of the prospectus.

Schedule 1 to the POS Regulations requires that the prospectus lists out all those persons who have statutory responsibility for the accuracy of the prospectus and so a careful judgement as to which persons have statutory responsibility by virtue of 'authorising the contents' of the prospectus will be required. The expression 'offeror' is significant because it is the offeror, and not the issuer, on whom most of the obligations in the POS Regulations fall. Regulation 5 makes it clear that an offeror, for the purposes of the POS Regulations, is the person making the offer as principal, not as agent.

The POS Regulations do not contain a requirement for a responsibility statement by any category of persons as to the information contained in the prospectus. However, a formal statement is required by the directors (of the issuer or, if different, the offeror) to the effect that, to the best of the knowledge of the directors, the information contained in the prospectus is in accordance with the facts and makes no omission likely to affect the import of such information.

## 5.8 Mutual recognition

The POS Regulations make provision for both the recognition in the United Kingdom of prospectuses produced elsewhere in the European Community and for the approval of prospectuses produced by United Kingdom issuers which are to be used outside the United Kingdom. If an offeror wants to rely on the mutual recognition provisions in using the prospectus outside the United Kingdom, the prospectus must comply with the Yellow Book requirements for contents of listing particulars and must be approved by the Stock Exchange. A prospectus or listing particulars produced outside the United Kingdom will be recognised in the United Kingdom if it is produced and approved by the competent authorities in another member state and is to be used in the United Kingdom, whether as listing particulars or as a prospectus.

# 6 CIVIL LIABILITY AND CRIMINAL LIABILITY UNDER PART IV

The FSA contains a number of civil remedies and criminal offences which are peculiar to Part IV. This section discusses:

(1) compensation for false or misleading listing particulars (s 150);
(2) exemption from liability under s 150 (s 151);
(3) persons responsible for listing particulars (s 152).

In this section the regulated investments which are the subject of the listing particulars or prospectus are termed 'securities'.

It is important to bear in mind that these statutory remedies do not displace other remedies such as for breach of contract or negligence.

## 6.1 Liability for untrue or misleading statements

Section 150(1) provides that liability may arise in respect of untrue or misleading statements in listing particulars or supplementary listing particulars, or the omission from listing particulars of information required under s 146 or 147.

> 150(1) Subject to s 151 below, the person or persons responsible for any listing particulars or supplementary listing particulars shall be liable to pay compensation to any person who has acquired any of the securities in question and suffered loss in respect of them as a result of any untrue or misleading statement in the particulars or the omission from them of any matter required to be included by s 146 or 147 above.

Liability under this section will be incurred by 'persons responsible for any listing particulars or supplementary listing particulars'. The persons who will fall into this category are referred to in s 152. They are:

(a) The person who has issued, or will issue, the securities.
(b) Every director (or shadow director) of the company who issues the particulars at the time when the particulars are submitted to the Stock Exchange, or prospectus delivered to the Registrar of Companies.
(c) Every person who, with his authority, is named in the particulars as a director of the company which issues them or as having agreed to become a director.
(d) Each person who accepts, and who is stated in the particulars as accepting, responsibility for any part of them.
(e) Any other person who has authorised any part of the particulars. We discuss the meaning of 'authorise' in Chapter 13.

These categories, of course, only relate to liability under s 150. Different people may be liable in an action for negligent misstatement. There are, furthermore, a number of disqualifications to this general position.

First, a person who is responsible by virtue of being a director of the issuer must be a director at the time when the particulars are submitted to the Stock Exchange.

Secondly, a director who would otherwise be responsible under (b) is not responsible for any particulars if they are published without his knowledge or consent and if, on becoming aware of their publication, he forthwith gives reasonable public notice that they were published without his knowledge or consent (s 152(2)). It is unlikely that this defence will have any practical application as a director will usually give express written confirmation of such particulars.

Thirdly, if the persons referred to in categories (d) and (e) have authorised or accepted responsibility for only part of the particulars, then their responsibility is limited to that part only. Moreover, if the information authorised or approved by them is included out of context, or in a form different to that agreed, then they may escape liability (s 152(3)). For example, a valuer authorising the publication of a report valuing specific assets cannot be held responsible for the entirety of the particulars.

If there is an agreed takeover in circumstances where the target and its directors accept responsibility for information about that company, then responsibility can be split so the bidder's directors take responsibility for all information in the document other than that relating to the target and its directors, while the target's directors will take responsibility for information about the target and themselves.

An issuer of Eurobonds is responsible under this section but its directors will not be (s 152(5) and (6)). If a director has a conflict of interest, then he will not be responsible if the Stock Exchange so certifies (s 152(5)).

A solicitor who gives professional advice on the contents of listing particulars does not become a person responsible solely by reason of giving such advice (s 152(8)) although he could be liable in some other capacity such as an expert whose statement appears in the particulars with his consent, or as a director of the issuer. However, the position is less clear where a solicitor goes beyond giving professional advice and assists the issuer in the preparation of the particulars for submission for listing. The question to be considered is whether by doing so he becomes a person responsible for the particulars either under category (d) or (e) above. Merely putting together information, it is submitted, does not amount to authorisation or acceptance of responsibility. It would be unrealistic to impose such responsibility given the fact that reliance will be placed on the issuer or its directors and officials to provide the relevant information. This would entail the solicitor making investigations into the books of the issuer to discover information or to verify the accuracy of information supplied to him, and it is submitted that the FSA could not have intended such a result.

*(a) Liable to whom?*
Any person who has acquired any of the securities in question may bring a claim under s 150, as may a person who has only contracted to acquire the investments or any interests in them (s 150(5)).

*(b) Liability in respect of what?*

A person may be liable either in respect of

(1) an untrue or misleading statement; or

(2) an omission of any matter required to be included.

*(c) What are untrue or misleading statements?*

The word 'untrue' qualifies the word 'statement'. Does it include forecasts and promises? Section 47 (discussed above) expressly mentions promises and forecasts and their exclusion from s 150 would seem to imply that they are not covered. Secondly, in any event, it is illogical to speak of promises and forecasts as being untrue. Forecasts may turn out to be inaccurate while promises may be broken. In other words, the FSA probably does not depart from the common law position that a statement must be a statement of fact rather than an opinion or a promise. A person making a statement of opinion implies that his opinion is based on facts, and third parties who rely on a his opinion are entitled to assume that they exist. Therefore, if a person were to state an opinion which is not founded on facts,he might be held to have misrepresented that such facts existed (see *Brown v Raphael* [1958] Ch 636). Similarly, a statement declaring future intention, though not relating to an existing fact, may amount to a statement of fact: *Edgington v Fitzmaurice* (1885) 29 Ch D 459. Thus, a statement assuring the payment of dividends for the next three years is not actionable if no dividend is paid during those years but liability may arise if, when making the assurance, the company never had any intention of doing so.

*(d) When is an omission actionable?*

An omission, to be actionable, must be an omission of any of the matters required to be included by ss 146 and 147. For example, s 146 requires disclosure of information relevant to the prospects of the issuer which would include profit forecasts (s 146(1)(a)): there is no limitation that an omission must relate to an existing fact. Ignorance of the omitted matter will not necessarily offer a defence because the duty is cast on a person to include information which it would be reasonable for him to obtain by making enquiries (s 146(2)).

Section 150(2) has the effect of rendering an omission of some matter required to be included by the listing rules as a negative statement that there is no such matter. In cases where information should be included, the omission will amount to an untrue statement. Section 150(2) provides the following:

150(2) Where listing rules require listing particulars to include information as to any particular matter on the basis that the particulars must include a statement either as to that matter or, if such is the case, that there is no such matter, the omission from the particulars of the information shall be treated for the purposes of subs (1) above as a statement that there is no such matter.

The Stock Exchange may, under s 148, authorise the omission from the particulars of information otherwise required by s 146: for example, information relating to debentures on the ground that its disclosure is unnecessary for persons of the kind expected normally to buy or deal in them. The Yellow Book authorises such omission with regard to specialist debt securities including Eurobonds for which the market consists principally of institutional investors. Since what is authorised to be excluded from s 146 is not required to be included by that section, omission of those particulars will not ground an action under s 150. Furthermore, s 150(6) states that no person shall be liable for failing to disclose information which he is entitled to omit by virtue of s 148.

> 150(6) No person shall by reason of being a promoter of a company or otherwise incur any liability for failing to disclose any information which he would not be required to disclose in listing particulars in respect of a company's securities if he were responsible for those particulars or, if he is responsible for them, which he is entitled to omit by virtue of s 148 above. The reference above to a person incurring liability includes a reference to any other person being entitled as against that person to be granted any civil remedy or to rescind or repudiate any agreement.

Can an action be based on s 150(1) in respect of an omission of information required by the continuing obligation provisions of the Yellow Book? Section 146 requires disclosure of the listing particulars to be submitted as part of an application under s 144, so information outside the listing particulars will not afford a basis for an action under s 150. However, failure to comply with s 147 (obligation to publish supplementary listing particulars) can give rise to a claim for compensation under s 150(3), discussed below.

*(e) Loss and causation*
The claimant must have suffered loss in respect of the securities as a result of any untrue or misleading statement or omission in the particulars. A loss resulting from some other aspect of the particulars will not be actionable under this section. It is unclear whether the claimant must have acquired the securities direct from the issuer. On a strict reading one could argue that there is no requirement for the claimant to prove reliance on the particulars, or for there to be a contract between the parties. If this is right, a purchaser in the secondary market may be able to sue. An alternative interpretation is that s 150 is not intended to protect someone who acquires securities in the secondary market within a reasonable period after publication of the listing particulars, and is only concerned with the time up to commencement of dealing and acquisition in the primary market. This latter argument can be supported on two limbs. First, that Part IV is only concerned with the listing of securities, and not with subsequent dealings.

Secondly, s 150 is intended to overturn the long established rule that a shareholder who retains his shares (and does not exercise a right to rescind) cannot bring an action against the company for misrepresentations or breaches of contract by which he was induced to take them (see *Houldsworth v City of Glasgow Bank* (1879) 5 AC 317; *re Addlestone Linoleum Company* (1888) 37 Ch 191).

It is not enough to prove that a loss has been suffered; it must also be proved to have been caused by the untrue or misleading statement or omission. It may be difficult to establish that a technical breach of the listing rules has caused loss.

In practice, causation may be difficult to establish, especially by a market purchaser. Presumably a claimant must show that, had the statement been true and fair, or had the omitted matter been included, the securities would have been bought or valued at a materially different price. Furthermore, if a long time has elapsed between admission to listing and the claimant buying the shares, it may be difficult to argue that the loss arose from some fault in the particulars rather than from some other factor.

The measure of damages in an action for compensation is likely to be the difference between the value of the shares and the price paid for them. There is no statutory right to rescission under s 150.

Section 150 does not preclude other legal action (s 150(4)). Other heads of action include

(1) negligent misrepresentation: however, a plaintiff may find it difficult to prove that he has suffered loss in consequence of the breach of a duty of care owed to him in respect of a negligent statement in listing particulars;

(2) deceit or fraudulent misrepresentation: the claimant must show he made a loss in reliance upon a material, and fraudulently made, misrepresentation of fact;

(3) misrepresentation: a contractual claim for damages may be available under the Misrepresentation Act 1967;

(4) rescission: if the subscriber is induced by, and relies upon, a material misrepresentation he can seek rescission and damages;

(5) professional advisers may be liable in negligence, and under s 62.

## 6.2 Defences

A defendant to an action under s 150(1) may avail himself of the defences contained in s 151. There are two principal (and a number of other) ways in which he may escape liability.

*(a) He believed the statement was true*
First, he may satisfy the court that he believed the statements were true or that omissions were properly made. To succeed, he must satisfy the court that at the time the particulars were submitted he reasonably believed that the statement was true and not misleading or that the omission was properly omitted. His belief must have been arrived at after having made such enquiries (if any) as are reasonable. Section 151(1) sets out the following:

151(1)　A person shall not incur any liability under s 150(1) above for any loss in respect of securities caused by any such statement or omission as is there mentioned if he satisfies the court that at the time when the particulars were submitted to the competent authority he reasonably believed, having made such enquiries (if any) as were reasonable, that the statement was true and not misleading or that the matter whose omission caused the loss was properly omitted and . . .

Circumstances where it may be reasonable to make no enquiries would be in a hostile takeover, where only public material about the merger is available.

In addition, in accordance with s 151(1) he must establish any one of the following:

    (a)　that he continued in that belief until the time when the securities were acquired; or

    (b)　that they were acquired before it was reasonably practicable to bring a correction to the attention of persons likely to acquire the securities; or

    (c)　that before they were acquired, he took reasonable steps to have the correction brought to the notice of the persons likely to acquire the securities; or

    (d)　that he continued in that belief until after the commencement of dealing in the securities after their admission and that the securities were acquired after such a lapse of time that he ought in the circumstances to be reasonably excused.

The defence includes both a subjective element and an objective element. The requirement that the belief must be reasonable imports an objective standard by reference to which the defendant's belief will have to be judged. This corresponds to the duty imposed under s 146 that a person responsible must disclose information of which he is aware or which it would be reasonable for him to obtain by making enquiries. These provisions may conceivably impose a duty to correct information even after the securities have been admitted. The most obvious way to do so will be to disclose the corrected information to the market. It may be difficult for a person to avoid liability if he makes no effort to correct the information after becoming aware that the particulars contained false or misleading information.

A person responsible for listing particulars may have a similar defence under s 151(2) in relation to loss resulting from experts' statements. An expert is defined by s 151(7).

*(b) Acquired with knowledge*

Secondly, the defendant may avoid liability for a claim under s 150(1) and (3) by showing that the claimant acquired the securities with the knowledge that the statement was false or misleading, or that he knew of the omitted matter. Strictly speaking, this is not a defence at all because a person who knew that the statement was misleading could not have been misled in the first place. But this places the burden on the defendant to show that he knew the statement was untrue or misleading.

> 151(5) A person shall not incur any liability under s 150(1) or (3) above if he satisfies the court that the person suffering the loss acquired the securities in question with knowledge that the statement was false or misleading, of the omitted matter or of the change or new matter, as the case may be.

There are three further possible defences, two of which relate to s 150(1) and one of which relates to s 150(3):

(1) where the person responsible publishes a correction, or takes all reasonable steps to do so (s 151(3));

> 151(3) Without prejudice to subss (1) and (2) above, a person shall not incur any liability under s 150(1) above for any loss in respect of any securities caused by any such statement or omission as is there mentioned if he satisfies the court—
> (a) that before the securities were acquired a correction, or where the statement was such as is mentioned in sub-s (2), the fact that the expert was not competent or had not consented had been published in a manner calculated to bring it to the attention of persons likely to acquire the securities in question; or
> (b) that he took all such steps as it was reasonable for him to take to secure such publication and reasonably believed that it had taken place before the securities were acquired.

(2) where the person responsible has reproduced an official statement or document (s 151(4));

> 151(4) A person shall not incur any liability under s 150(1) above for any loss resulting from a statement made by an official person or contained in a public official document which is included in the particulars if he satisfies the court that the statement is accurately and fairly reproduced.

(3) where the person responsible did not comply with s 147 because he reasonably thought the change or new matter was insignificant (s 151(6)).

> 151(6) A person shall not incur any liability under s 150(3) above if he satisfies the court that he reasonably believed that the change or new matter in question was not such as to call for supplementary listing particulars.

## 6.3 Failure to comply with section 147

Liability under s 150(3) for failure to comply with s 147 differs from liability under s 150(1). Under sub-s (1), liability arises in respect of any untrue or misleading statement in the particulars, or the omission from them of any matter to be included by ss 146 and 147. Liability under sub-s (3), however, only arises in respect of failure to comply with s 147. Section 150(3) provides the following:

> 150(3)   Subject to s 151 below, a person who fails to comply with s 147 above shall be liable to pay compensation to any person who has acquired any of the securities in question and suffered loss in respect of them as a result of the failure.

Sub-section (3) applies only if there has been a failure to publish supplementary listing particulars. Subsection (1) assumes that the listing particulars have been published, but that the particulars are defective.

Liability under s 150(3) attaches to 'a person who fails to comply with s 147'. It will be noted that the duty under s 147 is imposed on the issuer of the securities but he is excused if he is unaware of the change or new matter (s 147(3)). A further duty is cast in that sub-section on a person responsible who is aware of any change or new matter to inform the issuer who shall then notify the Stock Exchange. Thus, a director who is aware of any significant change must bring it to the notice of the company. When producing listing particulars each director usually undertakes to the others to bring such matters promptly to their attention.

Non-compliance with s 147 may take the form of a failure by the issuer to publish supplementary particulars, or a failure by a person responsible to notify the issuer. Once a director has fulfilled his duty to give notice to the issuer in terms of s 147 he cannot be held liable under s 150(3) if the issuer defaulted on the obligation to notify the Stock Exchange.

The nature of the obligation under s 147 is comparatively lighter than the obligation imposed by s 146. Under s 147 the issuer is required to furnish particulars of changes and new matters which he knows or which have been brought to his notice. By contrast, under s 146, a person must disclose both what he knows and what he ought to have known after making reasonable enquiries.

Liability under s 150(3) is stricter than liability under sub-s (1): most of the s 151 defences can be pleaded only in respect of an action based on sub-s (1).

## 7   INSIDER DEALING

### 7.1   Introduction

Insider dealing has been illegal in the United Kingdom since 1980. The relevant legislation used to be contained in the Company Securities (Insider Dealing) Act 1985 (the '1985 Act') and ss 173–176 of the FSA, although from 1 March 1994 the 1985 Act was replaced by:

(1) Part V of the Criminal Justice Act 1993 (the 'CJA').
(2) The Insider Dealing (Securities and Regulated Markets) Order 1994 (SI No 187), which specifies the securities to which the insider dealing provisions apply and identifies regulated markets.
(3) The Traded Securities (Disclosure) Regulations 1994 (SI No 188).

These give effect to the requirements of the EC Directive on the Co-ordination of Laws on Insider Dealing (Council Directive No 89/592/EEC OJ L334/30). The FSA's provisions for investigation of insider dealing offences continue to apply (ss 173–176), subject to several minor amendments to bring them into line with the CJA.

## 7.2   Criminal Justice Act 1993

The CJA maintains the three basic offences of dealing, encouraging dealing, and disclosing inside information (ss 52 and 53).

It is an offence for an *individual* who *has information as an insider* to *deal* on a *regulated market* or as a *professional intermediary* or *in reliance on* a professional intermediary in *securities* whose price would be significantly affected if the *inside information* were *made public* ('price-affected securities'). A number of these elements are repeated in the other two offences set out below.

It is also an offence for an individual who has information as an insider to encourage dealing (which he knows or has reasonable cause to believe will be dealing of the kind referred to above) in price-affected securities by another person (regardless of whether the other person knows this).

The third offence is constituted if an individual who has information as an insider discloses the information to another, except in the proper performance of his employment, office or profession.

The components of each offence are complex and it is necessary to consider a number of definitions in order to ascertain whether an offence has been committed.

(1) *'individual'*: an individual must be a human person. A company cannot commit the offences summarised above. Therefore there is still scope to use Chinese Walls within a company, in appropriate circumstances, to prevent individuals who will be making dealing decisions on one side of the wall from becoming insiders as a result of information held by employees on the other side (subject to any breaches of the wall). Dealings by a company can still include primary offences being committed by individuals. An employee of the company can still commit an offence as that company's agent or, for example, by 'encouraging' the company to commit the dealing offence.
(2) *'inside information'*: this definition has been widened from the previous law and has four elements:

(a) it must be information which relates either to particular securities or to the company which has issued the securities, or to several companies (perhaps within a particular sector of industry) but not to securities of companies generally. For example, a forecast might show that the profits of a particular company would be different from market expectations. It should be noted that information is treated as 'relating to' not only the company concerned but also other companies which might affect its business prospects. For example, information about Company A's main supplier, Company B, going into liquidation would be information which also relates to Company A;

(b) the information must be 'specific' or 'precise';

(c) the information must not have been 'made public' (see below);

(d) the information (if made public) must be likely to have a significant effect on the price of *any* 'securities'. The use of the word 'significant' suggests that the information must potentially have a more than trivial impact on the price of any securities.

(3) *'has information as an insider'* (insiders and inside source): this is defined by s 57 of the CJA which contains the concept of 'inside source'. An individual has information in this capacity if:

(a) information is, and the individual knows that it is, 'inside information' and

(b) he has it, and knows he has it, from an inside source.

Section 57(2) CJA states that a person has information from an inside source only if:

(c) he has it through:
   (i) being a director, employee or shareholder of an issuer of securities; or
   (ii) having access to the information by virtue of his employment, office or profession; or

(d) the direct or indirect source of his information is a person within paragraph (c).

The scope of the definition under the CJA is much wider than the old legislation which was mainly concerned with preventing people who are knowingly connected with a company from misusing information by dealing in that company's shares. The CJA no longer requires a connection between the 'inside source' and the company whose shares are price affected by the information.

(4) *'made public'*: There are two categories of information within this definition (s 58 CJA):

(a) Information which will definitely be regarded as made public (s 58(2) CJA). For example:

- information published in accordance with the rules of a regulated market in order to inform investors and their advisors. Thus, for example, once the announcement has been released through the Stock Exchange, it will be 'public';
- information included in a record required by any enactment to be open to public inspection;
- information which can be readily acquired by anyone likely to deal in any securities to which it relates, or in securities of an issuer to which it relates or
- information derived from public information.

(b) The CJA sets out a number of situations where information may, depending on the circumstances, be treated as made public despite certain features which limit its circulation (s 58(3) CJA):

- information obtainable only through 'diligence or expertise';
- information communicated only to a section of the public (this is likely to be relevant to analysts);
- information obtainable only by 'observation';
- information communicated only on payment of a fee; or
- information published only outside the United Kingdom.

(5) *'securities'*: These are set out in Sched 2 of the CJA and in the Insider Dealing (Securities and Regulated Markets) Order 1994 (SI No 187) and include company shares and stock, debt securities of companies and public sector bodies and related warrants, depository receipts, options, futures and contracts for differences.

The distinction in the old legislation between United Kingdom registered and foreign companies is now removed. Under the order mentioned above, the CJA regime will now apply to the Sched 2 securities which are either:

(a) officially listed in a State within the European Economic Area ('EEA'); or

(b) admitted to dealing on, or have their prices quoted on, or under the rules of a regulated market (as set out in the order referred to at (7) below).

Debt: Sched 2 debt securities are defined as 'any instrument creating or acknowledging indebtedness which is issued by a company or public sector body.' The CJA therefore widens the definition of securities to include not only corporate debt, debentures and Eurobonds but also debt securities of public sector bodies, such as gilts and local authority bonds.

Under the CJA regime, warrants, depository receipts and derivatives (including options, futures and contracts for differences) are treated as securities if the rights under those instruments relate to shares or debt securities which are either officially listed in a state within the EEA, or are admitted to dealing on or have their prices quoted on or under the rules of a regulated market.

(6) *'dealing'*: For the offence to be committed the relevant acquisition or disposal must be on a 'regulated market' or effected by a 'professional intermediary' or the relevant person dealing must be relying on a 'professional intermediary'.

The old legislation prevented an insider from dealing on a recognised stock exchange, but only prohibited off-market dealings if made through a 'market maker'. The CJA now greatly widens the scope of the offences in relation to private or off-exchange deals by catching off-market dealings by a person who 'relies on a professional intermediary' or is himself 'acting as a professional intermediary' (see below).

(7) *'regulated market'*: See the Insider Dealing (Securities and Regulated Markets) Order 1994 (SI No 187). The regulated markets listed in the order are in EEA Member States (which includes Scandinavia, Austria and Liechtenstein). The relevant regulated markets in the United Kingdom are the London Stock Exchange. LIFFE and OMLX.

(8) *'professional intermediary'*: A professional intermediary is someone who carries on a business of acquiring or disposing of securities or acting as an intermediary in such a transaction and who holds himself out as willing to do so in any of the following capacities:

- as a broker or other person dealing as an agent;
- as an 'intermediary between persons taking any part in any dealing in securities'; or
- as a market maker, or other person dealing as a principal.

Firms which only engage in these activities occasionally or incidentally are excluded from the definition.

Section 59(4) CJA states:

For the purposes of section 52, a person dealing in the securities relies on a professional intermediary if . . . a person who is acting as a professional intermediary carries out . . . in relation to that dealing' one of the following activities:

'(a) acquiring or disposing of securities (whether as principal or agent); or

(b) acting as an intermediary between persons taking part in any dealing in securities'.

## 7.3 Jurisdiction

There has to be a link with the United Kingdom. An individual is caught by the CJA if:

(1) he is in the United Kingdom when he commits the acts which constitute the dealing offence or form part of that offence; or

(2) the regulated market (in the case of the dealing offence) is regulated in the United Kingdom or the professional intermediary is in the United Kingdom at the time he acts; or

(3) the encouragement or disclosure (in the case of the encouraging and disclosing offences) was made or received in the United Kingdom.

Other elements of these offences may be carried out in other EU Member States, provided the individual falls within one of the above requirements.

## 7.4 Defences

The defences set out in the CJA fall into two categories.

(1) General defences (s 53).
(2) Specific defences (Sched 1).

*(a) General defences*
Section 53 contains defences for all three types of prohibited activity. The defences to the 'dealing' and 'encouraging' offences are similar.

For all three offences (dealing, encouragement and disclosure) it is a defence for the individual to show that he did not expect the dealing to result in a profit (or the avoidance of a loss) attributable to the inside information.

The dealing and encouragement offences are subject to two further defences:

(1) at the time of the dealing or encouragement the individual believed on reasonable grounds that the information was (or in the case of encouragement would be) disclosed widely enough to ensure that none of the parties to the dealing would be prejudiced by not having the information.

(2) the individual would have done what he did even without the information.

For the disclosure offence it is also a defence for the individual to show that he did not expect the disclosure to result in any person dealing on a regulated market or dealing as or through a professional intermediary.

*(b) Specific defences*
The specific defences are set out in Sched 1 to the CJA and only apply to the dealing and encouraging offences.

The market information defence to the dealing and encouraging offences may be available where the insider can show the information was market information that it was reasonable for an individual in his position to have acted upon as he did, or where:

(1) the inside information which the insider had was market information arising directly out of his involvement in the acquisition or disposal of securities, as distinct from the information about the issuer concerned; and

(2) he acted:

(i) in connection with an acquisition or disposal which was under consideration or the subject of negotiation; and

(ii) with a view to facilitating a proposed acquisition or disposal.

For this purpose market information is information consisting of one or more of the following facts:

(1) that particular securities have been or are to be purchased or sold;
(2) that particular securities have not been or are not to be purchased or sold;
(3) the price at which the securities are to be purchased or sold;
(4) the number of securities to be purchased or sold;
(5) the identity of anyone involved or likely to be involved in the acquisition or disposal.

There are also separate special defences for market makers and those involved in price stabilisation.

## 7.5 Penalties

The penalties under the insider dealing legislation remain unaltered. Under s 61 CJA:

– on summary proceedings the penalty is a fine and/or a period of imprisonment of up to six months
– on indictment the penalty is a fine and/or up to seven years imprisonment

The CJA also provides that 'no contract shall be void or unenforceable by reason only' of insider dealing.

## 7.6 Investigations

The investigation provisions are contained in the FSA. The Secretary of State has power under s 177 to appoint inspectors to investigate alleged offences. Inspectors have powers to require production of documents, attendance and reasonable assistance. It is expressly provided by s 177(6) that replies given to an inspector in response to his statutory powers may be used in evidence against the witness.

## 7.7 Conclusion

Under the Insider Dealing Directive, the CJA regime affects a broader range of individuals and information, and approaches liability on the basis of unfair informational advantage. The current legislation is as technical as before and defines insider dealing very widely, making it no easier to prove the offence. If a civil penalty for those who engage in such activities (and market manipulation) were introduced, then there could be a real disincentive to engage in such activities.

# 15 Banking Business

This chapter sets out to discuss, in outline, the impact of the FSA on banking business. We cover:

(1) the relevance of the regulated investments and investment activities to a bank's business.

(2) how the FSA may affect secured lending, syndicated lending and securitisation. These are complicated fields, so we concentrate on the principles rather than their application. In each case it will be necessary to consider the detailed documentation in order to determine the FSA's impact.

(3) advertising banking products.

(4) the exemption for listed money market institutions.

The regulation of banking business under the Banking Act 1987 is separate from, and complementary to, the FSA's regulation of investment business.

The FSA itself contains only a few references to banking, but its impact on business carried on by banks is very substantial.

First, a banking body, or more likely its subsidiary, may engage in activities other than the traditional business of banking such as investment broking or management. A stockbroking, investment management or life assurance or unit trust broking subsidiary will almost certainly be carrying on investment business in its own right and require authorisation under the FSA in the same way as any other investment business.

Secondly, while the activity of taking deposits falls wholly outside the FSA (being regulated under the Banking Act 1987), many kinds of lending involve investment activities in relation to regulated investments. Where a bank cannot take advantage of the FSA's exclusions it may be carrying on investment business and require to be authorised under the FSA.

Whether any specific activity amounts to carrying on investment business, and how a bank should obtain authorisation, will in each case be a question of fact depending entirely on the particular circumstances.

A bank considering authorisation under the FSA must address the same issues as any other potential investment business.

(1) First, do any of its activities constitute carrying on investment business? While the bank may be carrying on an investment activity in respect of regulated investments, it may be able to rely on one or more of the FSA's

exclusions. It may be an exempted person as a listed money market institution pursuant to s 43: this is discussed at the end of the Chapter. A number of banks, although not the principal United Kingdom clearing or merchant banks, have not obtained authorisation under the FSA.

(2) Secondly, if the bank is carrying on investment business, how should it obtain authorisation? Being an exempted person as a listed institution may not be sufficient in light of the restricted 'exempt' activities in Sched 5 discussed below. The authorisation which a bank or its subsidiary must obtain will depend on the investment business which it carries on, and the scope of the authorisation conferred on it will depend on the identity of the SRO, and the business profile which it has agreed with the SRO.

(3) Thirdly, once the bank is authorised, what is the impact of the conduct of business rules of its SRO? This, again, will depend on the nature of the investment business in question. The main rules and duties which are relevant to a person authorised under the FSA are discussed in Chapter 3.

# 1   THE REGULATED INVESTMENTS

We discuss these in detail in Chapter 7. It may, however, be helpful to emphasise how they may be relevant to banking business. Each number refers to a paragraph in Sched 1.

(1) *Shares*: A bank may take a security interest over shares when making a loan.

(2) *Debentures*: An instrument creating or acknowledging indebtedness is caught as a debenture, subject to the Note to para 2 to Sched 1. Many instruments such as commercial paper or promissory notes created or traded by a bank will fall within this paragraph, as will a charge.

(3) *Government securities*: A bank may trade in these, or take a security interest over them.

(4) *Instruments entitling to shares or securities*: A bank may trade in these, or take a security interest over them.

(5) *Certificates representing securities*: As well as trading in these certificates, a mortgage over the shares of one company will be an investment falling within para 5.

(6) *Collective investment scheme units*: These may be traded in or used as part of a security interest.

(7) *Options*: A bank may grant or acquire an option as part of a security interest, or over foreign currency in the course of its business.

(8) *Futures*: Banks often enter into futures contracts. The question to be considered in each case is whether such a contract is for commercial rather than investment purposes as determined by reference to the Notes to this paragraph. In the case of a contract for forward foreign exchange, this is

not immediately clear. Under a contract for forward foreign exchange, a bank converts one currency for another. The price is fixed at the date of the contract, but delivery may not always be within seven days. The 'conclusive' tests in para 8 to Sched 1 do not assist in determining whether such a contract is caught: for this example let us assume that delivery is not within seven days and the contract is not made on an exchange. One must then consider the 'pointers', which are also inconclusive in this example, although Note (4) is of some assistance. While neither party will 'produce' the foreign exchange, the bank could be said to use it in its business (Note 4(a)). Furthermore, depending on how the contract is drafted, at least one of the parties will at the date of the contract intend to deliver or take delivery of the foreign exchange, thereby fulfilling Note (4(b)). Provided the contract envisages that delivery will take place, this should be sufficient evidence that either (or both) parties intend to deliver at the date of the contract, even if the contract is subsequently cancelled. If delivery takes place, even if it is netted off, then Note (4(b)) will apply.

(9) *Contracts for differences*: A bank will often enter into a currency swap or an interest swap, and these may fall within this paragraph.

(10) *Life assurance*: A bank may take a security interest in a life assurance policy in connection with making a loan.

(11) *Rights and interests in investments*: This paragraph may include an interest in a regulated investment held under a trust or a mortgage over a regulated investment. A mortgage of shares falls within para 2, but is excluded by Note (c) because it is a disposition of property. It will also fall within para 5, since a mortgage of shares confers property rights in an investment, and will only be excluded by the Note to para 5 if it is a mortgage over two or more companies' shares. A mortgage over more than one company's shares may be an investment falling within para 11, since it does not fall within any other paragraph.

## 2   THE INVESTMENT ACTIVITIES

The ways in which a bank may engage in investment activities in relation to regulated investments are the same as for any other person.

(1) *Dealing*: A bank may deal in investments if, for example, it buys shares, takes an assignment of a life assurance policy, takes a security interest in shares, or a charge over units in a collective investment scheme. It may, however, be able to take advantage of the exclusions discussed below.

(2) *Arranging deals*: A bank may arrange for a third party to deal.

(3) *Managing*: A bank may manage investments.

(4) *Advice*: A bank may give investment advice.

(5) *Operating a collective investment scheme*: A bank may operate a collective investment scheme.

Bearing these general principles in mind, we now examine three particular areas: secured lending, syndicated lending and securitisation.

# 3 SECURED LENDING

We discuss the effect of the FSA on a secured lending transaction by reference to a particular example: a bank enters into a loan agreement under which the borrower has a right to borrow a sum of money which is repayable after five years. The borrower gives security over shares and a life assurance policy. Let us assume that both the bank and the borrower are effecting these transactions in the course of a business.

## 3.1 Is the loan agreement a debenture?

As discussed in Chapter 7, a loan agreement will not necessarily fall within the definition of a debenture under para 2 of Sched 1. It may just specify the terms that will apply to future indebtedness rather than itself create or acknowledge indebtedness, and in such a case it is unlikely to be a debenture for the purposes of the FSA. However, one or more debentures may well come into existence after drawdown because the documentation will then acknowledge existing indebtedness. It is important to emphasise that the position will in each case depend upon the construction of the documentation.

The exclusionary Note to para 2 must be considered when discussing debentures. Note (a) may exclude the debenture from para 2 if the loan is for goods or services. Note (b) is unlikely to apply since the loan agreement is not a bill of exchange or letter of credit, draft or cheque. Note (c) is also unlikely to assist since the loan agreement itself is probably not a disposition of property.

## 3.2 Are the security documents debentures or otherwise regulated investments?

A mortgage or charge over shares and an assignment of the life assurance policy potentially fall within para 2 by virtue of creating or acknowledging indebtedness. However, a mortgage or an assignment of either of these regulated investments will entail a disposition of property and should be excluded from para 2 by Note (c). A charge over shares will, however, fall within para 2.

A mortgage of the shares will also fall within para 5: it is an instrument which confers property rights over the shares, which are investments falling within para 1. If it were a mortgage of the shares of two or more companies, though, it would be excluded from para 5 by virtue of the Note.

Paragraph 11 takes in rights and interests in investments falling within Sched 1 which rights or interests are not already caught (see Note (2)). Accordingly, the assignment of the life policy (which falls within para 10) and the mortgage of the shares (if they are issued by two or more companies) will come within para 11.

We are therefore concerned in this transaction with:

(1) a debenture (para 2);
(2) a certificate representing securities (para 5) (but only if the mortgage is of one company's shares);
(3) rights and interests in investments (para 11).

We must now consider what investment activities may be engaged in, in relation to these regulated investments.

## 3.3 Investment activities relating to regulated investments

We must consider whether either of the parties is dealing in these regulated investments. Let us assume that neither the bank nor the borrower will be arranging (because both are parties to the resulting transaction), and also that the bank has not advised the borrower on the transaction (so it will not have engaged in the investment activity of advising), and that there is no question of either party managing investments or operating a collective investment scheme.

*(a) Is the bank dealing by entering into documents evidencing the loan?*
Possibly not. Some or all of these documents may constitute debentures falling within para 2 if they do not come within the Note to para 2 and, in principle, the bank will be dealing in them within para 12 by accepting them. However, if the debenture relates to a loan it has made then the bank should not be dealing on account of the exclusion in the Notes to para 12.

*(b) Is the bank dealing by taking a security interest over the shares and life assurance policy?*
Where the document representing the security interest is a debenture under para 2, the position will be as outlined in the preceding paragraph. In other cases, the bank probably will be dealing by taking a security interest, unless it can rely on the dealing as principal exclusions discussed below, or another of the FSA exclusions.

*(c) Is the borrower dealing by entering into documents evidencing the loan?*
If the loan agreement creates or acknowledges indebtedness then, subject to Note (a)–(c) to para 2, it may be a debenture. However, if it is not, then a debenture may be created on drawdown. In either case, though, the borrower will not be dealing since although it is issuing a debenture (and therefore dealing within para 12 by virtue of the extended definition given in para 28(2)(b)), the transaction is excluded by para 28(3), since the borrower is issuing its own debenture. If this

exclusion were unavailable, then the dealing as principal exclusions discussed below should be considered.

*(d)  Is the borrower dealing by mortgaging or charging the shares and assigning the life assurance policy?*
In principle 'yes'. The borrower will deal when it charges the shares; if the mortgage of shares falls within para 5, the borrower is dealing by creating the mortgage which grants rights to the lender for the valuable consideration of a loan. The borrower will also be disposing of its rights, and therefore dealing, by assigning the life policy or, if the mortgage of shares falls within para 11, by mortgaging the shares. However, before reaching any conclusion, we must consider the dealing as principal exclusions.

## 3.4   The application of the dealing as principal exclusions

The application of these exclusions for this loan transaction is relevant to both the borrower and the bank entering into the security documents.

We are here concerned with the wider 'dealing as principal' exclusion arising under para 17(3) because we are discussing debentures, a mortgage over shares and the assignment of a life assurance policy. In order to fall within this exclusion each party must show:

(1)  it is not engaging in an activity akin to market making in the investments; and
(2)  it does not hold itself out as engaging in the business of buying these investments with a view to selling them; and
(3)  it does not regularly solicit the public to induce them to enter into this kind of transaction.

Each of these elements must be considered in turn, and we discuss the considerations in detail in Chapter 8. However, for the purpose of this example, we can conclude by saying:

(1)  it is likely that the borrower will fall within this exclusion;
(2)  the lender will need to consider its position under (c) very carefully.

## 4   SYNDICATED LENDING

A syndicated loan agreement is an agreement entered into by a group of banks pursuant to which they lend directly to the borrower under a single loan agreement. Lending banks have always perceived such an agreement (a primary syndicated loan agreement) as a collection of individual loan contracts conveniently documented in one single agreement which effectively enables the participants to extend a facility they would not be prepared to advance individually, because of the value of the facility, current exposure to the borrower or some other reason. A primary syndicated loan agreement is usually arranged by one bank (often referred to as the lead bank) which commonly negotiates and documents the syndicated loan agreement on behalf of the participants. Once the syndicated loan agreement has been executed, the lead manager effectively drops out of the picture and the responsibility of administering the loan generally falls upon the agent bank who may, however, also be the lead bank.

The primary syndicated loan agreement differs from the secondary syndication agreements which come into existence when a single bank, which has lent directly to a borrower or as a participant in a primary syndicated loan agreement, sells all or part of its interest in that loan to other banks. Many primary syndicated loan agreements enable the participants to sell all or part of their interest in the syndicated loan to other banks who need not be party to the original syndicated loan agreement. A participation in a primary syndicated loan agreement may generally be transferred by way of an assignment, novation or participation. The nature and implications of these methods of transfer for the purposes of the FSA are considered below.

On account of the variety and complexity of syndicated lending arrangements it is not practicable to deal with the FSA's impact on all possible permutations. We therefore consider the FSA's general implications for the basic structure of a syndicated loan agreement, and the relationships between the parties involved. We aim to highlight the main consequences arising from these arrangements and, in practice, any specific arrangement should be considered in far greater detail. The regulated investment which is most relevant is the debenture, which falls within para 2 of Sched 1. The application of the exclusionary Note to para 2, and of the FSA's other exclusions, are discussed above.

## 4.1 The primary syndication

With regard to the primary syndicated arrangement, the initial arranging and promotion can be distinguished from the subsequent operation of the syndicated facility.

*(a) Arranging a syndicated loan*
To arrange a syndicated loan the lead or managing bank has to obtain a mandate from the prospective borrower or borrowers and then promote the availability of the syndicate to the potential participants. The detailed documentation then has to be negotiated.

*Obtaining the mandate*   Most mandates simply provide that the lead manager will use its 'best efforts' to arrange a suitable syndicate. Obtaining the mandate should not constitute dealing or arranging deals by the lead manager since no regulated investment is involved at this stage.

*Promotion*   The lead manager will generally only be soliciting interest from targeted potential participants to participate in the facility and to make syndicated funds available to the borrower. It is unlikely to be dealing, arranging deals or giving investment advice in relation to regulated investments. The promotion may, exceptionally, involve an investment agreement (discussed in Chapter 12) and in this case the restrictions on cold calling (s 56) and investment advertisements (s 57) may be relevant.

*Negotiation of the loan documentation*    There is some doubt as to whether at this stage the lead manager is acting on behalf of the participating banks. However, to the extent that it is only negotiating the terms of the syndicated loan agreement to be entered into, it will not be carrying on investment business.

As with normal term loan agreements, discussed above, the loan agreement itself will generally not constitute a debenture to the extent that it does not itself create or acknowledge any indebtedness, but only sets out the terms upon which future indebtedness will or may be incurred. Accordingly neither the lead manager, the participating banks, nor the borrower will be involved with dealing or arranging deals in a regulated investment when negotiating the loan documentation.

The lead bank will probably not give investment advice to potential participant banks who will be separately advised, particularly with regard to the regulated investments which may be involved.

The position may be different if security interests are provided for in the syndicated loan agreement. This is discussed below. However, even if security is provided for in the principal agreement, it may still not be a regulated investment although the security documentation entered into pursuant to the principal agreement may be debentures.

*Execution*    Provided no regulated investments are involved when the negotiated agreement is executed, none of the parties will be carrying on investment business by entering into it. If, however, the syndicated agreement provides for an immediate drawdown, then the agreement may be a debenture and entering into it may constitute dealing.

If the syndicated agreement provides for security, this may involve the creation of a debenture if those provisions acknowledge any amount of indebtedness, but subject to the exclusions in the Note to para 2. However, since no indebtedness will as yet have been incurred under the syndicated facility, the security documentation will probably not be a debenture since it will not create or acknowledge any existing indebtedness.

Even if there is an immediate drawdown, or the syndicate agreement provides for an immediate advance, and that indebtedness were acknowledged in the security documentation executed immediately after the syndicated loan agreement, one of the FSA's exclusions may be available. Note (a) to para 2 may be relevant if the syndicated loan is undertaken to finance a contract for the supply of goods or services. If the borrowing were incurred to finance general corporate or commercial activities, then the exclusion in the Note to para 12 and the dealing as principal exclusions in para 17 may be available. However, difficulties may arise with regard to the dealing as principal exclusions where the participant bank is generally involved with syndicated facilities, and so may fall within para 17(1)(c) to the extent that it could be said regularly to solicit such business.

If security interests were taken at the time the syndicated loan agreement was executed, then it is not clear whether the security granted in respect of future indebtedness not yet created by drawdown will constitute a debenture for the purposes of the FSA. It is considered that a debenture will not be created until the indebtedness is actually incurred and then evidenced by some written instrument.

Generally, only if security is granted at the same time as the indebtedness is created, or after the indebtedness has been incurred when the security documentation acknowledges that indebtedness, will the security instruments constitute debentures. This is again subject to the exclusions in the FSA and in particular the Note to para 2. These are difficult issues which await the decision of a court.

### (b) Operation of the syndicated facility

As noted above, the agent bank rather than the lead manager will be responsible for operating the syndicated facility once the syndicated loan agreement has come into force.

Provided the agent bank's functions are only administrative, it should not be carrying on investment business even if one or more regulated investment is involved although this will depend upon the terms of the syndicated agreement which specifies the agent bank's responsibilities. If some management of funds were involved beyond a purely administrative level, then it may be engaging in the investment activity of managing investments.

The agent bank should not be arranging deals in regulated investments where it arranges for finance to be made available in respect of each of the borrower's drawdowns under the facility.

As discussed above in relation to the definition of debentures and the constitution of term loan agreements, debentures will normally only be involved when there has been a drawdown under a particular facility. The drawdown notices or certificates provided for in the facility will then constitute debentures to the extent that indebtedness is created when the notice or certificate is sent to the agent bank, and funds made available after the conditions precedent for drawdown have been satisfied. The indebtedness will then be acknowledged by the drawdown notices unless separate notices or certificates are served by the agent bank in respect of each drawdown. Each separate drawdown will constitute a separate debenture.

Although the funds will be made available to the borrower by the agent bank in a single amount, each participating bank will have paid its proportion of the overall syndicated facility to the agent bank for the purposes of payment to the borrower. So while a single indebtedness will be acknowledged by the drawdown notice, that indebtedness will consist of a large number of separate payment obligations to each of the participating banks. The object of syndication is to administer these separate debts collectively, so it is thought that only one debenture is created on each drawdown, unless the separate composite amounts due to each participating bank are separately acknowledged.

## 4.2  Secondary participation

A secondary syndication agreement can arise as a result of the transfer of the primary syndication in one of three main ways.

*(a) Assignment*
This is the normal mechanism for transfer, and is usually provided for in the syndicated loan agreement.

An assignment of a debt may take the form of a legal or equitable assignment. A legal assignment is one which complies with the requirements of s 136 Law of Property Act 1925. An equitable assignment is one which does not comply with those requirements. Equitable assignments most commonly arise where only part of the debt due is assigned, or the assignment is not perfected by notice having been given to the obligor.

Although differences arise with regard to the legal consequences of these two forms of assignments, the effect in both cases is to transfer the benefit of the debt to the assignee. This involves an appropriation of property and has to be considered as such with regard to the application of the FSA.

It is likely that part, if not all, of the facilities made available under the syndicated participation will have been drawndown prior to assignment, so the parties may (subject to the exclusions discussed above) be dealing in a regulated investment to the extent that the benefit of the debentures so created on drawdown are transferred. If the borrower participates in the assignment, and separately acknowledges the indebtedness due to the new participant, then the existing debenture will be discharged in respect of that part of the debt due to the original participant, and a new debenture will be created and issued (subject to the exclusion available under para 28(3)).

However, in the case of an assigned participation, the rights of the assigning participant are simply transferred in terms of the assignment to the assignee, who may claim against the borrower under the earlier drawdown notices, the principal syndicated loan agreement and the assignment, but not under the assignment alone.

As the original debenture or debentures will not be affected (since only the rights of one participant under those debentures will have been transferred) there would appear to be no dealing with that debenture. The assignee acquires a right of action against the borrower, but only through the agent bank, subject to the terms of the syndicated loan agreement, and only through the original drawdown notices. Accordingly, it appears that no debenture is created or transferred since only the rights of the assigning participant in respect of the outstanding indebtedness of the borrower have been transferred. In these circumstances neither assignor nor assignee will be dealing in the debenture (although they may be dealing in a para 11 investment assuming that the security is held on trust for the various lenders). In the unlikely event that the amount due to the individual participating bank which is assigning all or part of its participation is separately acknowledged, then a separate debenture may be involved.

## (b) Novation

The same distinction has to be drawn between the novation of the participant's rights and obligations under the syndicated loan agreement itself, and the novation of rights and obligations in respect of any amounts drawdown under the syndicated facility.

As novation involves the new participant entering into an entirely new agreement to replace the earlier agreement from the date of its execution with all the existing parties other than the transferring participant, no regulated investment will be involved to the extent that the new agreement itself does not create or acknowledge any indebtedness. In this case neither the new nor the former participants will be engaging in an investment activity merely by being parties to the agreement.

Because novation involves all of the parties entering into a new agreement, it is common for the novation to be effected by the execution of an ancillary agreement to the principal syndicated agreement. If this, or a re-executed primary agreement, acknowledges any outstanding drawdowns under the syndicated facility, or provides for an immediate drawdown, then it may constitute a debenture, although subject to the FSA's exclusions.

The position of the parties entering into a novation will be the same as when entering into the primary participation, discussed above. However, as the outstanding indebtedness will generally be evidenced by the initial drawdown notices or receipts, the question as to whether any debentures will be dealt in will depend upon whether the rights and obligations under those notices are transferred, or new notices or receipts are executed in their place.

In practice, since the object of novation is to extinguish the rights and obligations existing under the original agreement, and to replace them with the new agreement, the debts of the borrower incurred under the earlier agreement may be extinguished, and reconstituted under the new agreement. The debentures corresponding to the earlier drawdowns would then be discharged, and replaced by one or more debentures created under the new agreement.

In this case the participant under the earlier syndicated loan agreement would be disposing of debentures in respect of existing drawdowns, and this would constitute dealing in investments (para 12 and 28(2)(c)). The borrower would then be issuing one or more new debentures, depending upon whether one or more documents were to evidence the reconstituted indebtedness under the new agreement. This activity may involve dealing in investments although it will probably fall within the exclusion in para 28(3).

In any particular case it will be necessary to study the detailed terms of the documentation to determine the FSA's application.

*(c) Participation*

A funded participation or sub-participation involves one or more of the original participants to a syndicated agreement entering into a separate contractual arrangement with a third party ('the sub-participant') to fund either the whole or part of the participant's current or outstanding participation in the syndicated facility.

The sub-participation agreement will not constitute a debenture provided it does not acknowledge any existing indebtedness, on principles similar to a term loan agreement or a syndicated loan agreement. However the sub-participation agreement may acknowledge the participant's present outstanding advances to the borrower; or it may evidence the indebtedness due by the participant to the sub-participant if the sub-participation involves an advance being made by the sub-participant to the participant to finance the participant's commitment to lend a portion of the syndicated amount to the borrower. In either case it may then be a debenture, but subject to the FSA's exclusions.

In any event the exclusion in para 28(3) in respect of persons issuing their own debentures will be available where the debenture is created in respect of advances made by the sub-participant to the participant.

The sub-participant may be acquiring a debenture, and dealing in investments, subject to the availability of the FSA's exclusions and, in particular, the dealing as principal exclusions in para 17.

## 4.3 Is a syndicated loan agreement a collective investment scheme?

The features of a collective investment scheme are discussed at length in Chapter 9. We also discuss the practical consequences of any arrangements constituting a collective investment scheme in that chapter. A collective investment scheme can be summarised as being arrangements for the participants to make money where their funds are pooled and managed by someone other than themselves. Looking in turn at each of the elements of a collective investment scheme specified by s 75:

(1) The arrangements contained in a syndicated loan agreement relate to money (s 75(1)).

(2) The purpose of the arrangements is to enable the lenders who are parties to the syndicated loan agreement to receive income from the management of the property: in other words, from its being lent to the borrower (s 75(1)).

(3) The participants may not have day-to-day control over the management of the subject property, in the sense that the day-to-day administration of the loan is carried out by the agent bank (s 75(2)).

(4) Their contributions and the income are pooled (s 75(3)(*a*)).

(5) The arrangements are managed as a whole by the agent bank (s 75(3)(*b*)).

If all the necessary features seem to be present, one must consider the exclusions contained in s 75 and Sched 1. Two of these exclusions are relevant and, taken together, make it unlikely that a syndicated loan agreement will be a collective investment scheme.

(1) Section 75(6)(*b*): arrangements which each participant enters into for commercial purposes relating to a non-investment business which it carries out will not be a collective investment scheme. This exclusion may be of assistance where each bank enters into a syndicated loan agreement for banking purposes in the course of ordinary bank lending. However, it may be difficult to show that each party carries on a non-investment business. Furthermore, difficulties may arise if part of the loan is transferred to a third party who does not qualify within this exclusion, since it seems to contemplate that all participants must qualify under it for the entire duration of the arrangements.

(2) Sched 1 para 35(d): arrangements where participants' rights are to money held in a common account in certain circumstances will not be a collective investment scheme. This is thought likely to exclude arrangements carried on by the agent acting under a collective investment scheme who pools depositors' funds and interest received from a borrower, from being a collective investment scheme.

## 5   SECURITISATION

Securitisation is an extremely complicated topic, and so it is practicable only to discuss the barest outlines in this section.

Securitisation of assets is a financing technique pursuant to which income-producing assets are transferred from the originating entity to another established solely for the purpose of holding those assets. This transfer can be by novation or, more commonly where there are numerous underlying credit transactions, by assignment. The new entity finances the acquisition by raising funds against the security of the assets themselves. The funds can be raised by a public issue or private placement of bonds or notes where the assets are charged in favour of a trustee for the noteholders; under a syndicated loan agreement against the security of the underlying assets which are secured in favour of the agent; or by other means of borrowing, including the issue of commercial paper. The method of securitisation used will depend upon the individual transaction concerned and the nature of the asset to be securitised.

We discuss this topic by reference to a mortgage securitisation where the originator assigns a portfolio of mortgages over a residential property to the acquirer and also assigns its rights in the security which it holds for the mortgage loans, such as its rights under life policies over each borrower's life. The purchaser of the mortgages, and assignee of the rights, issues floating rate notes ('FRNs') on the Euromarkets secured by charges over the underlying assets.

(1) Lending on the security of a mortgage over real property is not regulated by the FSA. While a mortgage on its own may amount to the creation or

acknowledgement of a debt, at first sight falling within para 2 of Sched 1, it is excluded by Note (c) so long as the mortgage is a disposition of property. If circumstances arise where the mortgage is not a disposition of property, and does fall within para 2, the original lending transaction should not amount to dealing by the lender on account of Note (1) to para 12 where the borrower creates the mortgage to secure a loan.

(2) When the lender takes an assignment of the borrower's life policy, it is in principle dealing within para 12. The lender may, however, be able to bring itself within the dealing as principal exclusion in para 17, discussed above.

(3) When the lender assigns its rights in the life policies to the acquirer, both parties will be dealing in investments falling within para 11. Both parties will also be dealing in debentures if the mortgage falls within para 2. In either case it is necessary to consider the availability of the FSA's exclusions. Of these, the dealing as principal exclusions at para 17 may be of assistance.

(4) When the new company issues the FRNs, they are likely to be regulated investments. However, if they will constitute debentures it will not be dealing (para 28(3) of Sched 1).

(5) Persons who manage or market the issue may require to be authorised and must observe the FSA's general restrictions on cold calling and advertising.

(6) If the FRNs are listed on the London Stock Exchange, or made the subject of a public offering, the regime summarised in Chapter 14 will be relevant.

# 6 ADVERTISING LOAN PRODUCTS AND BANKING BUSINESS

It is important to remember that almost any advertisement relating to a regulated investment will amount to an investment advertisement. As discussed in Chapter 13, an investment advertisement is (in summary) an advertisement which invites people to enter into an investment agreement, or which contains information which is likely to result in their doing so. An investment agreement is any agreement where either party is, by making or performing the agreement, engaging in one of the five investment activities ignoring whether or not that party is carrying on business and also ignoring the exclusions in paras 17–27 of Sched 1.

To take an example, a bank may make me a loan on the security of my assigning to the bank a life assurance policy. I am not carrying on investment business because I am a private individual, while the bank may not be carrying on investment business because of the dealing as principal exclusion in para 17. However, if the bank issues a brochure describing its secured lending facilities then this will potentially be an investment advertisement because, by entering into the transaction just described, both lender and borrower will be engaging in the investment activity of dealing: that one party is not carrying on investment business and the other party may otherwise rely on para 17 are irrelevant.

# 7 CAPITAL MARKETS AND BANK OF ENGLAND REGULATION

As mentioned in Chapter 2, s 43(1) provides that a person included in a list maintained by the Bank of England (known as a 'Listed Institution') is an exempted person in respect of certain specified capital market transactions as set out in Sched 5.

The Investment Services Directive will have implications for Listed Institutions which are currently exempted persons when carrying on business which comes within Sched 5 as this business falls within the Directive. In order to meet the Investment Services Directive's requirements, an investment firm seeking to do investment business covered by the Directive must be authorised to do so in its home Member State. In future, Listed Institutions will therefore need to be authorised to undertake wholesale money markets business instead of exempted, although it is intended that this will be a technical change and that most of the FSA will not apply to Listed Institutions in respect of their wholesale money markets business. A United Kingdom firm can become a Listed Institution if it satisfies the Bank of England that it fulfils the Directive's requirements. An EU firm can become a Listed Institution if it carries on business falling within s 43 FSA and is authorised by its home state to undertake such business.

Transactions falling within Sched 5 are regulated by the Bank of England on the basis contained in its paper 'The Regulation of the Wholesale Markets in Sterling, Foreign Exchange and Bullion' ('the Grey Paper'). Only market makers and brokers are intended to apply to be Listed Institutions: the exemption is not for customers or other persons who deal as principal.

This regime also only applies to dealing activities (buying or selling the instruments as principal or agent) and arranging for other persons to enter into such transactions, and does not apply to giving investment advice in relation to such transactions.

Transactions in the following instruments (which are regulated investments) are exempted from the FSA when undertaken by a Listed Institution in the circumstances specified below.

(1) Certificates of deposit, or other debt instruments, issued by institutions authorised under the Banking Act 1987 or by European deposit takers or by United Kingdom building societies, with an original maturity of not more than five years.

(2) Other debentures with an original maturity of not more than one year (including non-London certificates of deposit and commercial paper).

(3) Medium term notes issued under the terms of an exempt transaction.

(4) Local authority debt (bills, bonds, loan stock or other instruments) with an original maturity of not more than five years.

(5) Other public sector debt with an original maturity of not more than one year (such as Treasury bills, but not gilt edged securities).

(6) Any certificate or other instrument representing the securities covered in the four preceding items; or rights to, and interests in, these instruments.

(7) Options not regulated by, or made subject to the rules of, an RIE (including warrants) or futures contracts on these particular instruments; on any currency (including sterling); or on gold or silver. These include interest rate options.

(8) Forward rate agreements, or other contracts for differences involving arrangements to make a profit or avoid a loss by reference to movements in the value of certain instruments; the value of any currency; or in the interest on loans in any currency. These include interest rate and currency swaps regardless of their original maturity.

(9) Sale and repurchase agreements involving debentures, loan stock or other debt instruments of any original maturity where the repurchase will take place within 12 months of the sale.

The Bank of England also regulates transactions in the following instruments (which fall outside the FSA) on the basis contained in the Grey Paper:

(1) sterling wholesale deposits;
(2) foreign currency wholesale deposits;
(3) spot and commercial forward foreign exchange;
(4) spot and commercial forward gold and silver bullion;
(5) commercial bills including bankers' and other acceptances.

But the Bank of England does not regulate transactions involving instruments listed on, or subject to, the rules of an RIE.

Whether a transaction in these instruments is regulated by the Bank of England depends on the size of the transaction and the identity of the parties.

(1) For transactions involving debentures, bonds, loan stock and sale and repurchase agreements, the transaction must be of at least £100,000 or its equivalent in a foreign currency.

(2) For options, futures, forward rate agreements, swaps and other contracts for differences, the underlying value or price of the transaction must be at least £500,000 or its equivalent in a foreign currency.

Other transactions are exempted if:

(1) both parties are Listed Institutions; or
(2) one party is a Listed Institution and the other is a wholesale counterparty (defined below); or
(3) both parties are wholesale counterparties of a listed broker which has arranged the deal.

In addition, sale and repurchase transactions below the specified minimum value will only fall within Sched 5 where both parties are Listed Institutions acting as principal.

A wholesale counterparty is a person (other than a Listed Institution) who has entered into a transaction at or above the minimum limits during the previous 18 months with, or as a result of arrangements by, a Listed Institution in one of the instruments listed in Sched 5 (but excluding sale and repurchase transactions). Such a person is a wholesale counterparty only in relation to the Listed Institution with whom it carried out that transaction. Listed Institutions are obliged, before entering into transactions over the minimum limit with customers who would become wholesale counterparties, to warn them of the consequential loss of protection under the FSA.

In order to be included in the list the applicant must satisfy the Bank of England that:

(1)  it is a broker or market maker in such instruments; and

(2)  it is a fit and proper person; and

(3)  it fulfils the Bank's capital adequacy requirements.

Once included in the list, the institution must observe the Bank of England's code of conduct set out in the Grey Paper.

# 16 Regulation of Investment Vehicles

In previous chapters we have examined the principal provisions of the FSA as they relate to investment business. In this chapter we consider the impact of the FSA on a number of different investment vehicles.

## 1 UNIT TRUSTS AND COLLECTIVE INVESTMENT SCHEMES

A unit trust scheme is concisely defined as a collective investment scheme under which the property in question is held on trust for the participants (s 75(8)). A unit in a unit trust scheme or other collective investment scheme is a regulated investment falling under para 6 in Sched 1. The FSA regulates unit trusts and collective investment schemes in four ways.

(1) It controls their promotion to the public. Only an authorised unit trust scheme or a recognised overseas collective investment scheme may be promoted to the Untied Kingdom public (s 76). Section 76 is discussed in Chapter 9.

(2) It contains detailed provisions for the authorisation of United Kingdom unit trust schemes (ss 77–85), which implement the UCITS Directive.

(3) It provides for recognition of overseas collective investment schemes (ss 86–90). An overseas collective investment scheme may take the form of a unit trust scheme but will more often be an open-ended investment company, where the property belongs to the company and participants' rights are represented by securities in that company. An 'open-ended investment company' for the purposes of the FSA is defined in s 75(8). Section 86, which provides for the recognition of a collective investment scheme constituted in an EEA member state other than the United Kingdom, fulfils the requirements of the UCITS Directive.

(4) SIB is granted detailed powers of intervention in the operation of collective investment schemes under ss 91–95.

## 1.1 Regulation of the United Kingdom unit trusts

Prior to the FSA, the regime for the regulation of unit trust schemes was based on s 17 PFA 1958, which gave the Minister power to authorise a unit trust scheme and to revoke authorisation. Once authorised, the manager and trustee of the unit trust scheme did not need to obtain a licence under that Act, and managers and other persons authorised under that Act could promote the scheme to the public. Provided an order under s 17 PFA 1958 was in force in respect of a unit trust scheme on 29 April 1988 then that scheme is treated as an authorised unit trust scheme in accordance with the provisions of s 78 FSA (para 9 Sched 15).

## 1.2 Obtaining authorisation for United Kingdom unit trusts

In order to obtain authorisation for a United Kingdom unit trust scheme, the intending manager and trustee must apply to SIB in accordance with specified regulations (s 77). The manager and trustee must be companies incorporated in the United Kingdom or another EEA member state, be authorised to carry on investment business under the FSA, and be independent of each other (s 78). SIB will authorise the unit trust scheme if it complies with regulations made under s 81 (The Financial Services (Regulated Schemes) Regulations 1991, discussed at 1.3 below), and the FSA's other requirements. Authorisation can be revoked under s 79. The trustee and manager are under a continuing obligation to notify the SIB of proposed alterations to the scheme, or of proposals to replace the trustee or manager (s 82).

The manger of an authorised unit trust scheme may act as a manager of a collective investment scheme of a kind specified in s 83(2))(a), or engage in ancillary activities. Apart from these it may not engage in any other activities.

Once a unit trust scheme has been authorised, it may be freely marketed to any person by persons authorised under the FSA in accordance with their conduct of business rules, and by their appointed representatives.

The sections of the FSA relating to the authorisation of unit trust schemes, and the regulations made under them, are intended to fulfil the United Kingdom's obligations to authorise collective investment schemes in accordance with the UCITS Directive which may, once authorised, be marketed throughout the EEA. Under s 78(8) the SIB may certify that an authorised unit trust scheme complies with the UCITS Directive so it can be marketed throughout the EEA.

A manager or trustee of an authorised unit trust scheme who contravenes any regulations made under s 81, ss 75–95 or regulations made under them, is to be treated as having contravened rules made under Chapter V of Part I of the FSA, or those of its SRO or RPB (s 95(1)). Accordingly, ss 60–62 will apply to such contravention.

## 1.3 The regulations for United Kingdom unit trusts

The Financial Services (Regulated Schemes) Regulations 1991, as amended, contain:

(1) The secondary legislation relating to the constitution and management of authorised unit trust schemes.

(2) Most regulations concerning the marketing in the United Kingdom of collective investment schemes recognised under ss 86–88 FSA.

*(a) The regime for authorised unit trust schemes*
(1) SIB seeks to maintain a high standard of investor protection which includes requirements relating to:

(a) risk spreading;
(b) separation of management from custody;
(c) an obligation to deal in units at a price based on the net asset value;
(d) the trustee's supervision of the manager and the trustee's duty to act solely in the interests of unit-holders.

(2) An authorised unit trust scheme must fall into one of nine defined categories.
(3) The manager must prepare scheme particulars giving information about the constitution, objectives and operation of the scheme.
(4) An authorised unit trust scheme is constituted by a trust deed between the manager and the trustee. The manager manages the investments, performs valuations and determines prices. The trustee has oversight over the manger and safeguards title to investments. Their respective sources of remuneration are specified.
(5) The trustee creates units on the manager's instructions who then pays for them. The manager issues units to an applicant as principal or as agent for the trustee at a price fixed in accordance with the Regulations. If a unit-holder sells units to the manager, they will be redeemed at a price calculated in accordance with the Regulations.
(6) Investment restrictions for the various categories of scheme are specified.
(7) Each scheme has a six-monthly and an annual account period. The income for each period is calculated by the manager and distributed by the trustee to income unit-holders, and allocated to accumulation unit-holders, *pro rata* their holdings. The manager produces a report and accounts for each period.
(8) There are provisions for suspension and termination of unit trust schemes in defined circumstances.

*(b) The regime for recognised collective investment schemes*
(1) The scheme operator must prepare scheme particulars for schemes recognised under ss 87 and 88 FSA.
(2) The Regulations prescribe information which operators of schemes recognised under ss 86 and 87 must provide to SIB.
(3) The Regulations contain the requirements for the provision of facilities in the United Kingdom by any recognised scheme for inspection of scheme documents and for the sale and redemption of units.

## 1.4 Powers of intervention: United Kingdom unit trusts

SIB may give a direction for a manager of an authorised unit trust scheme to cease the issue or redemption of units or both, or require the manager and trustee to wind up the authorised unit trust scheme, if the authorisation order is no longer satisfied; if the exercise of this power is desirable in the interests of potential or actual participants; or if the manager or trustee has contravened the FSA or the rules made under it, or has furnished false, misleading or inaccurate information (s 91).

If a manager or trustee fails to observe SIB's direction, then SIB may make a public statement (s 60). It may also seek an injunction or restitution order (s 61), and any investor suffering loss may have a civil claim against the manager or trustee under s 62 (s 91(4)).

SIB may also, in circumstances where it could give a direction under s 91, apply to the court for an order to replace the manager or trustee or both, or for an order to appoint an authorised person to wind up the scheme (s 93).

SIB may additionally appoint inspectors to investigate and report on the affairs of an authorised unit trust scheme, or the manager or trustee of one (s 94). This section also relates to recognised and all other collective investment schemes.

## 1.5 Recognising an overseas collective investment scheme

A collective investment scheme constituted in another EU member state is a recognised scheme if it satisfies the requirements of s 86, which are that it complies with the UCITS Directive (The Financial Services (Schemes Constituted in Other Member States) Regulations 1989) (1989 SI No 1585). Section 86 implements the United Kingdom's obligations when acting as 'host' state in accordance with the UCITS Directive. Its 'home' state obligations under the Directive (authorising United Kingdom unit trusts) are discussed above.

The Directive on the Co-ordination of Laws relating to Undertakings for Collective Investment in Transferable Securities, its full name, provides that a collective investment scheme which complies with its conditions and is authorised in any EEA state may be marketed in accordance with local marketing laws and other local legislation in any other EEA state without needing further authorisation.

The UCITS Directive sets minimum standards. While an EEA state may set higher standards for domestic schemes which it authorises, it may not exclude schemes authorised in other EEA states which comply with the Directive's minimum standards.

A collective investment scheme is constituted in an EEA state if it is constituted under that state's law by contract or trust, and managed by a body corporate incorporated under that law, or if it is an open-ended investment company incorporated under that law (s 86(8)). If recognised, the overseas collective investment scheme can be marketed to the United Kingdom public by authorised or exempted persons in accordance with s 76.

In order for SIB to determine whether the scheme complies with United Kingdom marketing regulations, the operator must give notice to SIB in a specified form at least two months before it invites any United Kingdom persons to become participants (s 86(2)). The scheme shall not be recognised if within two months SIB gives the operator and its home regulator a reasoned notice that the manner in which it proposes to invite United Kingdom persons to become participants does not comply with United Kingdom law: in other words, its proposed marketing methods do not conform to the FSA or applicable conduct of business rules. If there is a refusal, the operator and home regulator may make representations to SIB.

Once an EEA collective investment scheme is recognised under s 86, the operator and trustee are automatically authorised to carry on investment business which consists of acting as operator or trustee of that scheme, and investment business carried on by them in connection with or for the purposes of that scheme (s 24). Only those parts of SIB Principles, conduct of business and other rules made under s 48 which relate to marketing and advising shall apply to the operator and trustee so authorised (s 86(7)).

## 1.6 Collective investment schemes authorised in designated countries

A collective investment scheme which is not recognised under s 86, but which is managed in and authorised under the laws of a designated country or territory outside the United Kingdom, is a recognised scheme under s 87.

A country or territory is designated by being named in an order made by the Treasury. A scheme managed or authorised in that place is recognised if it is of a class specified by that order.

The Treasury may only designate a country or territory if it is satisfied that the law under which the collective investment scheme is to be supervised in that place will afford United Kingdom investors protection at least equivalent to that provided for them by the FSA for authorised unit trust schemes.

Once a place is designated, the operator or scheme manager, in order to obtain recognition for the scheme, must give prescribed notice to SIB and obtain formal recognition in accordance with s 87.

Designated countries or territories at the time of writing are Jersey, Guernsey, the Isle of Man and Bermuda, and schemes capable of recognition are those falling within the terms of the individual designation orders.

## 1.7 Other countries

The operator of a scheme managed in an overseas country or territory which does not satisfy ss 86 or 87 may apply to SIB for recognition under s 88. Recognition may be granted if SIB considers that the scheme offers adequate protection to participants, there are adequate provisions for its constitution and management, and it otherwise fulfils the requirements of s 88.

## 1.8  Provisions relevant to sections 87 and 88

Schemes designated under ss 87 or 88 must maintain facilities and provide information in the United Kingdom as specified in s 90.

SIB may revoke or suspend recognition granted under ss 87 or 88 in accordance with ss 89 and 91(5). It also has powers to appoint an inspector in relation to any collective investment scheme under s 94.

## 2  INSURANCE

In this section, the Insurance Companies Act 1982 is referred to as 'the ICA'.

The FSA affects insurance business in three separate ways:

(1) Rights under most life assurance contracts are regulated investments under para 10 of Sched 1 to the FSA, so anyone carrying on investment activities in relation to such contracts will, subject to the FSA's exclusions, require to be authorised or exempted.

(2) There are special provisions governing the enforceability of general business insurance contracts contained in s 132 FSA. These provisions have no connection with the other subject matter of the FSA, as (with one exception) they are contracts which are not regulated investments. These provisions are discussed at the end of this section.

(3) The marketing of life assurance is restricted by s 130 FSA and, together with the promotion of collective investment schemes (restricted by s 76 FSA), is subject to a detailed regulatory regime contained in the rulebooks of the SIB and SROs. This is discussed in Chapters 3 and 17.

## 2.1  Regulated insurance contracts

Rights under an insurance contract the effecting and carrying out of which constitutes long-term business under the ICA falls within para 10 of Sched 1, but subject to two exceptions:

(1) a protection policy with all the characteristics contained in Note (1)(a)–(d) of para 10 of Sched 1;

(2) a long-term reinsurance contract (Note (3) of para 10).

Where effecting and carrying out a contract of insurance constitutes both long-term and general business under the ICA (by virtue of s 1(3) ICA or otherwise), then only the 'long-term' rights are regulated under the FSA (Note (2) of para 10).

Long-term business under the ICA is defined by Sched 1 ICA to be:

(1) life and annuity insurance contracts;

(2) contracts of insurance lasting over one year to pay money on birth or marriage;

(3) linked life and annuity insurance contracts;
(4) tontines;
(5) capital redemption;
(6) pension fund management.

Examples of investment activities which can be carried out in relation to regulated insurance contracts include:

*(a) Dealing*

A life assurance company will deal in investments (para 12 Sched 1) when it enters into a life assurance contract because it is then 'assuming the . . . corresponding liabilities under the contract' (para 28(2)(a) Sched 1). It will also deal when it accepts the surrender of, or converts, a contract (para 28(2)(c) of Sched 1). The 'dealing as principal' exclusion in para 17 Sched 1 is restricted insofar as it relates to life assurance contracts. The individual investor will also deal when he acquires, surrenders, converts or assigns his rights under the contract of insurance, but is unlikely to be doing so in the course of business.

*(b) Arranging*

A broker will be making arrangements (para 13 Sched 1) if he arranges for a life assurance company to issue a specific policy to an investor.

*(c) Managing*

A person may manage investments (para 14 Sched 1) where the assets under management include a life assurance policy. A life assurance company which manages regulated investments belonging to other persons (ie not own funds) will be engaging in the activity of managing investments.

*(d) Advising*

A broker will be giving investment advice (para 15 Sched 1) when advising a potential investor on the merits of acquiring or disposing of a specific life assurance policy.

*(e) Operating a collective investment scheme*

While a life assurance policy may be an asset of a CIS, s 75(6)(j) provides that a contract of insurance is not of itself a CIS.

*(f) Offering or agreeing*

A person who offers or agrees to do any of the activities at (a)–(d) is also engaging in an investment activity.

## 2.2 Authorisation

A body authorised under ss 3 or 4 ICA to carry on insurance business which is investment business is an authorised person under the FSA by virtue of s 22 FSA in relation to:

(1) carrying on in the United Kingdom that insurance business which is also investment business under the FSA; and

(2) carrying on any other investment business which does not contravene s 16 ICA. This provides that an insurance company of the kind specified in s 15 ICA may not carry on any activities in any part of the world other than in connection with or for the purposes of its insurance business.

This section is only concerned with the authorisation of insurance companies to carry on investment business under the FSA: it does not confer any authorisation in relation to activities regulated by the ICA (Sched 10 para 2(4) FSA).

An insurance company falling within s 22 will not require to obtain authorisation under the FSA by joining an SRO, or directly from the SIB, because it is granted automatic authorisation under this section. The reason for this is that an authorised United Kingdom insurer is already subject to financial regulation and prudential control by the DTI acting under powers conferred on it by the ICA.

However, an insurance company authorised under s 22 (or s 31: see below) does not thereby escape from the FSA's regulatory net: it is subject to the SIB conduct of business rules made under s 48(1) FSA (as varied by Sched 10 para 4 FSA) in relation to marketing its life assurance contracts unless it chooses to become a member of an SRO. The SRO is PIA, which will regulate the conduct of an insurance company's business but without conferring authorisation on it because an insurance company authorised under s 22 FSA may not be an authorised person except by virtue of that section (Sched 10 para 2(1) FSA).

In addition, an EEA insurer which is authorised in its state to carry on insurance business which is investment business is authorised under s 22 FSA to carry on that business in the United Kingdom, provided it fulfils Sched 2F ICA, together with any other investment business which it may carry on under the law of its home state (reg 57, Insurance Companies (Third Insurance Directives) Regulations 1994 (SI No 1696)). If an EEA insurer chooses to join an SRO, it is not subject to regulations regarding fitness, financial resources or other matters that are the preserve of its home state regulator (regs 56 and 58).

Schedule 10 FSA contains further detailed provisions regulating the application of the FSA to insurance companies authorised under the ICA or s 31, and also to EEA insurers. In particular, para 5 disapplies certain sections and regulations in or made under the ICA from insurance contracts which are regulated by the FSA. These include:

(1) insurance advertisement regulations made under s 72 ICA;

(2) the regulation of intermediaries under section 74 ICA;

(3) cancellation rights under sections 75 to 77 ICA.

The powers of intervention contained in ss 64–73 (discussed in Chapter 11) are disapplied or modified in relation to insurance companies authorised under the ICA or s 31 by para 6 of Sched 10 FSA. They are further modified in relation to EEA insurers exercising 'passport' rights under s 22 FSA (reg 59, Insurance Companies (Third Insurance Directives) Regulations 1994).

Other sections of the FSA which regulate insurance business are:

(1) ss 130 and 131 which regulate the promotion of life insurance contracts (discussed in Chapter 17);

(2) ss 132 and 133 which (with an exception) are concerned with general business insurance contracts (discussed below);

(3) ss 134 to 139 which make a number of miscellaneous and consequential amendments to the ICA and other statutes.

## 2.3 Provisions relating principally to general insurance business

Two sections of the FSA relate principally to insurance contracts which are not investments regulated by the FSA, and (with one exception) these sections do not relate to the FSA's principal provisions. They are as follows:

(1) s 132, which provides that the insured may generally enforce a general business insurance contract (and one kind of life insurance contract) entered into in contravention of the ICA; and

(2) s 133, which makes it a criminal offence to make a false or misleading statement about an insurance contract which is not an investment agreement. This corresponds to s 47 which is discussed in Chapter 11.

Section 132 FSA is (with the exception mentioned below) concerned with insurance contracts which are not otherwise regulated by the FSA: in other words, general (non-life) business contracts. This section regulates the enforceability of such insurance contracts entered into by someone who is carrying on insurance business in the United Kingdom without authorisation under the ICA, and is accordingly in breach of s 2 of the ICA.

Section 132 is extended by reg 64 of the Insurance Companies (Third Insurance Directives) Regulations 1994 to insurance contracts effected by EEA or United Kingdom insurers in breach of specified paragraphs of Scheds 2F and 2G ICA.

Prior to the enactment of s 132 FSA, which came into force on 12 January 1987 (although sub-s (6) came into force on 29 April 1988), the legal position of the enforceability of an insurance or reinsurance contract of an unauthorised insurer entered into in contravention of s 2 ICA was unclear.

In the *Bedford Insurance* case [1985] 1 QB 966 it was held at first instance that if an unauthorised overseas insurance company arranged for an unauthorised United Kingdom broker to write and reinsure insurance contracts on its behalf in the United kingdom, then these contracts were illegal and void, and the assured could not recover.

However, in the conflicting decision of *Stewart v Oriental Fire & Marine Insurance* [1985] 1 QB 988, also at first instance, a Lloyd's syndicate insured a risk which was reinsured by an unauthorised overseas insurer. It was held that the contract was not invalid because the insurer was in breach of the ICA, and the insured might enforce the contract.

The *Phoenix General* case [1986] 1 All ER 908, again at first instance, offered a middle way. Here a United Kingdom insurer placed reinsurance contracts outside the scope of its authorisation. The court held that the contracts were not void or illegal: the ultimate assured could enforce the contract against the insurer even though the insurer itself could not enforce them.

The *Phoenix General* was appealed in [1988] QB 216, and the Court of Appeal held that the insurer was, in fact, authorised to carry on the insurance business in the first place. It did however, consciously obiter, offer some observations on the earlier cases. In effect it approved *Bedford Insurance* on the grounds that the ICA prohibited effecting and carrying out unauthorised insurance contracts, which were in consequence illegal, void and unenforceable by both parties. In what the leading judgment described as an unfortunate effect of the wording, the contracts were void and, because the ICA prohibits the insurer from carrying out the contract, the insured cannot call on the insurer to do so, even though this was to the detriment of the very class of person whom the ICA is intended to protect. The Court of Appeal's obiter dicta in this case were followed in *Re Cavalier Insurance Co Ltd* (1989) (*The Times*, 31 May).

Whilst considering the effect of the enactment of s 132 FSA, the *Bedford Insurance* case and the obiter dicta in the *Phoenix General* case were followed in the *DR Insurance Company* case [1993] 1 Lloyd's Law Rep 210. It was held at first instance that certain reinsurance contracts entered into by unauthorised insurers before s 132 came into force were void and unenforceable as that section was intended to apply only to contracts entered into after it came into force. However the later first instance case of *Bates v Barrow* (1995) *The Times*, 9 February held that a person could claim for a loss that had arisen after s 132 came into force even though the contract of insurance had been entered into before that date in breach of the ICA.

Section 132 FSA returns to a position similar to that of the *Phoenix General* case at first instance. It is similar in concept to s 5 FSA (investment agreements made by or through unauthorised persons) and s 131 FSA (life assurance contracts made after contravention of s 130 FSA).

Section 132 provides that if an insurer who is not authorised under the ICA ('the insurer') enters

(1) either into an insurance contract falling outside para 10 Sched 1;

(2) or into an insurance contract which falls within para 10 of Sched 1, but to which s 5(1) FSA does not apply because the making or performance of the contract by the person seeking to enforce it or from whom money or other property would be recoverable (usually the insurer) is not an investment activity on account of one or more of the exclusions in paras 17–27 of Sched 1 FSA (s 5(7) FSA) for example, because the insurance company may be able to rely on the dealing as principal or overseas persons exclusions;

in the course of carrying on insurance business in the United Kingdom when it needs authorisation under the ICA, then the following applies:

(1) Subject to s 132(3) the insurer may not enforce the contract against the other party ('the insured') (s 132(1)).

(2) The contract is not otherwise illegal or invalid and the insured may enforce it (s 132(6)).

(3) The validity of a reinsurance contract entered into in respect of an insurance contract which contravenes s 132 is not affected (s 132(6)).

(4) If the insured chooses to exercise its rights under this section and elects not to perform the contract and to recover money or property paid under the contract, it must repay or return any benefits received (s 132(1) and (4)).

(5) The insured may also seek compensation for any loss it has sustained by reason of parting with money or property (s 132(1)). The compensation is to be agreed by the parties or determined by the court (s 132(2)).

(6) The court may, however, at the insurer's request, allow the insurer to enforce the contract under s 132(3) (or retain the insured's money or property transferred) if the court is satisfied that:

   (i) the insurer reasonably believed that entering into the contract did not contravene s 2 ICA. For example, it took appropriate legal advice and acted on it; *and*

   (ii) it is just and equitable for the court to allow the insurer to enforce the contract against the insured, or retain the insured's money or property transferred. For example, a court may well find it to be just and equitable to allow the insurer to enforce the contract where the insurer acted fairly, and the insured was not prejudiced by the fact that the insurer was not authorised under the ICA.

# 3   PENSIONS

There is an almost unlimited variety of pension arrangements, but only some of these are regulated by the FSA.

An occupational pension scheme, which is given a definition in s 207(1), is not regulated by the FSA. In broad terms the definition covers any scheme or arrangement providing an employee with benefit on death and/or on leaving service at or near retirement age. Interests under the trusts of an occupational pension scheme are not investments falling within Sched 1 (on account of Note (1) to para 11) and an occupational pension scheme, which may possess the characteristics of a collective investment scheme, will not be such a scheme on account of the express exclusion contained in s 75(6)(k).

In practical terms, this means that the marketing of pension rights in an occupational pension scheme will not be regulated by the FSA. An employer can establish an occupational pension scheme for its employees, administer it, and advise the employees on their rights without requiring to be authorised under the FSA. However, an employer must take care not to draw comparisons between the occupational scheme and other forms of pension provision that might be available to its employees, as those alternatives will most probably be regulated investments.

Assuming that the members' and the employer's contributions are invested in investments regulated by the FSA, the management of those investments is covered by s 191 FSA, which brings occupational pension schemes back within the FSA as regards management of their assets. Whoever manages the investments of such an occupational pension scheme, whether or not they are carrying on business, will be carrying on the investment activity of managing and will require to be authorised or exempted, subject to the FSA's general exclusions, and to the exemption contained in s 191(2). That exemption applies where all decisions, or all day-to-day decisions, regarding the management of a scheme's assets are taken by an authorised, exempted or overseas person. The power of investment under the scheme will generally be vested in the scheme's trustees. Provided that the trustees delegate this power to an appropriate investment manager they will not themselves require authorisation. Having delegated this function the trustees must take care over the extent to which they attempt to oversee the investment manager's activities. It must take all day-to-day decisions. However, the trustees may still take broad, generic decisions (for example, to follow a policy of ethical investment) without FSA authorisation (see 3.3 below).

A contract for a personal pension, a 's 32' buy-out policy or a free standing additional voluntary contribution scheme ('FSAVC') will be regulated by the FSA when the subject assets comprise investments regulated by the FSA since the contract will confer a right to, or an interest in, the subject investments and hence be caught by para 11 of Sched 1. A deposit-based personal pension or FSAVC contract whose assets are represented by deposits in a bank or building society will fall outside the FSA, whereas a contract based on shares or life assurance contracts would be caught.

Situations where a person may be carrying on an investment activity in relation to pensions are as follows. With the one exception noted, carrying on any of these activities will only amount to carrying on investment business when it amounts to, or is done in the course of, a business.

## 3.1 Dealing

You will be dealing in investments within para 12 of Sched 1 if you issue me with a personal pension or FSAVC contract which is invested in regulated investments such as life assurance contracts, shares or units in a unit trust scheme. You will not, however, be dealing in investments if you issue me with a contract relating to an occupational pension scheme, a personal pension or to an FSAVC contract which is based on money deposited in a bank account.

The trustees of an occupational pension scheme will be dealing when they buy or sell investments registered in their names. A trustee of an occupational pension scheme who is carrying on business may be able to rely on the 'dealing as principal' exclusion in para 17 Sched 1.

## 3.2 Arranging

A broker will probably be arranging a deal in regulated investments within para 13 of Sched 1 if he makes arrangements for a pension provider to issue me with a regulated investment-based personal pension contract.

## 3.3 Managing

If the assets of an occupational pension scheme, personal pension scheme or FSAVC include (or can at the manager's discretion include) investments regulated by the FSA, then the trustees or other operator of the arrangements will be managing these investments within para 14 of Sched 1 unless the management functions are delegated to a third party. This act of managing will amount to carrying on investment business if, in the case of a personal pension scheme or FSAVC, the manager is doing so in the course of, or as part of, a business.

The position is different with trustees or managers of an occupational pension scheme. Section 191 provides that someone who manages the assets of an occupational pension scheme where they are investments regulated by the FSA is deemed to be carrying on investment business, and the 'trustee' exclusions in para 22 of Sched 1 will not apply, unless:

(1) all, or all day-to-day decisions in respect of the investments, are delegated to an authorised, exempted or overseas person. The SIB has issued guidelines (summarised below) relating to this point. Provided a trustee of an occupational pension scheme takes no, or no day-to-day, decisions it is implicit that a trustee or other person falling within s 191 may perform other management functions which would not be categorised as 'taking decisions' (s 191(2)); or

(2) the occupational pension scheme falls within the exclusion set out in The Financial Services Act 1986 (Occupational Pension Schemes) (No 2) Order 1988 (s 191(3)). This covers 'small self-administered schemes', which are schemes of no more than 12 members, all of whom are trustees, and schemes of up to 50 members purely providing life cover.

The SIB guidelines in Guidance Release 2/88 are, in summary, as follows:

An initial decision taken by trustees to place the assets of an occupational pension scheme in, for instance, insurance policies does not amount to management, but subsequently switching investments may do.

If the trustees delegate day-to-day management to a manager, then their occasionally taking strategic decisions, or stipulating considerations in a particular case (for example, what action a manager should take in a takeover, or that a manager is not to invest in tobacco) will not amount to day-to-day decisions.

If the trustees have delegated day-to-day management to a manager, then their making occasional suggestions to the manager, or making recommendations during regular or quarterly reviews, will not amount to making day-to-day decisions.

However, frequent interventions outside regular scheduled meetings, or frequently participating in sale or purchase decisions, would be viewed as taking day-to-day decisions (unless they could be justified as covering exceptional matters).

## 3.4 Advising

Whether someone is advising on investments in accordance with para 15 of Sched 1 will depend on the nature of the pension arrangements. A person is likely to be carrying on the investment activity of advising an investor or potential investor on the merits of acquiring or disposing of regulated investments if, for example:

(1) you advise me on the merits of the purchase of an FSAVC contract which is invested in regulated investments; or

(2) you advise members of an occupational pension scheme to purchase an annuity or surrender a life assurance policy which falls within para 10 of Sched 1, since neither of these is an interest in an occupational pension scheme; or

(3) you advise me on the merits of acquiring an investment based personal pension contract.

You are probably not, however, advising within para 15 if you:

(1) advise scheme members of their rights under an occupational pension scheme;

(2) advise me on the merits of buying a deposit- (not investment-) based personal pension contract; or

(3) advise me on the merits of joining an occupational pension scheme unless in connection with the surrender of a personal pension policy.

## 3.5 Collective investment scheme

An occupational pension scheme falls outside the definition of a collective investment scheme on account of s 75(6)(k), but a personal pension or FSAVC contract is capable of constituting a collective investment scheme. The position will depend on whether it has the necessary attributes to fall within s 75 and there is a surprising degree of uncertainty here. It is considered that a unit trust-based personal pension contract may be a collective investment scheme, whereas an insurance based personal pension contract or FSAVC contract will probably not. This is not a result of the exclusion in s 75(6)(j), which excludes contracts of insurance from being a collective investment scheme, because the scheme will usually be separate from the units, but because the characteristics of pooling and management by another contained in s 75(3)(a) and (b) may not be present.

## 3.6 The Pensions Bill

At the time of writing, the legislation which emanated from the Report of the Pension Law Review Committee chaired by Professor Goode is still only at Bill stage. It looks set to reach the statute book during 1996. The Pensions Bill contains some fairly detailed provisions regarding the management of the assets of occupational pension schemes. To a large extent, these simply spell out the legal constraints that have evolved through case law. They also impose a more formal structure than exists at present on trustees and their delegates regarding investment strategy.

Clause 30 of the Bill expressly permits a scheme's trustees to delegate their investment powers and discretions to a fund manager who is an authorised person for the purposes of s 191 FSA. The trustees will not be liable for the acts or defaults of any such fund manager, provided that they have taken all reasonable steps to establish that their delegate has 'the appropriate knowledge and experience' for managing the scheme's investments. They must also ensure that the fund manager carries out his work competently, and in accordance with a statement of matters to which the trustees must have regard in the exercise of their investment powers. This statement is another new requirement introduced by the Bill.

Trustees may delegate their investment function to a non-authorised person, but they would remain liable for that person's acts or defaults after they had done so.

This statutory power of delegation is always subject to any restriction contained in the scheme itself, whether or not the delegation is to a person authorised under the FSA.

The Bill prohibits any purported exclusion or restriction of liability regarding investment activity, either by a scheme's trustees or by a person to whom the trustees have delegated those functions.

## 4   ENTERPRISE INVESTMENT SCHEMES

Under an EIS (the successor to the Business Expansion Scheme), an investor investing up to a maximum of £100,000 in any one tax year in shares in a qualifying company can receive relief from income tax at the 20% lower rate of income tax, and may, if the shares are retained for at least five years, be eligible for exemption from capital gains tax on the ultimate disposal of those shares. The investment must be in the ordinary shares of an unquoted company which carries on one or more qualifying trades.

A share in the capital of an EIS company will be an investment under para 1 of Sched 1, and its treatment will be no different from those of any other shares. An EIS company itself cannot constitute a collective investment scheme on account of the exclusion for companies in s 75(7). An EIS, however, has the characteristics of a collective investment scheme and accordingly para 34 Sched 1 FSA is intended to exclude EIS funds from the definition of collective investment schemes.

## 5   EMPLOYEE SHARE OWNERSHIP PLANS

An ESOP is a trust, usually with independent trustees, set up by a company for the benefit of its workforce which purchases shares in the company. The trust will distribute shares to employees, quite possibly in conjunction with a share option scheme, and may act as a market-maker, buying or selling the shares with the employees.

Depending on how the trust operates in any particular circumstances, it seems possible that the trustees of the trust may be carrying on an investment activity because they will be dealing in shares when they buy or sell, and the exclusions in para 17 of Sched 1 will not apply where the trustees offer a 'market-making' service between employees; and because they may hold themselves out as buying shares with a view to selling them and may regularly solicit employees to induce them to buy shares. For the same reasons the exclusion for trustees in para 22 of Sched 1 may also not be available. Whether the trustees are carrying on this activity as a business is an additional consideration.

## 6   VENTURE CAPITAL

The treatment of a company in which a venture capital fund makes an investment is no different under the FSA from that of any other company. The company itself will not be dealing in the shares it allots on account of the exclusion in para 28(3) of Sched 1 and, although the investors will be dealing under para 12, they may be able to take advantage of the 'dealing as principal' exclusion.

Where the investment takes the form of a limited partnership, it is likely that this will constitute a collective investment scheme. The general partner or other manager may be carrying on the investment activities of operating the scheme and also managing investments, and will need to observe the restrictions contained in s 76, which are discussed in Chapter 9.

## 7   PERSONAL EQUITY PLANS

Personal equity plans ('PEPs') were created by the Finance Act 1986 and their operation is governed by the Personal Equity Plan Regulations 1989. PEPs are intended to encourage direct investment in United Kingdom companies by giving tax relief on such investments. Any United Kingdom resident over 18 years old can invest in a PEP up to a yearly subscription limit of £6,000. In addition, a further £3,000 may be invested in any year in a single company PEP.

A PEP is a service rather than an investment product in its own right, although under SIB and SRO rules certain kinds of PEP are treated as products for the purpose of applying certain of the conduct of business rules, such as 'best advice' and polarisation. The plan manager holds the investment in its name on behalf of the investors who are the beneficial owners. The manager of a PEP will require to be authorised as it will be carrying on the investment activity of managing. A PEP also possesses the characteristics of a collective investment scheme, but is intended to be excluded from the definition of a collective investment scheme by s 75(5).

# 8  EMPLOYEE SHARE SCHEMES

There are a number of employee share schemes, of which the most common are the three Revenue-approved profit sharing, savings related and executive share option schemes.

The exclusion in para 20 of Sched 1 provides that neither a company, a connected company, nor a relevant trustee (all as defined) is dealing or arranging deals in shares or debentures (as defined) in relation to certain transactions done for the benefit of current and past employees and their dependants (but excluding non-executive directors). A company issuing its own shares or debentures or warrants is already excluded by para 28(3) of Sched 1. An instrument entitling the holder to subscribe for shares in a company falls within para 4 rather than para 7 of Sched 1 (Note (2) to para 4) and hence is also covered by paragraph 28(3). Paragraph 20 stipulates the following:

20(1)  Paragraphs 12 and 13 above do not apply to anything done by a body corporate, a body corporate connected with it or a relevant trustee for the purpose of enabling or facilitating transactions in shares in or debentures of the first-mentioned body between or for the benefit of any of the persons mentioned in sub-paragraph (2) below or the holding of such shares or debentures by or for the benefit of any such persons.

(2)  The persons referred to in sub-paragraph (1) above are:—

(a)  the bona fide employees or former employees of the body corporate or of another body corporate in the same group; or

(b)  the wives, husbands, widows, widowers, or children or step-children under the age of eighteen of such employees or former employees.

(3) In this paragraph 'a relevant trustee' means a person holding shares in or debentures of a body corporate as a trustee in pursuance of arrangements made for the purpose mentioned in sub-paragraph (1) above by, or by a body corporate connected with, that body corporate.

(4) In this paragraph 'shares' and 'debentures' include any investment falling within paragraph 1 or 2 above and also include any investment falling within paragraph 4 or 5 above so far as relating to those paragraphs or any investment falling within paragraph 11 above so far as relating to paragraph 1, 2, 4 or 5.

(5) For the purposes of this paragraph a body corporate is connected with another body corporate if:—

(a) they are in the same group; or

(b) one is entitled, either alone or with any other body corporate in the same group, to exercise or control the exercise of a majority of the voting rights attributable to the share capital which are exercisable in all circumstances at any general meeting of the other body corporate or of its holding company.

This should enable a company to establish an employee share scheme, and to set up a 'share shop' without thereby dealing or arranging deals. These exclusions do not, however, exclude the following:

(1) the employees themselves who (in the unlikely event that they are carrying on business in relation to dealing in the shares) may presumably rely on the dealing as principal exclusions in para 17; or

(2) the company or others giving advice to employees on the share scheme. The exclusions in para 24 are unlikely to apply here.

If the company issues promotional material relating to its employee share scheme it may be an investment advertisement but should be excluded under s 58(3) by virtue of art 6 of the Investment Advertisement (Exemptions) Order 1995 (SI No 1266).

One needs to consider an employee share scheme in detail in order to identify how it is affected by the FSA. It is likely that any of the three Revenue approved schemes will fall within paras 20(1) and (2) as they will normally be employees' share schemes so as to qualify for the exemption from the prohibition on financial assistance available to such schemes. Paragraph 20(2) follows the wording in s 743 Companies Act 1985. With unapproved schemes, however, the position may well be less clear-cut.

## 8.1  Profit-sharing schemes

Under a profit-sharing scheme a company constitutes a trust and pays money to the trustees to purchase its shares. These are registered in the trustees' names and, while appropriated to particular employees who receive dividends and distributions, the shares are usually not registered in the employees' names until the fifth year, otherwise an income tax liability arises. A profit-sharing scheme possesses the characteristics of a collective investment scheme, but is intended to be excluded by s 75(6)(*d*). This exclusion requires that there is a scheme operator in the same group as the company.

## 8.2 SAYE share option schemes

Under this kind of scheme employees are granted an option to subscribe for shares with money from the proceeds of a save-as-you-earn contract with a bank or building society. The price of the shares, and monthly contributions to the savings contract, are fixed when the option is granted. The company is neither dealing nor arranging deals on account of the exclusion in para 20.

## 8.3 Executive share option schemes

This is where a company grants a fixed-price share option to its executives and the same exclusion should apply.

## 8.4 Financial assistance

Section 196 FSA amends s 153 Companies Act 1985 and lifts the restriction on a company providing financial assistance for the purchase of its own shares in some circumstances in connection with an employees' share scheme, as defined in s 743 Companies Act 1985.

# 17 Marketing Investments and Money Laundering

This chapter examines those aspects of the financial services regime principally concerned with the marketing of investments and also summarises the United Kingdom's money laundering regime.

## 1  THE ACT'S IMPACT

The marketing of regulated investments falls within the ambit of the FSA because the investment activities of dealing, arranging, managing and advising include 'offering or agreeing' to do so. An invitation to treat amounts to an offer (para 28(1) Sched 1). Issuing an advertisement or making a cold call may therefore amount to engaging in an investment activity.

## 2  INVESTMENT ADVERTISEMENTS

Any kind of written or oral publicity which relates to the marketing may be an investment advertisement. This is discussed in Chapter 13.

## 3  LISTED SECURITIES AND PUBLIC OFFERS

The listing of securities on the London Stock Exchange is regulated by ss 142–157 which are discussed in Chapter 12, together with the regime governing public offers of securities.

## 4  OVERSEAS PERSONS

An overseas person is defined as someone who carries on investment business in the United Kingdom other than from a permanent place of business which he maintains there (para 26(2) of Sched 1). If such a person wishes to market regulated investments in the United Kingdom without obtaining authorisation or being an exempted person it must, where that marketing would amount to carrying on investment business, fall within either the general exclusions contained in paras 17–25 of Sched 1, or the overseas person exclusions in paras 26 and 27. When dealing direct with United Kingdom residents it must also ensure that it does not infringe s 56 which, subject to the regulations discussed below, prohibits unsolicited calls, or s 57, which regulates the issue of investment advertisements.

The position of an overseas person is discussed in Chapter 6.

## 5   COLLECTIVE INVESTMENT SCHEMES

The promotion of collective investment schemes is regulated by s 76, which is discussed in Chapter 9.

## 6   PROMOTION OF LIFE ASSURANCE CONTRACTS

Section 130 restricts the promotion of insurance contracts falling within the FSA (here called 'life assurance contracts') to those issued by specified classes of insurer. Unlike the corresponding provisions restricting promotion of collective investment schemes contained in s 76, there are no categories of person to whom contracts falling outside s 130 (here referred to as 'unapproved contracts') can be promoted, presumably because life assurance contracts are predominantly promoted to private individuals who are felt to deserve this level of protection.

Section 130 operates in addition to s 57. Section 57 provides that only an authorised person may issue (or cause to be issued) an investment advertisement in the United Kingdom unless it has been approved by an authorised person. Section 130 imposes an additional restriction: even an authorised person cannot issue or cause to be issued an advertisement relating to a life assurance contract unless it conforms to the categories in ss 130(2) or (3). Section 130 goes further still in providing that a person may not in the course of business advise or procure United Kingdom persons to enter into an unapproved contract. It specifies the following:

130(1)   Subject to subsections (2) and (3) below, no person shall—
    (a)   issue or cause to be issued in the United Kingdom an advertise-ment—
        (i)   inviting any person to enter or offer to enter into a contract of insurance rights under which constitute an investment for the purposes of this Act; or
        (ii)   containing information calculated to lead directly or indirectly to any person doing so; or
    (b)   in the course of a business, advise or procure any person in the United Kingdom to enter into such a contract.

The restriction in (a) is almost identically worded to that in s 57, which is described in Chapter 13.

The life assurance contracts which are not caught by s 130(1), and in respect of which persons may issue an advertisement, or advise or procure persons to enter into, are set out in sub-ss (2) and (3) as follows:

130(2)  Subsection (1) above does not apply where the contract of insurance referred to in that subsection is to be with—

    (a)  a body authorised under section 3 or 4 of the Insurance Companies Act 1982 to effect and carry out such contracts of insurance;

    (b)  a body registered under the enactments relating to friendly societies;

    (c)  an insurance company the head office of which is in a member State other than the United Kingdom and which is entitled to carry on there insurance business of the relevant class;

    (d)  an insurance company which has a branch or agency in such a member State and is entitled under the law of that State to carry on there insurance business of the relevant class;

and in this subsection 'the relevant class' means the class of insurance business specified in Schedule 1 or 2 to the Insurance Companies Act 1982 into which the effecting and carrying out of the contract in question falls.

A body falling within (a) will be authorised under s 22 FSA and one falling within (b) will be authorised under s 23. An insurance company which intends to rely on (c) or (d) must first ascertain whether it is entitled to carry on insurance business under the law of the relevant state.

A contract with an insurance company authorised in a country or territory designated under s 130(3) may also be promoted in the United Kingdom.

130(3)  Subsection (1) above also does not apply where—

    (a)  the contract of insurance referred to in that subsection is to be with an insurance company authorised to effect or carry out such contracts of insurance in any country or territory which is for the time being designated for the purposes of this section by an order made by the Secretary of State; and

    (b)  any conditions imposed by the order designating the country or territory have been satisfied.

The Minister will only designate a country or territory if he is satisfied that its laws for authorising and supervising insurance companies adequately protect actual and potential policy-holders against risk of default (s 130(4)).

The territories of Guernsey and the Isle of Man, the Commonwealth of Pennsylvania and the State of Iowa have been the subject of a designation order made by the Minister.

## 6.1 Contravention of section 130

*(a) Criminal offence*

It is a criminal offence to promote an insurance contract which does not conform to s 130(6).

Subject to subsections (7) and (8) below, any person who contravenes this section shall be guilty of an offence and liable—

130(6)(a) on conviction on indictment, to imprisonment for a term not exceeding two years or to a fine or to both;

(b) on summary conviction, to imprisonment for a term not exceeding six months or to a fine not exceeding the statutory maximum or to both.

However, a defence is available in sub-s (7) to someone who in the ordinary course of carrying on a non-investment business (such as publishing a newspaper) issues an advertisement promoting an insurance contract not conforming to s 130 on the instructions of someone whom he believes on reasonable grounds after due enquiry to be an authorised person and provided he did not devise the advertisement. It may be difficult to establish 'due enquiry' unless he has consulted the SIB central register of authorised persons, or questioned the advertiser itself. Section 130(7) states the following:

130(7) A person who in the ordinary course of a business other than investment business issues an advertisement to the order of another person shall not be guilty of an offence under this section if he proves that the matters contained in the advertisement were not (wholly or in part) devised or selected by him or by any person under his direction or control and that he believed on reasonable grounds after due enquiry that the person to whose order the advertisement was issued was an authorised person.

Someone who promotes an unapproved insurance contract may have a defence under s 130(8) provided he is not the insurance company (as defined by the ICA) with which the contract was made. This defence will be available if a promoter can prove that he believed on reasonable grounds after due enquiry that the contract of insurance fell within sub-ss (2) or (3). Section 130(8) is as follows:

130(8) A person other than the insurance company with which the contract of insurance is to be made shall not be guilty of an offence under this section if he proves that he believed on reasonable grounds after due enquiry that sub-section (2) or (3) above applied in the case of the contravention in question.

*(b) Civil consequences*

*Unenforceable contracts*    If there has been a contravention of s 130, and someone has promoted an unapproved contract in the United Kingdom, then the insurance company may not enforce the contract; and the insured may recover money or property transferred together with compensation for loss. Section 131(1) states the following:

> 131(1)    Where there has been a contravention of section 130 above, then, subject to subsections (3) and (4) below—
>
> (a) the insurance company shall not be entitled to enforce any contract of insurance with which the advertisement, advice or procurement was concerned and which was entered into after the contravention occurred; and
>
> (b) the other party shall be entitled to recover any money or other property paid or transferred by him under the contract, together with compensation for any loss sustained by him as a result of having parted with it.

This corresponds to the provisions relating to the unenforceability of agreements made by or through unauthorised persons which are contained in s 5, discussed in Chapter 11. The provisions relating to the insured's recovery (sub-s (1)), compensation (sub-s (2)), repayment of any benefits received (sub-s (5)) and third party rights (sub-s (6)) are substantially the same as in s 5.

If an insurance company contravenes s 130 the court may allow it to enforce the contract where the insured was not materially influenced by the advertisement or advice to enter into the insurance contract, or the advertisement or advice was fair and not misleading. This corresponds to s 57(8) which relates to the enforcement of contracts entered into in consequence of unauthorised persons' investment advertisements. Section 131(3) reads as follows:

> 131(3)    In a case where the contravention referred to in subsection (1) above was a contravention by the insurance company with which the contract was made, the court may allow the contract to be enforced or money or property paid or transferred under it to be retained if it is satisfied—
>
> (a) that the person against whom enforcement is sought or who is seeking to recover the money or property was not influenced, or not influenced to any material extent, by the advertisement or, as the case may be, the advice in making his decision to enter into the contract; or
>
> (b) that the advertisement or, as the case may be, the advice was not misleading as to the nature of the company with which the contract was to be made or the terms of the contract and fairly stated any risks involved in entering into it.

Where someone other than the insurance company with which the unapproved contract was made has contravened s 130, then the court may enforce the contract if it is satisfied that the company had no reason to believe there was any breach of s 130 when that particular contract was made. For example, the company may have been unaware that its advertisements for the unapproved contract were circulating in the United Kingdom, or that an insurance broker had advised the United Kingdom person to enter into such a contract. This may be difficult to establish in practice if, for instance, the insurer receives a proposal from a United Kingdom broker. Section 131(4) states:

131(4)    In a case where the contravention of section 130 above referred to in subsection (1) above was a contravention by a person other than the insurance company with which the contract was made the court may allow the contract to be enforced or money or property paid or transferred under it to be retained if it is satisfied that at the time the contract was made the company had no reason to believe that any contravention of section 130 above had taken place in relation to the contract.

*Recovery of loss*    If an authorised person contravenes s 130 by promoting an unapproved contract to a United Kingdom person, then anyone who suffers loss as a result may claim compensation from the authorised person. This differs from s 131(1)(b) where compensation is only payable to the insured, although the insurer does not need to be an authorised person to be liable. Section 131(7) states:

131(7)    A contravention of section 130 above by an authorised person shall be actionable at the suit of any person who suffers loss as a result of the contravention.

This sub-section is difficult to understand because, unlike s 62, it does not expressly provide that the loss is actionable as if it were a breach of statutory duty. It is, however, submitted that this will be the case because where an Act of Parliament states that a breach is civilly actionable, that action will lie for breach of statutory duty. Accordingly, the 'defences and other incidents applying to breach of statutory duty' which are discussed in Chapter 11 in relation to s 62 should apply here. The omission, however, is curious.

*Injunctions and restitution orders*    The SIB may take action under s 61 in circumstances where someone has contravened, or will contravene, section 130. Subsection 8 provides

130(8)    Section 61 above shall have effect in relation to a contravention or proposed contravention of section 130 above as it has effect in relation to a contravention or proposed contravention of section 57 above.

# 7 THE MARKETING REGIME FOR RETAIL INVESTMENTS

In this section we outline the regulations which are relevant principally to the sale of life assurance and units in regulated collective investment schemes (ie authorised unit trust schemes and recognised CISs).

## 7.1 Polarisation

A firm should take reasonable steps to ensure private customers are given adequate information about its polarisation status (in other words, whether it is tied or independent). This should be made clear when first meeting or speaking with a potential investor; in premises, on advertisements and on stationery.

Polarisation is the name given to the set of rules which require that persons who market retail investment products—principally life assurance, unit trusts and recognised CISs—to the public do so as either independent financial advisers, who must offer a choice of products drawn from all providers, or as tied agents offering only the products of their company or its group. These two clearly opposed positions are meant to represent the two 'poles' of retail financial services and, as in physics where iron filings attach to the positive and negative poles, nothing is left in between.

Polarisation is an entirely artificial concept, introduced by SIB when the FSA regime was brought in. It is intended to protect investors from the risks associated with the position prior to implementation of the FSA, when life assurance and unit trust products were available from numerous suppliers who might represent a single product company or several product companies; or who might act as an independent intermediary yet only offer the products of a few companies. There were no clear rules requiring them to disclose their status as the agent of a company or the investor, and the scope of duties they owed to the investor was correspondingly uncertain.

SIB recognises that polarisation 'exerts a significant influence on the structure and evolution of the retail investment sector' and 'involves substantial restrictions on commercial freedom' (SIB Consultative Paper 60, March 1992 para 45). However the outcome of SIB's review of retail regulation in 1991–92 (see Chapter 1) was to affirm its commitment to polarisation since 'where the consumer's investment choice is guided by the advice of an intermediary, a vital component of *informed* choice is an appreciation of the scope and limitation of the advice on which it is based.' (Consultative Paper 60 para 47). In other words, investor protection requires that investors know whether the advice is coming from a tied or an independent agent. SIB therefore rejected proposals that a tied agent could represent unconnected life assurance companies ('multi-tying') or that a life assurance company could fill gaps in its product range by offering the products of an unconnected life assurance company but under its own label ('badging').

The basic elements of polarisation are as follows. This summary is taken from Core Rule 4, which although now de-designated, was implemented by SFA and

IMRO. PIA, which is not adopting Core Rules, may have a different approach although it is expected that these principles will be preserved.

(1) Polarisation applies to firms which advise private customers. It does not apply when dealing with business investors.

(2) Polarisation applies to packaged products. These are:

    (a) Life policies, being investments falling within para 10 Sched 1 FSA.

    (b) Units in an authorised unit trust scheme or collective investment scheme recognised under ss 86–88 FSA.

    (c) Investment trust saving schemes.

(3) A firm which advises a private customer on packaged products must either:

    (a) Act as an independent adviser; or

    (b) Be the issuer of the policy or operator of the scheme ('product company') or one of a number of firms allied together for marketing the group's packaged products ('marketing group associate'). The product company and its marketing group associates are together called a marketing group.

(4) A firm which acts as an independent adviser must always advise a private customer about all packaged products which are generally available on the market and on which it can advise. It must advise the customer to purchase that generally available packaged product of which it is aware which is most suitable for his needs. In practice an independent adviser will not survey the entire market every time it advises a customer; it will normally have identified the best providers of different kinds of packaged products already and will review this 'panel' regularly. An independent adviser may not advise a private customer to buy a packaged product issued by a member of its group (for example, where an independent adviser is a member of the same corporate group as a life assurance company) unless it is better than any other generally available packaged product—a difficult task to prove.

(5) A firm which is a product company or its marketing group associate may only advise private customers to buy a packaged product which is issued by the members of that marketing group. It must advise the customer to purchase the packaged product of the marketing group which is most suitable for his needs. In other words Lifeco plc can only advise on Lifeco products and must recommend the best Lifeco policy; it cannot (subject to (6) below) advise an investor to buy an Otherco product.

(6) But when a firm (whether generally acting as an independent intermediary or otherwise) acts as an investment manager for a private customer, it may advise the customer on any packaged product and should advise on, or buy, that which is most suitable for his needs. Acting as an investment manager in this context means providing discretionary management or continuing

advice on an investment portfolio when acting as an agent of the investor (as distinct from the agent of a product company).

## 7.2 Product disclosure

Before or when making a personal recommendation to a private customer to buy a packaged product, the firm should give him adequate information about the product, including risks and costs, to enable him to make an informed decision.

SIB made detailed rules for disclosure of information about life assurance products in 1992, but upon review by the Director General of Fair Trading they were found to be significantly anti-competitive. In July 1993 the Treasury directed SIB to amend the rules. A further impetus for change was the Third Life Directive, which requires the provision of specified information before a contract is entered into.

The Treasury direction, made under ss 120(2) and 121(3) FSA required, in summary:

(1) illustrations should be based upon the actual charges and expenses of a life company, and not upon the regulator's standard figures. Previously life offices had used a standard set of charges issued by LAUTRO when drawing up illustrations. This meant that if a potential investor seeking, for instance, a 25-year endowment policy to pay off his or her mortgage obtained illustrations of projected future benefits for endowment policies issued by three different life offices, the figures would be identical as they were all required to use the same charges and assumptions when producing illustrations. This was done with the intention that investors would not rely upon illustrations as estimates of likely future returns when making comparisons between different product providers on account of the uncertainty of future investment performance;

(2) sellers' commission should be disclosed to an investor in cash terms;

(3) a life company should be allowed (but not required) to sell the same product at different premium rates through different appointed representatives or branches. This is known as differential pricing.

The current rules relating to disclosure were published in draft by SIB in Consultative Paper 77 (January 1994), where it stated that an 'essential feature of investor protection is timely and clear disclosure of information to investors: how the product works, what it costs, and what the advice costs.'

The disclosure notice will, in summary, include information relating to the following matters, although the disclosure requirement differs in detail between life and non-life products:

(1) the product provider's own charges and expenses, and how they affect the value of the investment. As with projections of future benefits, these were previously based upon standard LAUTRO figures;

(2) surrender values, to make clear the effect of surrender before maturity;

(3) commission or equivalent paid to the salesperson should be disclosed in cash terms to enable investors to identify the incentive to sell the product. An IFA will disclose commission in cash terms; a salesperson working for a life assurance company or its appointed representative would disclose 'commission equivalent' which takes into account any payments received, and benefits and assistance provided.

Any forecast of realisable value or illustration of benefits must comply with detailed rules and, as mentioned, be based upon the costs and projections calculated by each product provider.

## 7.3 Explanation of suitability

A firm may not recommend a private customer to buy, sell or surrender a life policy unless the customer has been provided with a written notice explaining why the firm believes the transaction is suitable for him. This requirement for a firm to explain its judgment on the suitability of the product in writing is intended to make clear the link between the client's circumstances, as disclosed to the firm, and its recommendation.

## 7.4 Cancellation

Section 51 FSA empowers SIB to make rules to enable a person who has entered, or offered to enter, into an investment agreement with an authorised person to rescind the agreement or withdraw the offer. There are two sets of cancellation regulations. The Financial Services (Cancellation) Rules 1994, which came into force on 1 January 1995, apply exclusively to life policies falling within para 10 Sched 1 FSA; the Financial Services (Cancellation) Rules 1989 (as amended) continue to apply but only to unit trusts and PEPs. Reference should be made to the text of the rules to determine the circumstances in which they apply. We now summarise the 1994 rules; while these apply exclusively to life assurance products they are broadly similar in operation to the 1989 rules.

The purpose of the 1994 rules is to give a policyholder the opportunity to make a considered investment choice by giving him a right to cancel which commences no later than receipt of the product and commission disclosure notices. By making a policyholder's decision revocable, the rules are intended to reduce the incentive for pressure selling techniques.

In summary the 1994 rules provide as follows:

(1) Cancellation is generally available only to individual policyholders and in respect of buying a life policy, or agreeing a variation to a regular premium life policy, of the kind specified in the rules.

(2) Where there is a right to cancel, the firm making the sale must post to the investor a notice in specified form within 14 days from making the agreement, and the investor then has 14 days in which to cancel.

(3) If the investor exercises his right to cancel, this rescinds the agreement, and each party returns to the position they were in before entering into the contract. The one exception is that the investor may have to pay for an element of shortfall in relation to a single premium policy where there has been a market fluctuation.

# 8  UNSOLICITED CALLS (COLD CALLING)

The making of unsolicited calls, generally known as cold calling, is restricted by s 56(1):

56(1) Except so far as permitted by regulations made by the Secretary of State, no person shall in the course of or in consequence of an unsolicited call—
(a) made on a person in the United Kingdom; or
(b) made from the United Kingdom on a person elsewhere,
by way of business enter into an investment agreement with the person on whom the call is made or procure or endeavour to procure that person to enter into such an agreement.

An unsolicited call is defined by s 56(8) as:

56(8) In this section 'unsolicited call' means a personal visit or oral communication made without express invitation.

This restriction relates to calls which are:

(1) Uninvited. For example, stopping people in the street, telephoning them or, indeed, canvassing off-the-street customers in a bank. It has no relevance to calls made by agreement.

(2) Personal or oral, but not in writing. While logic may suggest that an oral advertisement (whether made in person or over the telephone) falls within s 56 rather than s 57, there is a potential overlap since there is no requirement for an investment advertisement, regulated by s 57, to be in writing. The definition of 'advertisement' in s 207(2) includes reference to sound broadcasting and 'any other manner of advertising'.

(3) Made with a view to entering into a contract. The restriction does not relate to cold calls made without this intention, or with a view to an investor entering into a contract with a third party unless that person could be said to be entering into the contract in consequence of the cold call.

(4) By way of business. The meaning of this is discussed in Chapter 6.

If the person making the cold call offers or agrees to perform an investment activity in relation to regulated investments in the course of carrying on business (for example, offers to buy shares), then that person may as a result be carrying on investment business.

The meaning of 'in consequence of' and 'investment agreement' are discussed in Chapters 11 and 12 respectively.

It is not an offence to contravene s 56(1), but any resulting investment agreement may be unenforceable on principles similar to those contained in ss 5 and 131.

An investment agreement entered into in the course of, or in consequence of, the unsolicited call is unenforceable against the person called upon, who can recover any money or property transferred together with compensation for loss as agreed or determined by a court. Section 56 provides the following:

> 56(2)  A person shall not be guilty of an offence by reason only of contravening subsection (1) above, but subject to subsection (4) below—
>
> (a)  any investment agreement which is entered into in the course of or in consequence of the unsolicited call shall not be enforceable against the person on whom the call was made; and
>
> (b)  that person shall be entitled to recover any money or other property paid or transferred by him under the agreement, together with compensation for any loss sustained by him as a result of having parted with it.
>
> (3)  The compensation recoverable under subsection (2) above shall be such as the parties may agree or as a court may, on the application of either party, determine.

If the person called upon does not perform the agreement or recovers money or other property from the caller, he must hand back anything he has received under the agreement. Provision is made for this in s 56(5) which is as follows:

> 56(5)  Where a person elects not to perform an agreement which by virtue of this section is unenforceable against him or by virtue of this section recovers money paid or other property transferred by him under an agreement he shall repay any money and return any other property received by him under the agreement.

A court may allow the investment agreement to be enforced, or money or property to be retained by the caller if:

> (1)  the person called on was not materially influenced by the call; or
>
> (2)  the person called on entered into the agreement in consequence of subsequent discussions and understood the nature of the agreement and any risks involved; or
>
> (3)  the call was made by a third party and not by the person seeking to enforce the agreement or his agent or someone receiving remuneration from them.

Section 56(4) provides as follows:

56(4) A court may allow an agreement to which subsection (2) above applies to be enforced or money and property paid or transferred under it to be retained if it is satisfied—

    (a) that the person on whom the call was made was not influenced, or not influenced to any material extent, by anything said or done in the course of or in consequence of the call;

    (b) without prejudice to paragraph (a) above, that the person on whom the call was made entered into the agreement—

        (i) following discussions between the parties of such a nature and over such a period that his entering into the agreement can fairly be regarded as a consequence of those discussions rather than the call; and

        (ii) was aware of the nature of the agreement and any risks involved in entering into it; or

    (c) that the call was not made by—

        (i) the person seeking to enforce the agreement or to retain the money or property or a person acting on his behalf or an appointed representative whose principal he was; or

        (ii) a person who has received or is to receive, or in the case of an appointed representative whose principal has received or is to receive, any commission or other inducement in respect of the agreement from a person mentioned in sub-paragraph (i) above.

The Common Unsolicited Calls Regulations are made by SIB under s 56(1). Subject to their detailed provisions, to which reference must be made, they permit cold calls to be made in a number of defined circumstances. The three most common are:

(1) on non-private investors;

(2) on private investors to sell certain packaged products;

(3) on private investors, to enable an authorised or exempted person to sell certain readily realisable securities.

# 9 THE MONEY LAUNDERING REGIME IN THE UNITED KINGDOM

## 9.1 Introduction

*(a) What is money laundering?*

Money laundering is defined as the process by which criminals attempt to conceal the true origin and ownership of the proceeds of their criminal activities. The laundering process is usually accomplished in three successive stages.

(1) *Placement*: this is usually the first stage in the money laundering process and involves the physical disposal of cash proceeds derived from illegal activity;

(2) *Layering*: this is usually the second stage in the laundering of dirty money whereby illicit proceeds are separated from their source through a succession of financial transactions;

(3) *Integration*: this, the final part of the process, occurs when the proceeds of criminal activity re-enter the financial system and appear as legitimate business funds.

*(b) Vulnerability to money laundering*

Banks and building societies are particularly vulnerable at the placement stage and hence efforts to combat money laundering focus on the deposit-taking procedures of these institutions. However, as banks and building societies provide an ever-widening range of services they are also increasingly vulnerable to being used in the layering and integration stages.

The investment industry is less likely to be used in the initial placement stage where cash settlement of investment business is rare. However, caution is advised, for example, when dealing with bearer securities delivered other than through an established clearing system. The liquidity of many investment products makes them particularly attractive to sophisticated money launderers.

In relation to retail product providers and intermediaries, the use of unit trusts in particular is of concern. These tend to be liquid and allow quick and easy movement from one product to another, thus integrating illicit proceeds into the economy. In all of these industries, and others, the maintenance of accurate records can provide useful information in compiling an audit trail to help combat money laundering activities.

## 9.2 The regime in the United Kingdom

*(a) The EU Directive*

Money laundering legislation was introduced in the United Kingdom to implement the EU Directive on prevention of the use of the financial system for the purpose of money laundering (Council Directive No 91/308) (the 'Directive'). The Directive is based on two principles: repression and prevention of money laundering activities.

Equivalent provisions will apply in all EU member states. The Directive also falls within the scope of the European Economic Area Agreement (the EEA Agreement). According to a report issued by the Commission in March 1995 the Directive has been implemented in all EU member states except Greece and in all EFTA states which have ratified the EEA Agreement except Liechtenstein. This is particularly important when dealing with the exemptions from the identification requirements, discussed below.

The Directive fits within an international framework including, in particular, the UN Convention against illicit traffic in narcotic drugs and psychotropic substances (December 1988) and the Council of Europe Convention on laundering, search, seizure and confiscation of the proceeds from crime (November 1990).

*(b) United Kingdom money laundering legislation*
The Directive has been implemented by way of a mixture of primary, secondary and tertiary legislation.

Primary legislation is predominently set out in the Criminal Justice Act 1993 (the 'CJA') although United Kingdom law relating to money laundering is contained in several different Acts. The CJA, which came into force in several stages in 1993 and 1994, lays the foundations of the present law and consolidates the provisions of pre-existing legislation. The Drug Trafficking Act 1994, which came into force on 3 February 1995, consolidated the Drug Trafficking Offences Act 1986 and certain provisions of the Criminal Justice (International Co-operation) Act 1990 relating to drug trafficking. The provisions of the CJA dealing with money laundering mainly cover the definition of money laundering, the obligation to report suspicions, tipping-off and immunity. The primary legislation, it should be noted, is applicable to the general public and is not solely the concern of financial institutions.

The secondary legislation is the Money Laundering Regulations 1993 (SI 1993 No 1933) (the 'Regulations') which came into force on 1 April 1994. This concerns procedures of control (for example, customer identification, record keeping and staff training). The Regulations do not lay down detailed requirements but rely on guidance notes produced by the supervisory authorities of those institutions which fall under the Regulations.

The third tier of the United Kingdom system consists of guidance notes which were first issued between December 1990 and September 1991 (the 'Guidance Notes'). In October 1993 the Guidance Notes were updated by the Joint Money Laundering Steering Group and then further revised in February 1995.

The three sets of Guidance Notes issued by the steering group are:

(1) Guidance Notes for mainstream banking, lending and deposit-taking activities (the 'Red Book');
(2) Guidance Notes for wholesale, institutional and private client investment business (the 'Yellow Book'); and
(3) Guidance Notes for insurance and retail investment products (the 'Green Book').

All three versions follow a common format and provide a practical interpretation of the Regulations.

Various other bodies have issued guidance notes including the Law Society, the Institute of Chartered Accountants and several trade associations in the insurance business. This section however concentrates on the provisions of the Red, Yellow and Green Books.

*(c) Overall effect of the legislation*

The legislation introduced in the United Kingdom to implement the Directive has widened the definition and scope of money laundering and introduced new offences. The primary legislation covers not only the proceeds of drug trafficking but also the proceeds of terrorism and general crime. Under the EU regime preventative measures such as client identification procedures have become compulsory for institutions covered by the Regulations.

## 9.3 Money laundering offences

One of the most significant changes introduced by the CJA is to extend money laundering offences to all types of criminal offences triable on indictment (except for reporting of suspicions, which is discussed below). It appears to include, for instance, the most serious tax frauds such as conspiracy to cheat the Revenue. This is much wider than the scope of the previous money laundering regime, which was limited to laundering of proceeds of drug trafficking and terrorism.

Furthermore the term 'criminal conduct' used in the CJA covers not only indictable offences committed in the United Kingdom but also any offence committed outside the United Kingdom which would constitute an indictable offence if committed in the United Kingdom.

The most relevant offences are set out below as they appear in the CJA:

(1) *Assisting another to retain the benefit of crime (s 29).* It is an offence for any person to provide assistance to a money launderer to obtain, conceal, retain or invest funds if that person knows or suspects (or in the case of terrorist activities should have known or suspected) that those funds are the proceeds of criminal conduct.

(2) *Acquisition, possession or use of the proceeds of criminal conduct (ss 16 and 30).* A person is guilty of an offence if, knowing that any property is, or in whole or in part directly or indirectly represents, another person's proceeds of criminal conduct, he acquires or uses that property or has possession of it.

(3) *Concealing or transferring proceeds to avoid prosecution or a confiscation order (s 31).* Under the CJA it is an offence for a person to conceal, disguise, convert, transfer or remove from the jurisdiction of the courts any property which directly or indirectly, in whole or part, represents the proceeds of his criminal conduct. It should be noted that this offence concerns only an offender and no-one else who may be involved in the laundering of the proceeds of criminal conduct to avoid confiscation or prosecution.

(4) *Failure to disclose knowledge or suspicion of money laundering (s 18).* The CJA requires that anybody who, in the course of his trade, profession, business or employment knows or suspects that another person is engaged in money laundering must report this knowledge or suspicion to the police

as soon as it is reasonably practicable after it comes to his attention. This reporting obligation is limited to drug money and terrorism-related money rather than the proceeds of general crime. This covers drug money laundering committed in the United Kingdom and outside the United Kingdom if this would constitute an offence in the United Kingdom.

This dual regime may leave in a difficult position the person who suspects that laundered money is involved but cannot determine the kind of crime the proceeds come from. The position is even more difficult where this person, although not bound to report these suspicions, is still liable to be prosecuted for assisting the money launderers. The CJA contains a defence of reasonable excuse for failure to report a suspicion to the police. The concept of reasonable excuse is not defined in the CJA. The CJA expressly provides that where an employee has reported his suspicion through an internal procedure, he will have a defence to a charge under those provisions.

(5) *Tipping-off (ss 18 and 32).* Under the CJA it is an offence to disclose to a customer or any third party that information has been passed to the authorities or that a money laundering investigation is being carried out or planned. The prohibition contained in earlier legislation against tipping-off only applied where, for example, a warrant had already been issued for the arrest of the suspected offender.

It was necessary to ensure that the positive duty to supply information concerning money laundering created by the CJA would not constitute a breach of, for example, the banker's duty of confidentiality or of the rules regarding banking secrecy. Disclosure made under the CJA will not be considered a breach of any restriction on the disclosure of information imposed by statue or otherwise. The CJA, however, may be more restrictive than the Directive. It seems that the Directive went further than the CJA in providing that disclosure in good faith will not involve an institution in liability of any kind. What will happen where a credit institution discloses information about a client who in fact has not been involved in any money laundering activities? Could the client, for instance, bring an action for defamation against the institution if such a report proved to be unfounded? Is it implied in the CJA that such a disclosure made in good faith cannot lead to any liability? These are, at present, undecided questions.

## 9.4    The Regulations and Guidance Notes

The Regulations require credit and financial institutions to put into place systems 'to deter money laundering and to assist the relevant authorities to detect money laundering activities'. The Regulations apply to all those carrying on 'relevant financial business'. This definition in reg 4 includes amongst others those carrying on banking business under the Banking Act 1987, investment business under the Financial Services Act 1986 and life insurance business. The Regulations also cover most activities listed in the Second Banking Directive. Even where the Regulations are not directly applicable, the scope of the primary legislation is such that money laundering preventative procedures may nevertheless be needed by certain other institutions to avoid breaking the law.

Under reg 5, the setting up of procedures to prevent money laundering is compulsory. Failure effectively to comply with these procedures is an offence. It will be a defence if it can be shown that all reasonable steps were taken and due diligence exercised to avoid failing to comply with reg 5.

Whilst the Guidance Notes are not mandatory and only provide an illustration of good industry practice, the Regulations provide that, in determining whether an institution has complied with the Regulations, a court may take account of relevant Guidance Notes. Although failure to comply with the Guidance Notes does not mean that an institution has automatically breached the Regulations, it is expected that the institution would be required to demonstrate the adequacy of any alternative procedures adopted.

The Guidance Notes each cover a different type of business and are intended to provide a practical interpretation of the Regulations. Each set of Guidance Notes deals with the same topics tailored to the relevant needs of the different types of institution.

The Guidance Notes begin with a background section which deals with the question 'what is money laundering?' and the vulnerability of institutions to money laundering schemes. The next section on the requirements of United Kingdom law deals with money laundering offences. The Guidance Notes then deal in different sections with the practical application of the Regulations. Summaries of money laundering schemes uncovered and examples of transactions which ought to be viewed with suspicion are appended to the Guidance Notes.

*(c) Internal controls, policies and procedures*

Under reg 5 those covered by the Regulations are required to maintain 'procedures of internal control and communication for the purposes of forestalling and preventing money laundering'. The Regulations do not set out in detail the type of controls required nor the rights, duties and responsibilities of those within the control system. This is due to the divergence between the institutions covered by the Regulations and the wish to leave details regarding implementation to the relevant supervisory authorities.

To comply with the Regulations the respective sets of Guidance Notes state the need for institutions to establish clear responsibilities and accountabilities within their organisations to ensure that policies, procedures, and controls are introduced and maintained which can deter criminals from using their facilities for money laundering.

The Guidance Notes point out that reg 14 requires all businesses to establish a central point of contact with the law enforcement agencies in order to handle the reported suspicions of their staff regarding money laundering. The Guidance

Notes state that an 'appropriate person' must be appointed to undertake this role, such person being referred to as the money laundering reporting officer.

The Guidance Notes suggest that institutions operating within the United Kingdom should:

(1) introduce procedures to ensure the prompt validation of suspicions and subsequent reporting to the authorities;

(2) provide the money laundering reporting officer with the necessary access to systems and records in this regard; and

(3) establish close co-operation and liaison with the National Criminal Intelligence Service.

As good practice, institutions are recommended to make arrangements to satisfy management about compliance with policies, procedures and controls relating to money laundering. The Guidance Notes observe that there is no need to introduce systems to *detect* money laundering activities.

### (b) Identification procedures

**When do they apply? (reg 7)**
The identification procedures must be applied in four situations:

(1) In any case where the parties form or resolve to form a business relationship between them. This could be an established customer for which work will be undertaken on a frequent, habitual or regular basis.

(2) In any case where, in respect of any 'one-off transaction' (for example, other than in the course of business), payment is to be made by or to the applicant for business if the amount is ECU 15,000 or more.

(3) In any case of two or more transactions where it appears at the outset or at any later stage that the transactions are linked and that the total amount which is payable is ECU 15,000 or more.

(4) In any case where, in respect of any one-off transaction, any person handling the transaction knows or suspects that the applicant for business is engaged in money laundering or that the transaction is carried out on behalf of another person engaged in money laundering. This requirement applies whatever the amount of the transaction.

The requirement to verify identity is not retrospective and only applies to one-off transactions and business relationships entered into since 1 April 1994.

**Whose identity must be established? (reg 7)**
The person whose identity must be verified is the 'applicant for business'. Under the Regulations, the applicant for business is defined as a person seeking to form a business relationship, or carry out a one-off transaction, with a person who is carrying out relevant (financial) business in the United Kingdom. The Guidance Notes deal with many situations including the following:

(1) A customer or counterparty dealing with an institution on its own behalf would be an applicant for business.

(2) When a customer or counterparty is acting as agent for a principal and deals in its own name on behalf of an underlying client then it is the counterparty as the agent, and not its client, who is the institution's applicant for business.

(3) The Guidance Notes refer to trust, nominee and fiduciary accounts. They provide that when it is known or suspected that an account is being opened, or a transaction is being undertaken, on behalf of a third party without that being disclosed, reasonable measures should be taken to obtain information as to the identity of the person on whose behalf the customer is acting and, if the identity of the principal cannot be ascertained, the account activity should be monitored.

(4) The Guidance Notes refer to 'client accounts' opened by intermediaries. They stress that stockbrokers, fund managers, solicitors, accountants, estate agents and other intermediaries frequently hold funds on behalf of their clients in 'client accounts' opened with banks and building societies. Such accounts may be omnibus accounts holding the funds of many clients, or may be opened specifically for a single client either undisclosed to the bank or building society or identified for reference purposes only. In each case it is the intermediary who is the bank's customer and these situations should be distinguished from those where an intermediary introduces a client who himself becomes a client or customer of the institution.

**What happens if the applicant for business is an agent? (reg 9(2))**

The regulations provide that reasonable measures must be taken for the purpose of establishing the identity of any person on whose behalf the applicant for business is acting, namely the principal. Reasonableness must be assessed by reference to all the circumstances of the case and, in particular, to the best practice which for the time being is followed in the relevant field of business and which is applicable to those circumstances. Certain exemptions are mentioned below.

**Timing of identity verification (reg 11(2))**

Where evidence of identity is required, the Regulations provide that it must be obtained 'as soon as is reasonably practical' after the applicant for business makes contact with the firm involved or applies to enter a business relationship. Reasonableness will be assessed by reference to all the circumstances including, in particular, the nature of the business relationship or one-off transaction concerned, the geographical locations of the parties, and whether it is practicable to obtain the evidence before commitments are entered into between the parties or before money passes.

The institution's internal procedures must provide that where evidence is not obtained, the business relationship or one-off transaction cannot proceed any further.

**What is satisfactory evidence of identity? (reg 11(1))**
The Regulations provide that evidence of the applicant's identity must be reasonably capable of establishing that the applicant is the person he claims to be and is acceptable to the institution. Satisfactory evidence is not defined further. The various Guidence Notes recommend certain forms of identification. Whenever possible prospective customers should be interviewed personally.

The information required to verify identity depends on whether the applicant for business it is a personal or corporate applicant and whether it is a United Kingdom or non-United Kingdom resident.

For United Kingdom resident personal customers the Guidance Notes suggest that the following information should be obtained:

(1) true name used;
(2) correct permanent and United Kingdom address including postal code;
(3) date of birth.

Ideally the true name should be verified by reference to a document obtained from a reputable source which bears a photograph. Wherever possible a current valid full passport or a national identity card should be requested and a number registered. In addition to the name verification, it is important that the current permanent address should also be verified. Some of the best means of verifying an address depending on the circumstances are:

– personal visit to customer's home;
– checking the electoral register;
– making a credit reference agency search;
– checking a local telephone directory;
– checking an original recent utility bill.

For non-United Kingdom personal applicants for business who make face-to-face contact it is recognised in the Guidance Notes that address verification procedures may be difficult, but passport or national identity cards will normally be available. Where contact is by post or telephone, verification ought to be sought from a reputable credit or financial institution or professional adviser known to the institution in the applicant's country of residence.

For corporate customers (United Kingdom registered companies) the following documents should be obtained:

(1) the original or certified copy of the certificate of incorporation;
(2) resolution of the board of directors to open an account and confer authority on those who will operate it;
(3) a search of the file at Companies Registration Office.

In the case of a United Kingdom private company whose directors are not known to the institution, the identity of at least one director and/or shareholder should be verified in line with the requirements for personal customers.

In relation to non-United Kingdom registered companies comparable documents to those required for United Kingdom companies should be obtained so far as is practicable.

**Exemption from the identification requirements**

The Regulations provide various exemptions from the identification requirements. Where those exemptions apply, there is either no need to check identity or less burdensome requirements. None of the exemptions applies where it is known or suspected that money laundering activity is involved.

(1) *Payment by post or by any electronic means (reg 8)*. In the case of transactions where it is reasonable in the circumstances for payment to be sent through the post or by electronic means, identity does not need to be verified where payment is to be made from an account held in the applicant's name at an United Kingdom or EEA credit institution. This exemption does not apply when the applicant for business is opening a bank or building society account which provides cheques or other facilities for transferring funds to third parties. This exemption must be restrictively applied and should not be used where face-to-face contact is possible.

(2) *The status of the applicant for business (reg 10(1)(a)(b)*. The identification requirements do not apply where there are reasonable grounds for believing that the applicant for business (being either an agent or acting as principal) is a United Kingdom, or EEA institution subject to the Regulations or the Money Laundering Directive. Reasonable grounds according to the Guidance Notes might normally constitute ensuring that the institution does actually exist and is contained on the relevant regulator's list of regulated institutions. Unregulated United Kingdom or EEA institutions should be subject to further verification.

Where the applicant for business is an agent and is a regulated institution from a non-EEA country with equivalent money laundering legislation, it will be reasonable to accept a written assurance from the applicant for business that it will have obtained and recorded evidence of the identity of any principal for whom it acts as agent.

(3) *Introduction of one-off transactions (reg 10(1)(c))*. Where an applicant for business who is effecting a one-off transaction is introduced by an institution in the United Kingdom or EEA subject to the Regulations or the Money Laundering Directive, or a regulated institution from a country with equivalent legislation, the Regulations provide that there is no need to verify identity provided the introducer has disclosed the name of the underlying client and given the firm a written assurance that evidence of identity will have been taken and recorded. This assurance can be given separately by the introducer for each customer or by way of a written general assurance.

This exemption only applies in the case of one-off transactions. Where business relationships are established, identity must be fully checked by the firm.

(4) *Policies of insurance in connection with a pension scheme (reg 10(1)(e).* No steps are necessary to verify identity in respect of a policy of insurance in connection with a pension scheme taken out by virtue of a person's contract of employment or occupation, provided the policy contains no surrender clause and may not be used as collateral for a loan.

(5) *Small insurance contracts (reg 10(1)(f)).* If a transaction involves insurance premiums below specified levels the identification requirements do not apply.

*(c) Record-keeping (regs 12 and 13)*

Regulation 12 requires those subject to the Regulations to implement and maintain procedures to retain records concerning (a) customer identification and (b) transactions carried out, for use as evidence in any investigation into money laundering. This is an essential constituent of the audit trail procedures that the Regulations seek to establish.

The Regulations provide that where evidence of a person's identity is required, the records retained must indicate the nature of the evidence of identity obtained. The records of identity must be kept for at least five years after the relationship with the customer has ended.

In the case of transactions undertaken on behalf of customers, the Regulations require that the supporting evidence and records, consisting of the original documents or copies admissible in court proceedings, must be retained for a period of at least five years following the date on which the relevant transaction or series of transactions is completed. These could be evidence in support of entries in accounts in the form of credit/debit slips, cheques or bank waste-sheets.

Under reg 13, appointed representatives' principals are held responsible for ensuring that record-keeping procedures under reg 12 are maintained unless the appointed representative (as defined under s 44(2) FSA) is authorised under the FSA, Banking Act 1987, Building Societies Act 1986 or is a European Institution.

The Guidance Notes set out the types of information which should be included in the records and how they should be held. The Regulations do not specify the form in which records are to be kept; however, it is generally recognised that they should be in a format capable of being retrieved or reconstituted following demand within a reasonable time span.

Under the provisions set out in the Red Book, transaction records should include details of the beneficial owners of the account; the volume of funds flowing through the account; the origin of the funds (if known); the form and destination of the funds; the identity of the person undertaking the transaction; and the form of instruction and authority. The overriding objective is for banks and building societies to be able to retrieve relevant information, to the extent it is available, without undue delay.

In respect of insurance and retail investment and private client investment business under the Green Book and Yellow Book, firms should consider retaining a record of the name and address of the customer and counterparty (or the counterparty's identification code); the investment dealt in, including its price and size; whether the transaction was a purchase or a sale; the form of instruction; the account details, and the form in which the funds were paid by the customer; the form and destination of payment made by the business; and whether the investments were held in safe custody by the business or sent to the customer or the customer's order (and, if so, where that was). For bearer securities not held in a clearing system or in a safe custody, records should be kept of receipt and delivery by the firm.

Under the Green Book, insurance businesses should retain records adequate to provide initial proposal documentation (including, where completed, the fact find), needs analysis and copies of regulatory documentation and, where the insurance business verified the client's identification, a copy of that documentation. In addition, post-sale records associated with the maintenance of the contract up to maturity should be provided, together with details of maturity processing and/or claim settlement.

*(d) Recognition and reporting of suspicious transactions (reg 14)*
The internal reporting procedures of a financial institution must identify the person to whom handlers of financial business within that institution must direct any information which gives rise to a knowledge or suspicion of money laundering activity.

This person is known in the Guidance Notes as the money laundering reporting officer (the MLRO) and it is incumbent upon him to evaluate information provided in the light of all other relevant information to ascertain whether it does give rise to knowledge or suspicion of money laundering. All other relevant information must be made available to the MLRO to assist him in his task. If the MLRO knows or suspects money laundering activity, he is required to inform the police.

No attempt is made in the Guidance Notes to define a 'suspicious transaction'. It is, however, noted that such a transaction will often be one which is inconsistent with an investor's/customer's known legitimate business or activities, or with the normal business for that type of account/investor. It is suggested that the key to recognising the unusual is to know enough about a customer/investor to know what is normal in the circumstances.

The Guidance Notes recommend establishment of clear reporting lines within institutions, and that the person charged with responsibility for ensuring the system works has sufficient seniority and time to enable it to work as an effective deterrent. The MLRO should also be given sufficient powers (including access to the board of directors, where applicable, and to confidential information) to enable him to carry out his function effectively.

Firms may choose to combine the roles of MLRO and of prevention officer, the latter being in charge, in particular, of monitoring the proper implementation of the procedure.

It is also recommended in the Guidance Notes that reports of suspicions should be recorded in writing, and records should be made of reasons for non-submission of reports passed to the MLRO. The latest Guidance Notes state that, provided the MLRO acts in good faith in deciding not to pass on any suspicious report, there shall be no liability for non-reporting.

The reporting procedures section states that sufficient information should be disclosed as to the nature and reason for the suspicion, to enable a court order, if necessary, to investigate. It is further noted that the present legislation does not permit the passing of information held by Police or Customs to the Inland Revenue, either in the United Kingdom or overseas, for non-criminal investigations. In the event of a prosecution, the source of information is protected as far as the disclosure of evidence rules allow and there is protection against breach of confidentiality claims.

*(e) Staff training (reg 5(1)(b)(c))*

Another important aspect of the Regulations is that employees must receive appropriate training in the recognition and handling of suspicious transactions. The Guidance Notes develop the training principles identified in the Regulations which do not themselves specify the nature of the training to be given. They highlight the need for staff awareness and suggest specific training programmes for five different categories of employee in the recognition and handling of suspicious transactions.

(1) *New employees.* Training should cover background to money laundering; reporting conditions; the legal obligation to report and personal statutory obligations.

(2) *Dealers and sales persons/advisory staff.* Training should cover legal responsibilities; recognition of suspicious factors; firm policy on exceptional cases; reporting systems; dealing with occasional customers (large cash transactions/bearer securities).

(3) *Account opening/processing staff.* Identification and verification training procedures (for example, matching identity of investor to cheque); recognition of abnormal settlement/payment/delivery instructions.

(4) *Supervisors/managers.* Higher level of instruction, more detail on legislation including penalties and identification, recording and reporting procedures.

(5) *Reporting officers.* In depth training concerning all aspects of legislation. Regulations and internal procedures; validation, and reporting suspicious transactions; working relationships with NCIS.

Refresher training is recommended at regular intervals, which should be at least once a year, to ensure staff do not forget their responsibilities.

# *Index*

---